GENO...?

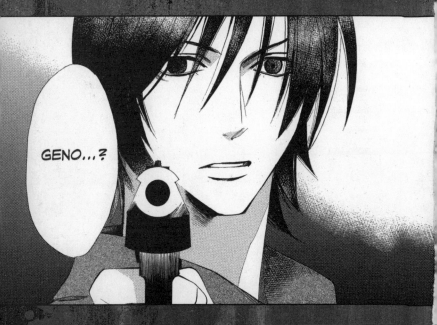

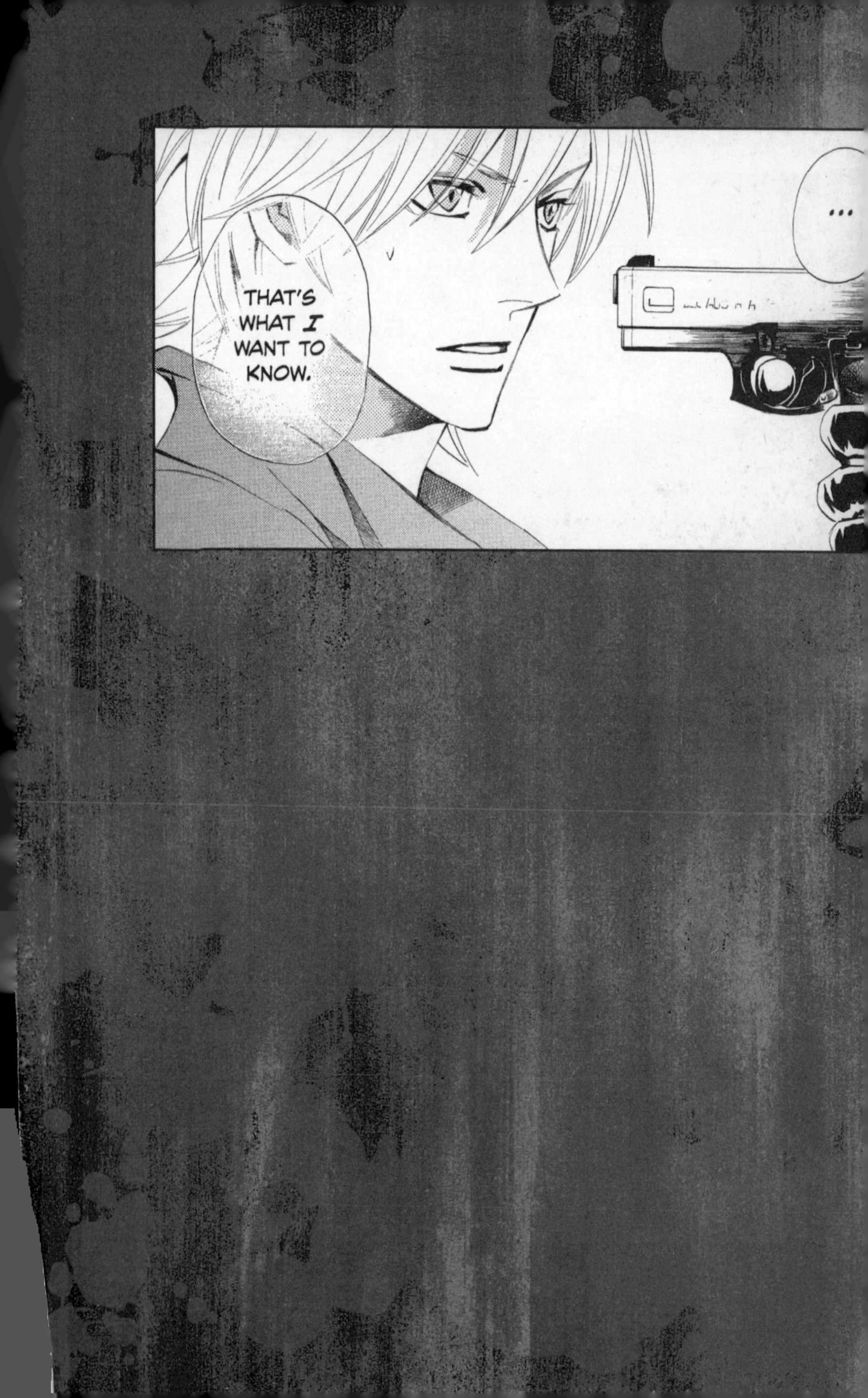
...
THAT'S WHAT *I* WANT TO KNOW.

Shojo Beat

BLANK SLATE

Vol. 2

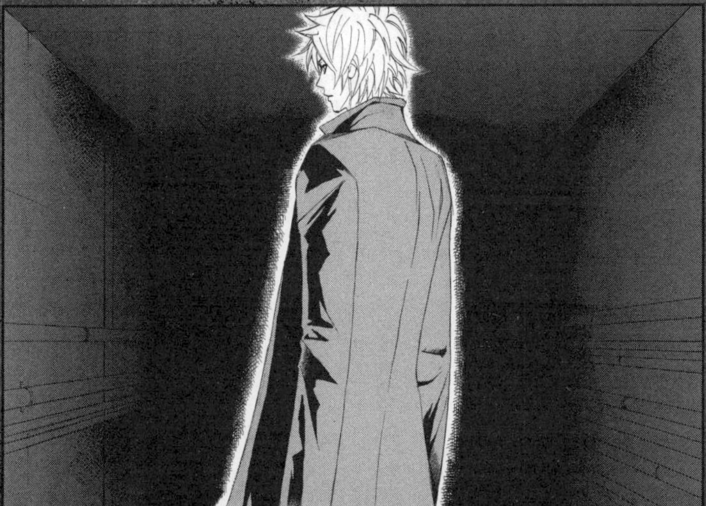

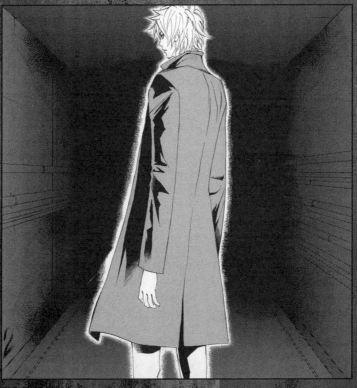

Story & Art by Aya Kanno

Vol. 2

Contents

BLANK SLATE

Chapter Five

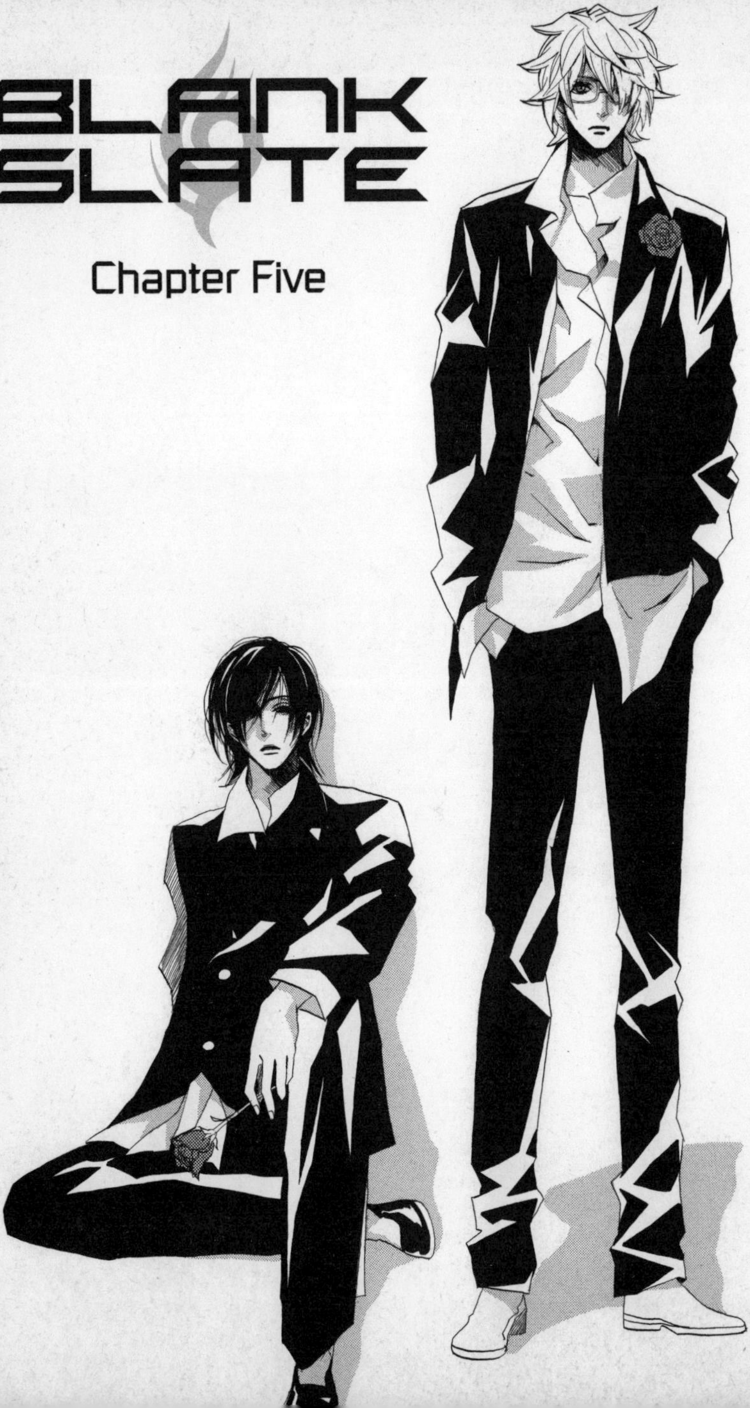

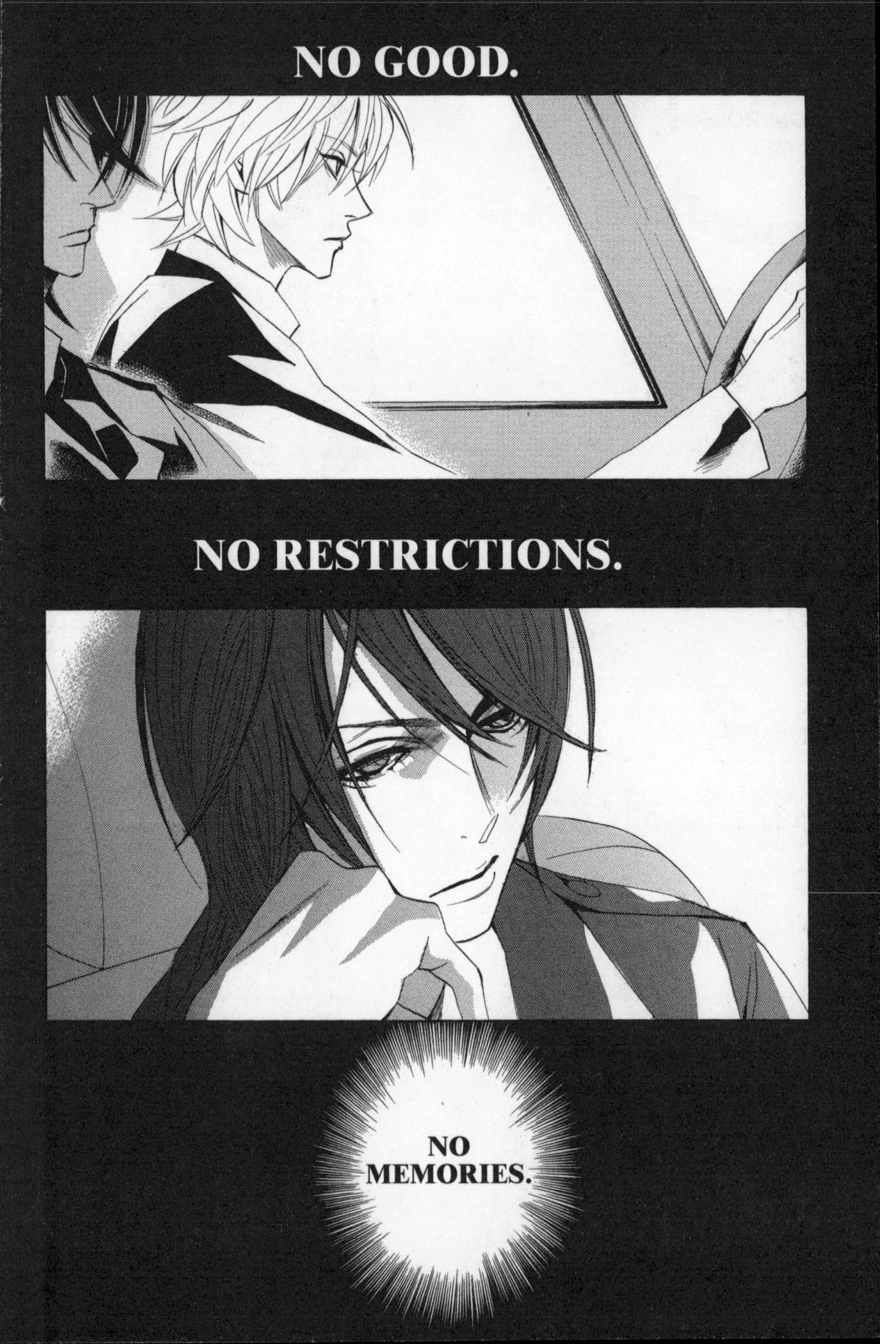
NO GOOD.
NO RESTRICTIONS.
NO MEMORIES.

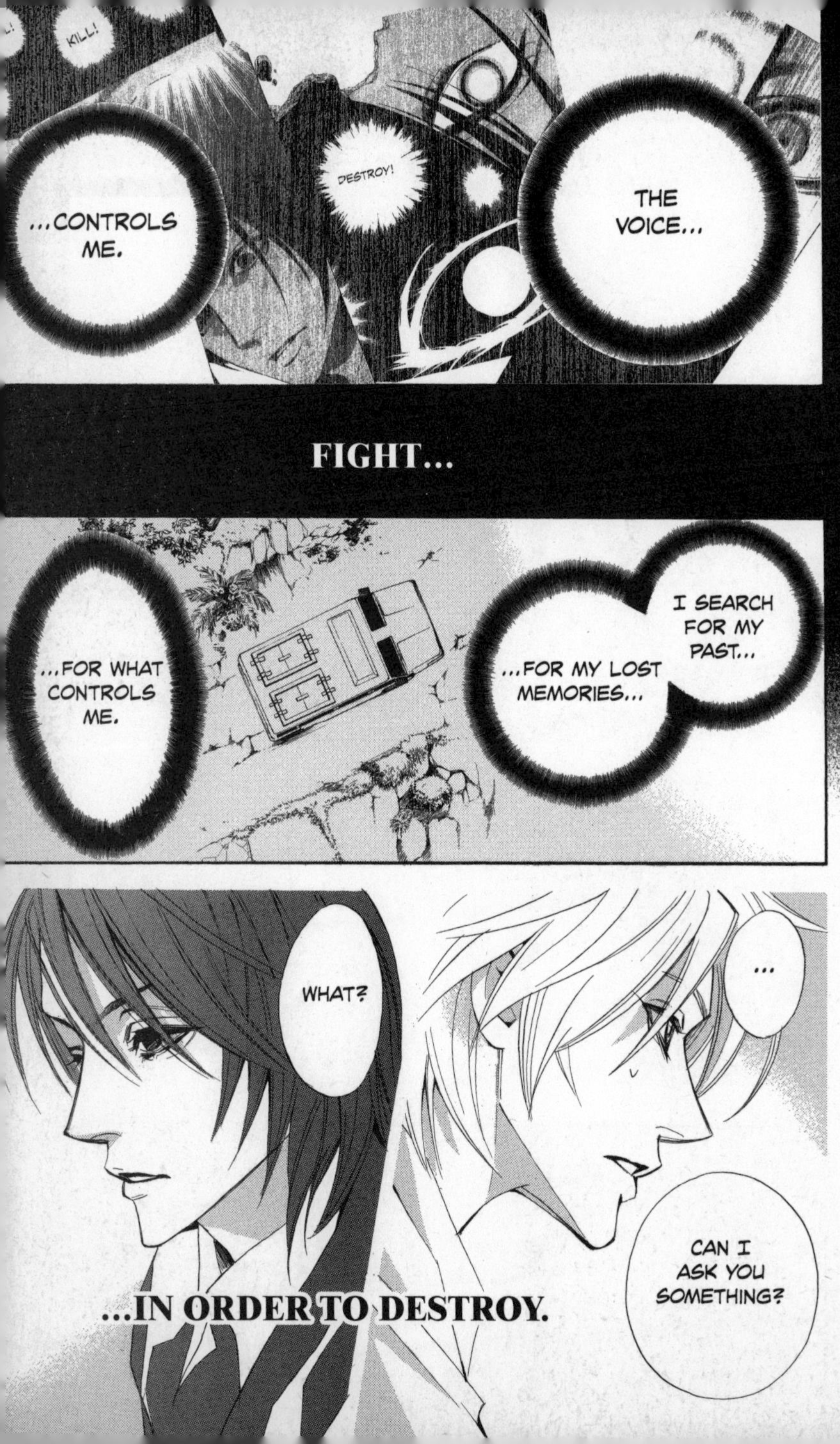
THE VOICE...
DESTROY!
KILL!
...CONTROLS ME.
FIGHT...
I SEARCH FOR MY PAST...
...FOR MY LOST MEMORIES...
...FOR WHAT CONTROLS ME.
...
WHAT?
CAN I ASK YOU SOMETHING?
...IN ORDER TO DESTROY.

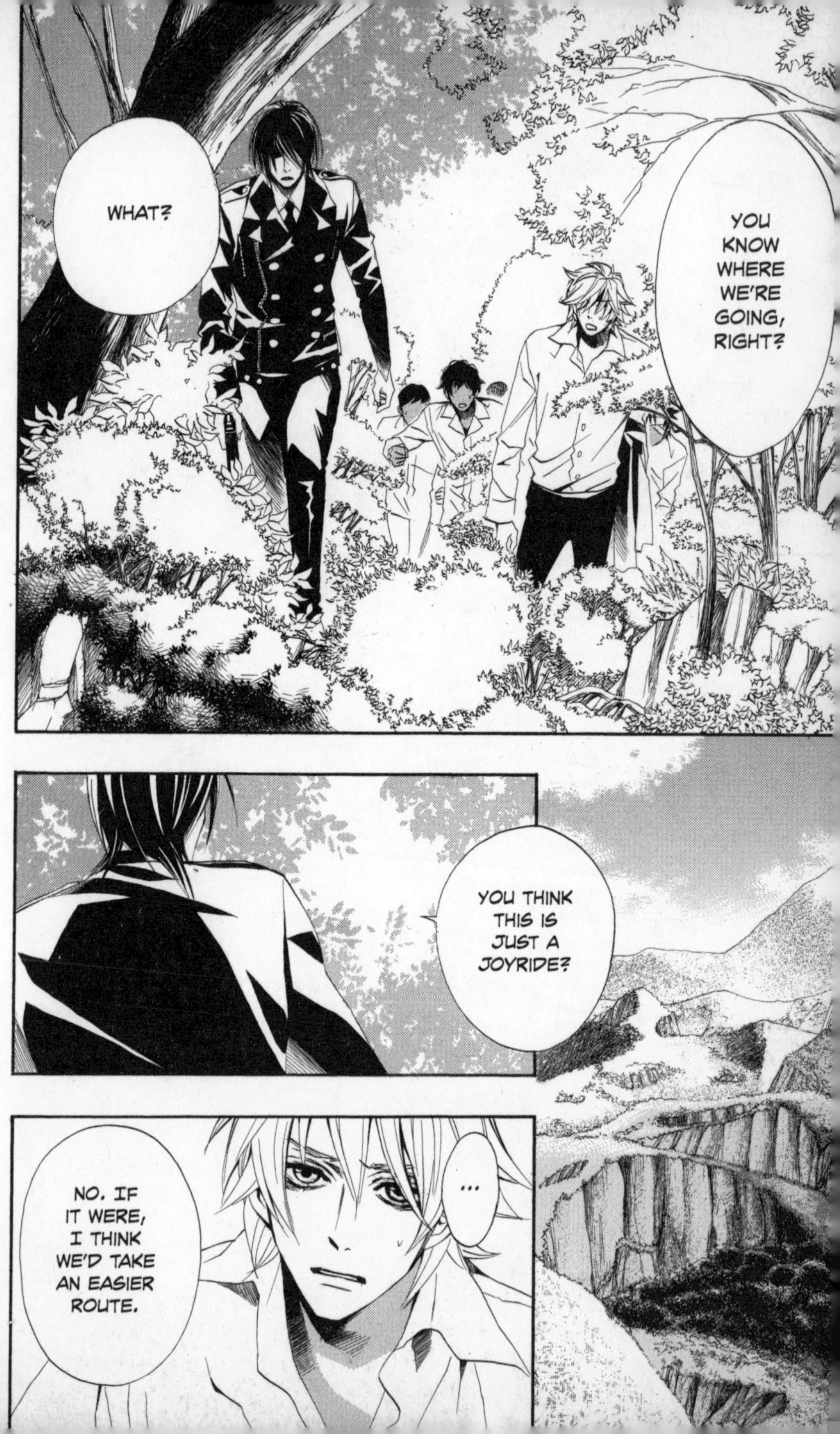
YOU KNOW WHERE WE'RE GOING, RIGHT?
WHAT?
YOU THINK THIS IS JUST A JOYRIDE?
...
NO. IF IT WERE, I THINK WE'D TAKE AN EASIER ROUTE.

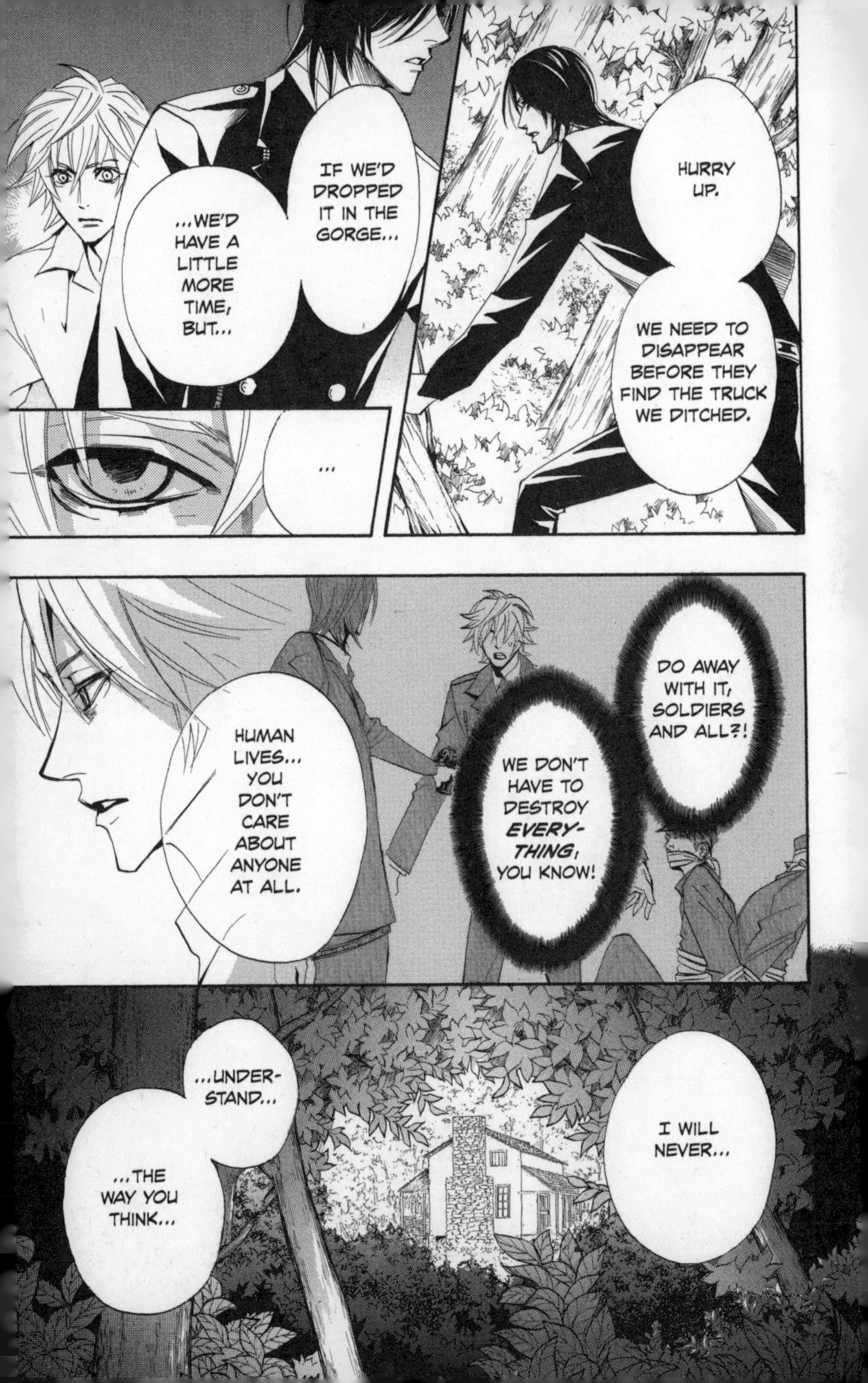
HURRY UP.
WE NEED TO DISAPPEAR BEFORE THEY FIND THE TRUCK WE DITCHED.
IF WE'D DROPPED IT IN THE GORGE...
...WE'D HAVE A LITTLE MORE TIME, BUT...
...
DO AWAY WITH IT, SOLDIERS AND ALL?!
WE DON'T HAVE TO DESTROY *EVERYTHING*, YOU KNOW!
HUMAN LIVES... YOU DON'T CARE ABOUT ANYONE AT ALL.
I WILL NEVER...
...UNDERSTAND...
...THE WAY YOU THINK...

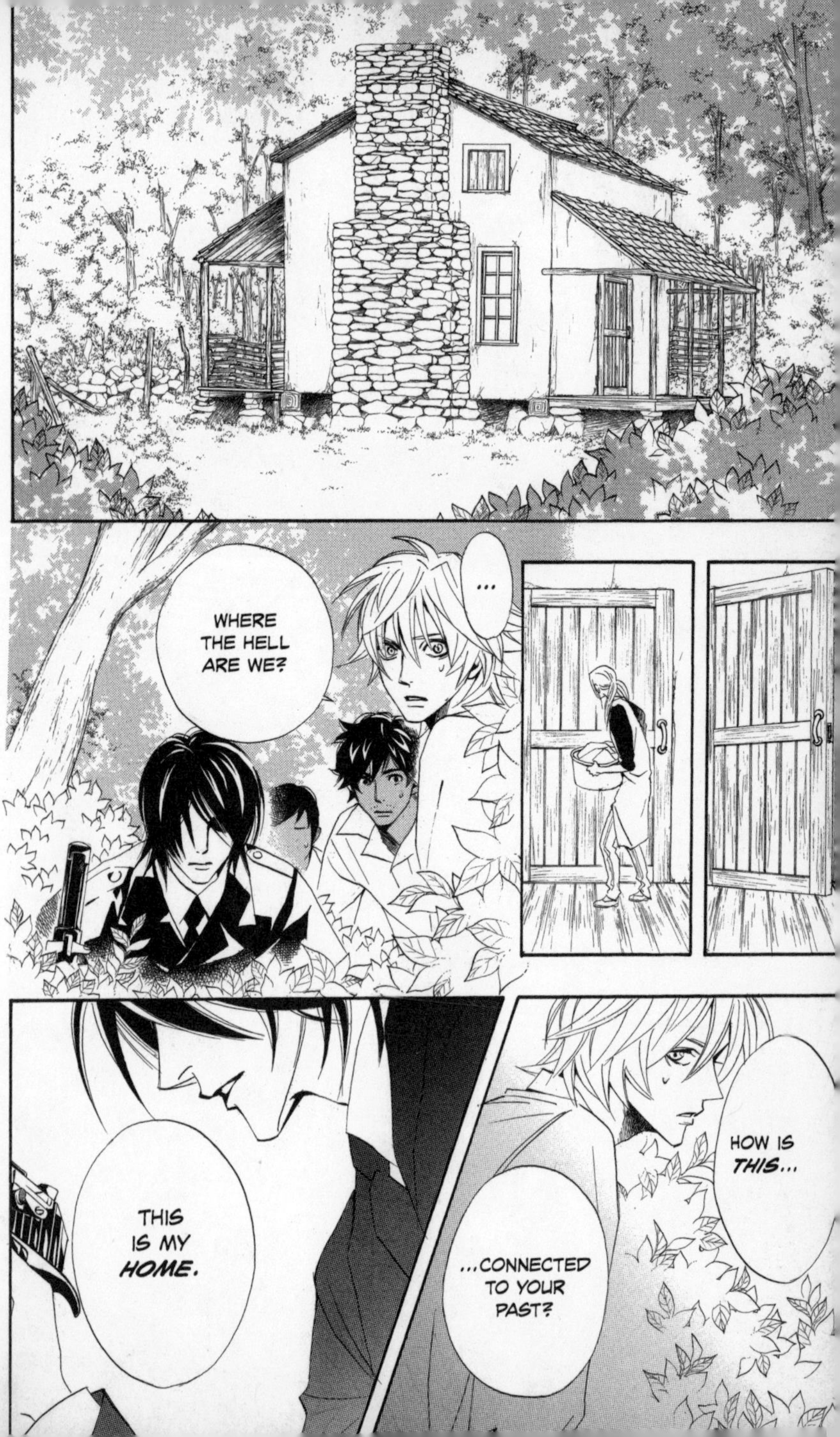
...
WHERE THE HELL ARE WE?
HOW IS *THIS*...
...CONNECTED TO YOUR PAST?
THIS IS MY *HOME*.

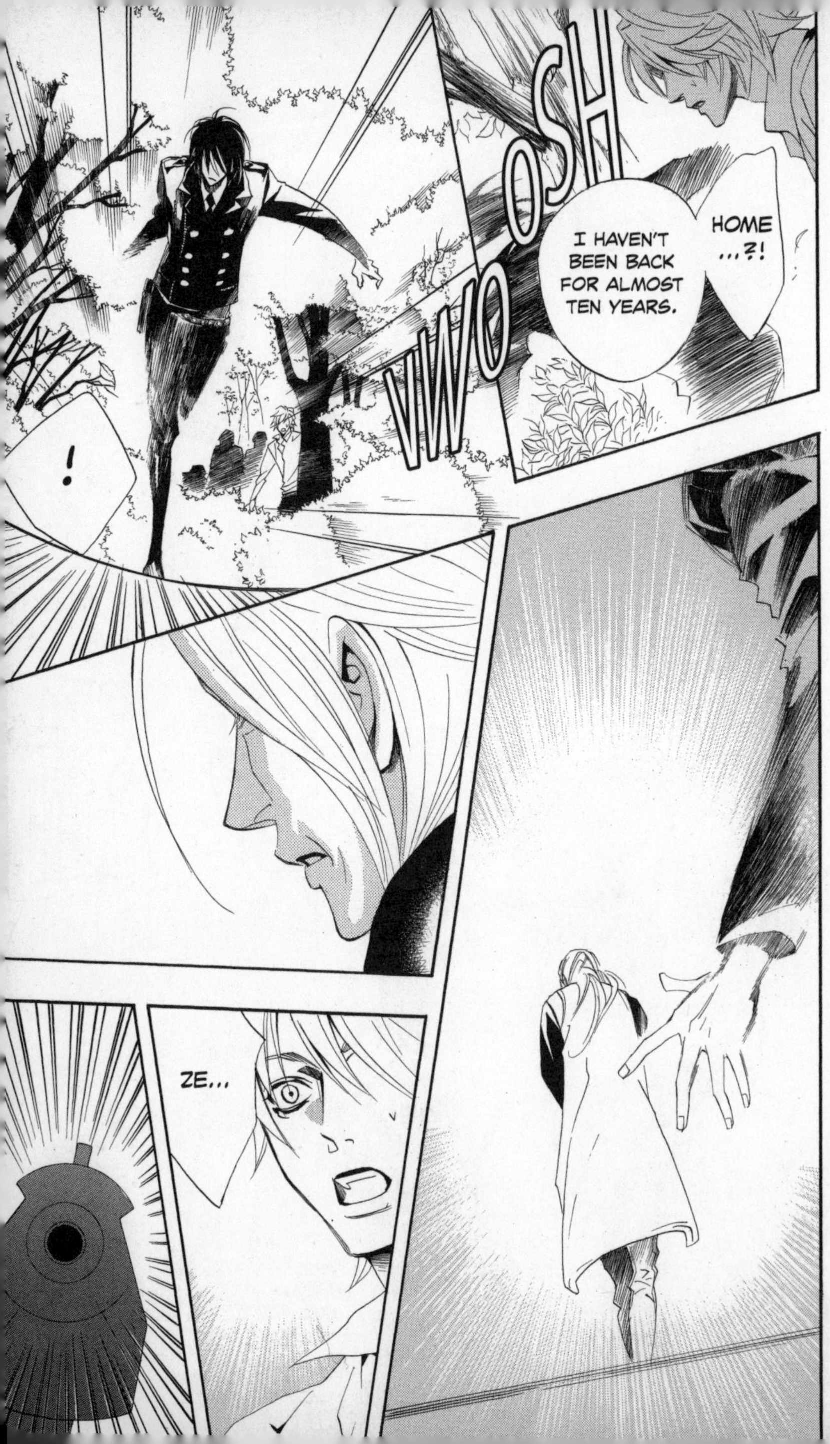
HOME ...?!
I HAVEN'T BEEN BACK FOR ALMOST TEN YEARS.
VWOOSH
!
ZE...

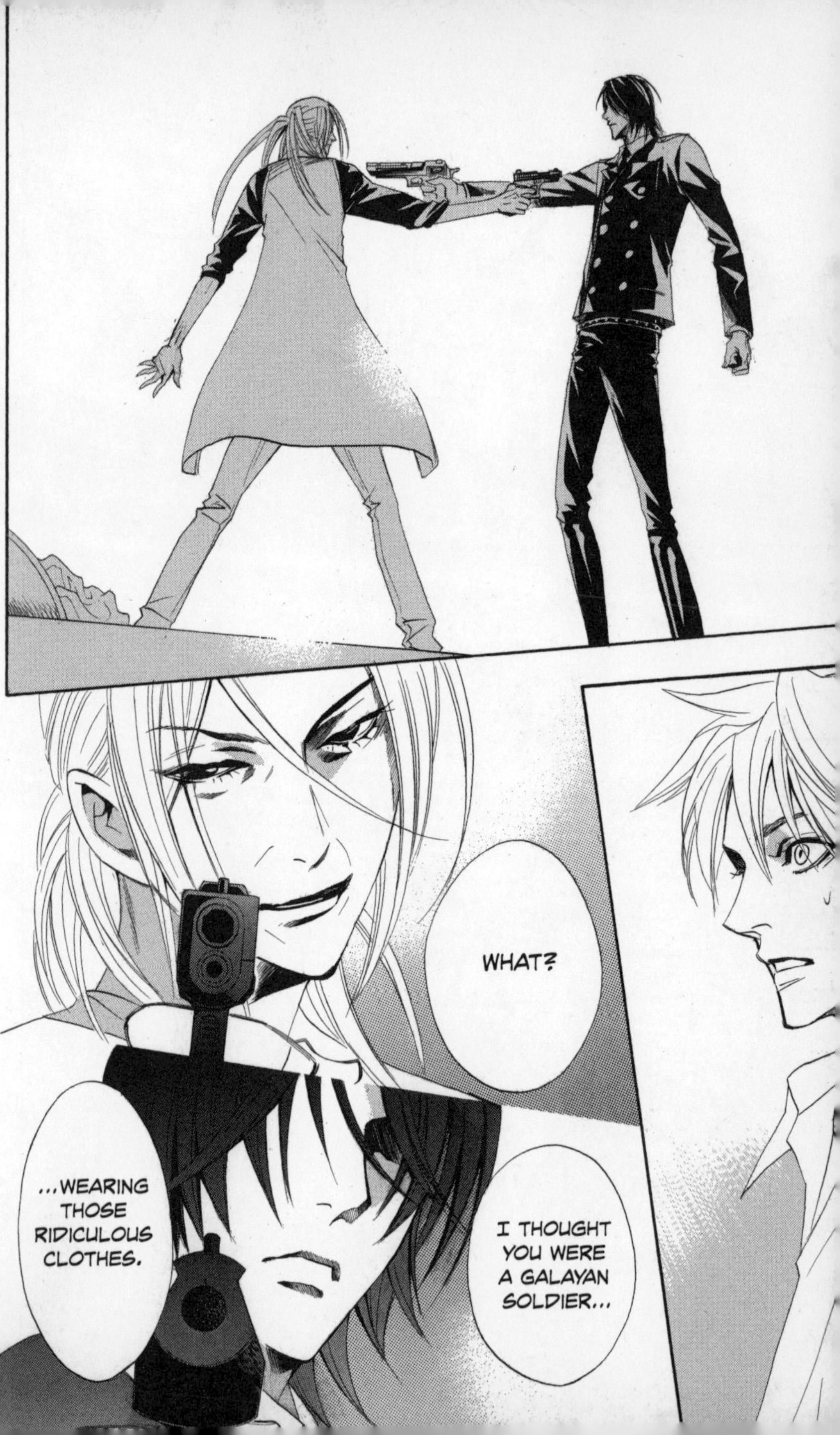
WHAT?
I THOUGHT YOU WERE A GALAYAN SOLDIER...
...WEARING THOSE RIDICULOUS CLOTHES.

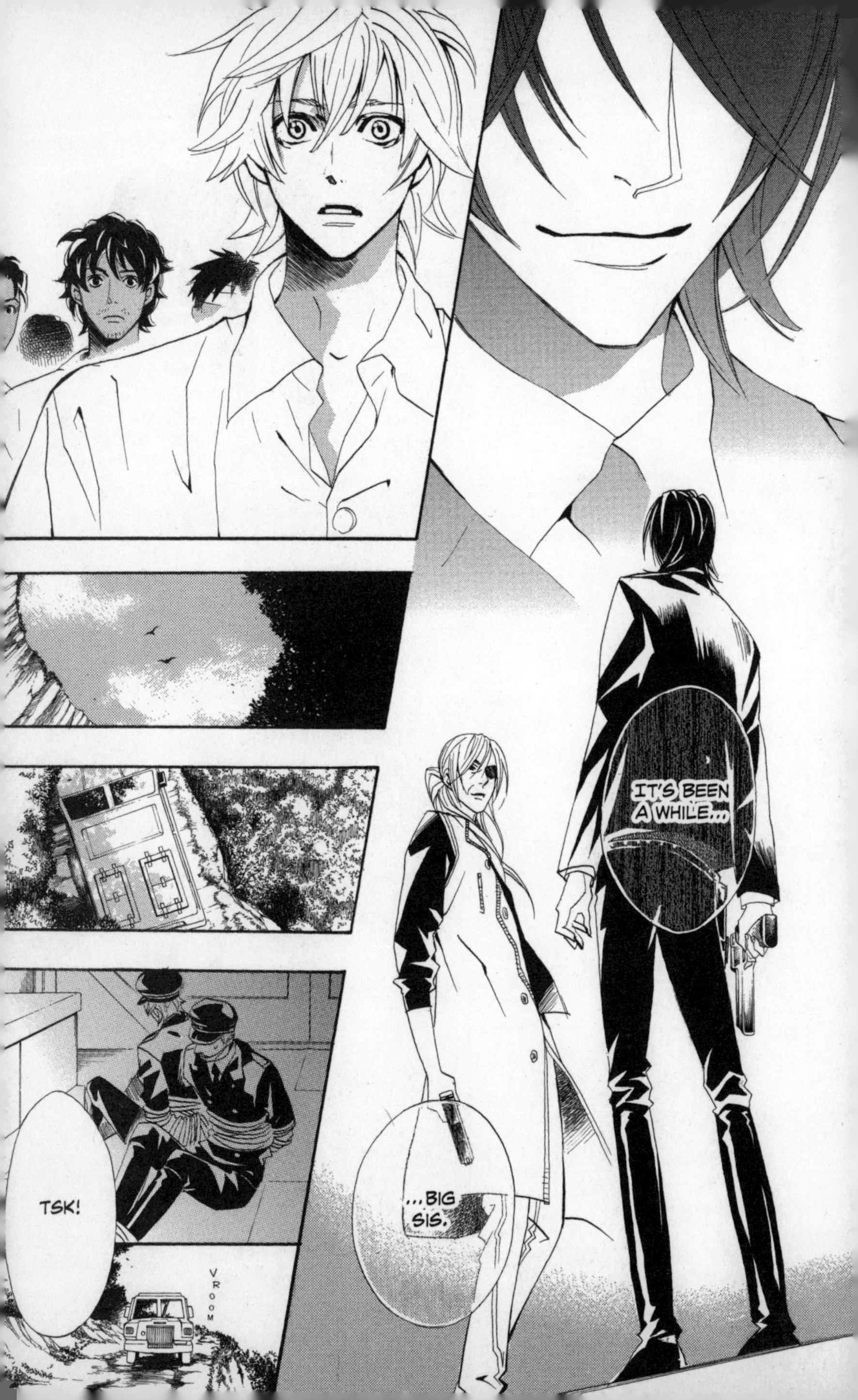
IT'S BEEN A WHILE...
...BIG SIS.
TSK!
VROOM

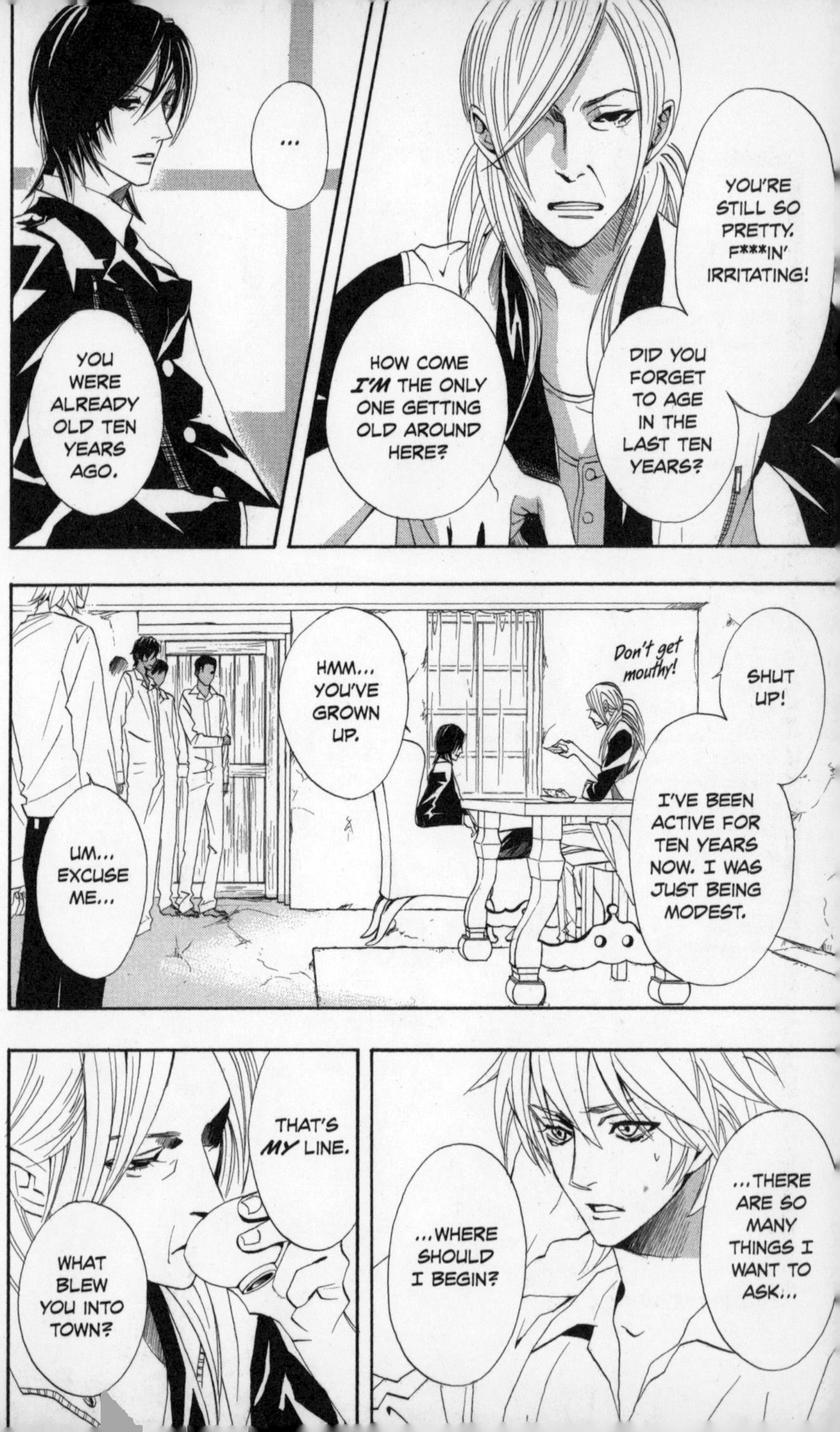

YOU'RE STILL SO PRETTY. F***IN' IRRITATING!
DID YOU FORGET TO AGE IN THE LAST TEN YEARS?
HOW COME *I'M* THE ONLY ONE GETTING OLD AROUND HERE?
...
YOU WERE ALREADY OLD TEN YEARS AGO.
SHUT UP!
Don't get mouthy!
I'VE BEEN ACTIVE FOR TEN YEARS NOW. I WAS JUST BEING MODEST.
HMM... YOU'VE GROWN UP.
UM... EXCUSE ME...
...THERE ARE SO MANY THINGS I WANT TO ASK...
...WHERE SHOULD I BEGIN?
THAT'S *MY* LINE.
WHAT BLEW YOU INTO TOWN?

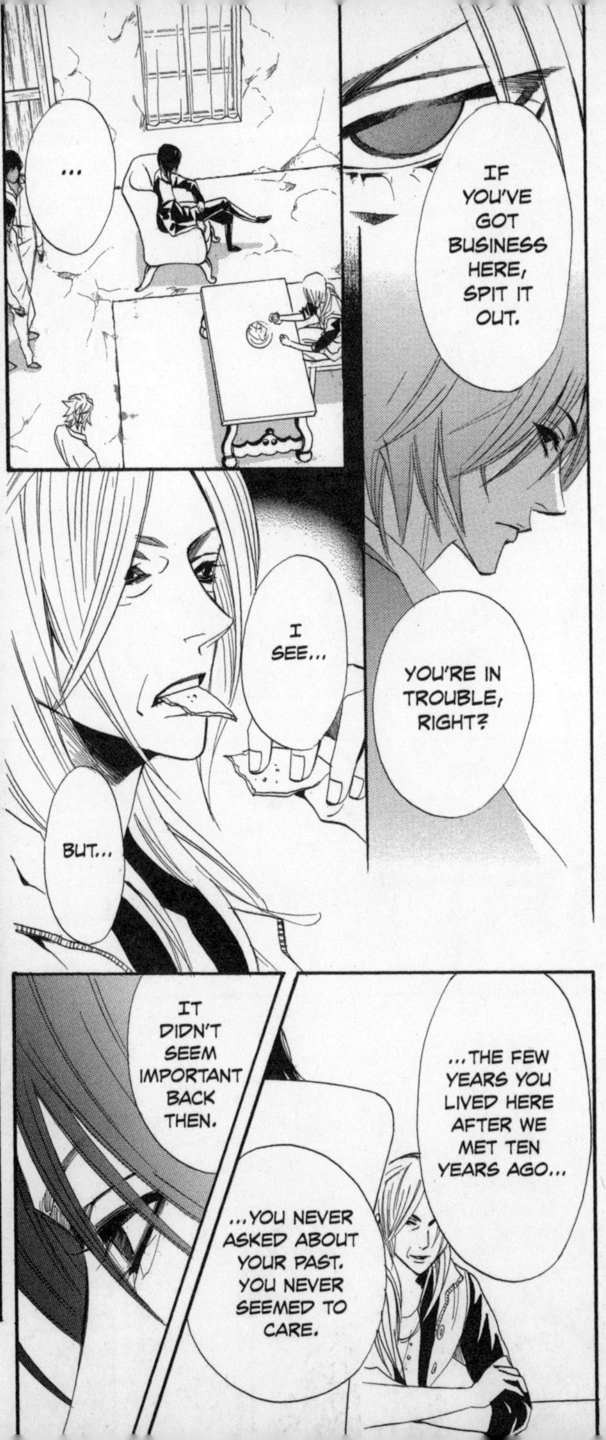
IF YOU'VE GOT BUSINESS HERE, SPIT IT OUT.
YOU'RE IN TROUBLE, RIGHT?
...
I SEE...
BUT...
...THE FEW YEARS YOU LIVED HERE AFTER WE MET TEN YEARS AGO...
...YOU NEVER ASKED ABOUT YOUR PAST. YOU NEVER SEEMED TO CARE.
IT DIDN'T SEEM IMPORTANT BACK THEN.

1

Hello! I'm glad to see you here again! This is Volume 2!

This time I'm thinking about revealing some spoilers and doing a little behind-the-scenes talk here.

So for those of you who don't like that sort of thing, and those of you reading *Blank Slate* for the first time in the graphic novels, read with caution.

So then...see you in the next sidebar.

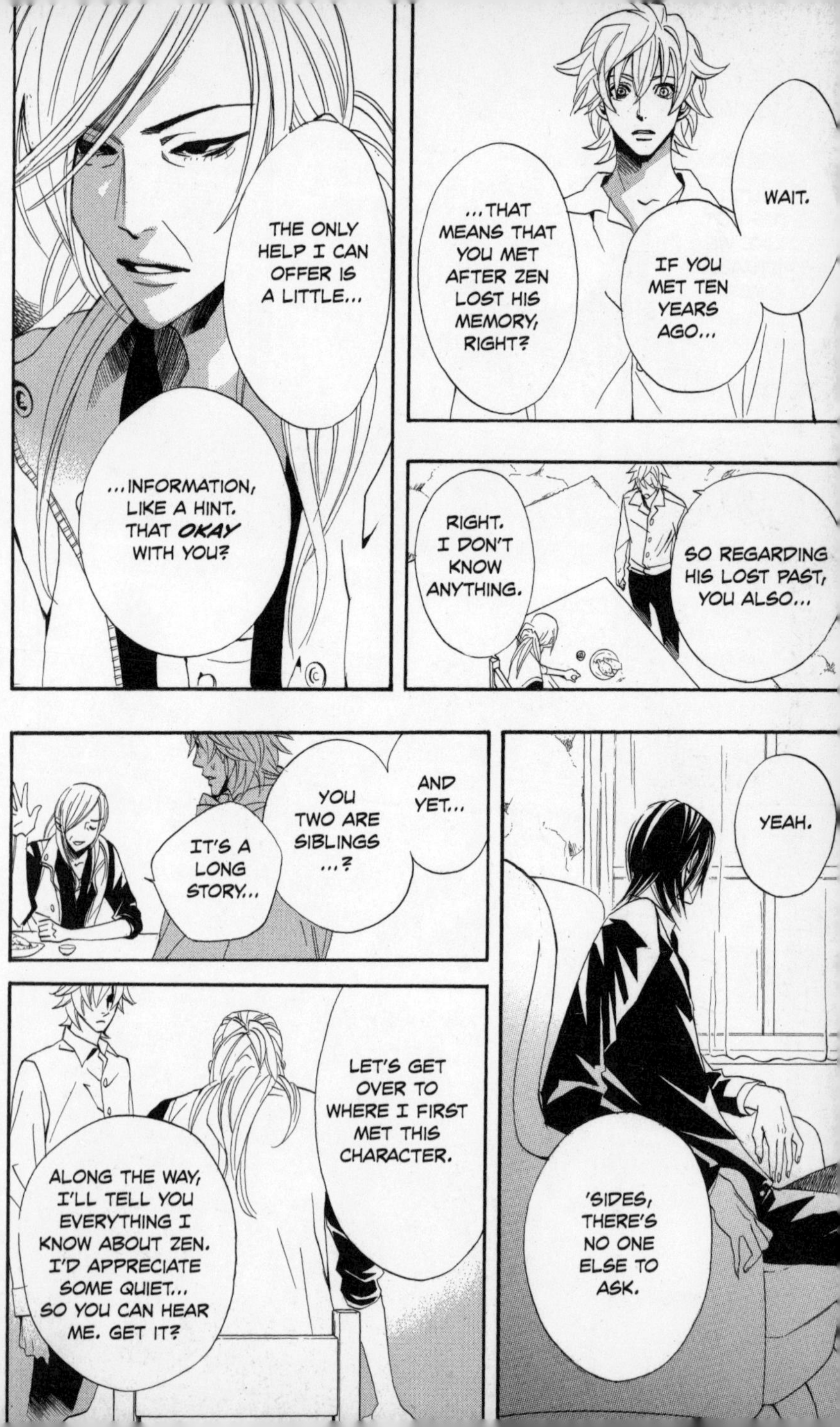
WAIT.
IF YOU MET TEN YEARS AGO...
...THAT MEANS THAT YOU MET AFTER ZEN LOST HIS MEMORY, RIGHT?
SO REGARDING HIS LOST PAST, YOU ALSO...
RIGHT. I DON'T KNOW ANYTHING.
THE ONLY HELP I CAN OFFER IS A LITTLE...
...INFORMATION, LIKE A HINT. THAT OKAY WITH YOU?
YEAH.
'SIDES, THERE'S NO ONE ELSE TO ASK.
AND YET...
YOU TWO ARE SIBLINGS ...?
IT'S A LONG STORY...
LET'S GET OVER TO WHERE I FIRST MET THIS CHARACTER.
ALONG THE WAY, I'LL TELL YOU EVERYTHING I KNOW ABOUT ZEN. I'D APPRECIATE SOME QUIET... SO YOU CAN HEAR ME. GET IT?

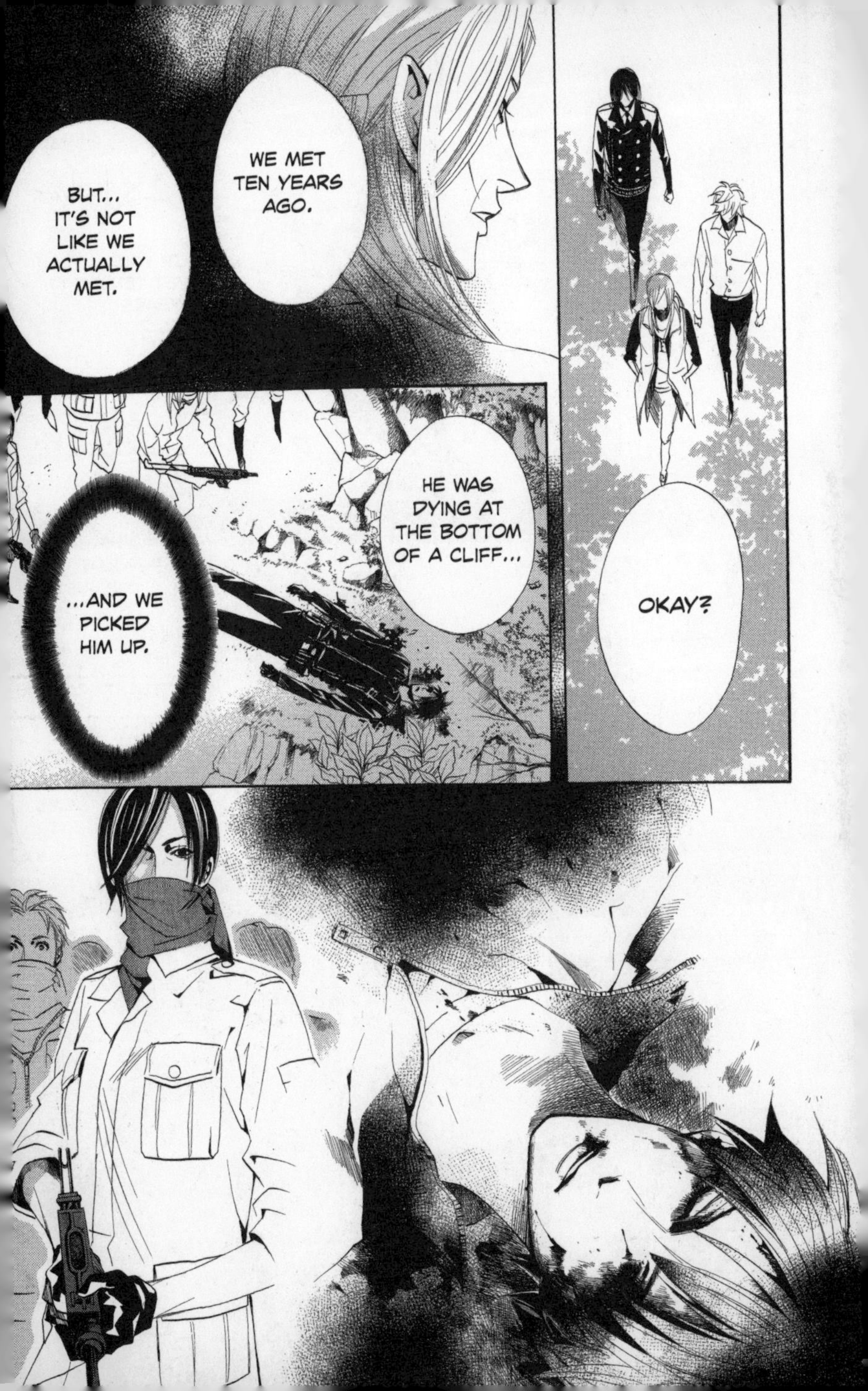
OKAY?
WE MET TEN YEARS AGO.
BUT... IT'S NOT LIKE WE ACTUALLY MET.
HE WAS DYING AT THE BOTTOM OF A CLIFF...
...AND WE PICKED HIM UP.

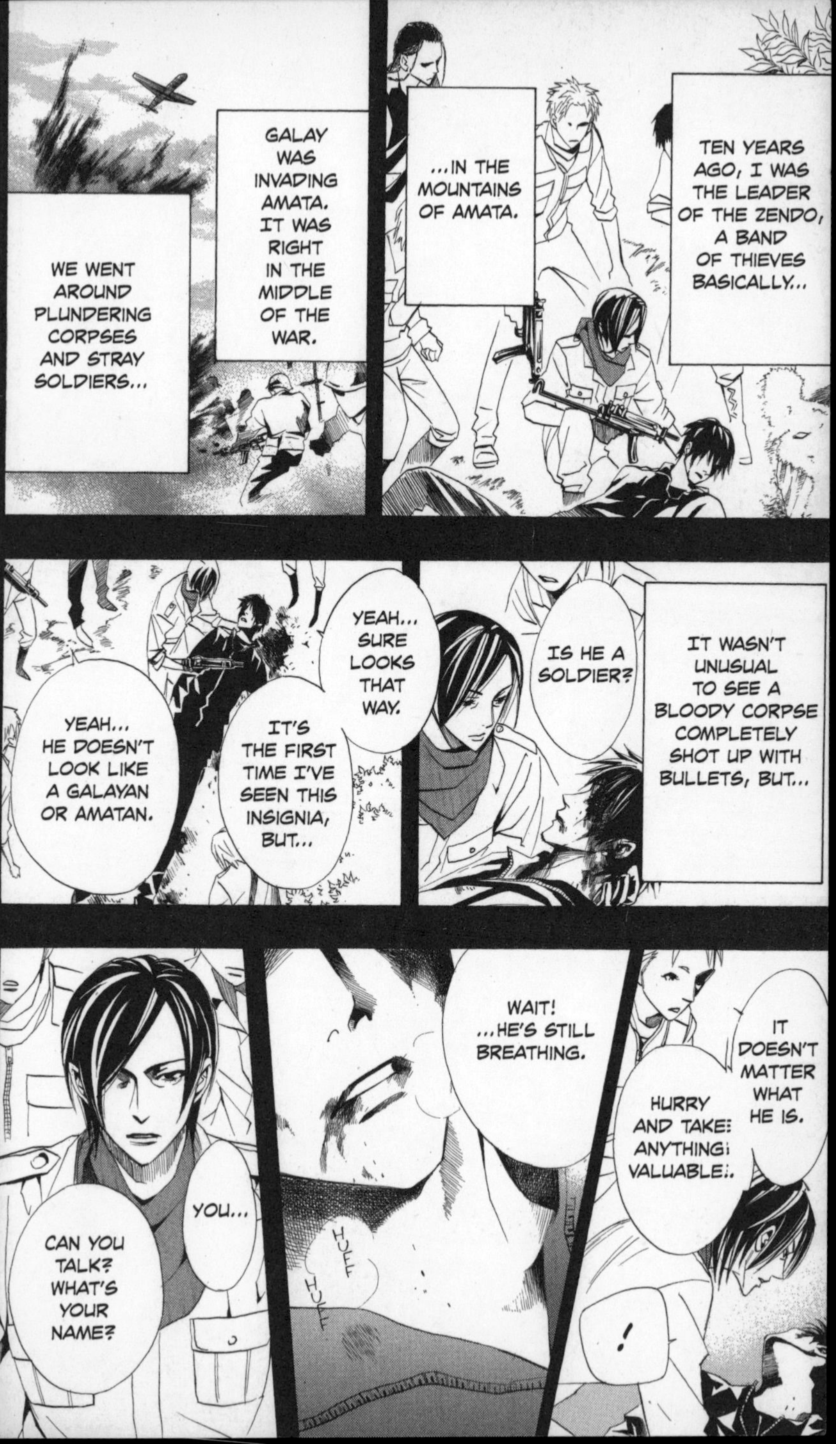
TEN YEARS AGO, I WAS THE LEADER OF THE ZENDO, A BAND OF THIEVES BASICALLY...
...IN THE MOUNTAINS OF AMATA.
GALAY WAS INVADING AMATA. IT WAS RIGHT IN THE MIDDLE OF THE WAR.
WE WENT AROUND PLUNDERING CORPSES AND STRAY SOLDIERS...
IT WASN'T UNUSUAL TO SEE A BLOODY CORPSE COMPLETELY SHOT UP WITH BULLETS, BUT...
IS HE A SOLDIER?
YEAH... SURE LOOKS THAT WAY.
IT'S THE FIRST TIME I'VE SEEN THIS INSIGNIA, BUT...
YEAH... HE DOESN'T LOOK LIKE A GALAYAN OR AMATAN.
IT DOESN'T MATTER WHAT HE IS.
HURRY AND TAKE ANYTHING VALUABLE.
!
WAIT! ...HE'S STILL BREATHING.
HUFF
HUFF
YOU...
CAN YOU TALK? WHAT'S YOUR NAME?

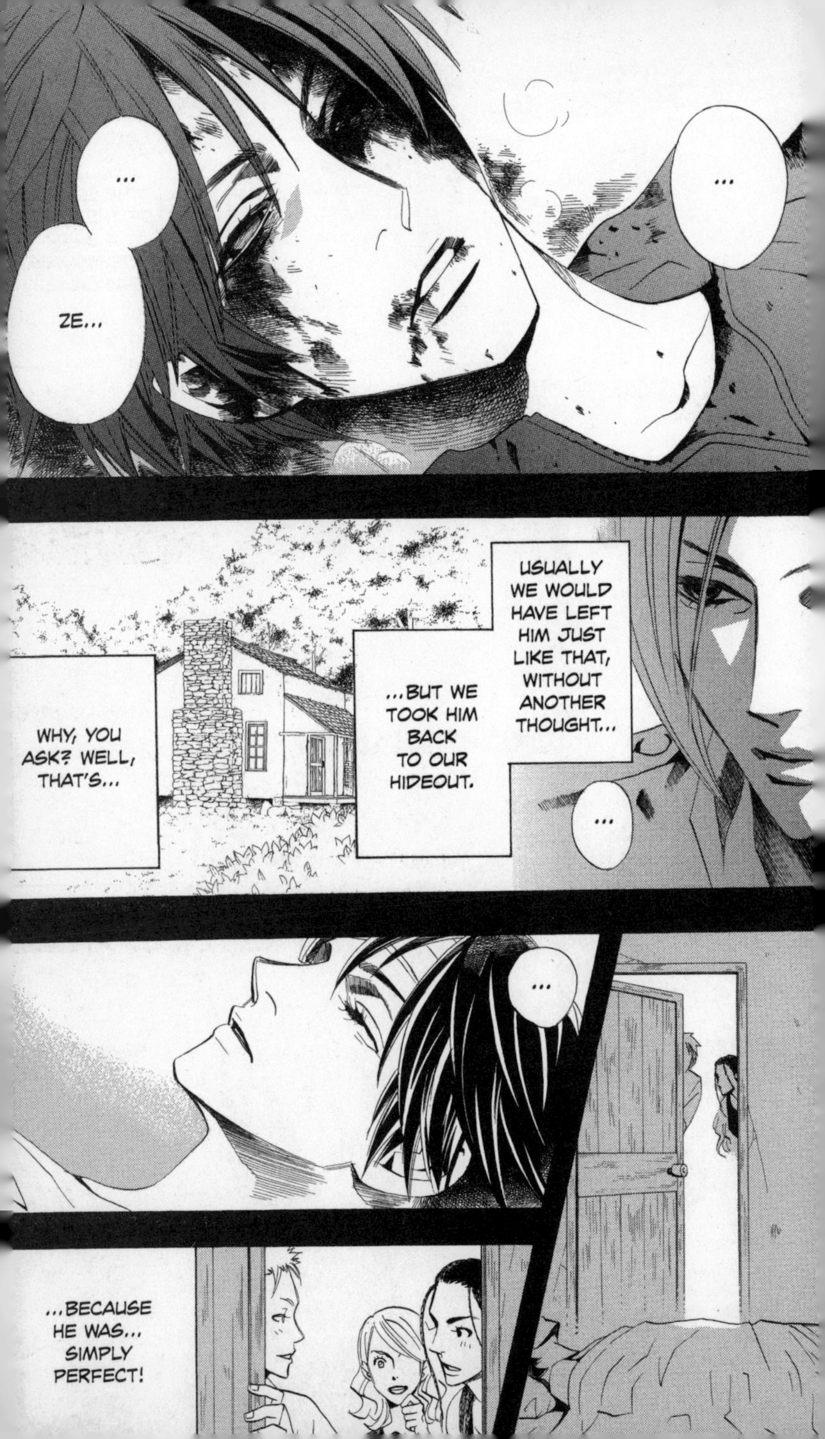
...
...
ZE...
USUALLY WE WOULD HAVE LEFT HIM JUST LIKE THAT, WITHOUT ANOTHER THOUGHT...
...BUT WE TOOK HIM BACK TO OUR HIDEOUT.
...
WHY, YOU ASK? WELL, THAT'S...
...
...BECAUSE HE WAS... SIMPLY PERFECT!

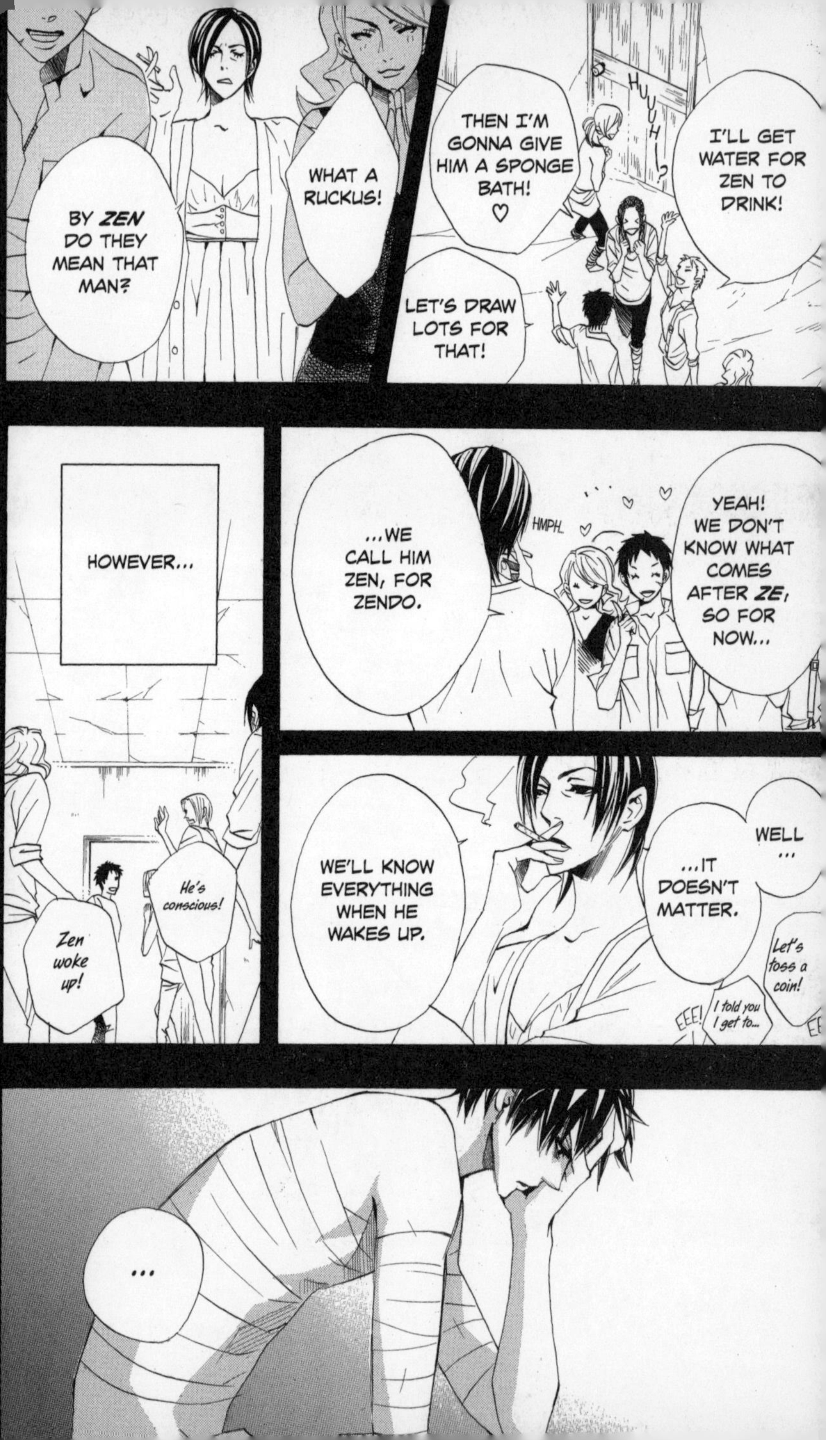
I'LL GET WATER FOR ZEN TO DRINK!
HUUUH!?
THEN I'M GONNA GIVE HIM A SPONGE BATH! ♡
LET'S DRAW LOTS FOR THAT!
WHAT A RUCKUS!
BY ZEN DO THEY MEAN THAT MAN?
YEAH! WE DON'T KNOW WHAT COMES AFTER ZE, SO FOR NOW...
HMPH.
...WE CALL HIM ZEN, FOR ZENDO.
WELL...
...IT DOESN'T MATTER.
Let's toss a coin!
I told you I get to...
EEE!
WE'LL KNOW EVERYTHING WHEN HE WAKES UP.
HOWEVER...
He's conscious!
Zen woke up!
...

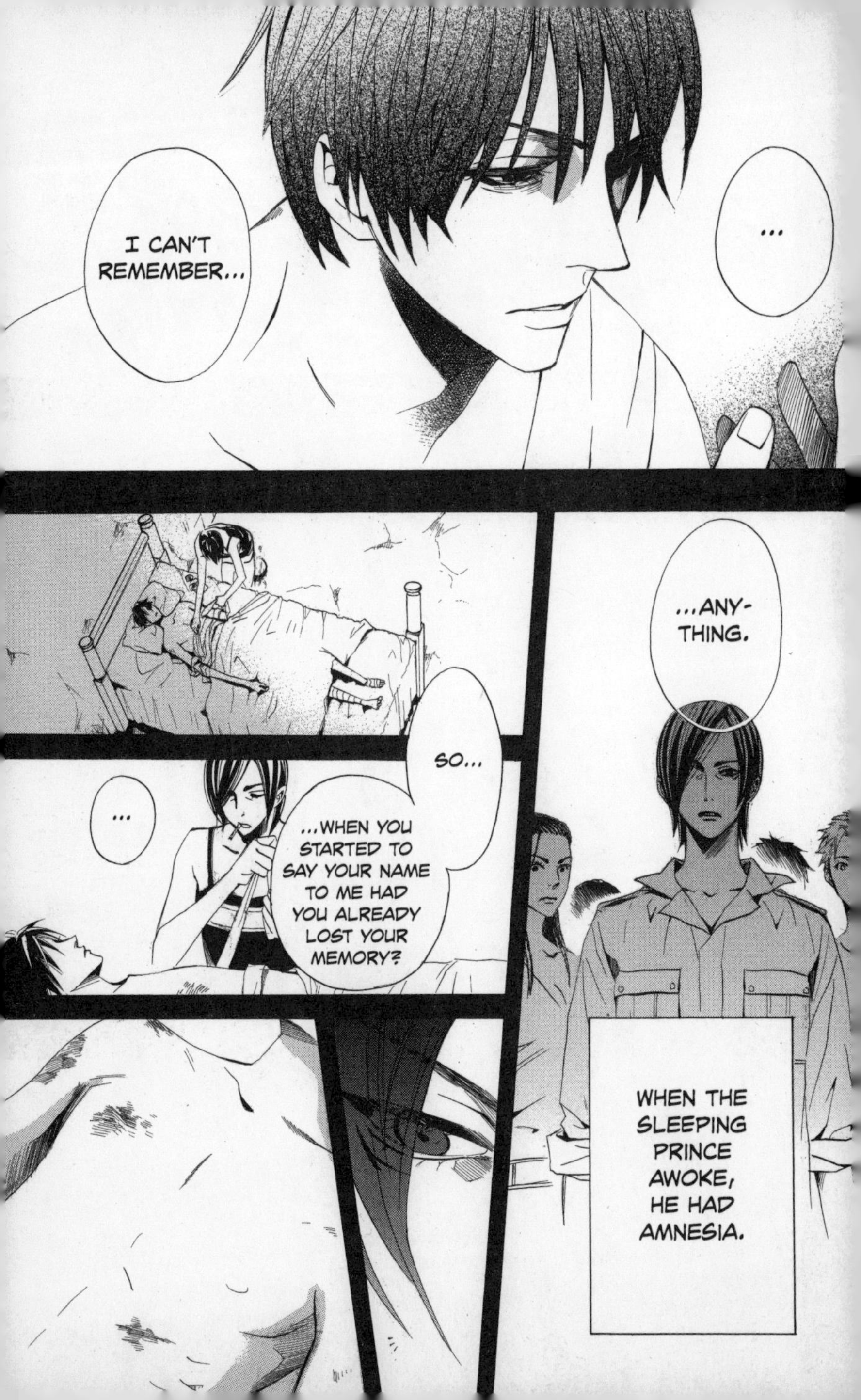
...
I CAN'T REMEMBER...
...ANY-THING.
WHEN THE SLEEPING PRINCE AWOKE, HE HAD AMNESIA.
SO...
...WHEN YOU STARTED TO SAY YOUR NAME TO ME HAD YOU ALREADY LOST YOUR MEMORY?
...

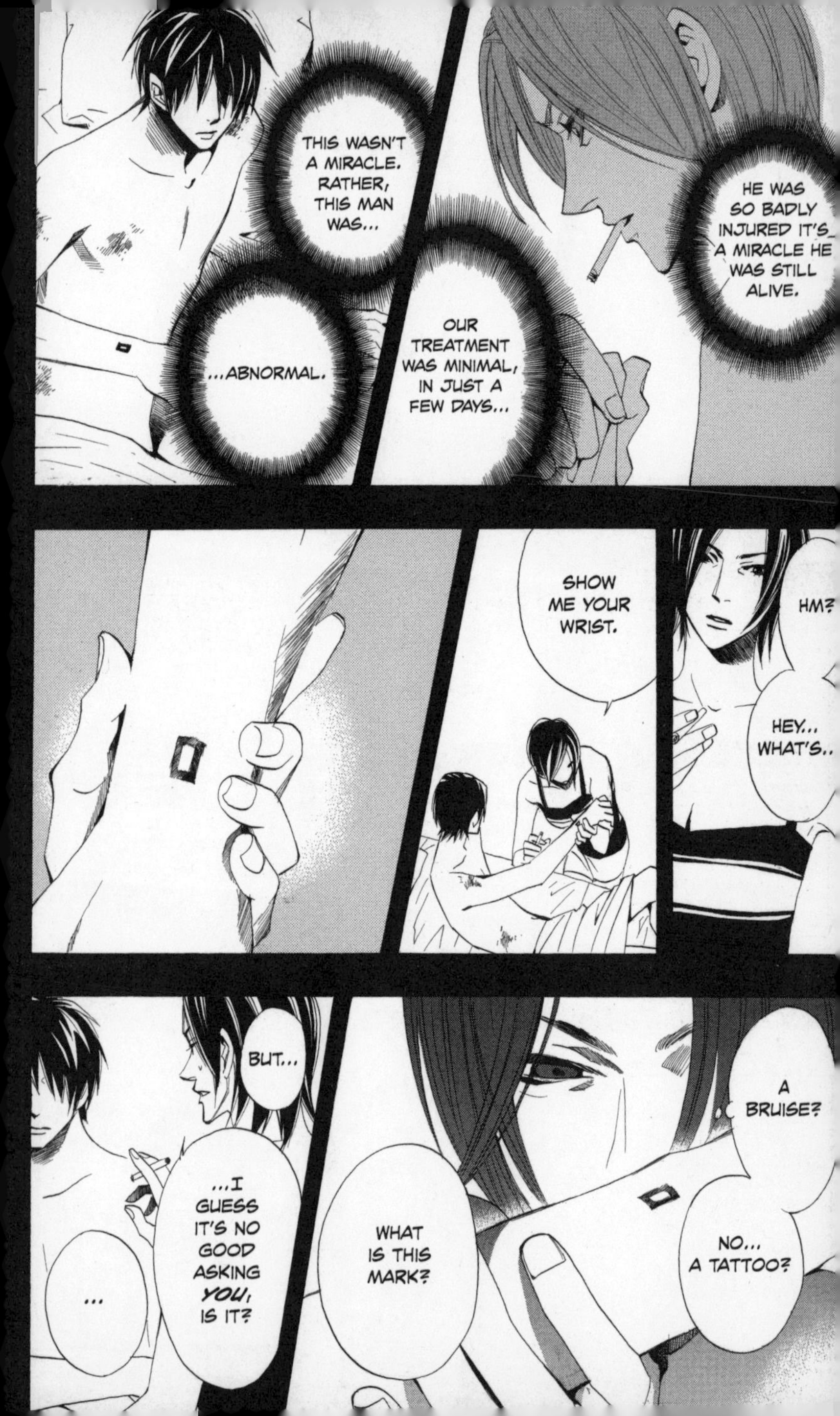
HE WAS SO BADLY INJURED IT'S A MIRACLE HE WAS STILL ALIVE.
OUR TREATMENT WAS MINIMAL, IN JUST A FEW DAYS...
THIS WASN'T A MIRACLE. RATHER, THIS MAN WAS...
...ABNORMAL.
HM?
HEY... WHAT'S..
SHOW ME YOUR WRIST.
A BRUISE?
NO... A TATTOO?
WHAT IS THIS MARK?
BUT...
...I GUESS IT'S NO GOOD ASKING *YOU*, IS IT?
...

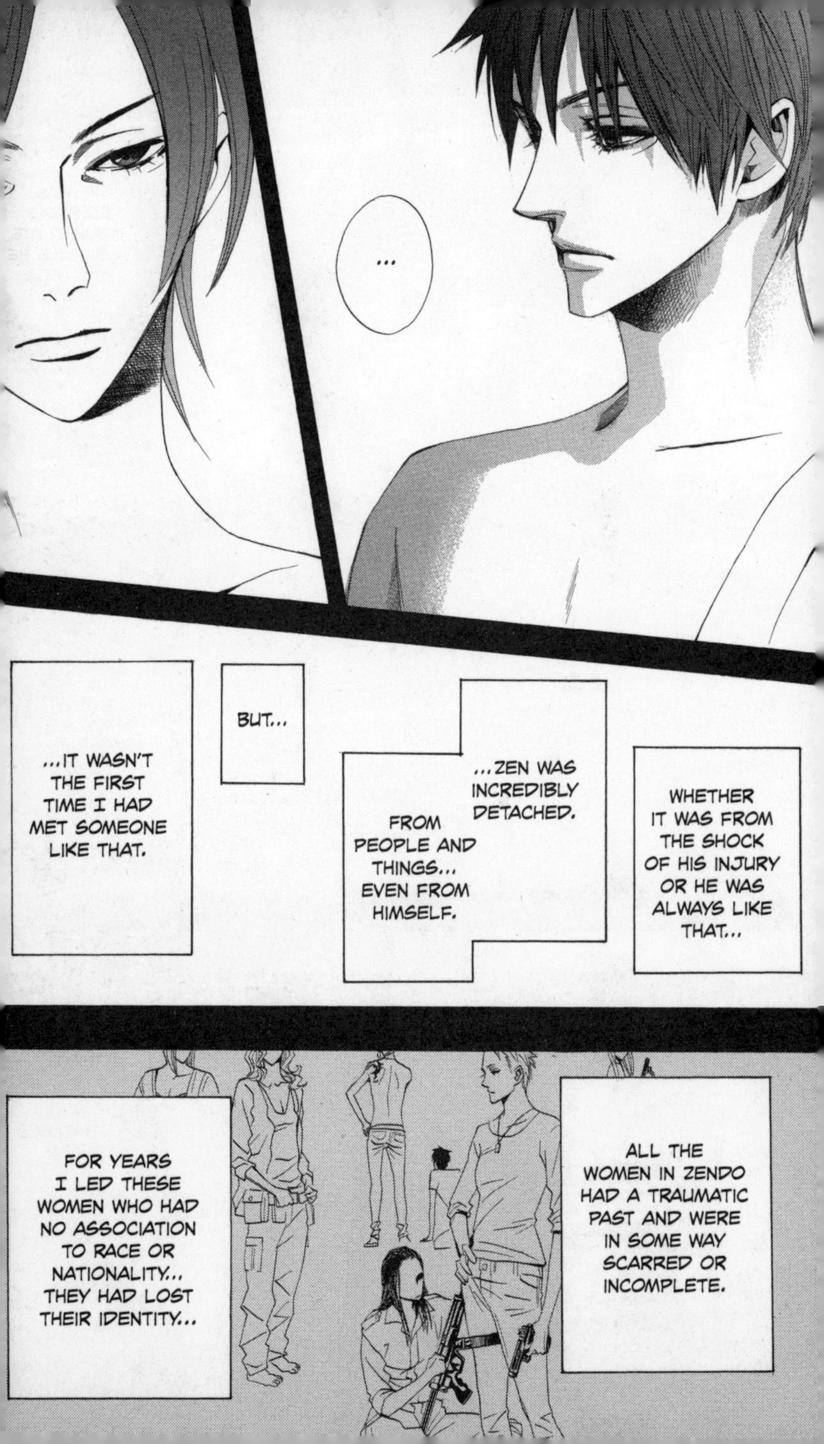
...
WHETHER IT WAS FROM THE SHOCK OF HIS INJURY OR HE WAS ALWAYS LIKE THAT...
...ZEN WAS INCREDIBLY DETACHED.
FROM PEOPLE AND THINGS... EVEN FROM HIMSELF.
BUT...
...IT WASN'T THE FIRST TIME I HAD MET SOMEONE LIKE THAT.
ALL THE WOMEN IN ZENDO HAD A TRAUMATIC PAST AND WERE IN SOME WAY SCARRED OR INCOMPLETE.
FOR YEARS I LED THESE WOMEN WHO HAD NO ASSOCIATION TO RACE OR NATIONALITY... THEY HAD LOST THEIR IDENTITY...

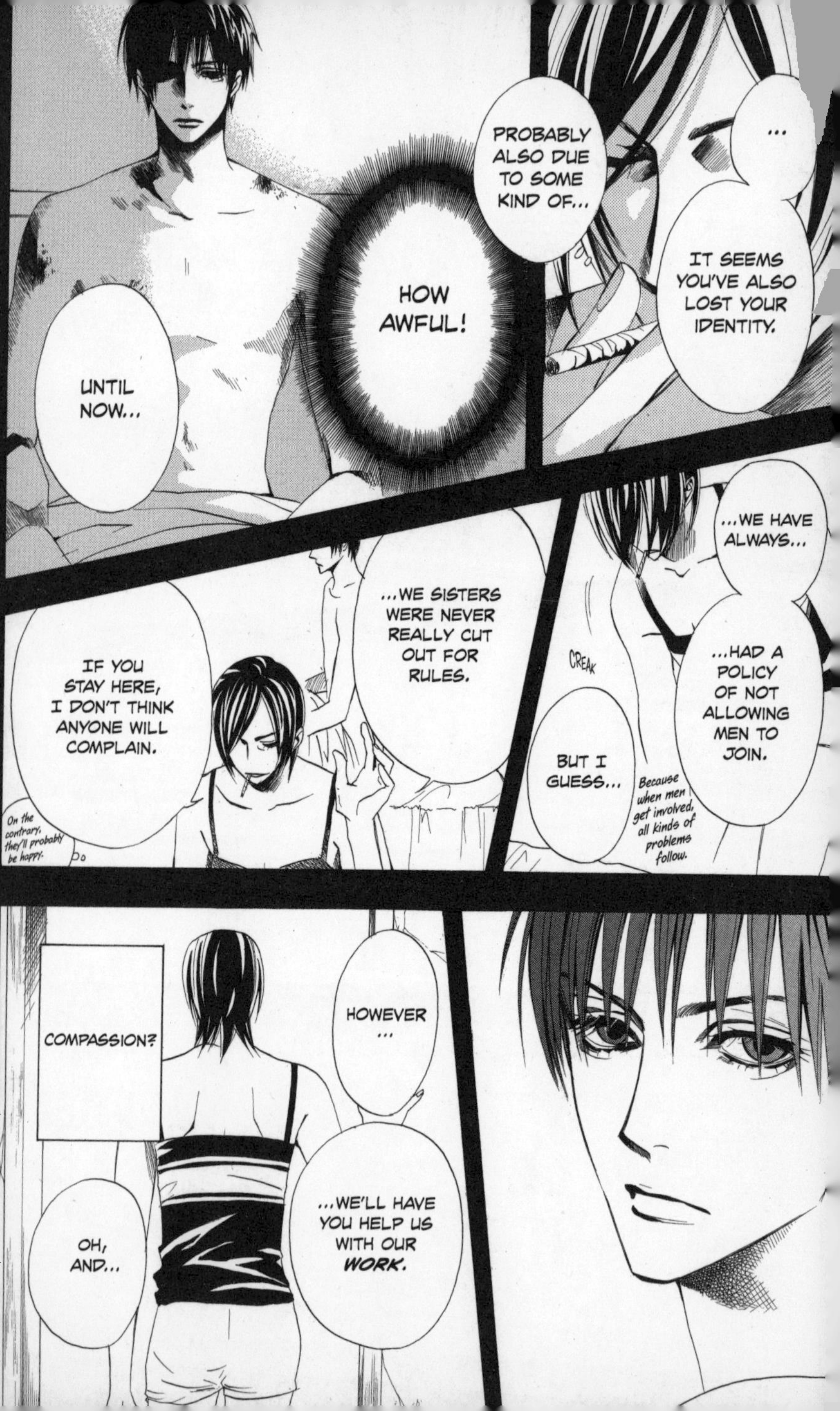
...
IT SEEMS YOU'VE ALSO LOST YOUR IDENTITY.
PROBABLY ALSO DUE TO SOME KIND OF...
HOW AWFUL!
UNTIL NOW...
...WE HAVE ALWAYS...
...HAD A POLICY OF NOT ALLOWING MEN TO JOIN.
Because when men get involved, all kinds of problems follow.
CREAK
BUT I GUESS...
...WE SISTERS WERE NEVER REALLY CUT OUT FOR RULES.
IF YOU STAY HERE, I DON'T THINK ANYONE WILL COMPLAIN.
On the contrary, they'll probably be happy.
HOWEVER...
COMPASSION?
...WE'LL HAVE YOU HELP US WITH OUR *WORK*.
OH, AND...

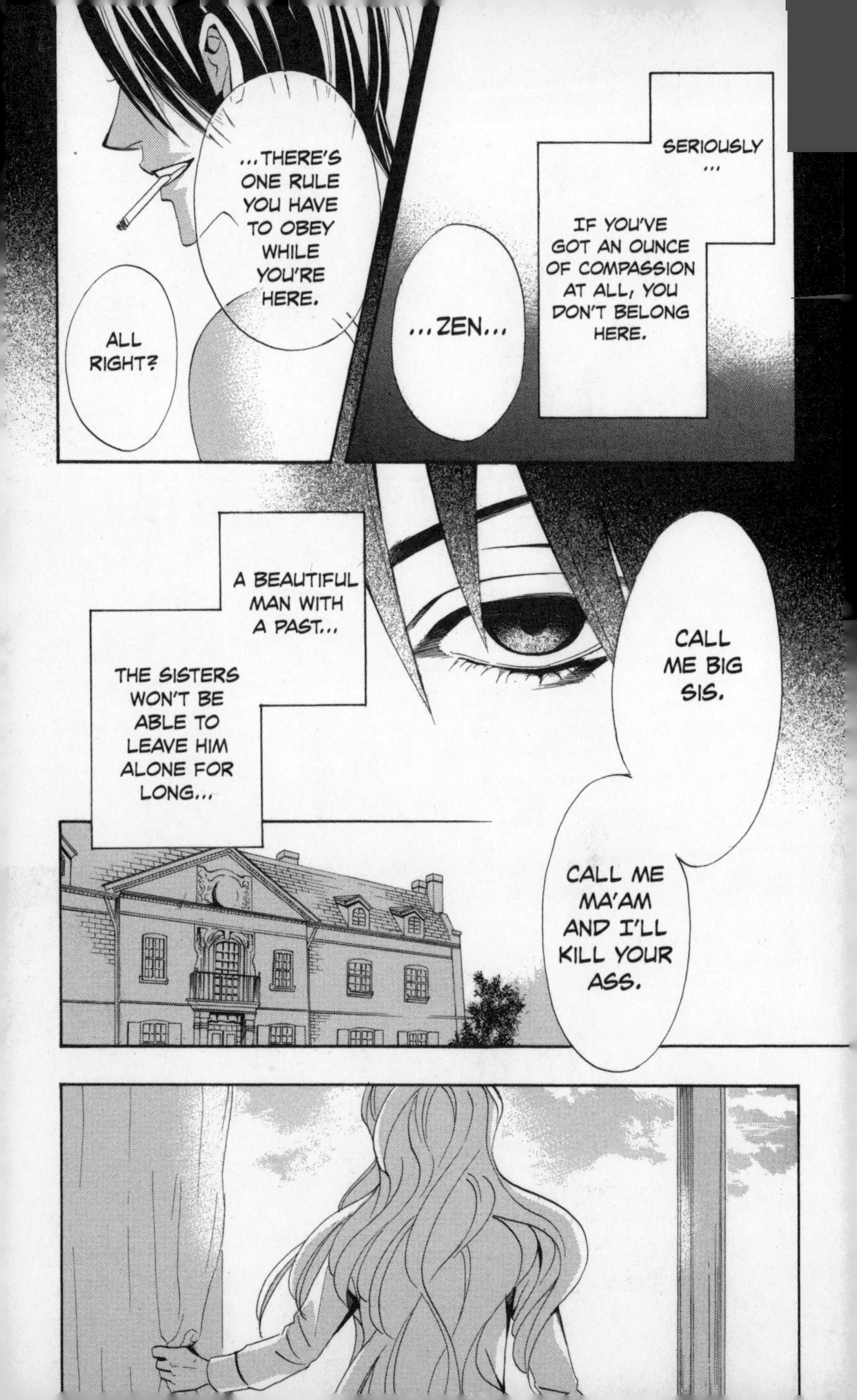
SERIOUSLY ...
IF YOU'VE GOT AN OUNCE OF COMPASSION AT ALL, YOU DON'T BELONG HERE.
...ZEN...
...THERE'S ONE RULE YOU HAVE TO OBEY WHILE YOU'RE HERE.
ALL RIGHT?
CALL ME BIG SIS.
CALL ME MA'AM AND I'LL KILL YOUR ASS.
A BEAUTIFUL MAN WITH A PAST...
THE SISTERS WON'T BE ABLE TO LEAVE HIM ALONE FOR LONG...

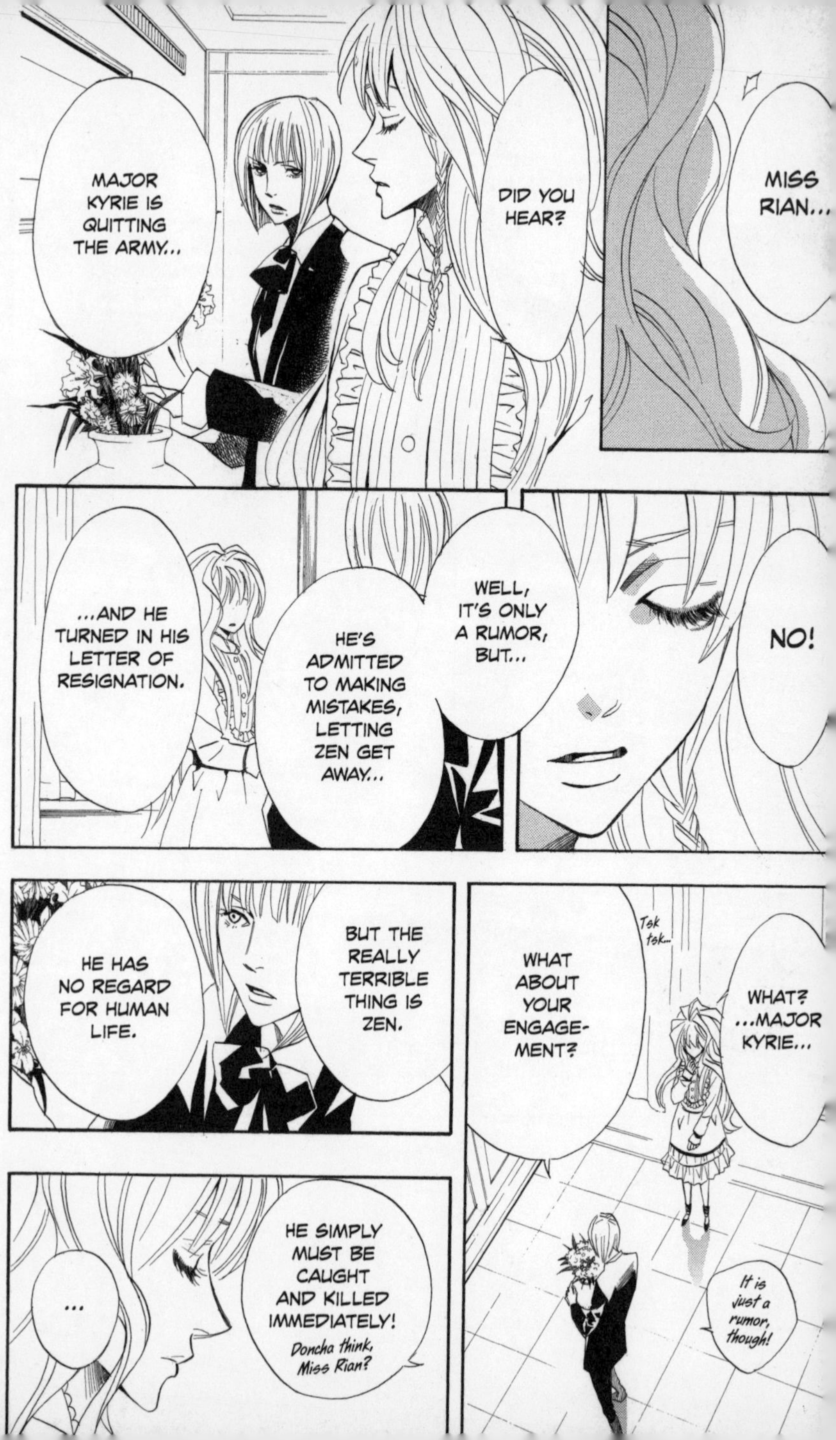
MISS RIAN...
DID YOU HEAR?
MAJOR KYRIE IS QUITTING THE ARMY...
NO!
WELL, IT'S ONLY A RUMOR, BUT...
HE'S ADMITTED TO MAKING MISTAKES, LETTING ZEN GET AWAY...
...AND HE TURNED IN HIS LETTER OF RESIGNATION.
WHAT? ...MAJOR KYRIE...
Tsk tsk...
WHAT ABOUT YOUR ENGAGEMENT?
It is just a rumor, though!
BUT THE REALLY TERRIBLE THING IS ZEN.
HE HAS NO REGARD FOR HUMAN LIFE.
HE SIMPLY MUST BE CAUGHT AND KILLED IMMEDIATELY!
Doncha think, Miss Rian?
...

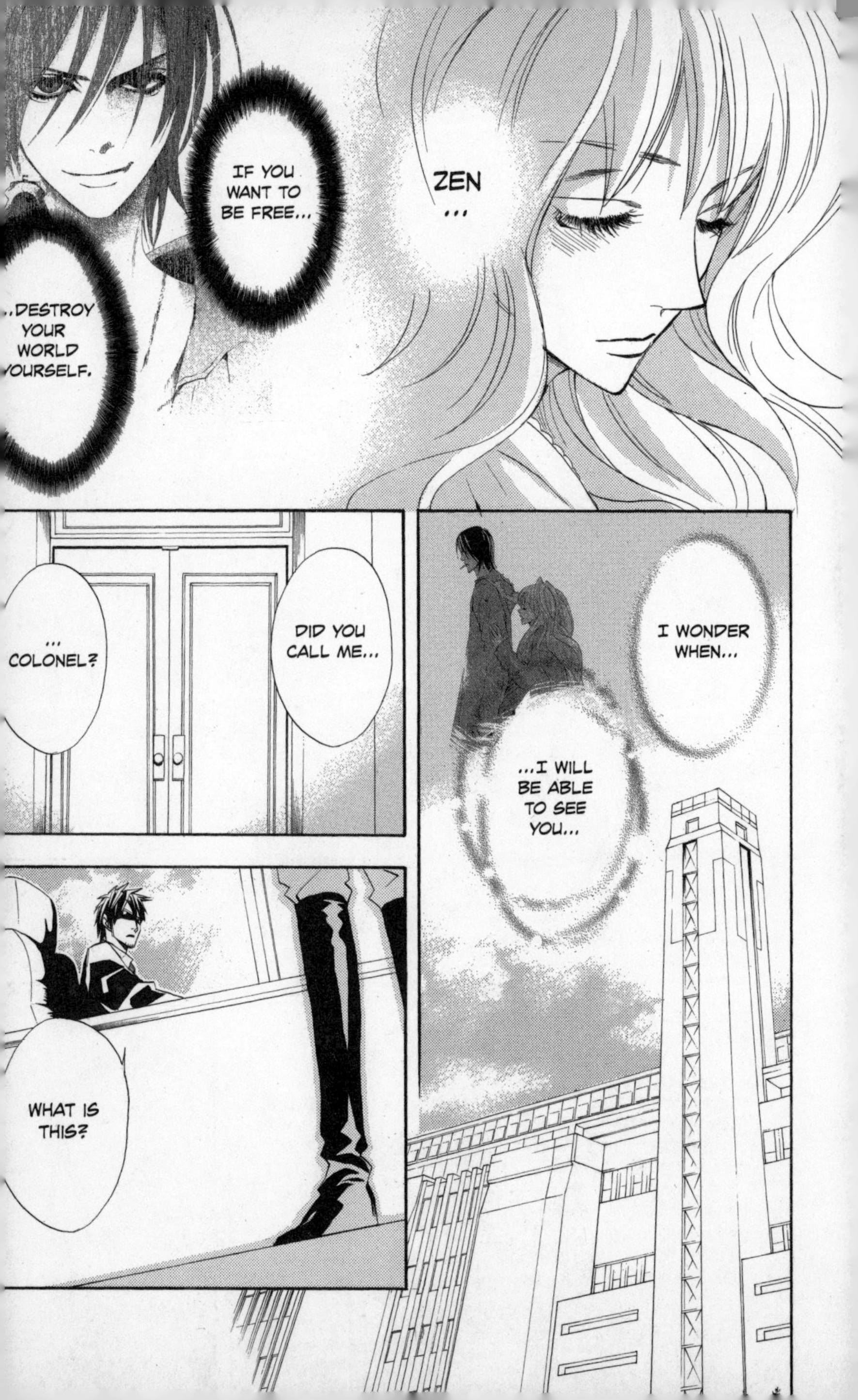
ZEN...
IF YOU WANT TO BE FREE...
..DESTROY YOUR WORLD YOURSELF.
I WONDER WHEN...
...I WILL BE ABLE TO SEE YOU...
DID YOU CALL ME...
...COLONEL?
WHAT IS THIS?

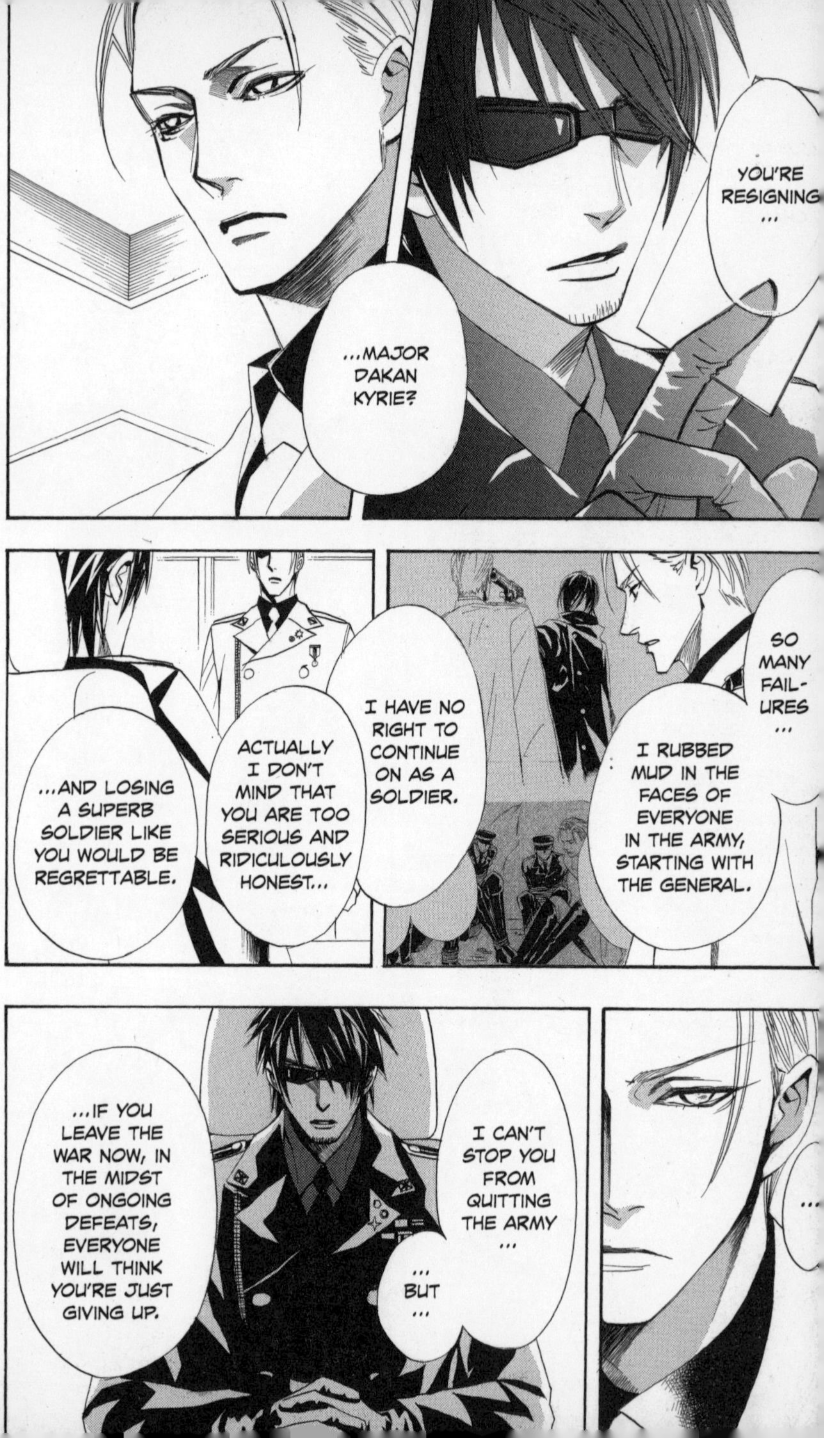
YOU'RE RESIGNING ...
...MAJOR DAKAN KYRIE?
SO MANY FAIL-URES ...
I RUBBED MUD IN THE FACES OF EVERYONE IN THE ARMY, STARTING WITH THE GENERAL.
I HAVE NO RIGHT TO CONTINUE ON AS A SOLDIER.
ACTUALLY I DON'T MIND THAT YOU ARE TOO SERIOUS AND RIDICULOUSLY HONEST...
...AND LOSING A SUPERB SOLDIER LIKE YOU WOULD BE REGRETTABLE.
...
I CAN'T STOP YOU FROM QUITTING THE ARMY ...
... BUT ...
...IF YOU LEAVE THE WAR NOW, IN THE MIDST OF ONGOING DEFEATS, EVERYONE WILL THINK YOU'RE JUST GIVING UP.

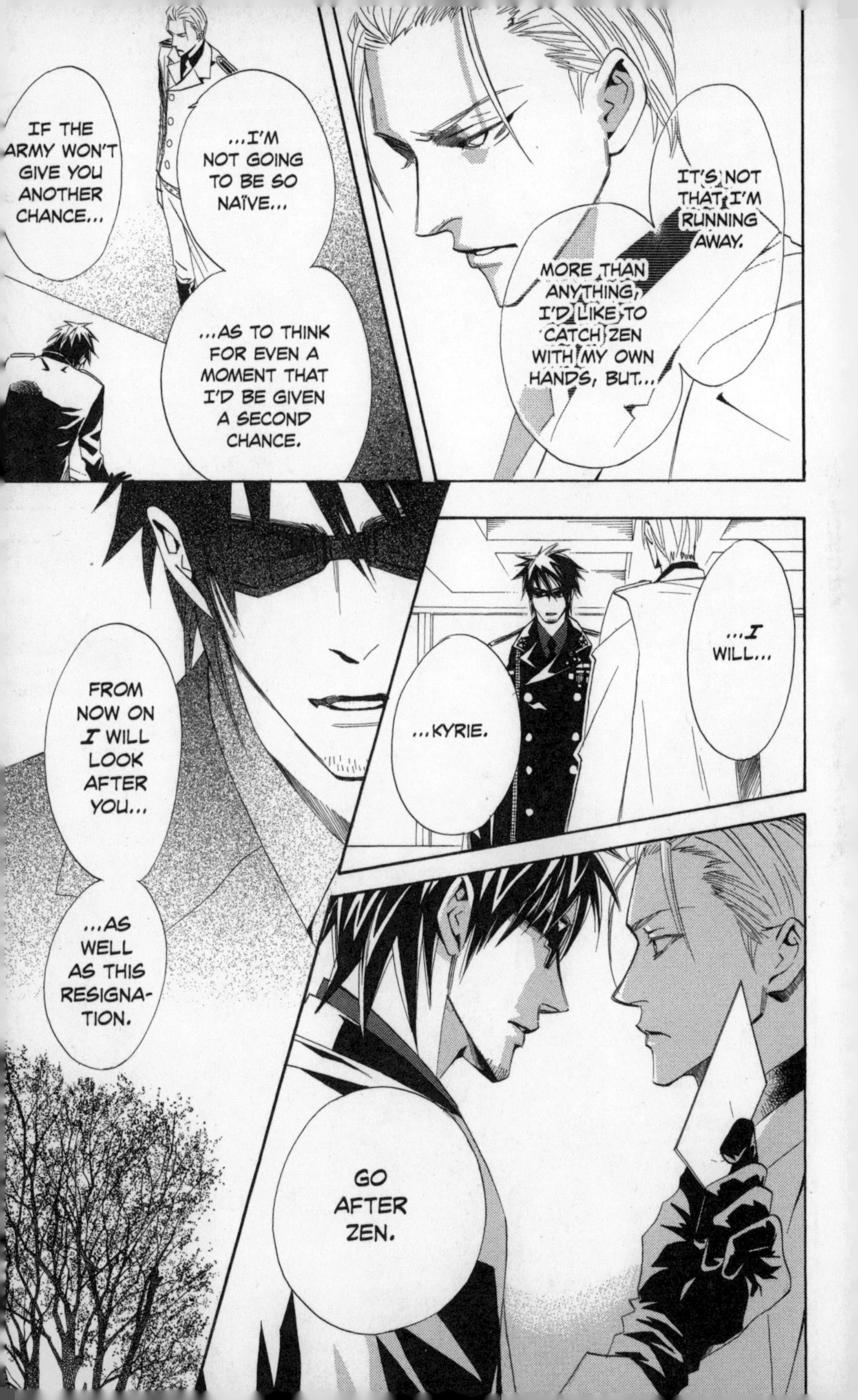
IT'S NOT THAT I'M RUNNING AWAY.
MORE THAN ANYTHING, I'D LIKE TO CATCH ZEN WITH MY OWN HANDS, BUT...
...I'M NOT GOING TO BE SO NAÏVE...
...AS TO THINK FOR EVEN A MOMENT THAT I'D BE GIVEN A SECOND CHANCE.
IF THE ARMY WON'T GIVE YOU ANOTHER CHANCE...
...*I* WILL...
...KYRIE.
GO AFTER ZEN.
FROM NOW ON *I* WILL LOOK AFTER YOU...
...AS WELL AS THIS RESIGNATION.

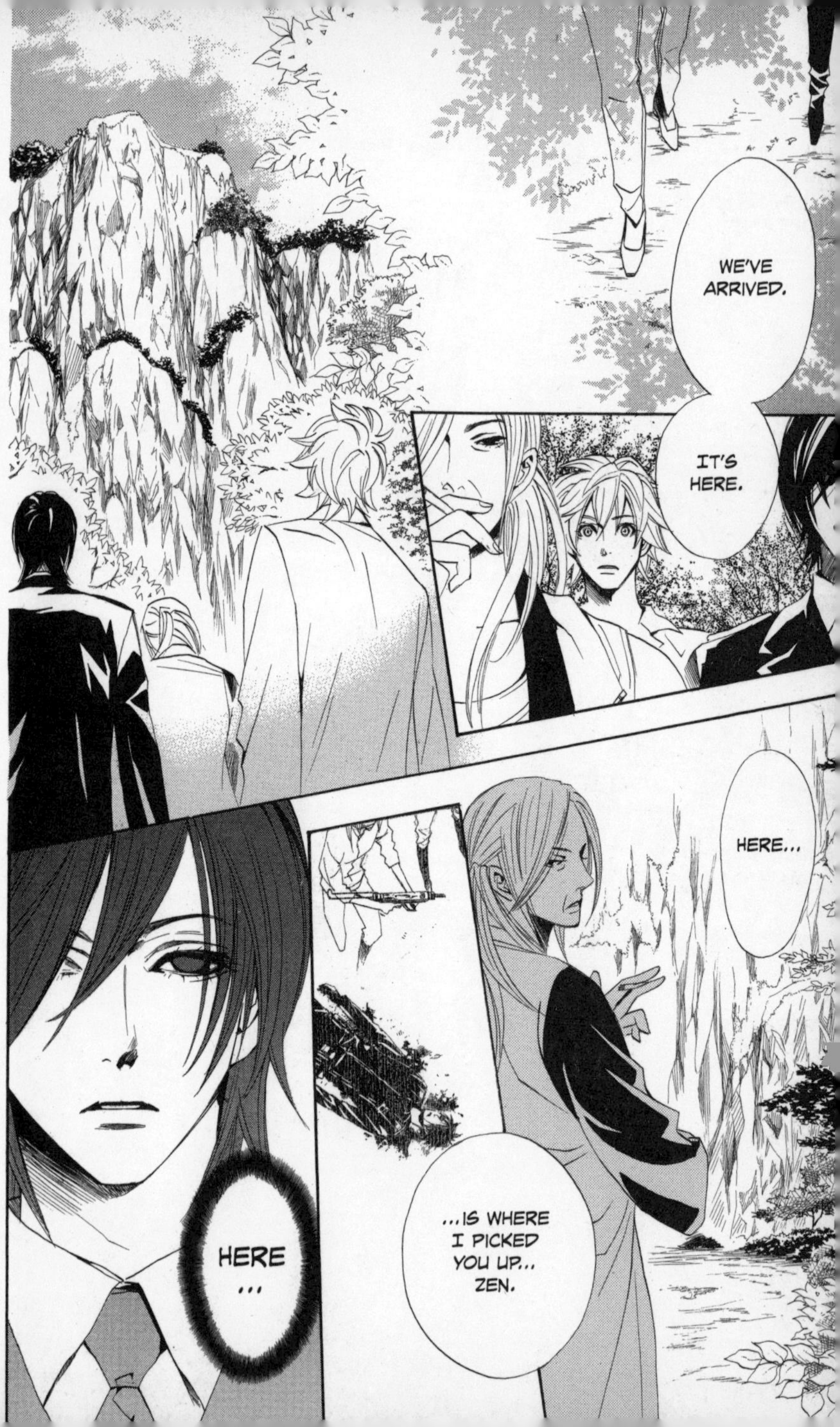
WE'VE ARRIVED.
IT'S HERE.
HERE...
...IS WHERE I PICKED YOU UP... ZEN.
HERE ...

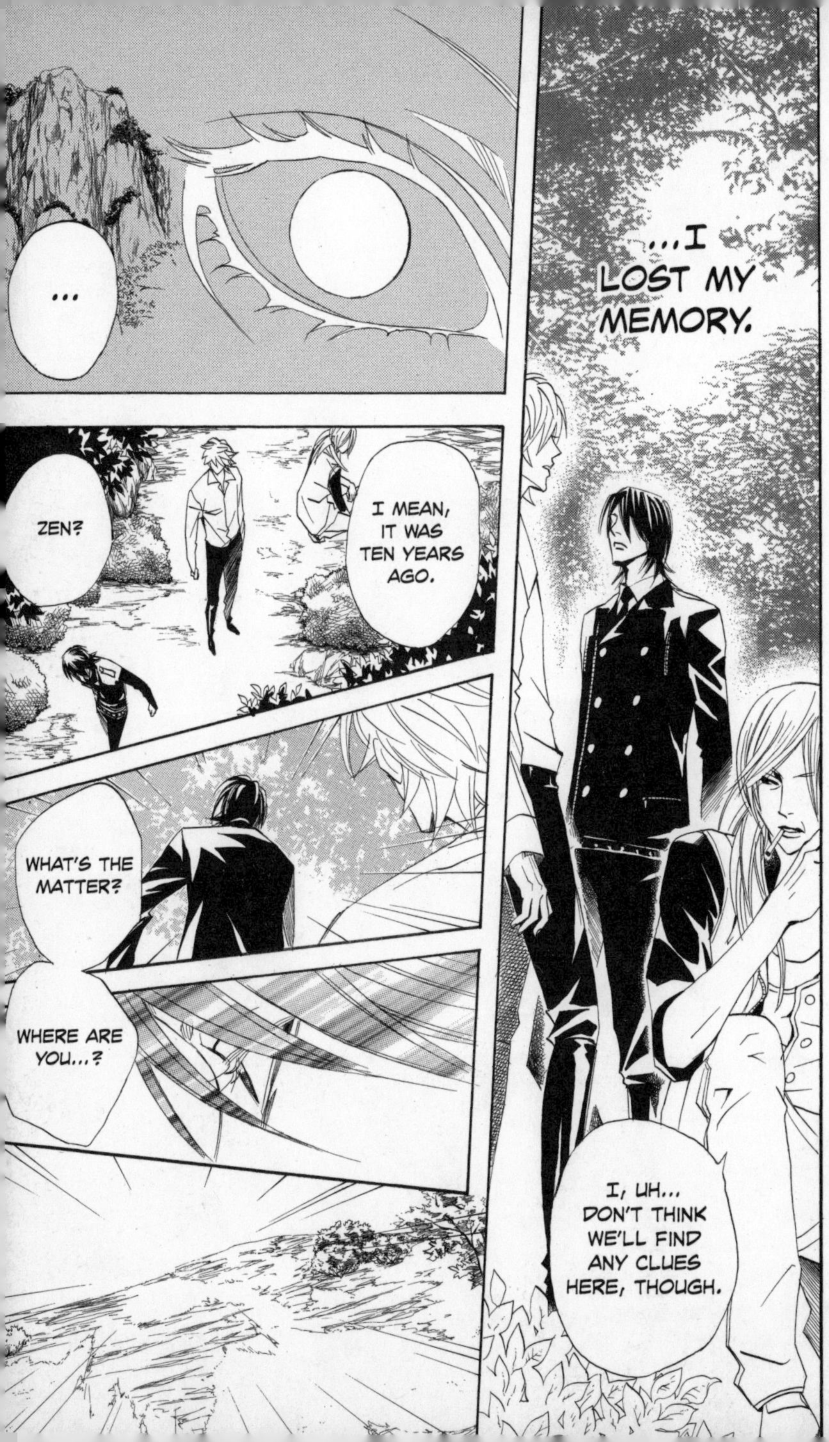
...I LOST MY MEMORY.
I, UH... DON'T THINK WE'LL FIND ANY CLUES HERE, THOUGH.
...
I MEAN, IT WAS TEN YEARS AGO.
ZEN?
WHAT'S THE MATTER?
WHERE ARE YOU...?

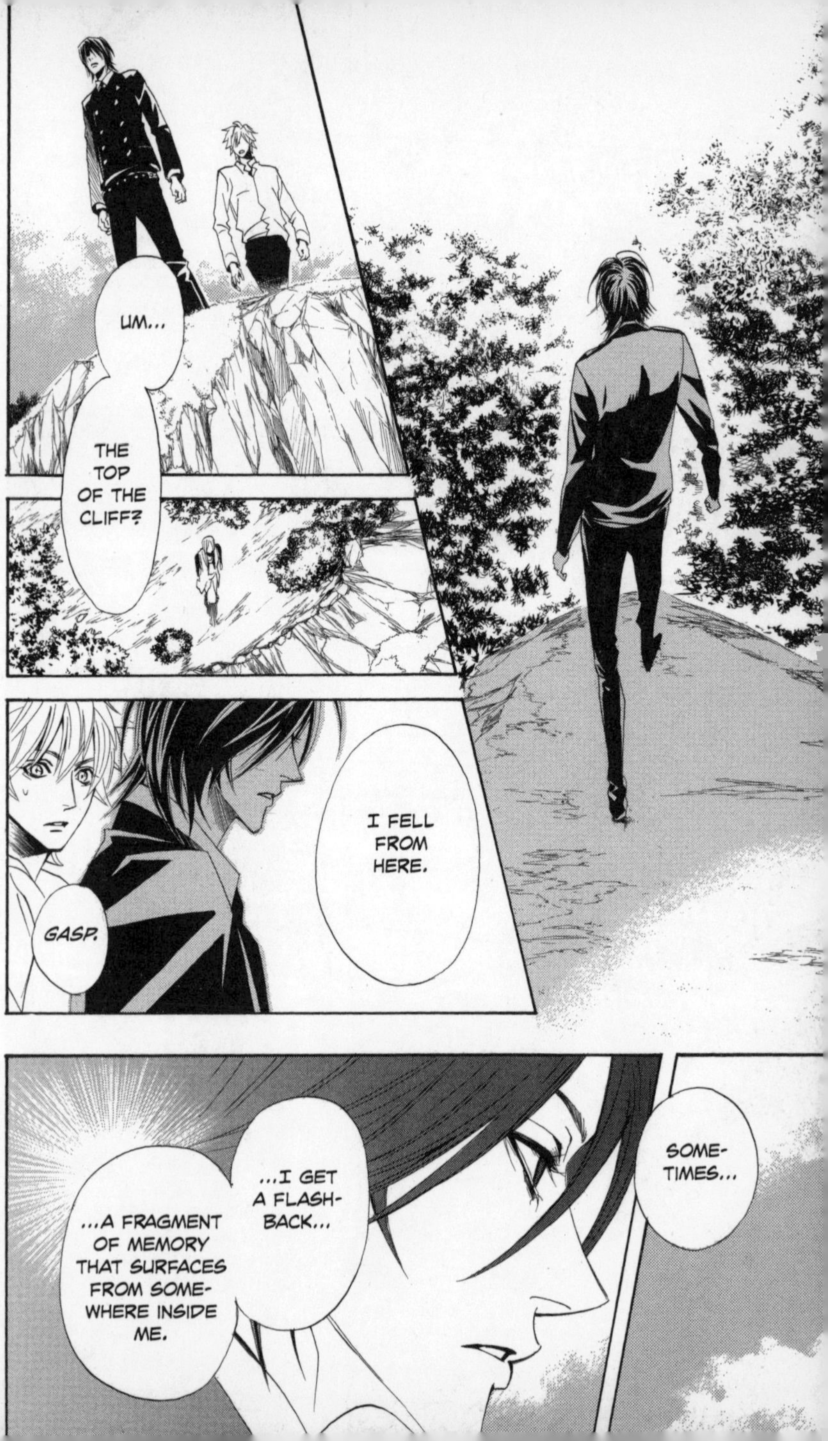
UM...
THE TOP OF THE CLIFF?
I FELL FROM HERE.
GASP.
SOME-TIMES...
...I GET A FLASH-BACK...
...A FRAGMENT OF MEMORY THAT SURFACES FROM SOME-WHERE INSIDE ME.

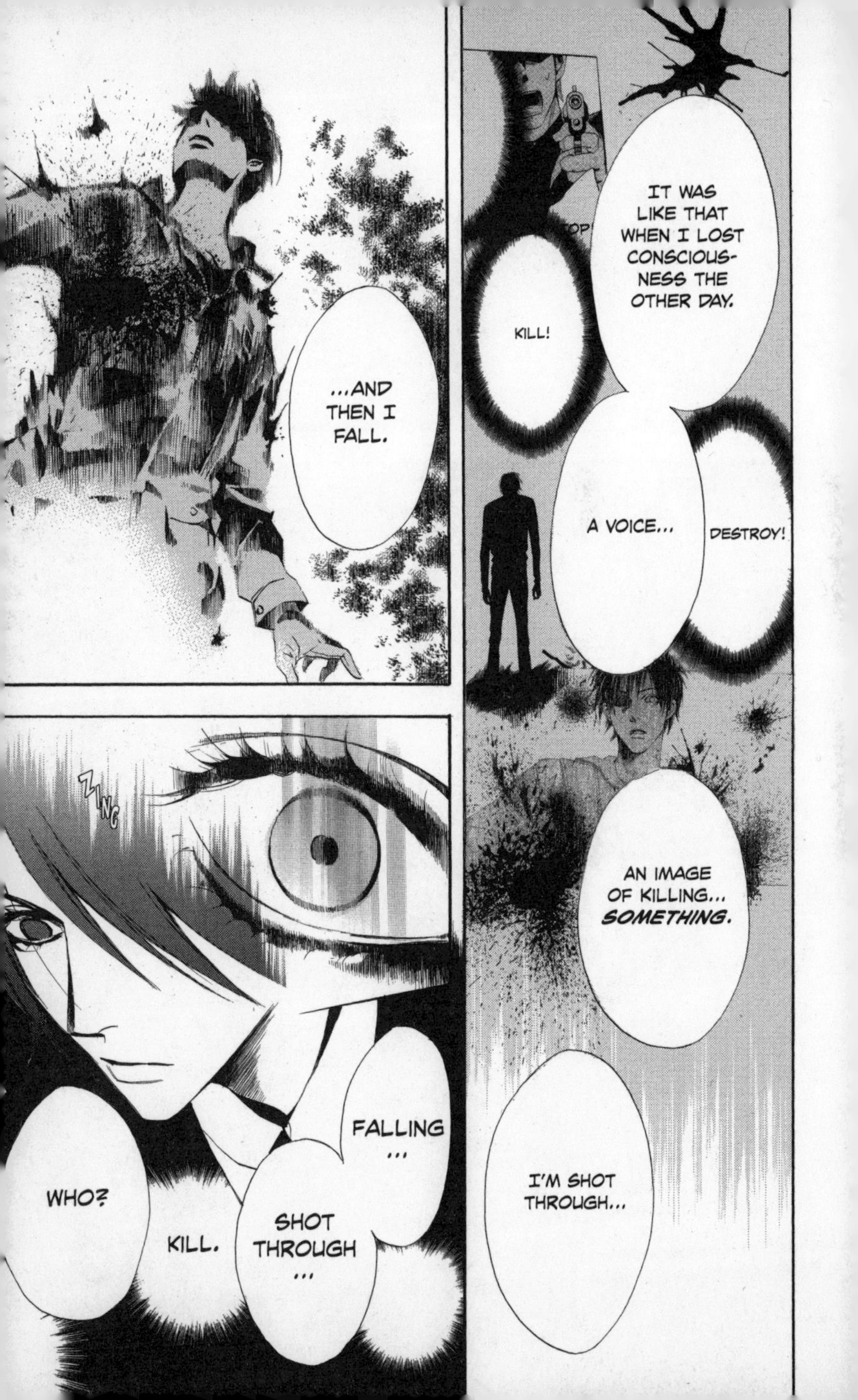
IT WAS LIKE THAT WHEN I LOST CONSCIOUS-NESS THE OTHER DAY.
KILL!
DESTROY!
A VOICE...
AN IMAGE OF KILLING... *SOMETHING*.
I'M SHOT THROUGH...
...AND THEN I FALL.
ZING
FALLING ...
SHOT THROUGH ...
KILL.
WHO?

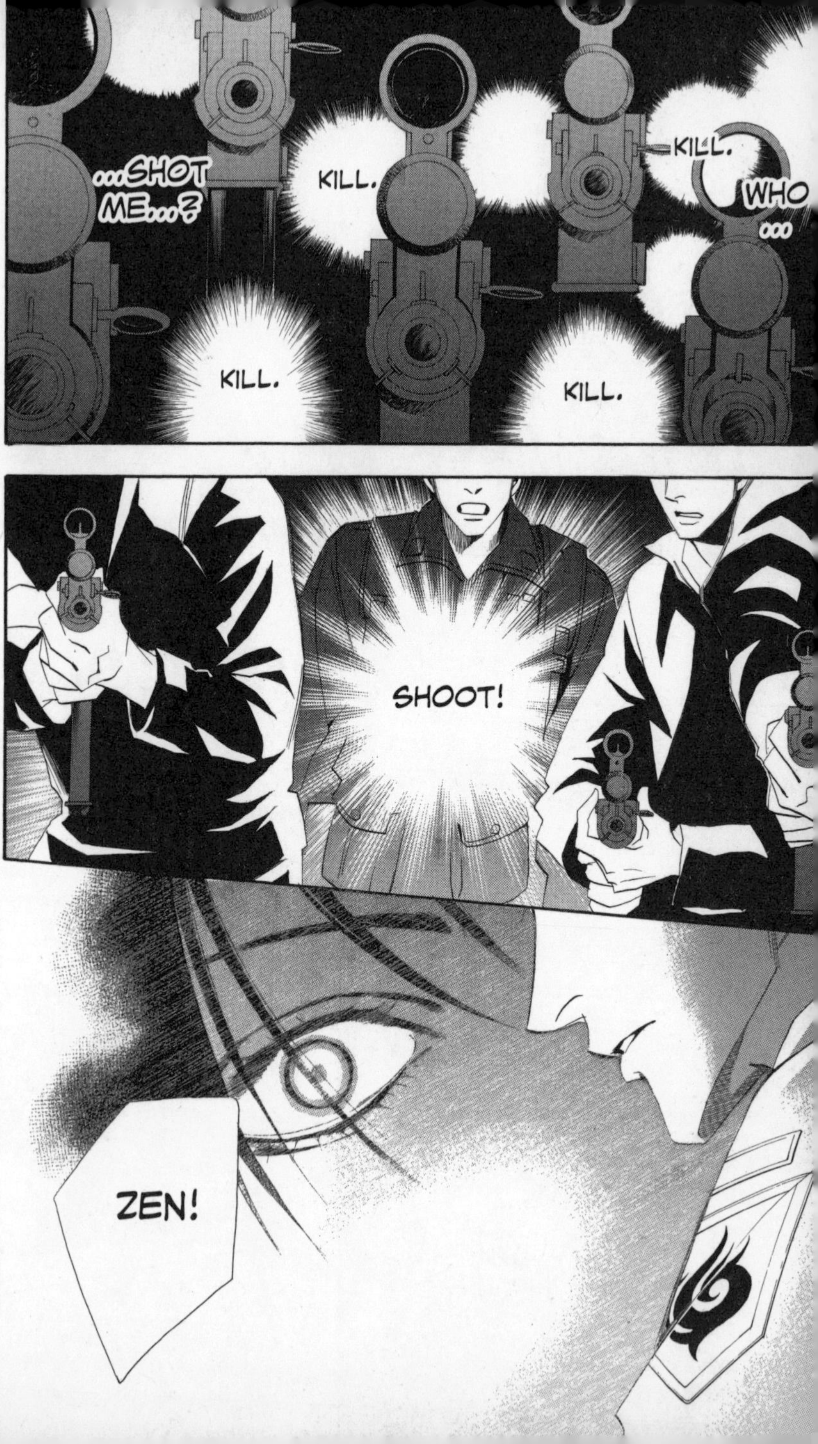
WHO ...
KILL.
KILL.
KILL.
KILL.
...SHOT ME...?
SHOOT!
ZEN!

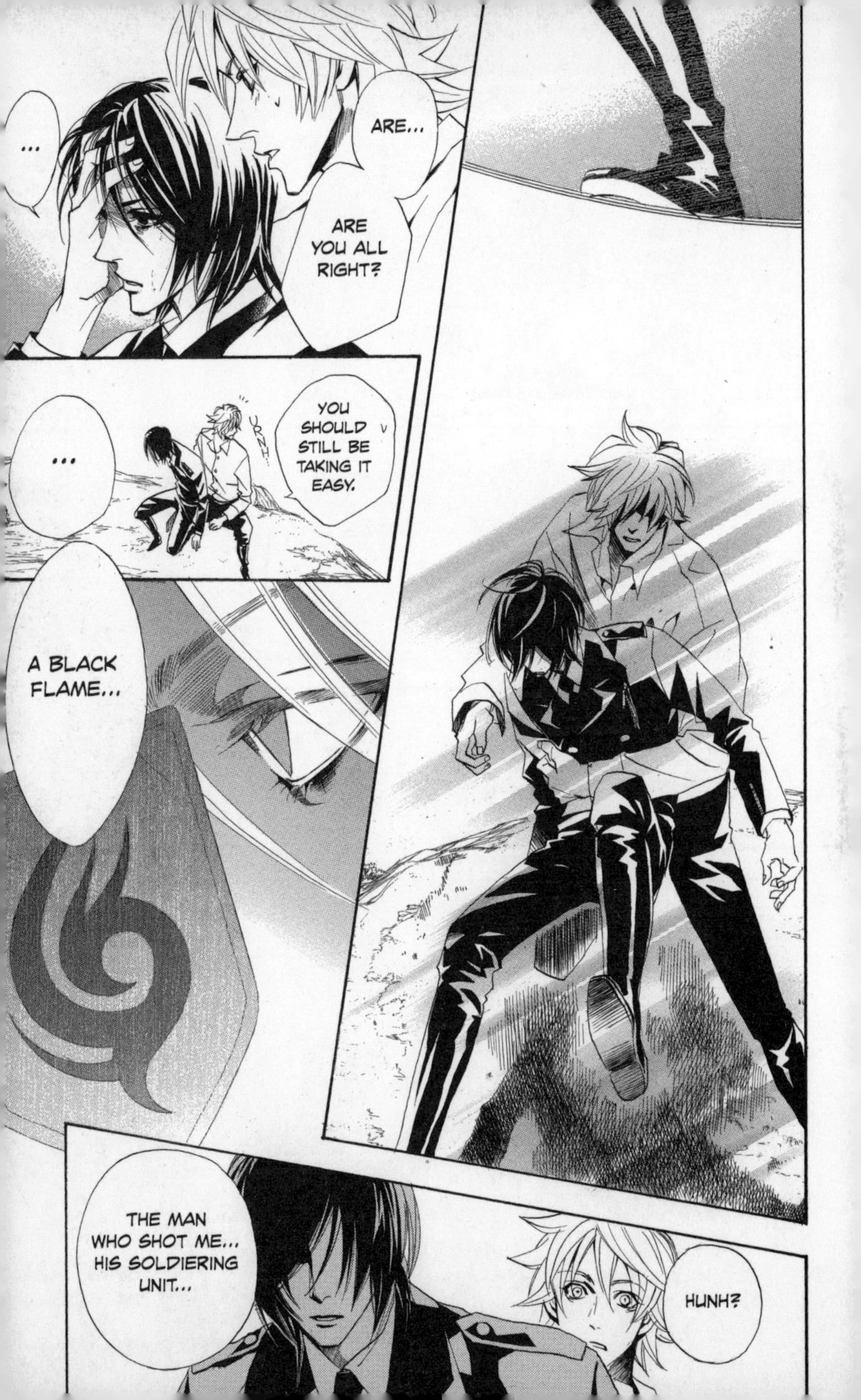
ARE...
ARE YOU ALL RIGHT?
...
URNH
YOU SHOULD STILL BE TAKING IT EASY.
...
A BLACK FLAME...
THE MAN WHO SHOT ME... HIS SOLDIERING UNIT...
HUNH?

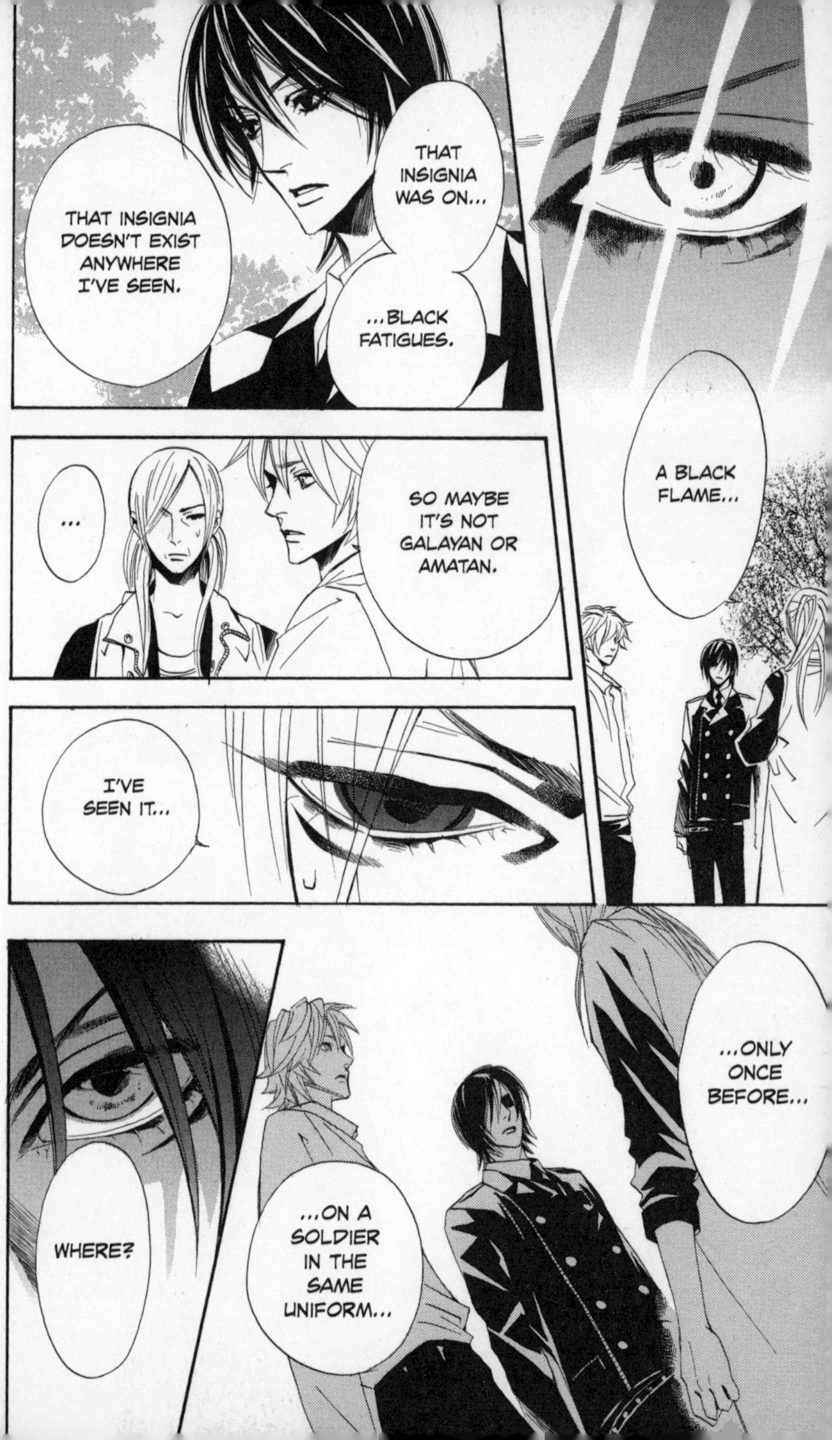
A BLACK FLAME...
THAT INSIGNIA WAS ON...
...BLACK FATIGUES.
THAT INSIGNIA DOESN'T EXIST ANYWHERE I'VE SEEN.
SO MAYBE IT'S NOT GALAYAN OR AMATAN.
...
I'VE SEEN IT...
...ONLY ONCE BEFORE...
...ON A SOLDIER IN THE SAME UNIFORM...
WHERE?

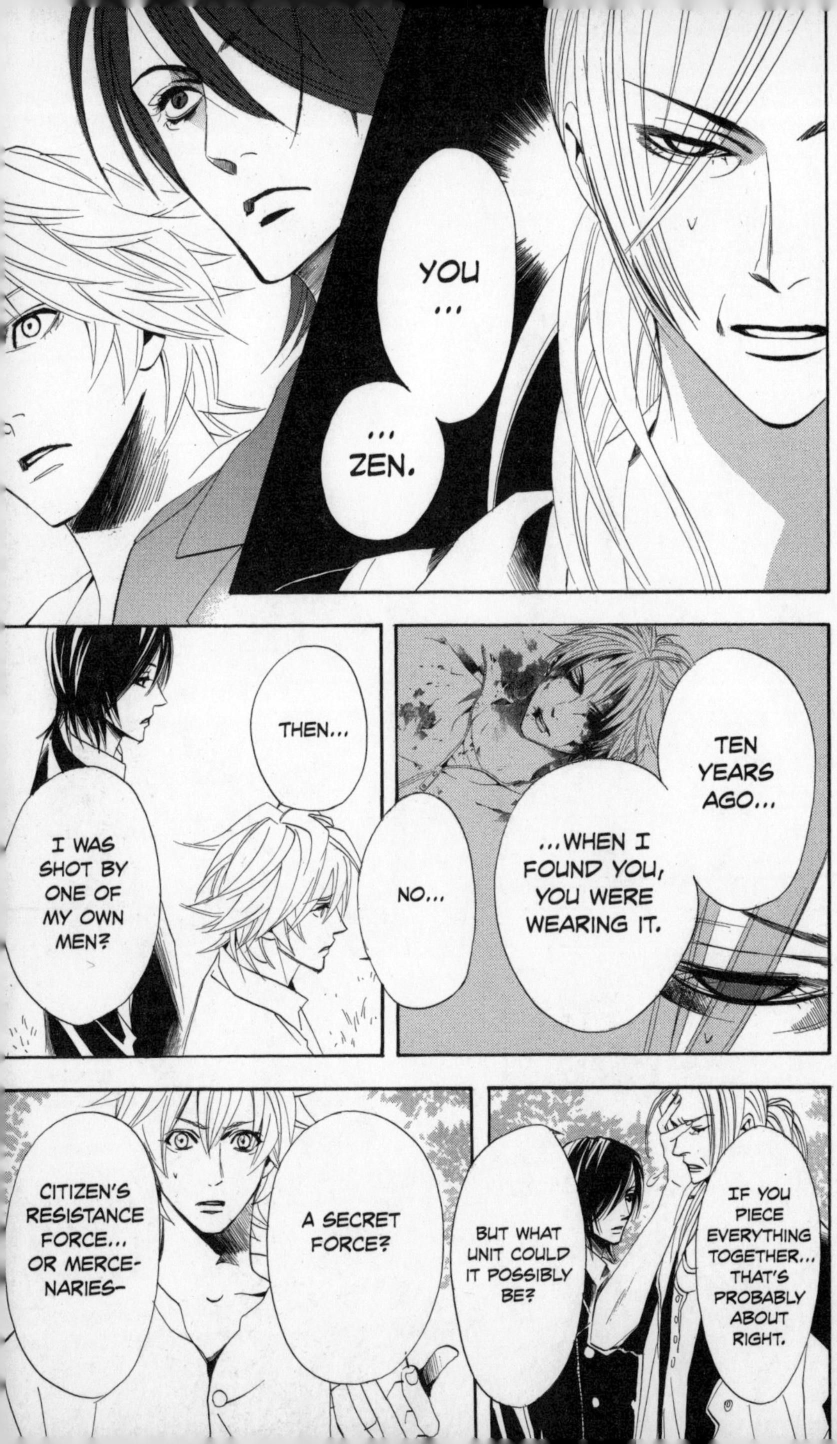
YOU...
...ZEN.
TEN YEARS AGO...
...WHEN I FOUND YOU, YOU WERE WEARING IT.
THEN...
NO...
I WAS SHOT BY ONE OF MY OWN MEN?
IF YOU PIECE EVERYTHING TOGETHER... THAT'S PROBABLY ABOUT RIGHT.
BUT WHAT UNIT COULD IT POSSIBLY BE?
A SECRET FORCE?
CITIZEN'S RESISTANCE FORCE... OR MERCE-NARIES-

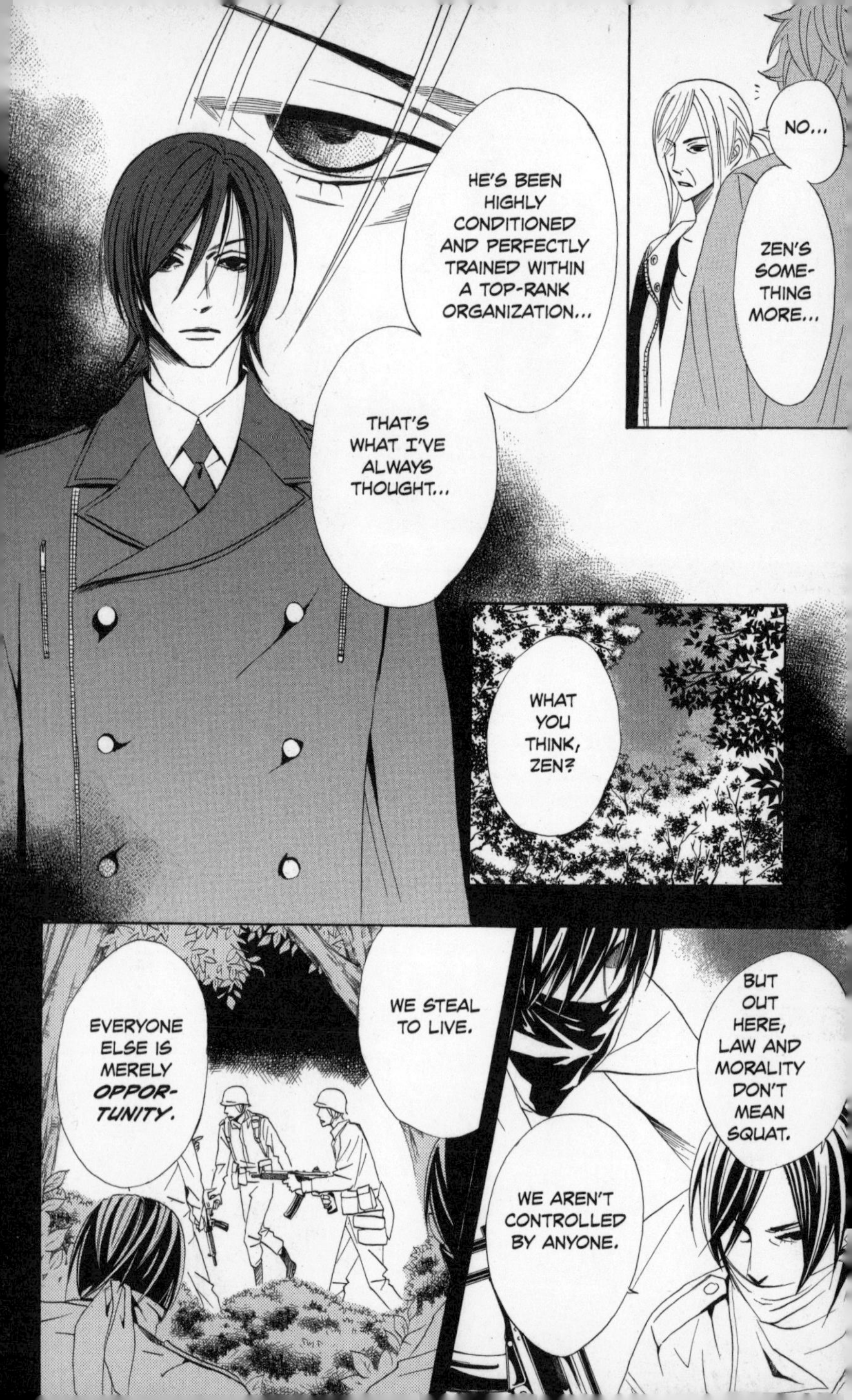
NO...
ZEN'S SOMETHING MORE...
WHAT YOU THINK, ZEN?
HE'S BEEN HIGHLY CONDITIONED AND PERFECTLY TRAINED WITHIN A TOP-RANK ORGANIZATION...
THAT'S WHAT I'VE ALWAYS THOUGHT...
BUT OUT HERE, LAW AND MORALITY DON'T MEAN SQUAT.
WE AREN'T CONTROLLED BY ANYONE.
WE STEAL TO LIVE.
EVERYONE ELSE IS MERELY *OPPORTUNITY*.

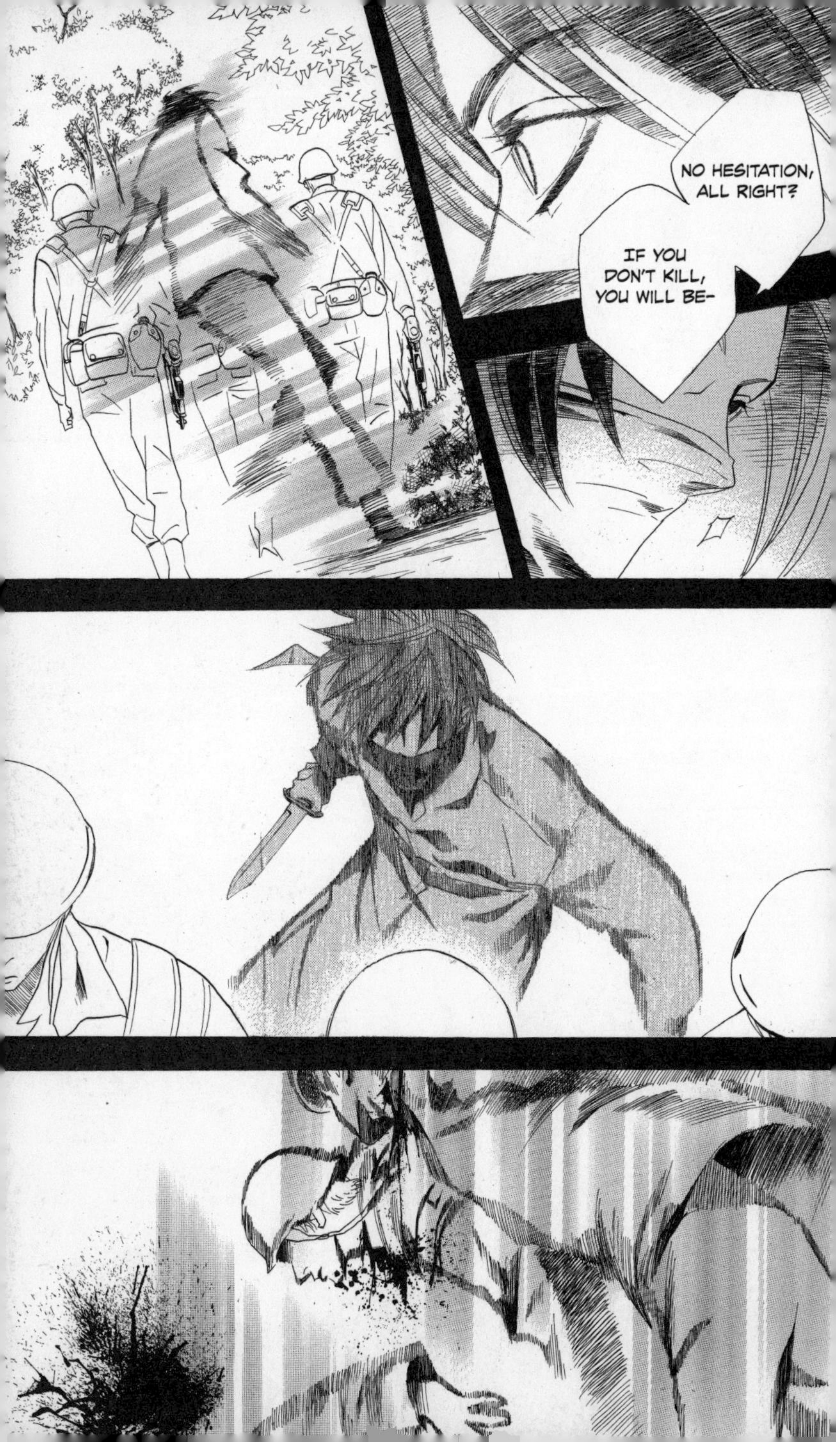
NO HESITATION, ALL RIGHT?
IF YOU DON'T KILL, YOU WILL BE-

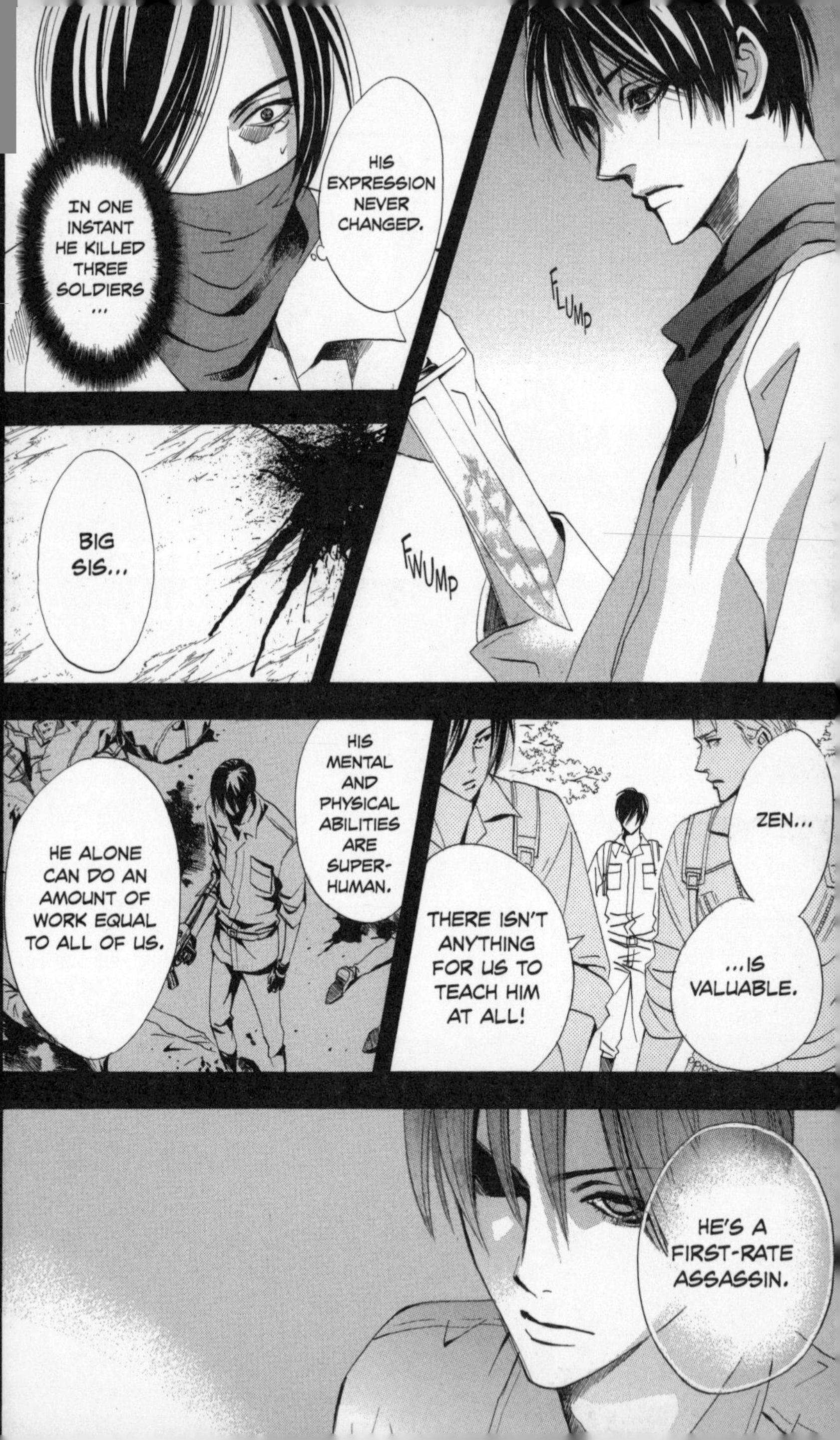
FLUMP
FWUMP
HIS EXPRESSION NEVER CHANGED.
IN ONE INSTANT HE KILLED THREE SOLDIERS ...
BIG SIS...
ZEN...
...IS VALUABLE.
THERE ISN'T ANYTHING FOR US TO TEACH HIM AT ALL!
HIS MENTAL AND PHYSICAL ABILITIES ARE SUPER-HUMAN.
HE ALONE CAN DO AN AMOUNT OF WORK EQUAL TO ALL OF US.
HE'S A FIRST-RATE ASSASSIN.

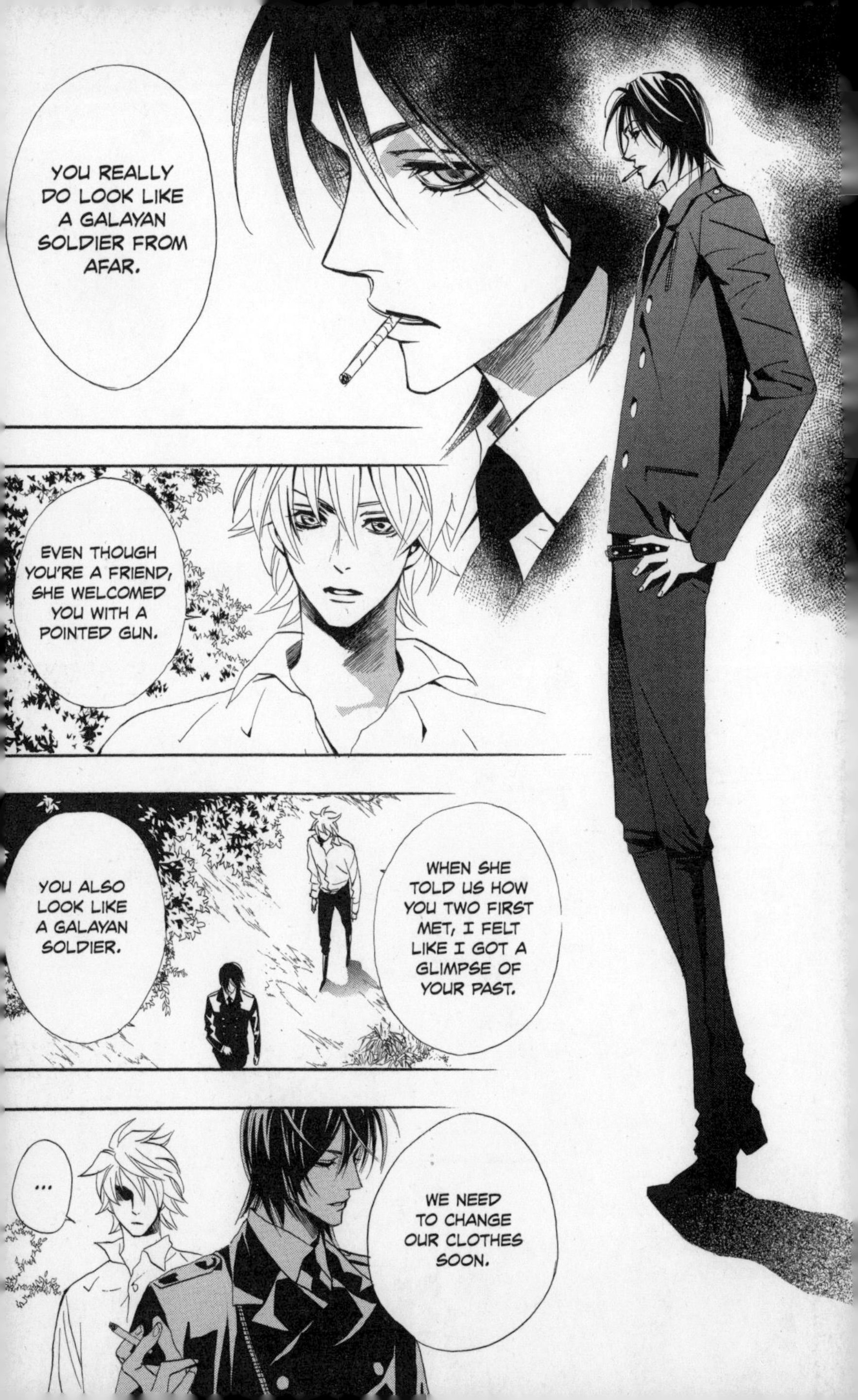
YOU REALLY DO LOOK LIKE A GALAYAN SOLDIER FROM AFAR.
EVEN THOUGH YOU'RE A FRIEND, SHE WELCOMED YOU WITH A POINTED GUN.
WHEN SHE TOLD US HOW YOU TWO FIRST MET, I FELT LIKE I GOT A GLIMPSE OF YOUR PAST.
YOU ALSO LOOK LIKE A GALAYAN SOLDIER.
WE NEED TO CHANGE OUR CLOTHES SOON.
...

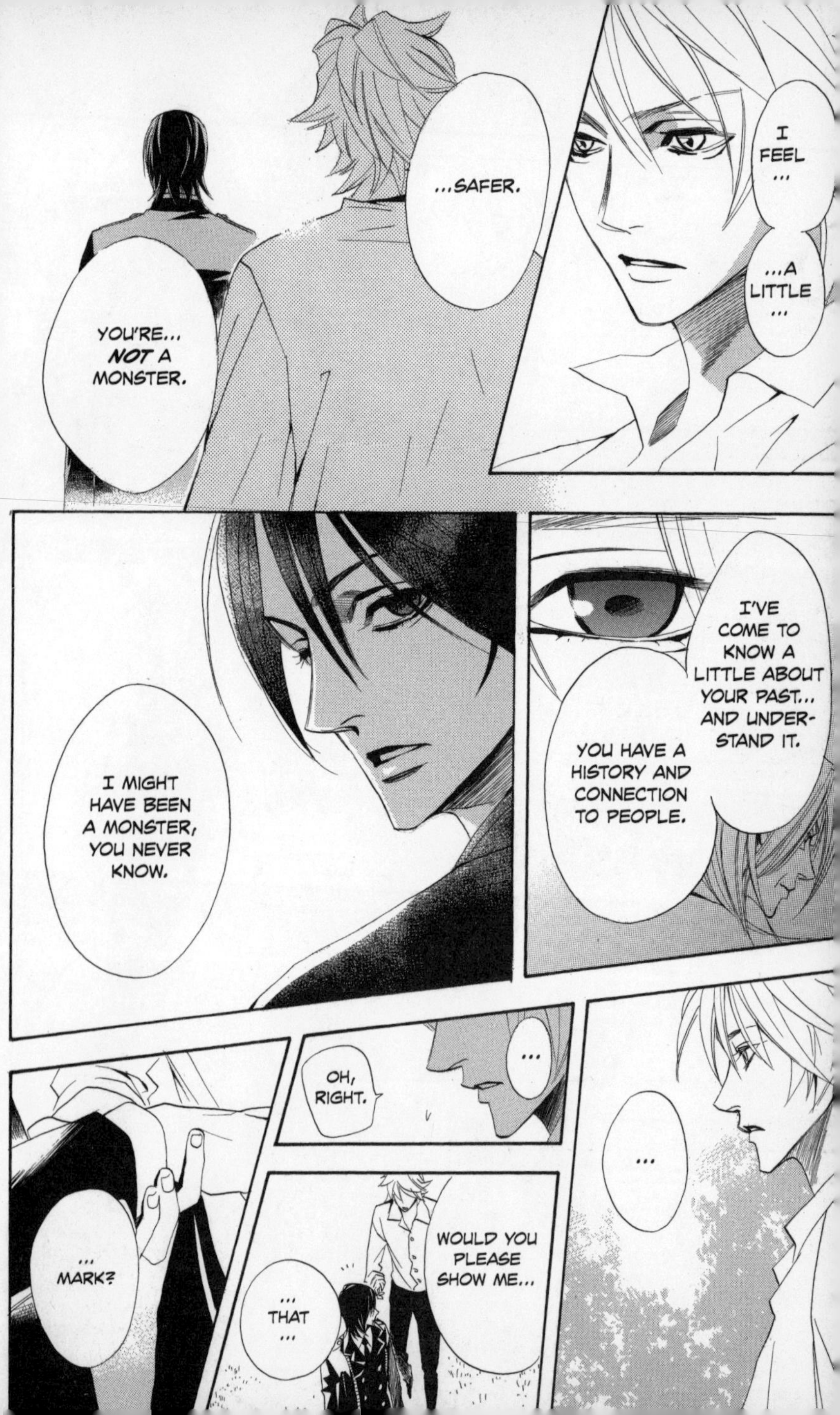
I FEEL ...
...A LITTLE ...
...SAFER.
YOU'RE... *NOT* A MONSTER.
I'VE COME TO KNOW A LITTLE ABOUT YOUR PAST... AND UNDER-STAND IT.
YOU HAVE A HISTORY AND CONNECTION TO PEOPLE.
I MIGHT HAVE BEEN A MONSTER, YOU NEVER KNOW.
...
...
OH, RIGHT.
WOULD YOU PLEASE SHOW ME...
...THAT...
...MARK?

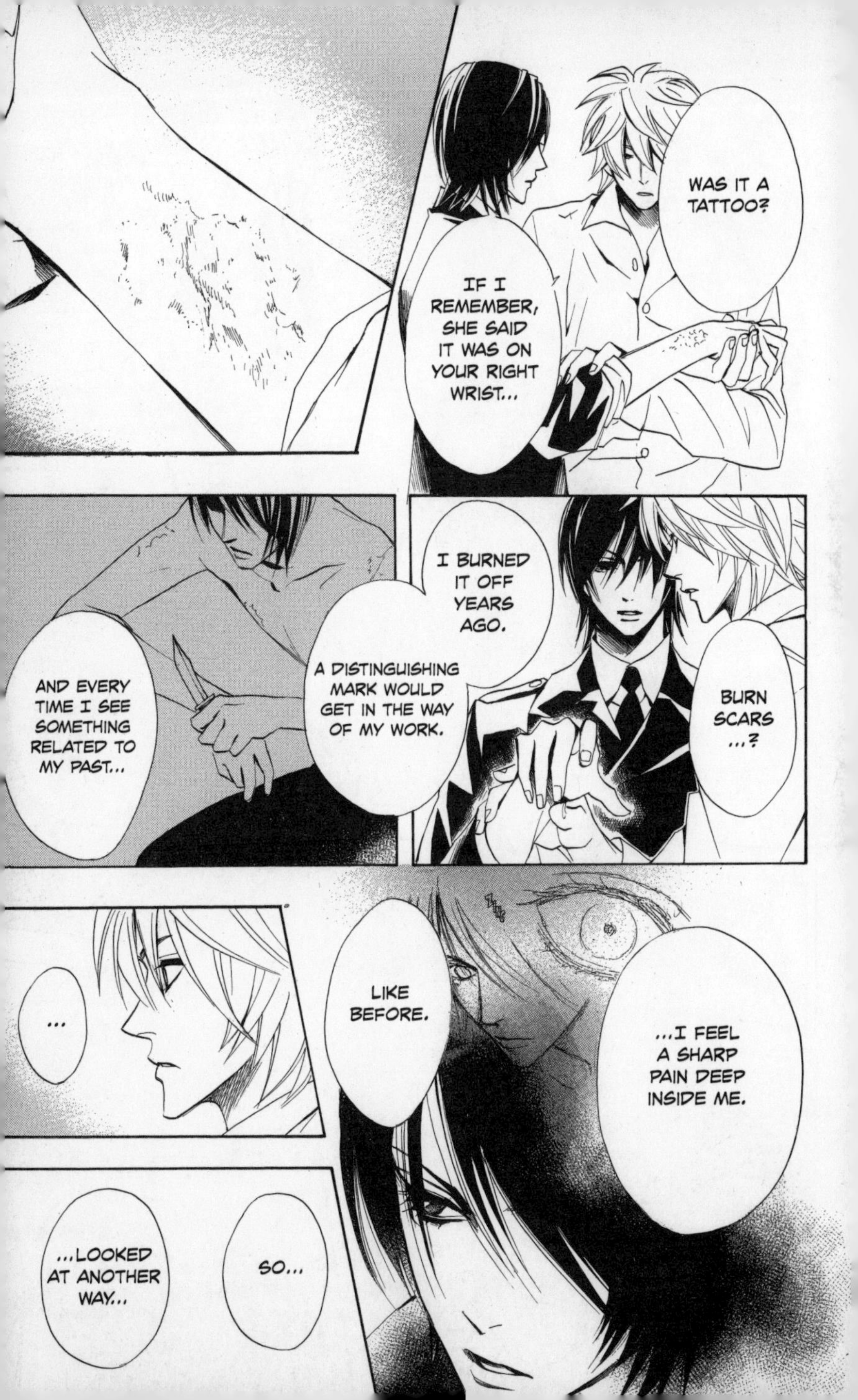
WAS IT A TATTOO?
IF I REMEMBER, SHE SAID IT WAS ON YOUR RIGHT WRIST...
BURN SCARS ...?
I BURNED IT OFF YEARS AGO.
A DISTINGUISHING MARK WOULD GET IN THE WAY OF MY WORK.
AND EVERY TIME I SEE SOMETHING RELATED TO MY PAST...
...I FEEL A SHARP PAIN DEEP INSIDE ME.
LIKE BEFORE.
...
SO...
...LOOKED AT ANOTHER WAY...

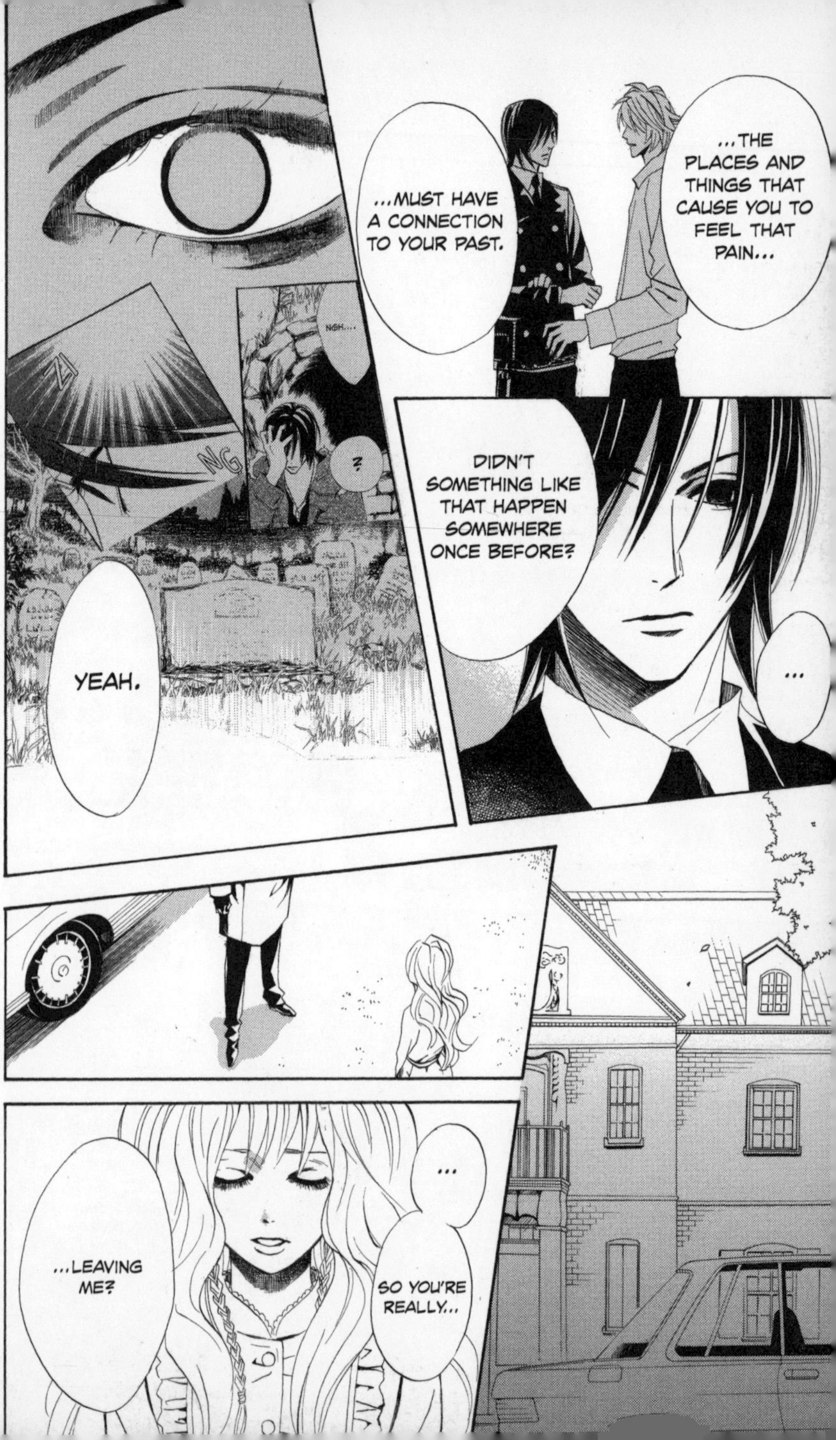
...THE PLACES AND THINGS THAT CAUSE YOU TO FEEL THAT PAIN...
...MUST HAVE A CONNECTION TO YOUR PAST.
DIDN'T SOMETHING LIKE THAT HAPPEN SOMEWHERE ONCE BEFORE?
...
NGH....
?
NG
YEAH.
...
SO YOU'RE REALLY...
...LEAVING ME?

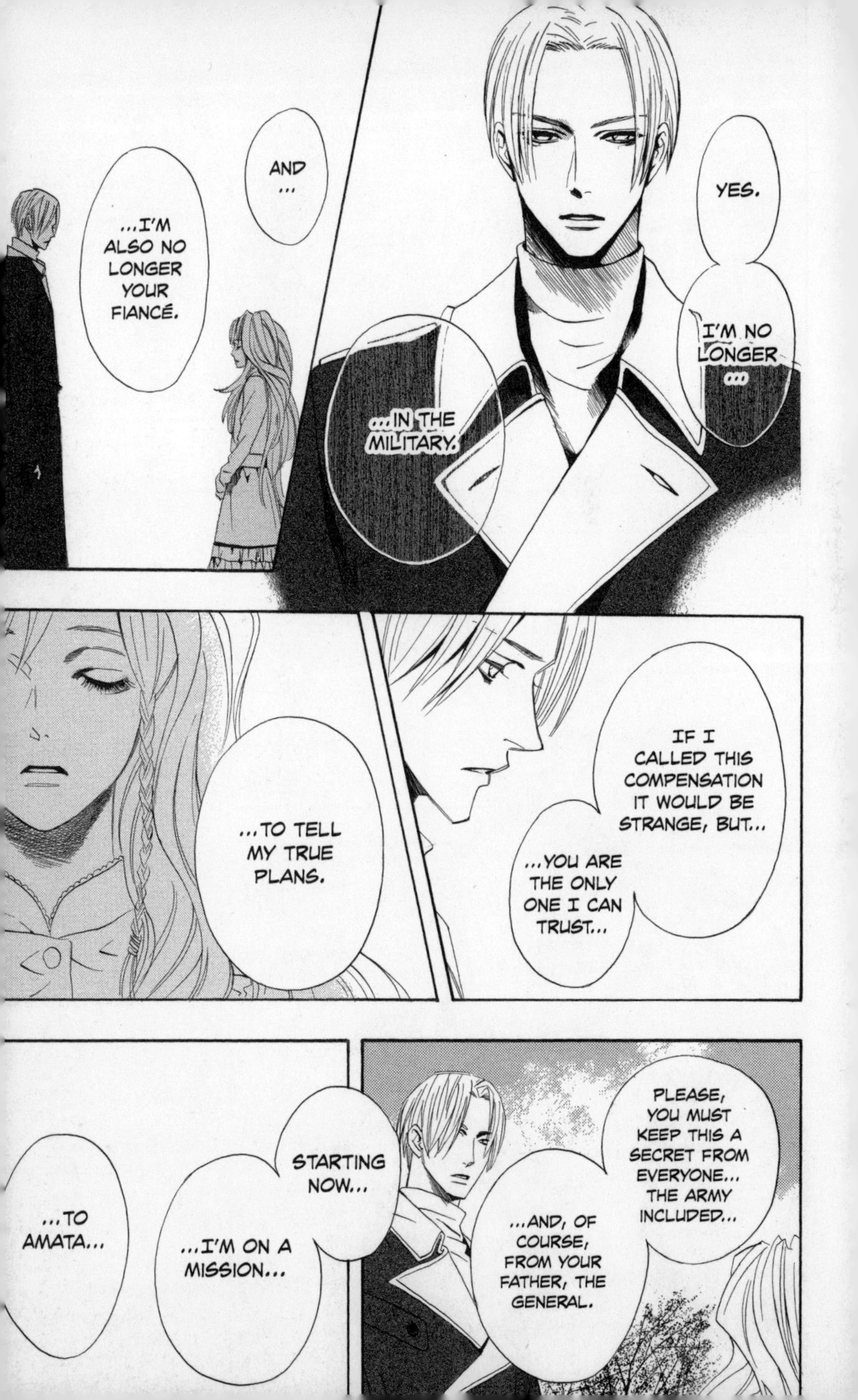
YES.
I'M NO LONGER...
...IN THE MILITARY.
AND...
...I'M ALSO NO LONGER YOUR FIANCÉ.
IF I CALLED THIS COMPENSATION IT WOULD BE STRANGE, BUT...
...YOU ARE THE ONLY ONE I CAN TRUST...
...TO TELL MY TRUE PLANS.
PLEASE, YOU MUST KEEP THIS A SECRET FROM EVERYONE... THE ARMY INCLUDED...
...AND, OF COURSE, FROM YOUR FATHER, THE GENERAL.
STARTING NOW...
...I'M ON A MISSION...
...TO AMATA...

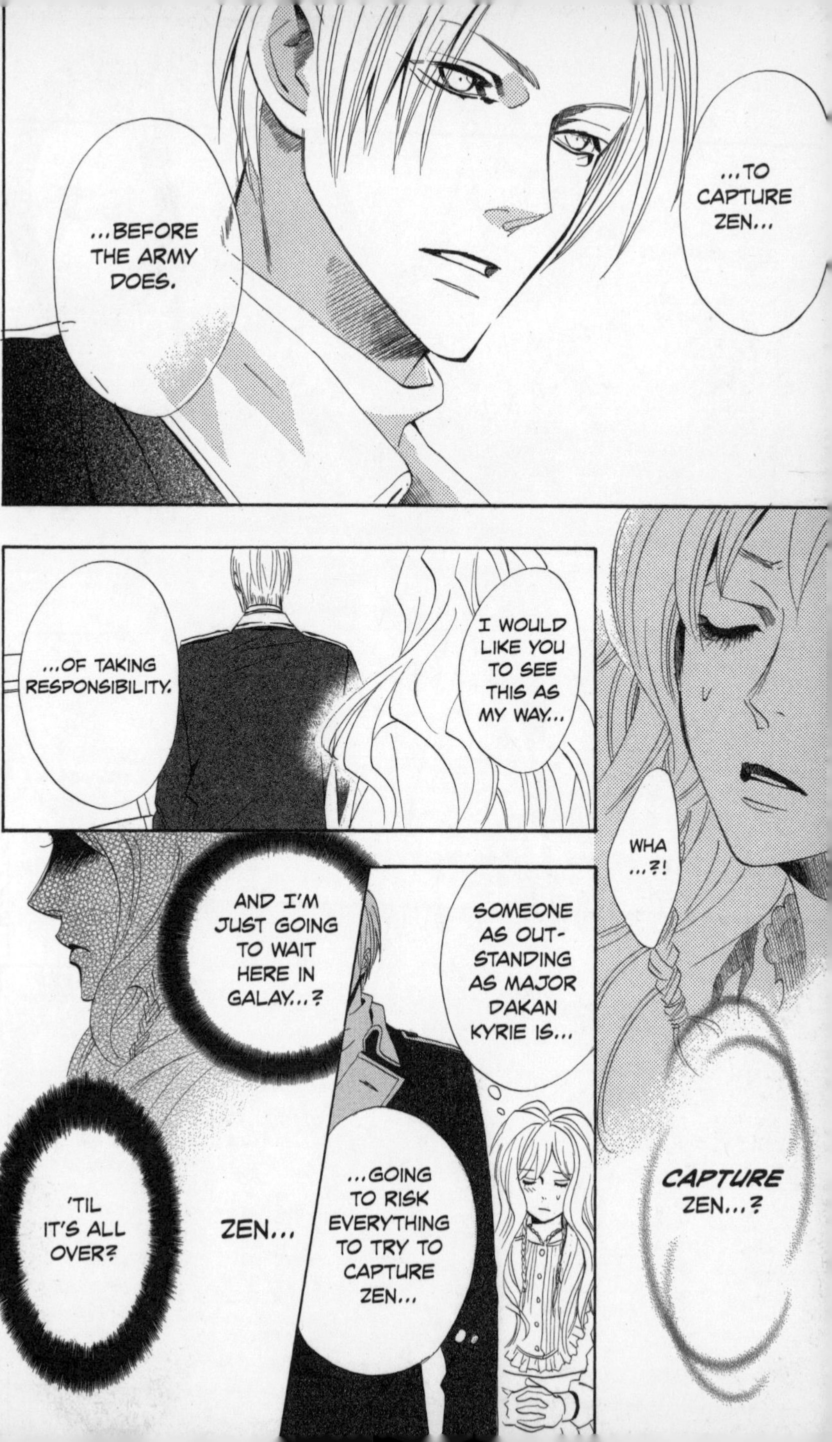
...TO CAPTURE ZEN...
...BEFORE THE ARMY DOES.
WHA ...?!
CAPTURE ZEN...?
I WOULD LIKE YOU TO SEE THIS AS MY WAY...
...OF TAKING RESPONSIBILITY.
SOMEONE AS OUT-STANDING AS MAJOR DAKAN KYRIE IS...
...GOING TO RISK EVERYTHING TO TRY TO CAPTURE ZEN...
ZEN...
AND I'M JUST GOING TO WAIT HERE IN GALAY...?
'TIL IT'S ALL OVER?

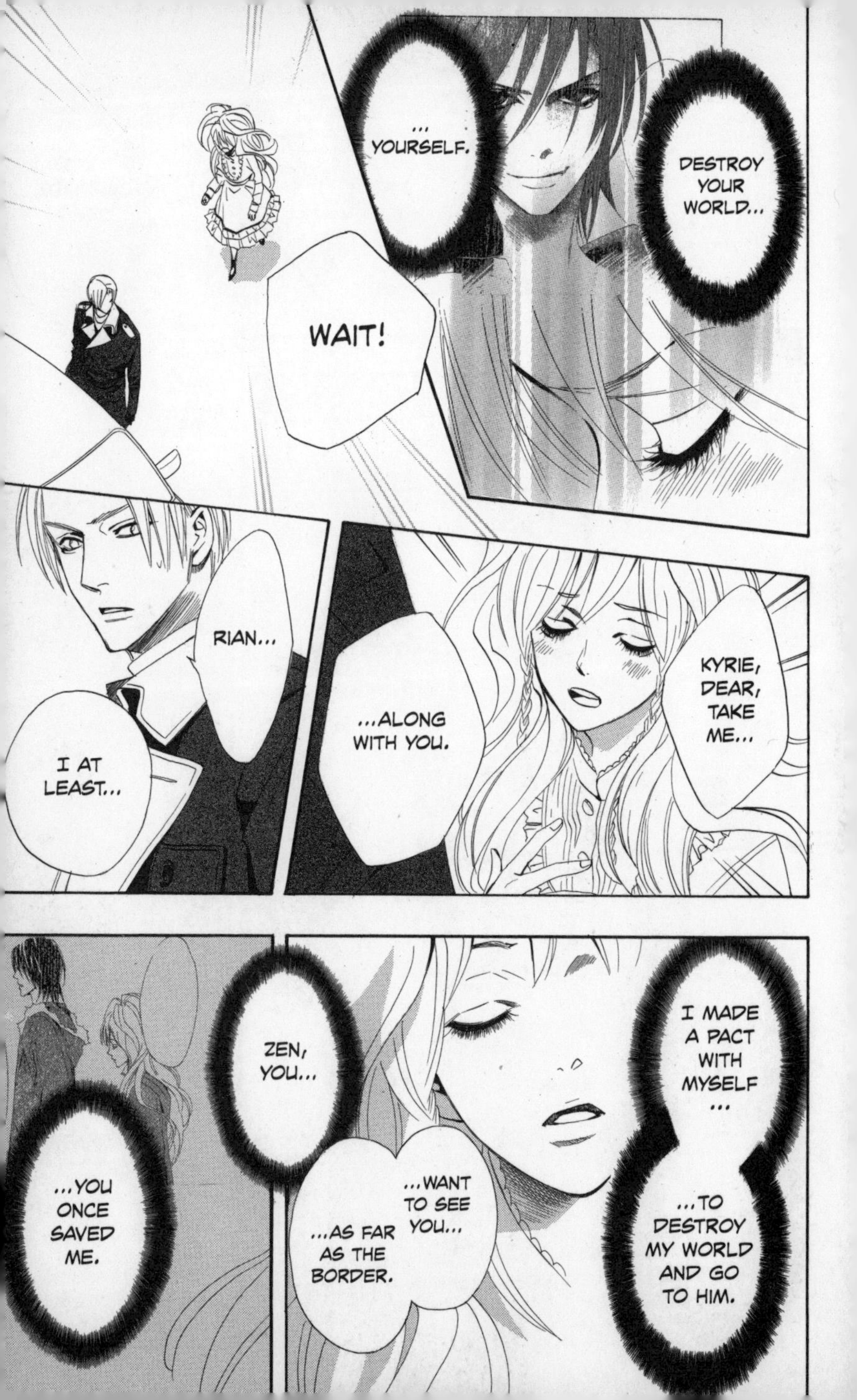
DESTROY YOUR WORLD...
...YOURSELF.
WAIT!
KYRIE, DEAR, TAKE ME...
...ALONG WITH YOU.
RIAN...
I AT LEAST...
I MADE A PACT WITH MYSELF...
...TO DESTROY MY WORLD AND GO TO HIM.
ZEN, YOU...
...WANT TO SEE YOU...
...AS FAR AS THE BORDER.
...YOU ONCE SAVED ME.

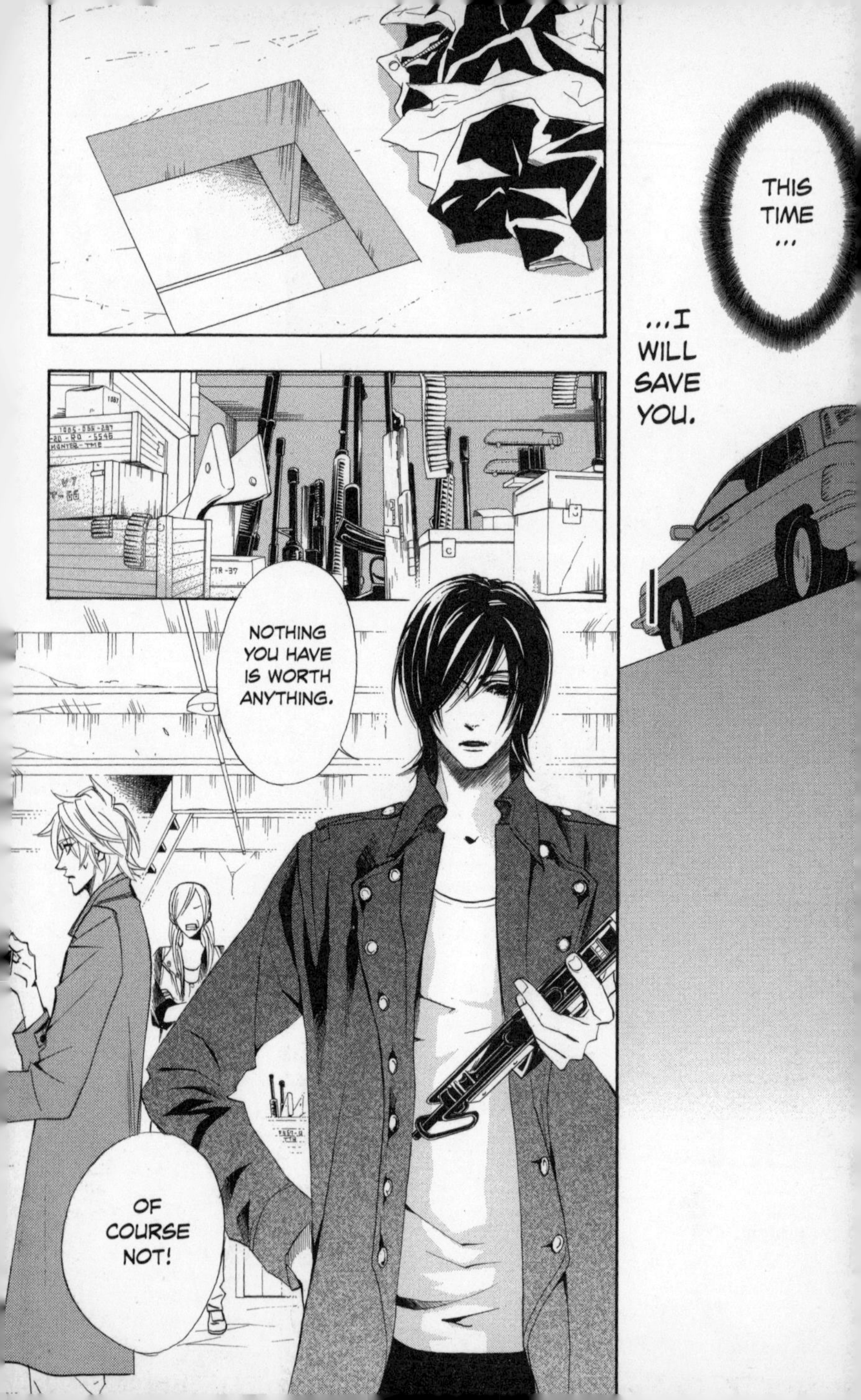
THIS TIME ...
...I WILL SAVE YOU.
NOTHING YOU HAVE IS WORTH ANYTHING.
OF COURSE NOT!

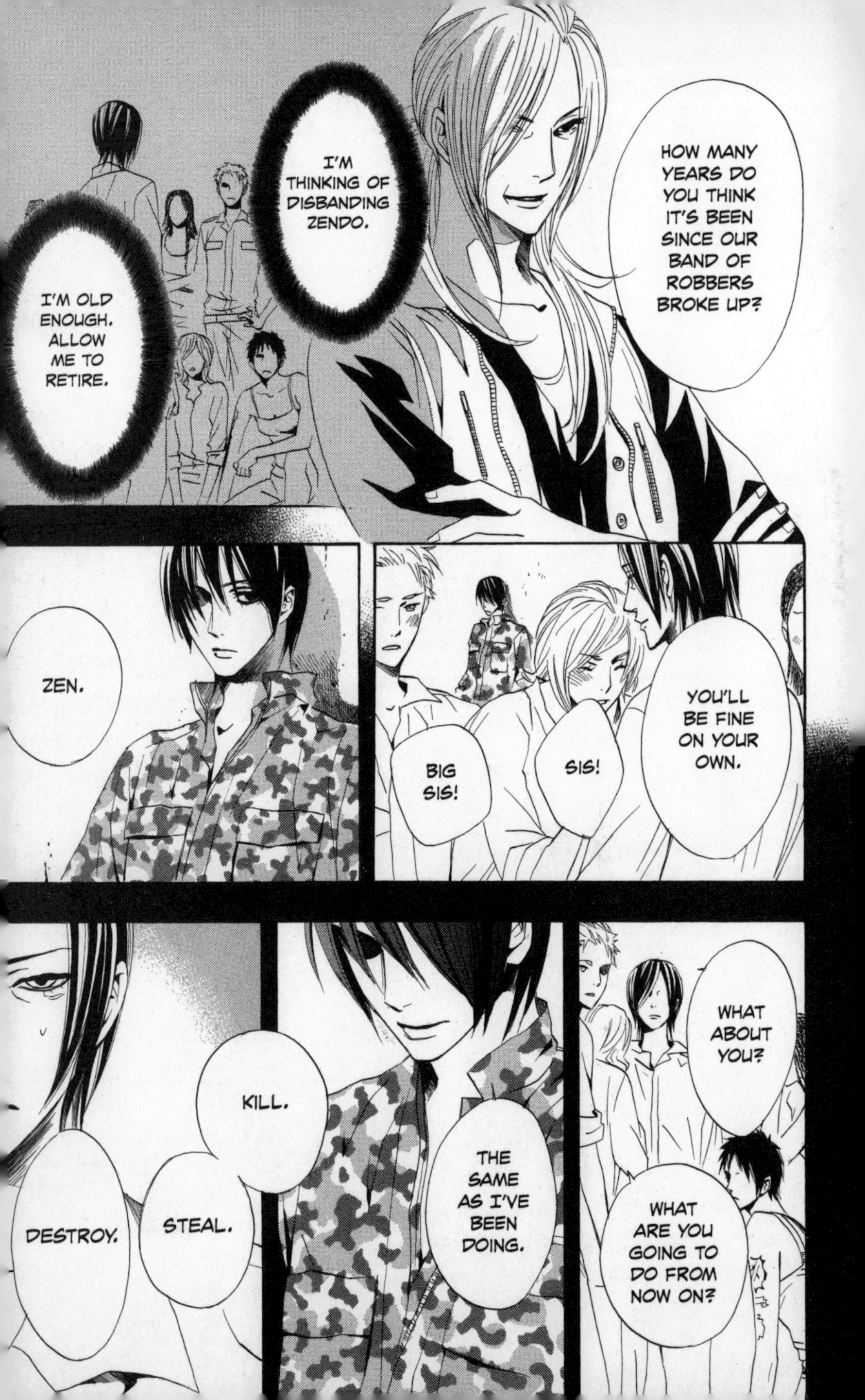
HOW MANY YEARS DO YOU THINK IT'S BEEN SINCE OUR BAND OF ROBBERS BROKE UP?
I'M THINKING OF DISBANDING ZENDO.
I'M OLD ENOUGH. ALLOW ME TO RETIRE.
YOU'LL BE FINE ON YOUR OWN.
SIS!
BIG SIS!
ZEN.
WHAT ABOUT YOU?
WHAT ARE YOU GOING TO DO FROM NOW ON?
THE SAME AS I'VE BEEN DOING.
KILL.
STEAL.
DESTROY.

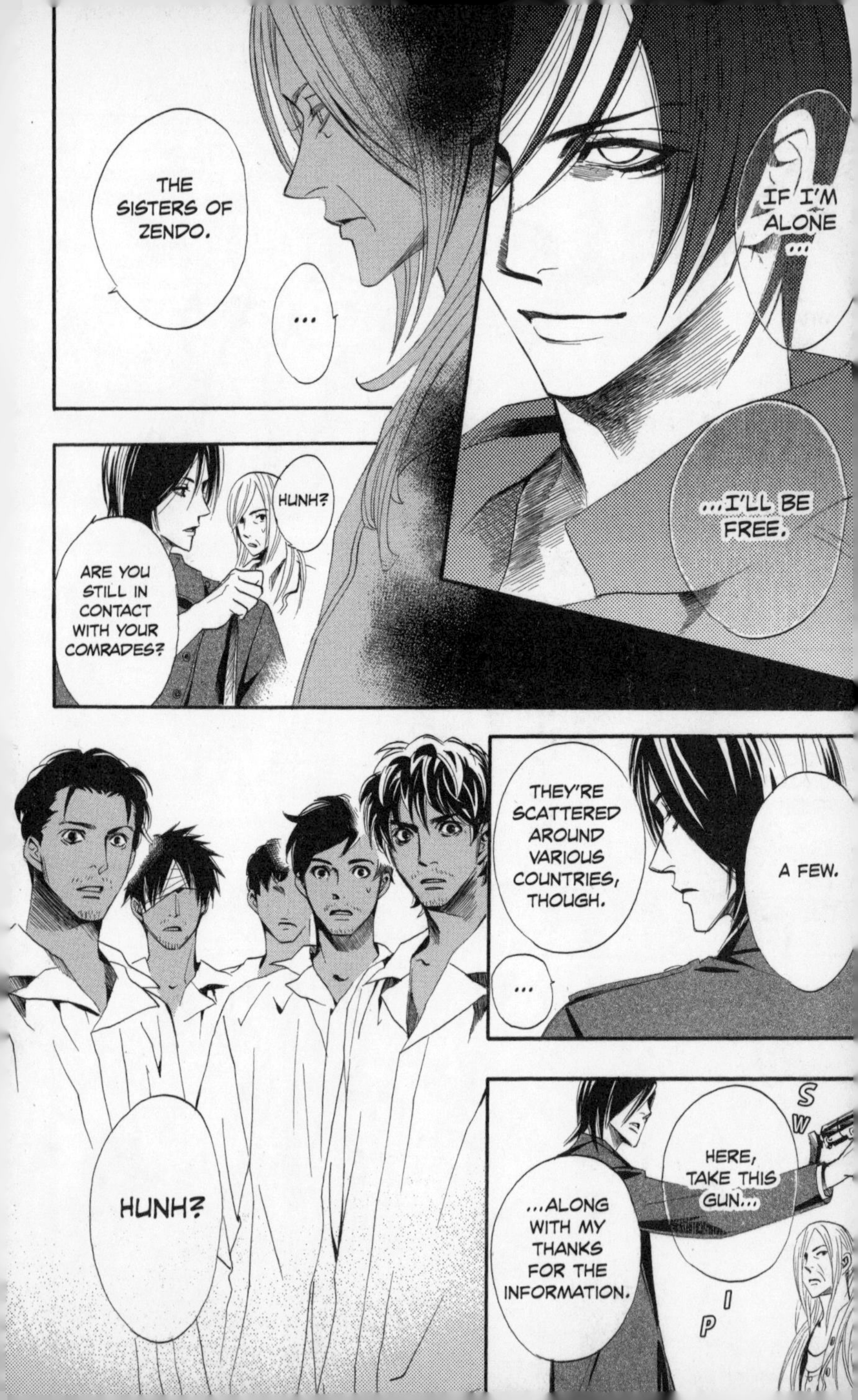
IF I'M ALONE...
...I'LL BE FREE.
THE SISTERS OF ZENDO.
...
HUNH?
ARE YOU STILL IN CONTACT WITH YOUR COMRADES?
A FEW.
THEY'RE SCATTERED AROUND VARIOUS COUNTRIES, THOUGH.
...
SWIP
HERE, TAKE THIS GUN...
...ALONG WITH MY THANKS FOR THE INFORMATION.
HUNH?

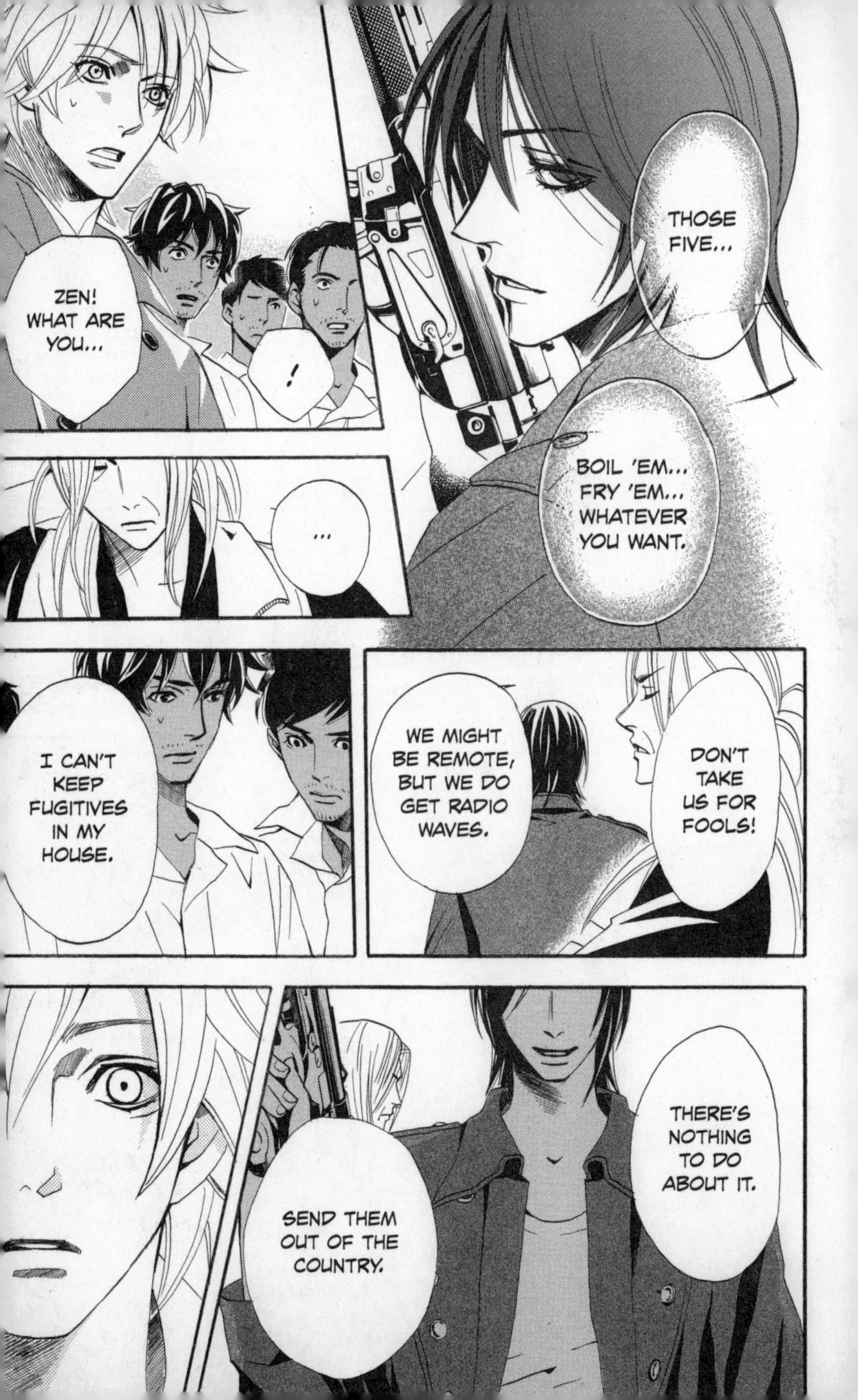
THOSE FIVE...
BOIL 'EM... FRY 'EM... WHATEVER YOU WANT.
ZEN! WHAT ARE YOU...
!
...
DON'T TAKE US FOR FOOLS!
WE MIGHT BE REMOTE, BUT WE DO GET RADIO WAVES.
I CAN'T KEEP FUGITIVES IN MY HOUSE.
THERE'S NOTHING TO DO ABOUT IT.
SEND THEM OUT OF THE COUNTRY.

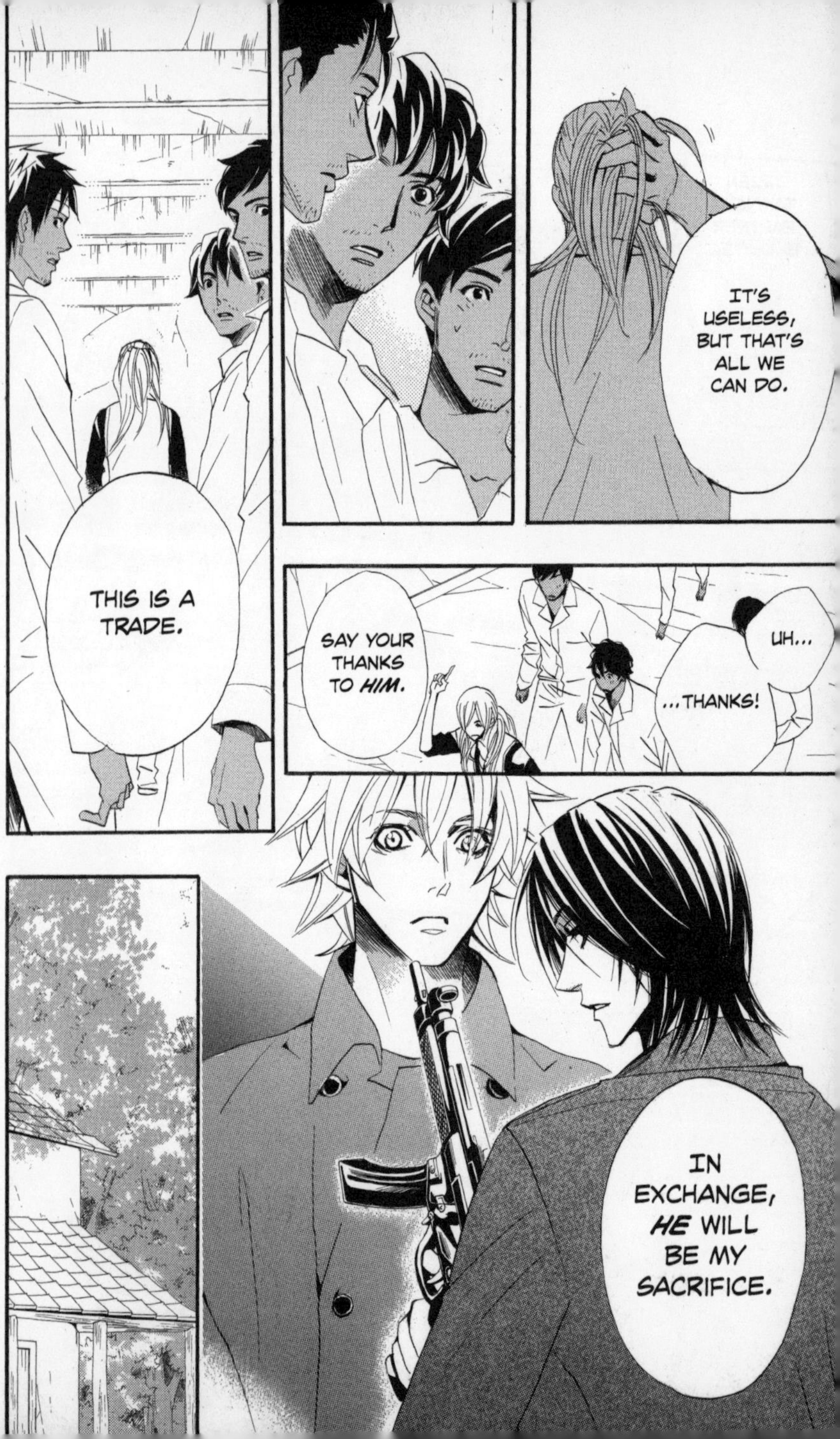
IT'S USELESS, BUT THAT'S ALL WE CAN DO.
SAY YOUR THANKS TO *HIM*.
UH...
...THANKS!
THIS IS A TRADE.
IN EXCHANGE, *HE* WILL BE MY SACRIFICE.

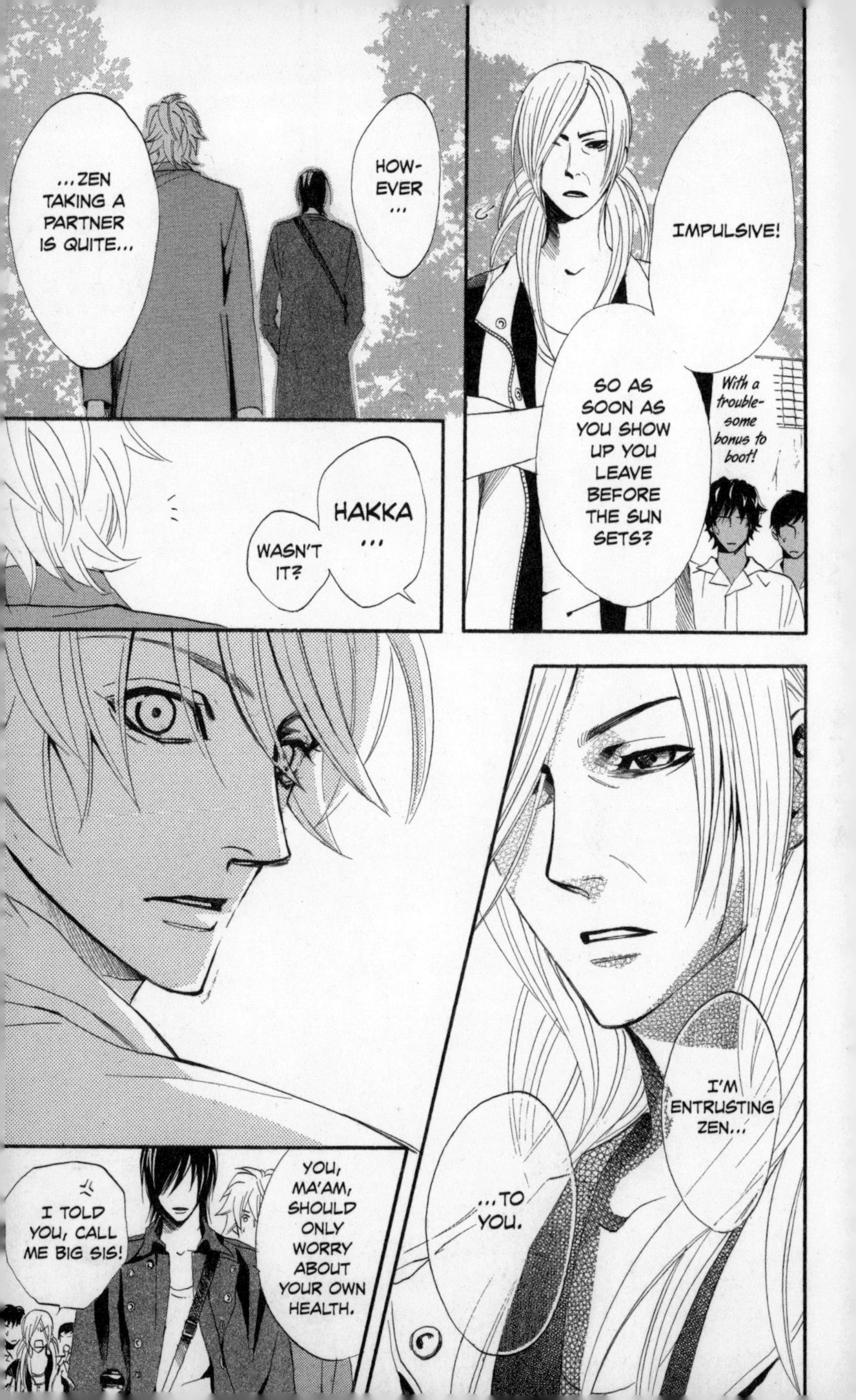
IMPULSIVE!
SO AS SOON AS YOU SHOW UP YOU LEAVE BEFORE THE SUN SETS?
With a trouble-some bonus to boot!
HOW-EVER...
...ZEN TAKING A PARTNER IS QUITE...
HAKKA...
WASN'T IT?
I'M ENTRUSTING ZEN...
...TO YOU.
YOU, MA'AM, SHOULD ONLY WORRY ABOUT YOUR OWN HEALTH.
I TOLD YOU, CALL ME BIG SIS!

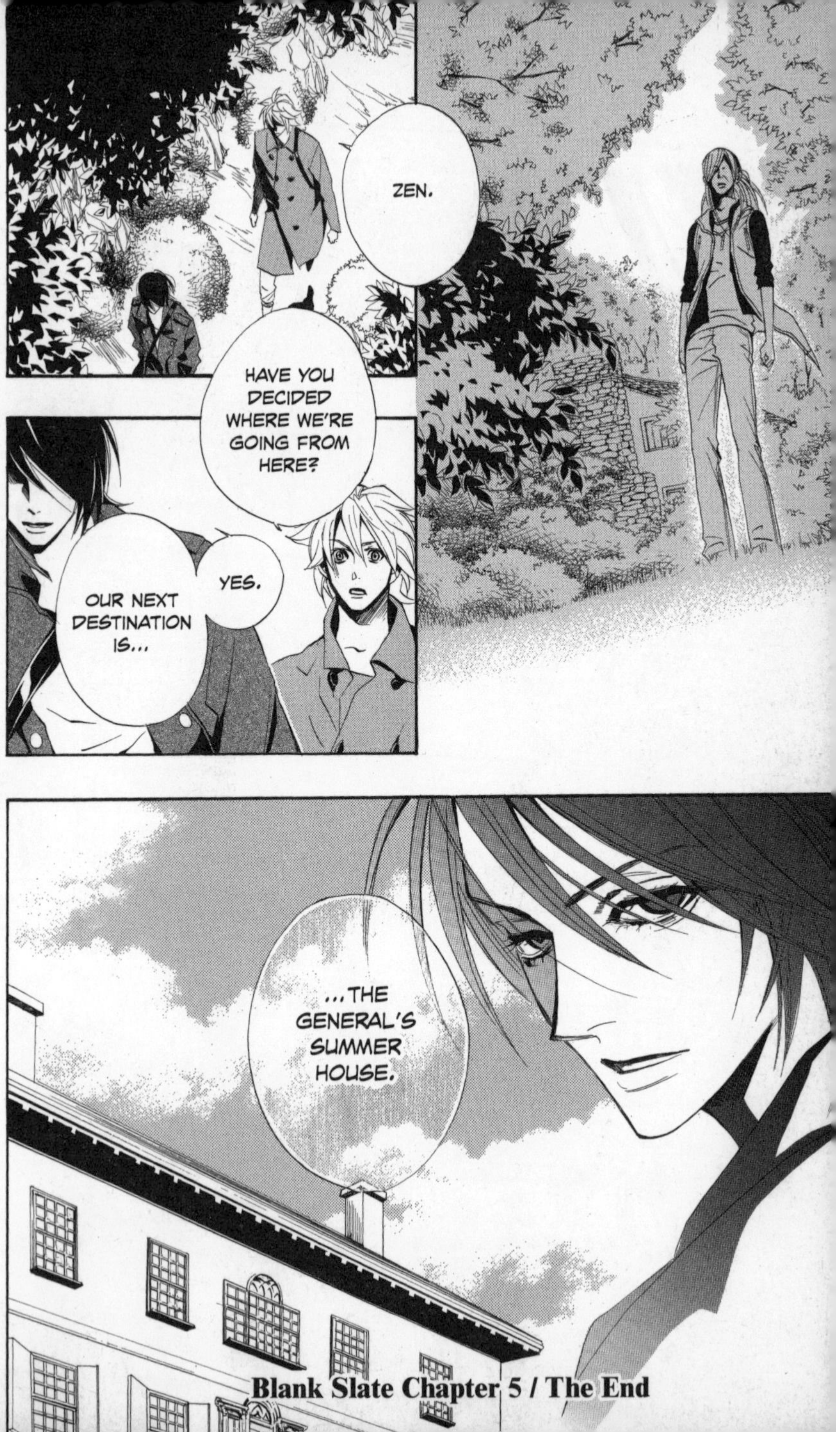
ZEN.
HAVE YOU DECIDED WHERE WE'RE GOING FROM HERE?
YES.
OUR NEXT DESTINATION IS...
...THE GENERAL'S SUMMER HOUSE.
Blank Slate Chapter 5 / The End

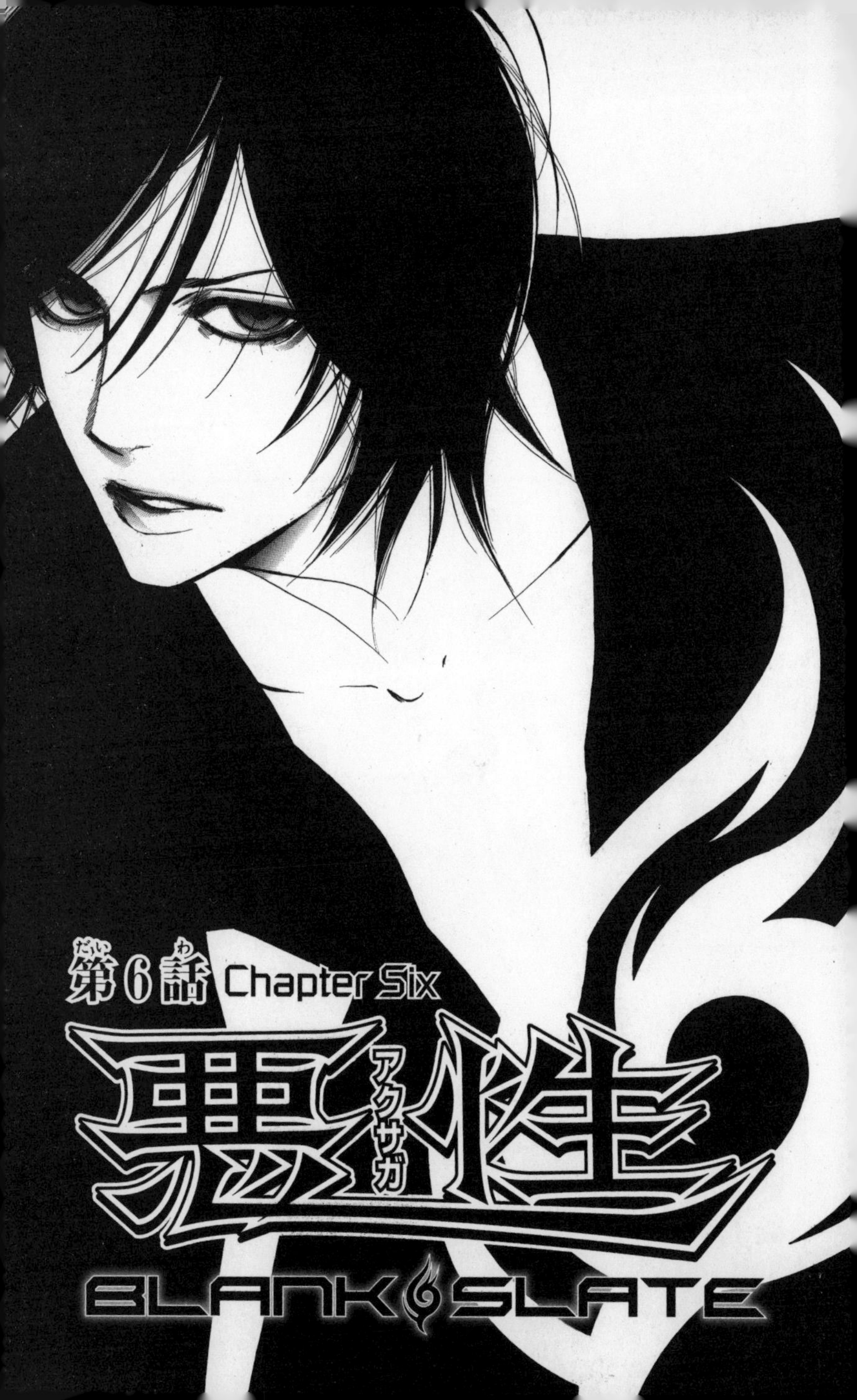
第6話 Chapter Six
悪性
アクサガ
BLANK SLATE

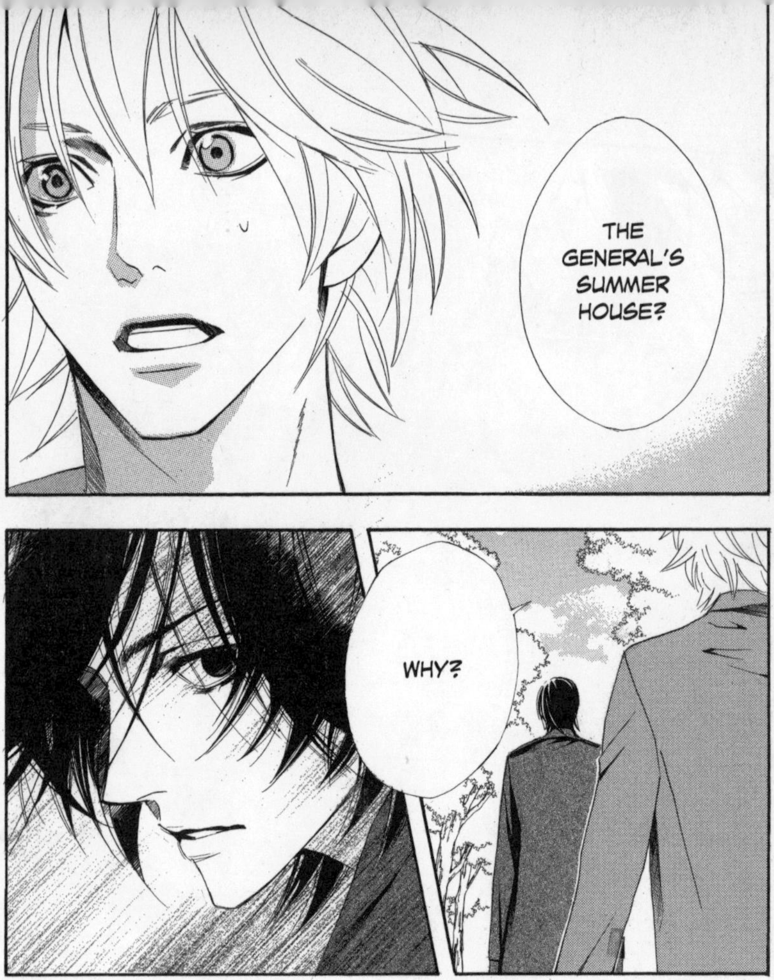
THE GENERAL'S SUMMER HOUSE?
WHY?

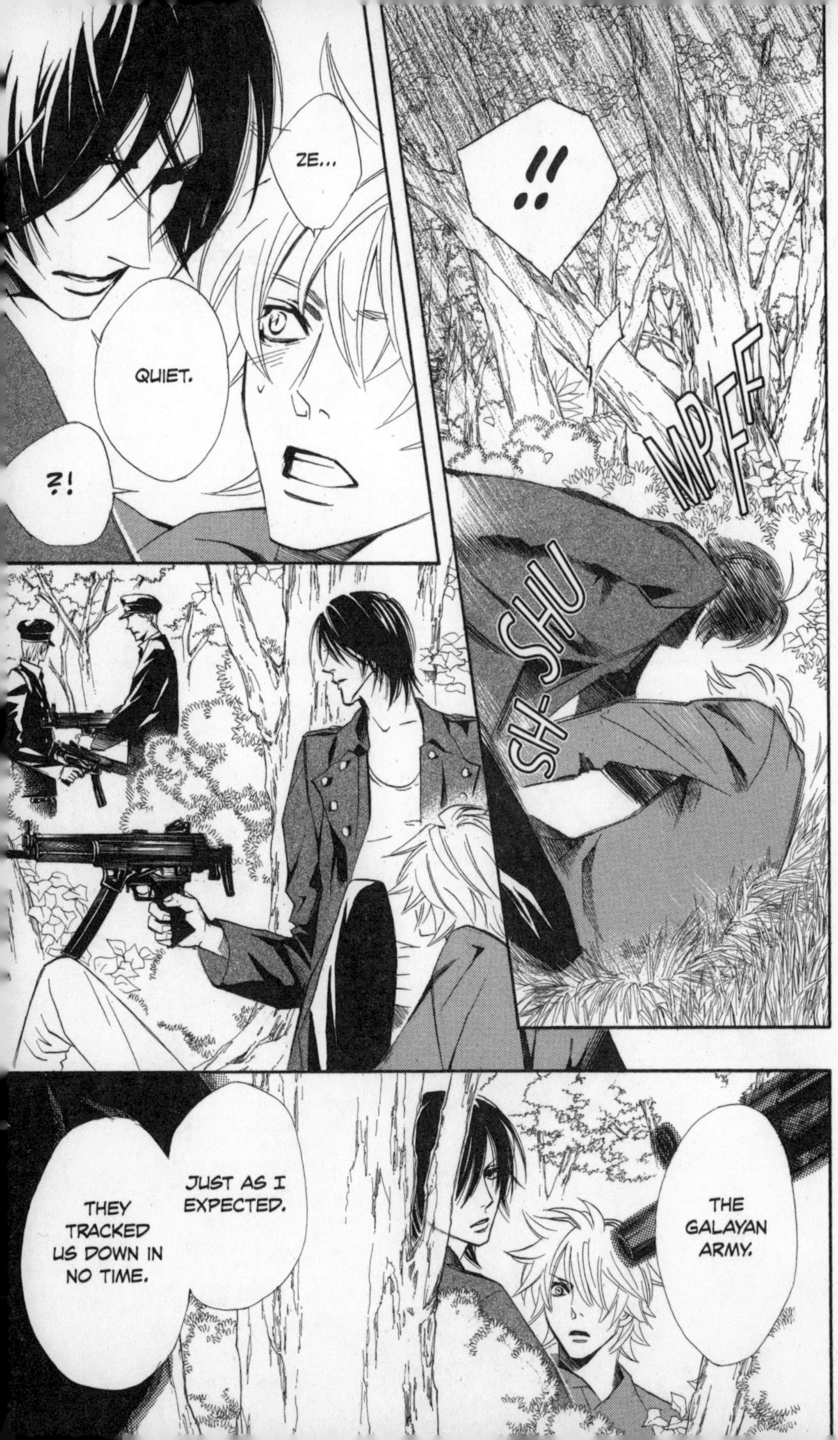
!!
MPFF
SH-SHU
ZE...
QUIET.
?!
THE GALAYAN ARMY.
JUST AS I EXPECTED.
THEY TRACKED US DOWN IN NO TIME.

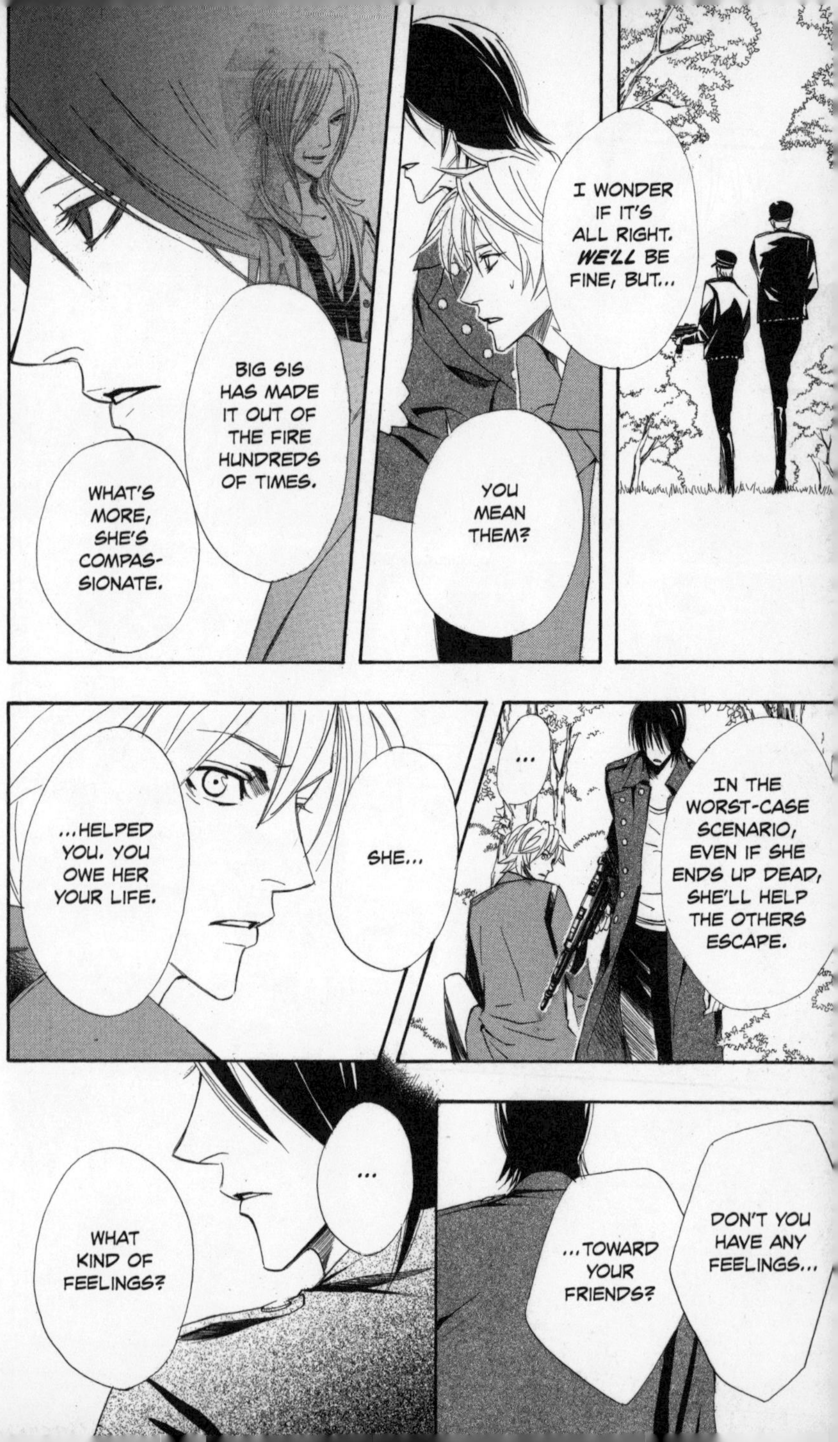
I WONDER IF IT'S ALL RIGHT. *WE'LL* BE FINE, BUT...
YOU MEAN THEM?
BIG SIS HAS MADE IT OUT OF THE FIRE HUNDREDS OF TIMES.
WHAT'S MORE, SHE'S COMPASSIONATE.
IN THE WORST-CASE SCENARIO, EVEN IF SHE ENDS UP DEAD, SHE'LL HELP THE OTHERS ESCAPE.
...
SHE...
...HELPED YOU. YOU OWE HER YOUR LIFE.
DON'T YOU HAVE ANY FEELINGS...
...TOWARD YOUR FRIENDS?
...
WHAT KIND OF FEELINGS?

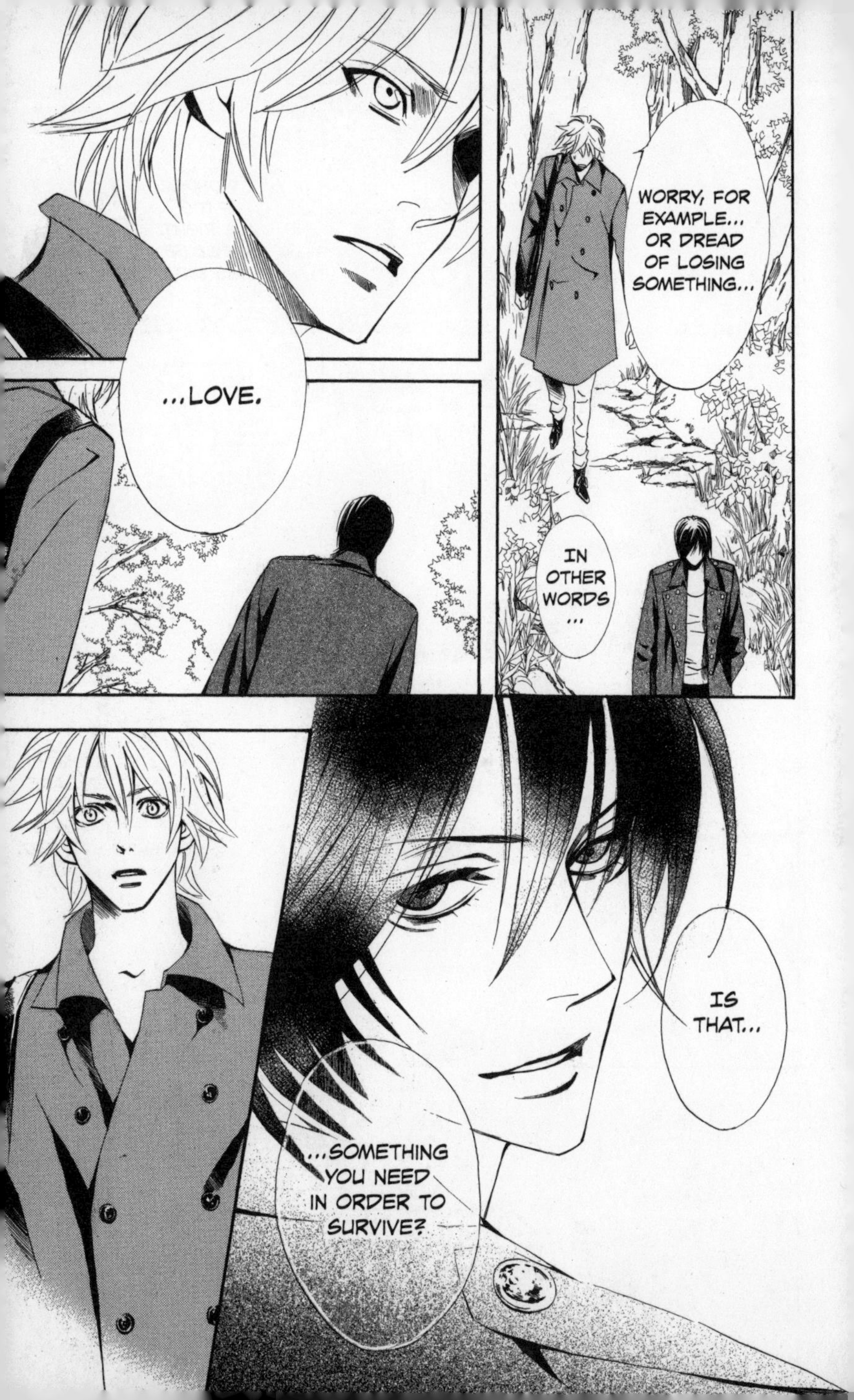
WORRY, FOR EXAMPLE... OR DREAD OF LOSING SOMETHING...
IN OTHER WORDS ...
...LOVE.
IS THAT...
...SOMETHING YOU NEED IN ORDER TO SURVIVE?

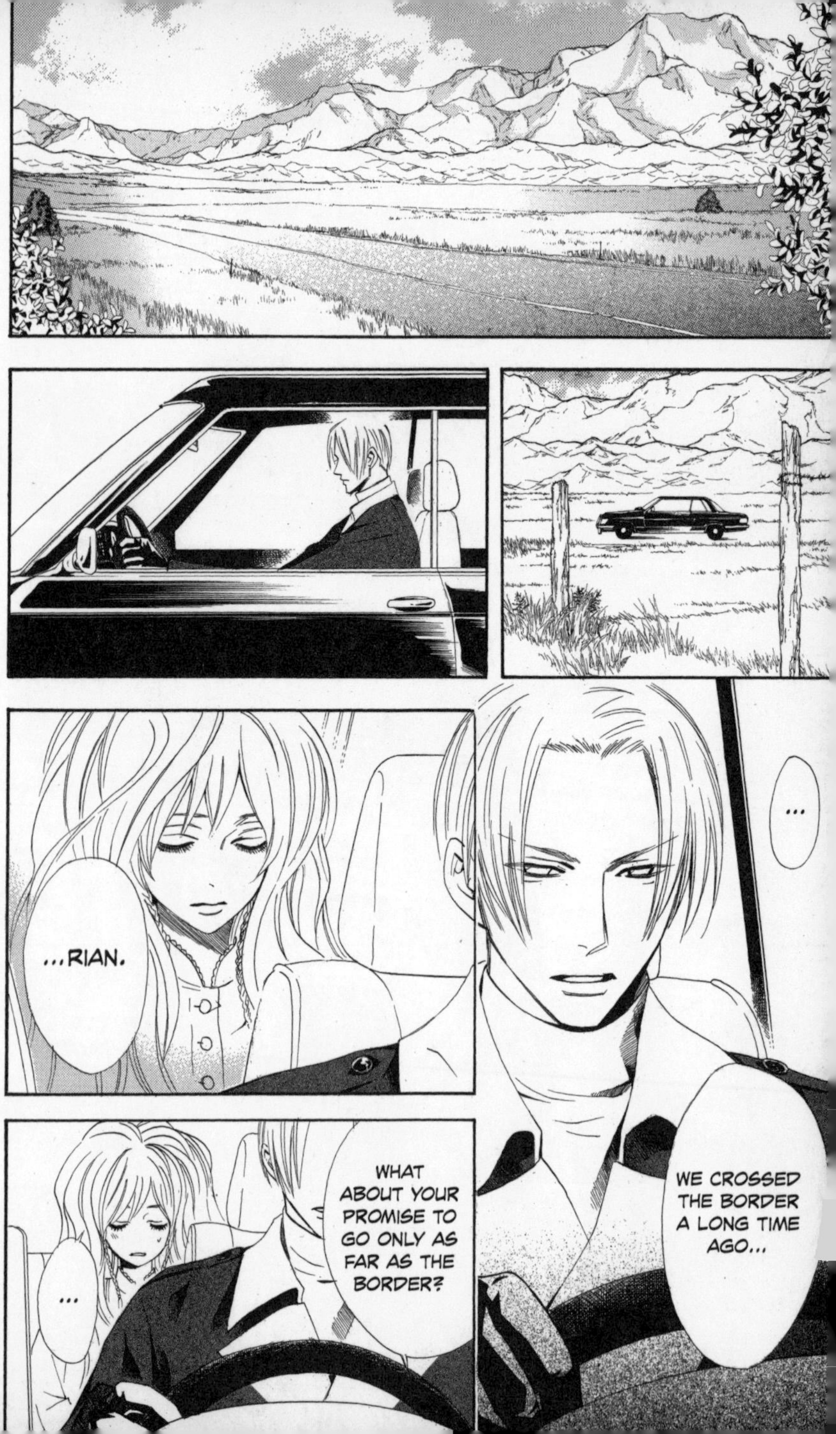
...
WE CROSSED THE BORDER A LONG TIME AGO...
...RIAN.
WHAT ABOUT YOUR PROMISE TO GO ONLY AS FAR AS THE BORDER?
...

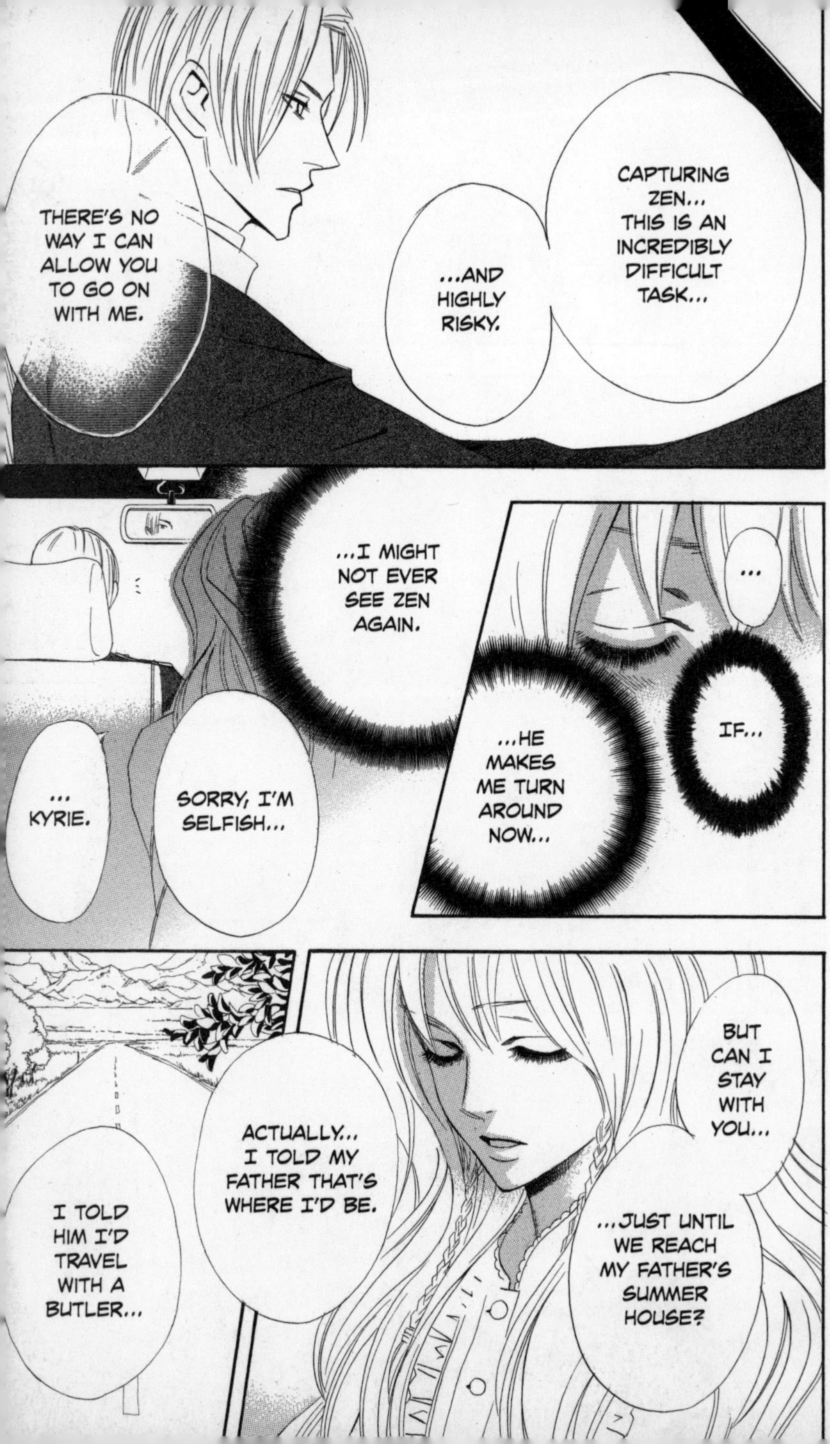
CAPTURING ZEN... THIS IS AN INCREDIBLY DIFFICULT TASK...
...AND HIGHLY RISKY.
THERE'S NO WAY I CAN ALLOW YOU TO GO ON WITH ME.
...
IF...
...HE MAKES ME TURN AROUND NOW...
...I MIGHT NOT EVER SEE ZEN AGAIN.
SORRY, I'M SELFISH...
... KYRIE.
BUT CAN I STAY WITH YOU...
...JUST UNTIL WE REACH MY FATHER'S SUMMER HOUSE?
ACTUALLY... I TOLD MY FATHER THAT'S WHERE I'D BE.
I TOLD HIM I'D TRAVEL WITH A BUTLER...

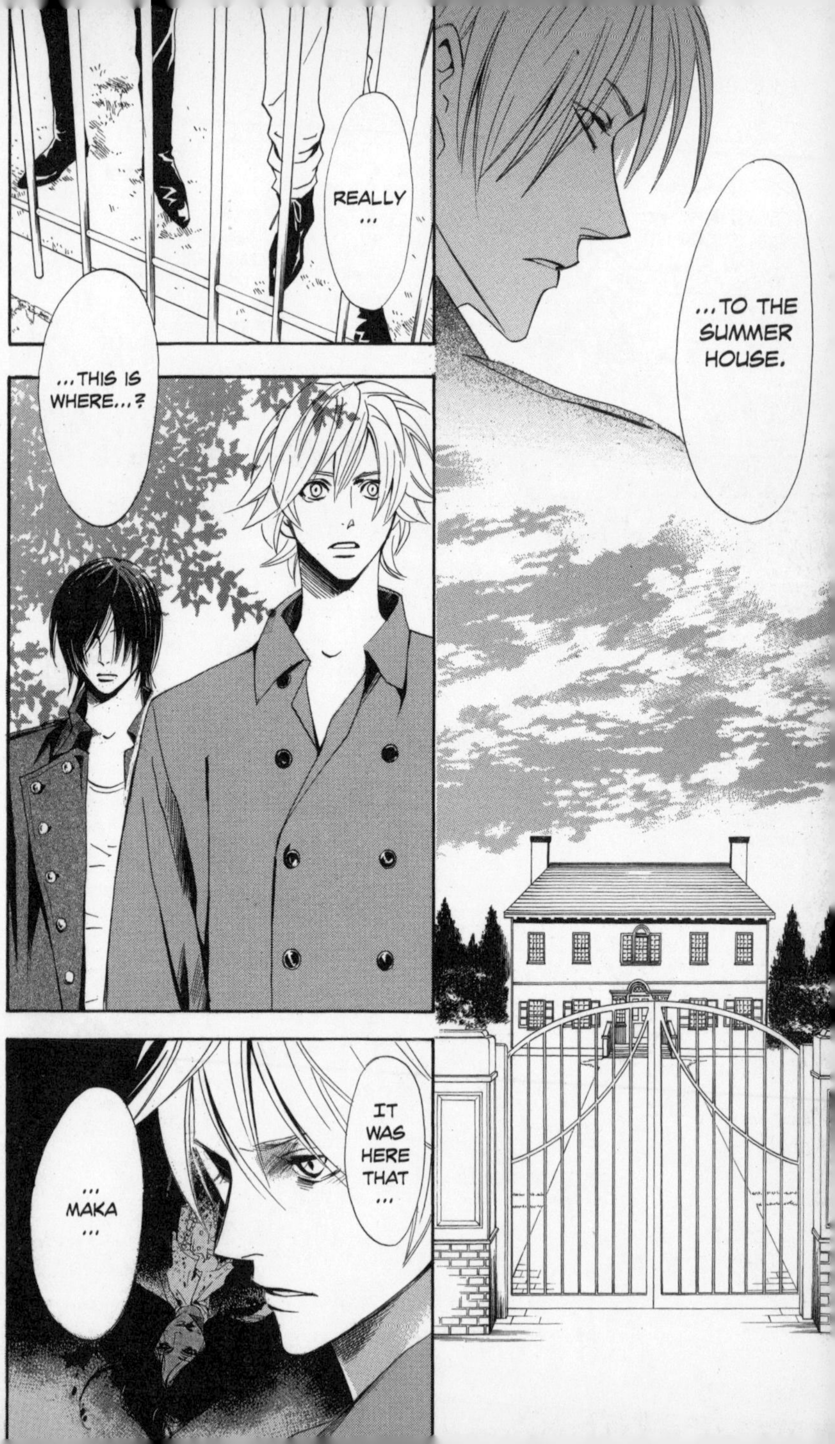
...TO THE SUMMER HOUSE.
REALLY ...
...THIS IS WHERE...?
IT WAS HERE THAT ...
... MAKA ...

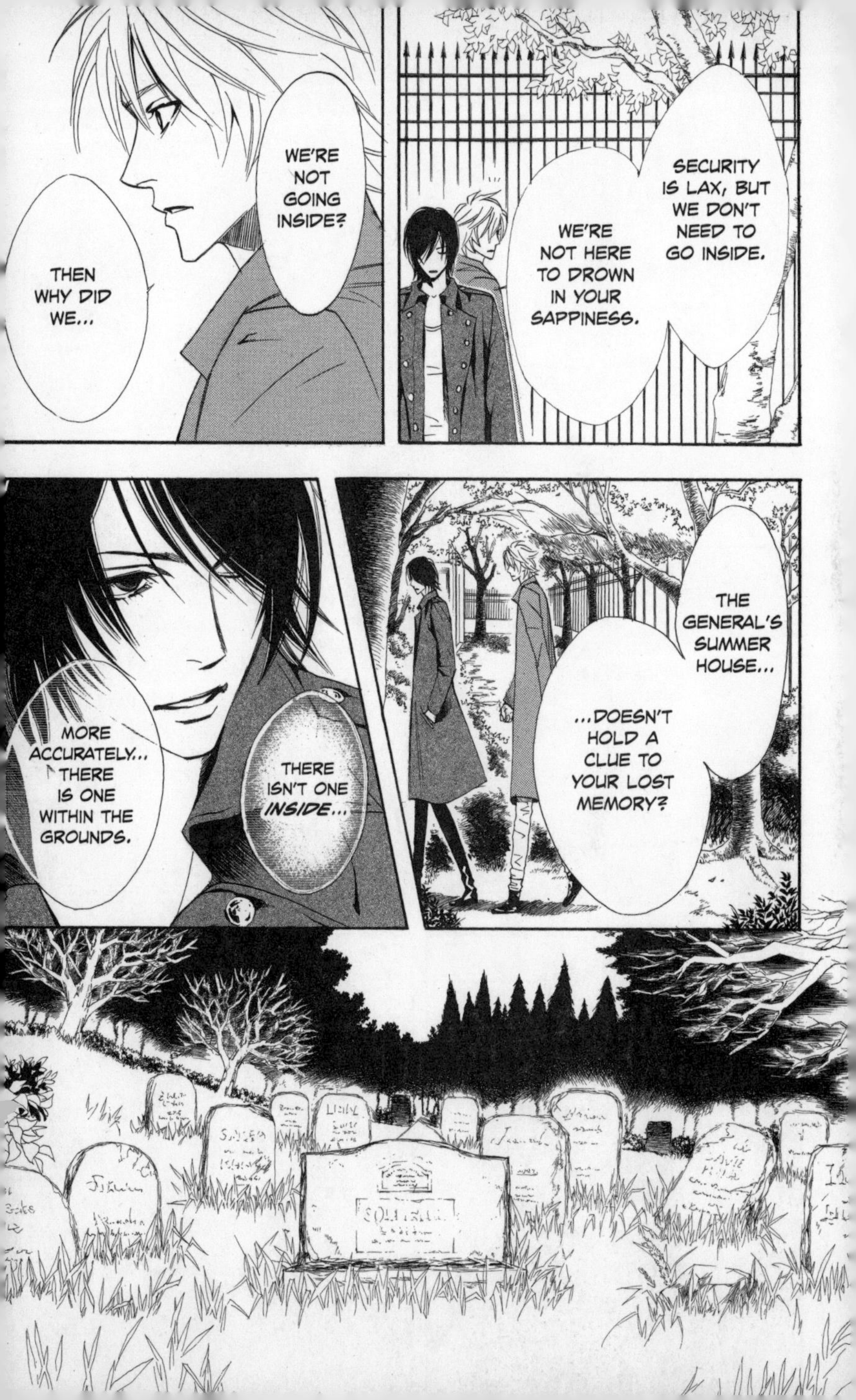
SECURITY IS LAX, BUT WE DON'T NEED TO GO INSIDE.
WE'RE NOT HERE TO DROWN IN YOUR SAPPINESS.
WE'RE NOT GOING INSIDE?
THEN WHY DID WE...
THE GENERAL'S SUMMER HOUSE...
...DOESN'T HOLD A CLUE TO YOUR LOST MEMORY?
THERE ISN'T ONE *INSIDE*...
MORE ACCURATELY... THERE IS ONE WITHIN THE GROUNDS.

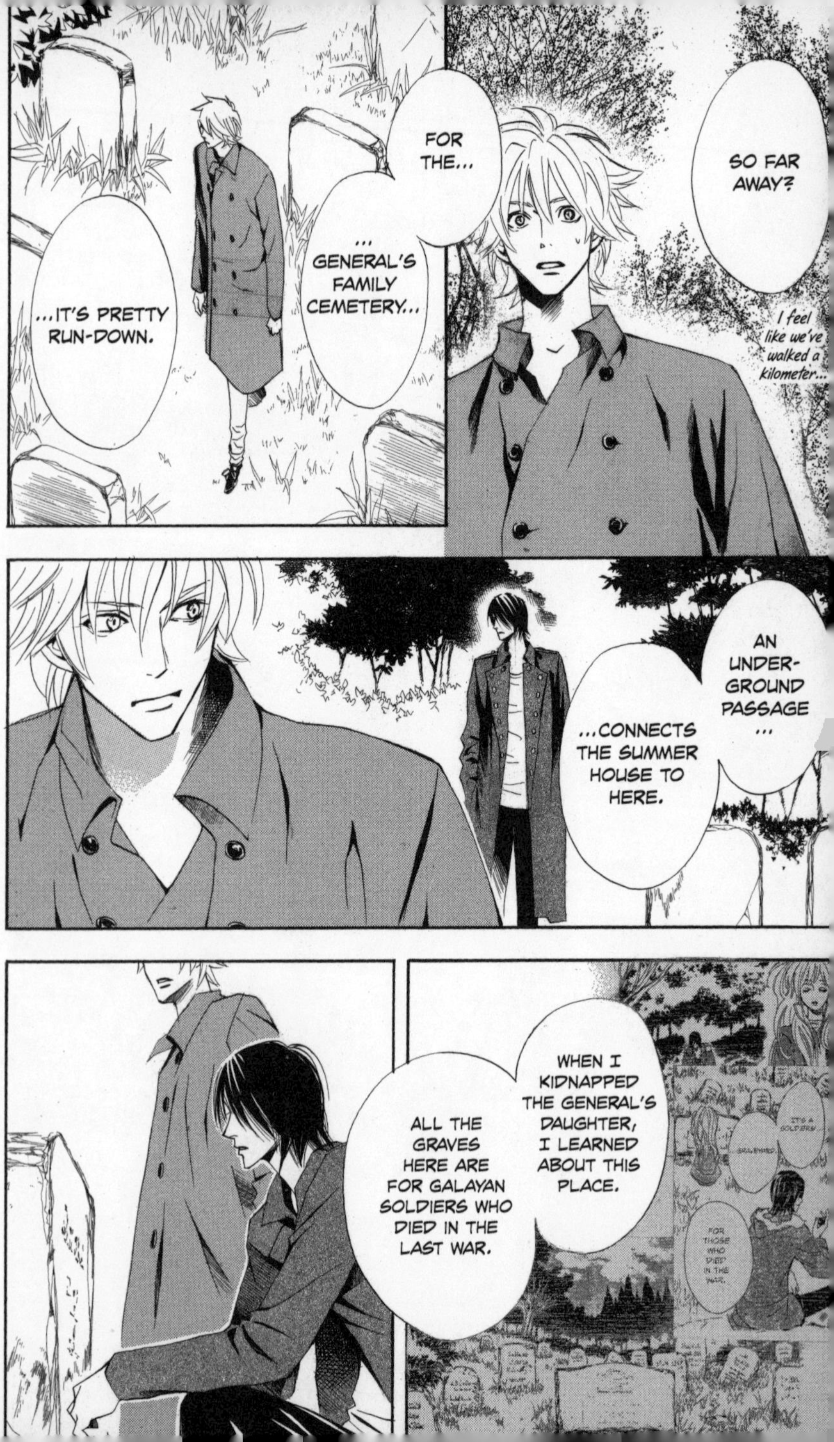
SO FAR AWAY?
I feel like we've walked a kilometer...
FOR THE...
...GENERAL'S FAMILY CEMETERY...
...IT'S PRETTY RUN-DOWN.
AN UNDER-GROUND PASSAGE...
...CONNECTS THE SUMMER HOUSE TO HERE.
WHEN I KIDNAPPED THE GENERAL'S DAUGHTER, I LEARNED ABOUT THIS PLACE.
FOR THOSE WHO DIED IN THE WAR.
ALL THE GRAVES HERE ARE FOR GALAYAN SOLDIERS WHO DIED IN THE LAST WAR.

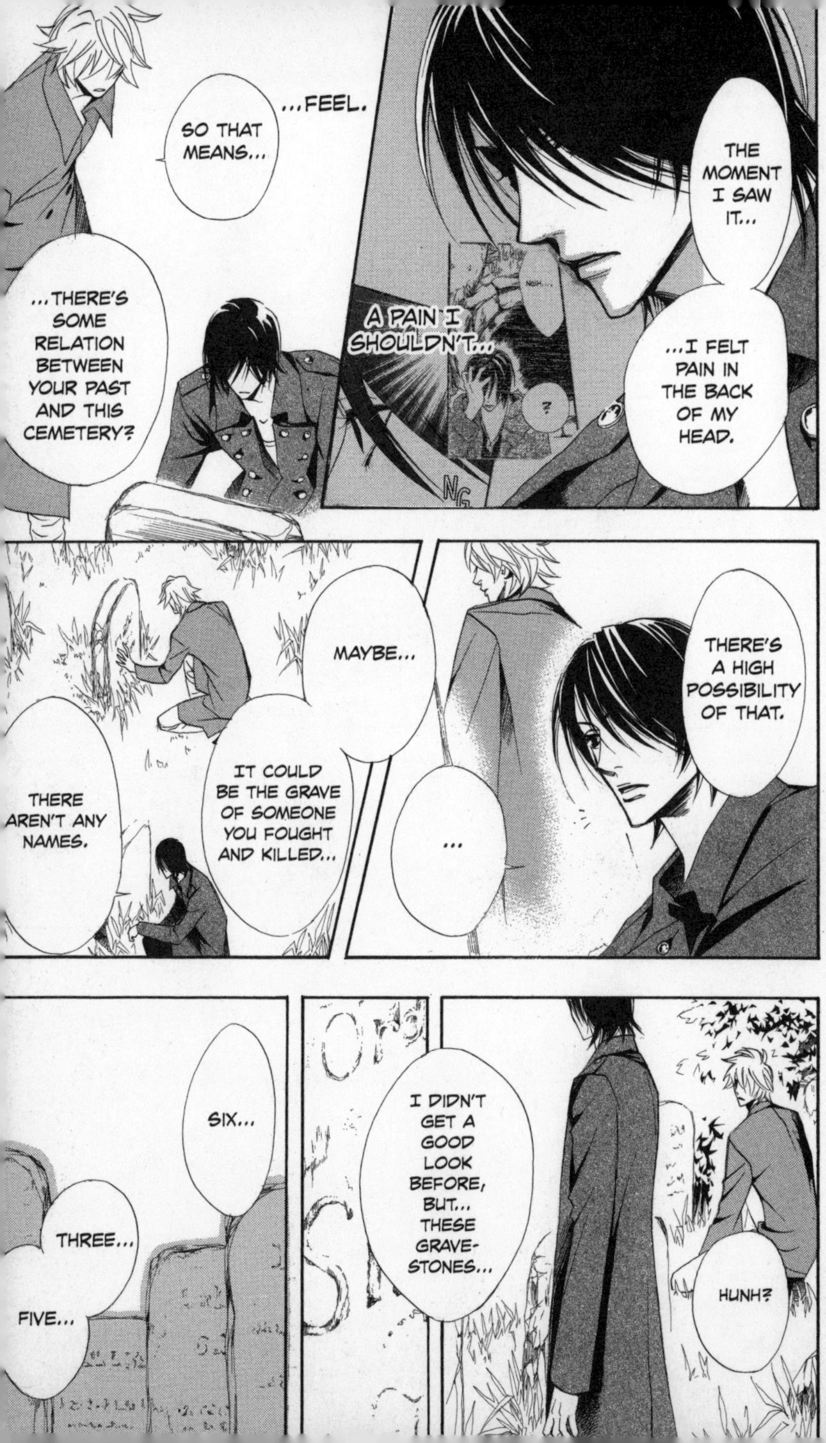
THE MOMENT I SAW IT...
...I FELT PAIN IN THE BACK OF MY HEAD.
?
A PAIN I SHOULDN'T...
...FEEL.
SO THAT MEANS...
...THERE'S SOME RELATION BETWEEN YOUR PAST AND THIS CEMETERY?
THERE'S A HIGH POSSIBILITY OF THAT.
...
MAYBE...
IT COULD BE THE GRAVE OF SOMEONE YOU FOUGHT AND KILLED...
THERE AREN'T ANY NAMES.
HUNH?
I DIDN'T GET A GOOD LOOK BEFORE, BUT... THESE GRAVE-STONES...
SIX...
THREE...
FIVE...

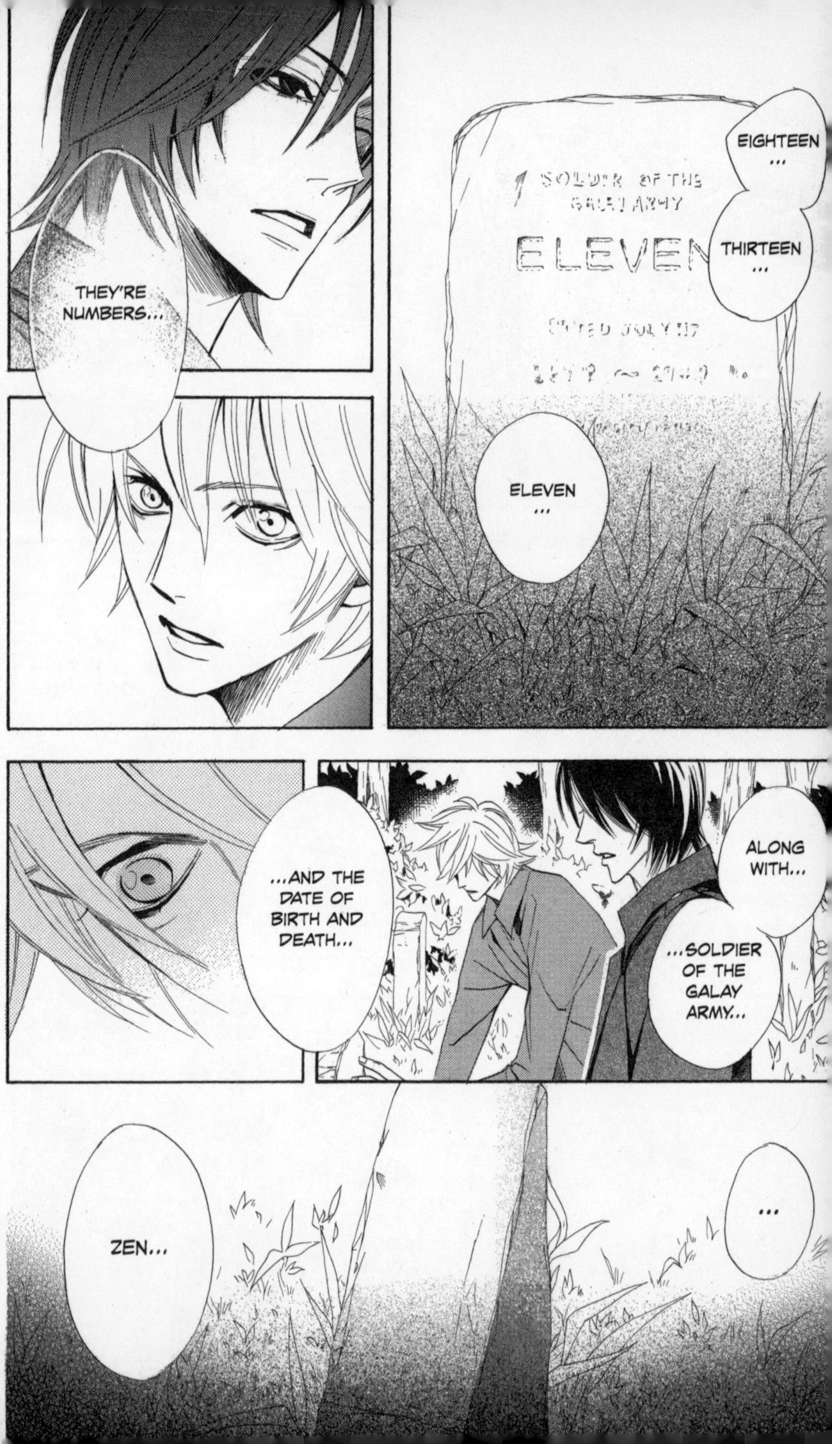
EIGHTEEN...
THIRTEEN...
ELEVEN
ELEVEN...
THEY'RE NUMBERS...
ALONG WITH...
...SOLDIER OF THE GALAY ARMY...
...AND THE DATE OF BIRTH AND DEATH...
...
ZEN...

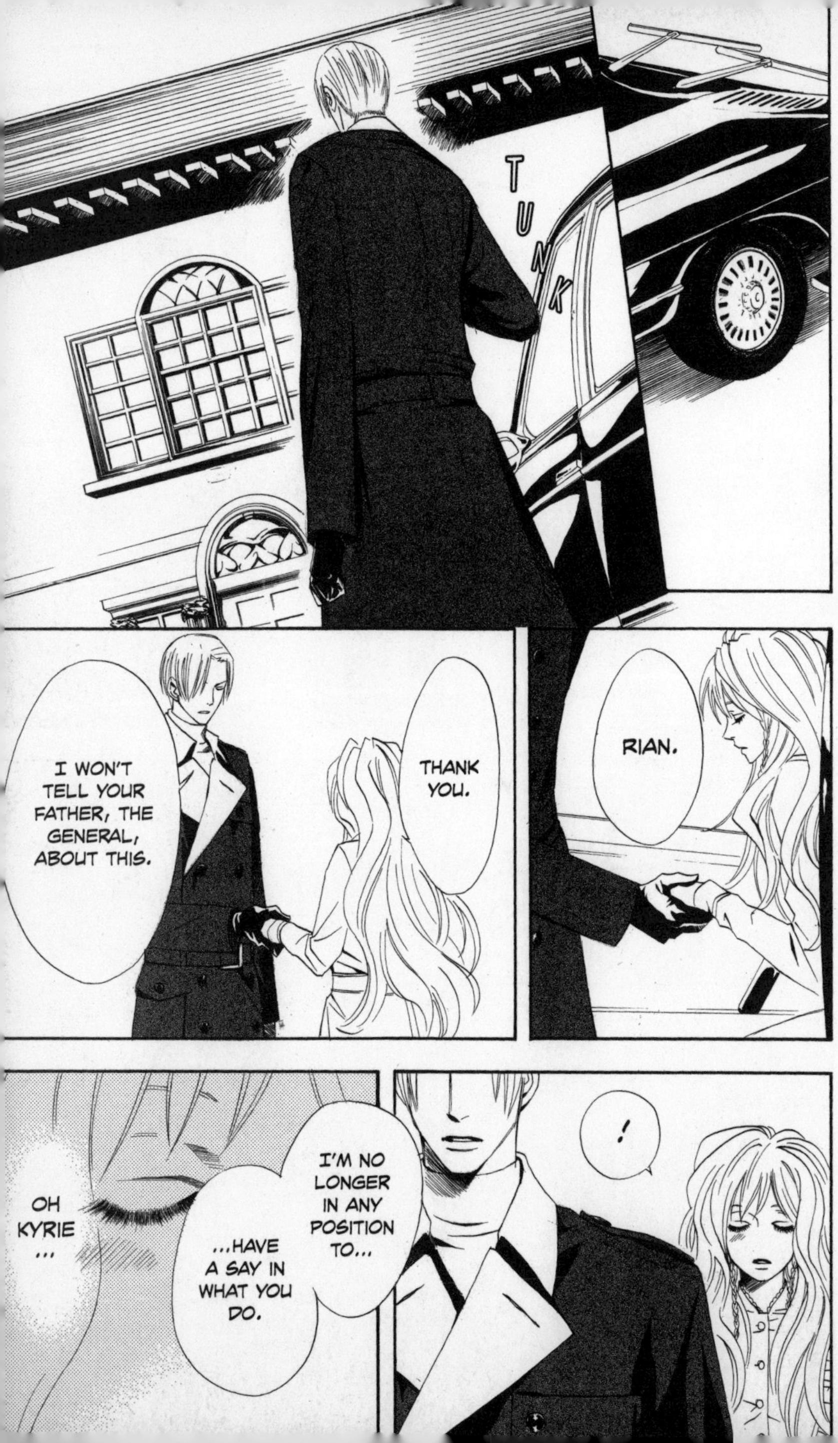
TUNK
RIAN.
THANK YOU.
I WON'T TELL YOUR FATHER, THE GENERAL, ABOUT THIS.
!
I'M NO LONGER IN ANY POSITION TO...
...HAVE A SAY IN WHAT YOU DO.
OH KYRIE ...

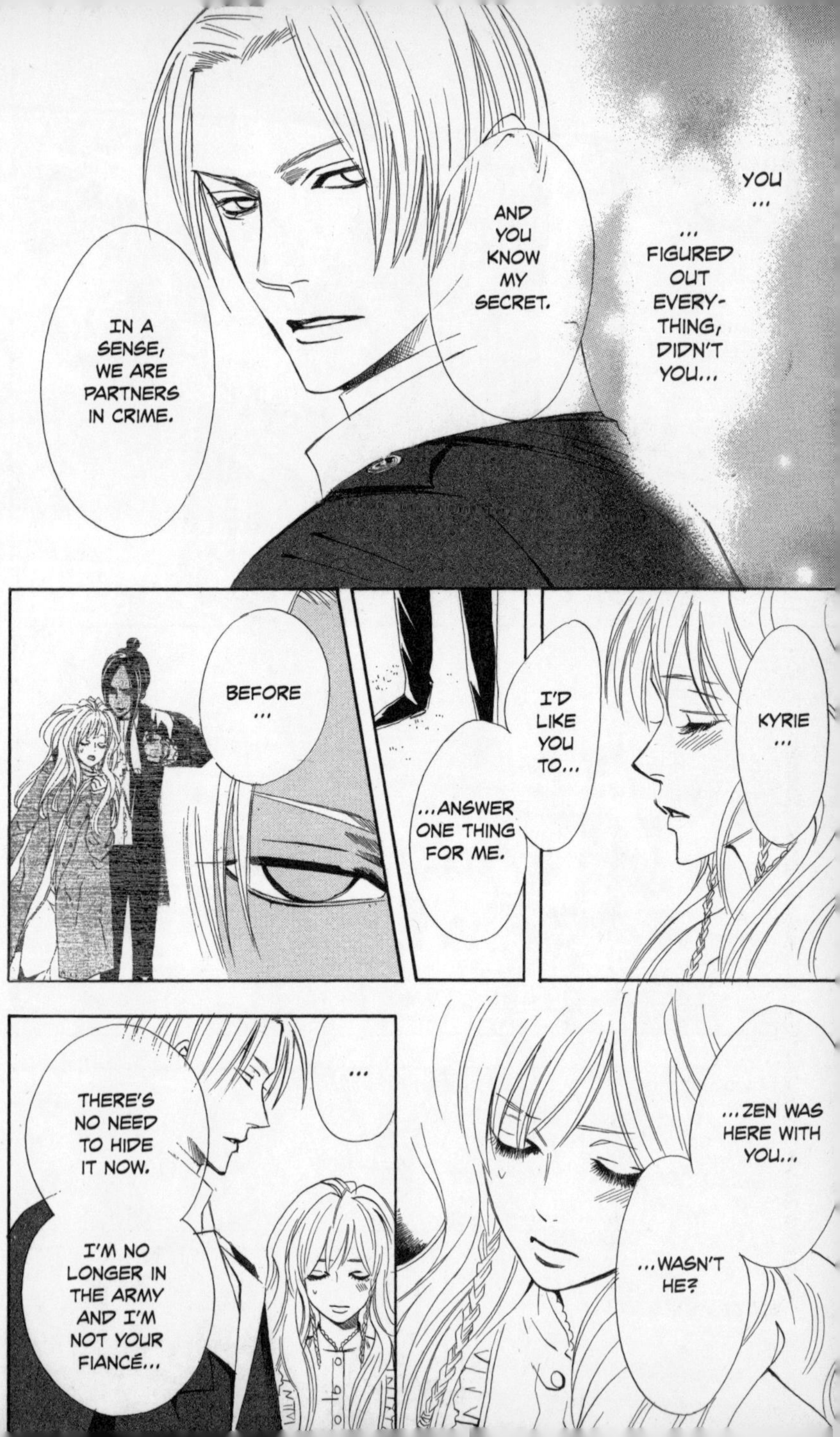
YOU ...
... FIGURED OUT EVERY-THING, DIDN'T YOU...
AND YOU KNOW MY SECRET.
IN A SENSE, WE ARE PARTNERS IN CRIME.
KYRIE ...
I'D LIKE YOU TO...
...ANSWER ONE THING FOR ME.
BEFORE ...
...ZEN WAS HERE WITH YOU...
...WASN'T HE?
...
THERE'S NO NEED TO HIDE IT NOW.
I'M NO LONGER IN THE ARMY AND I'M NOT YOUR FIANCÉ...

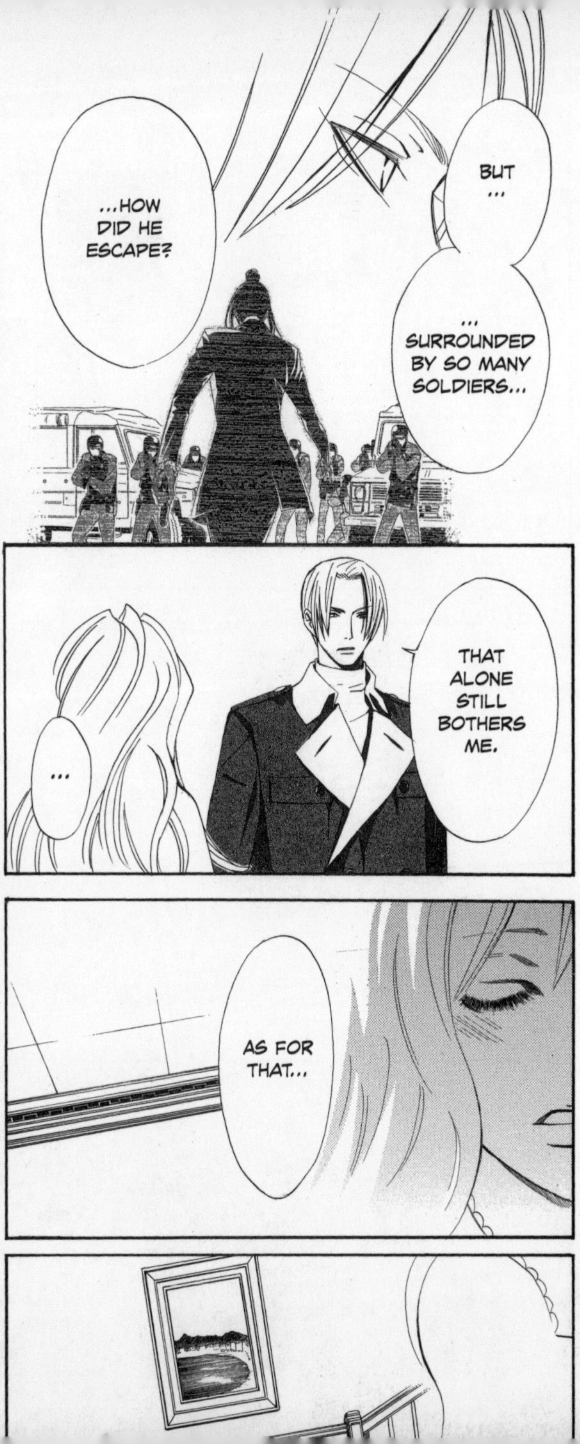
BUT ...
... SURROUNDED BY SO MANY SOLDIERS...
...HOW DID HE ESCAPE?
THAT ALONE STILL BOTHERS ME.
...
AS FOR THAT...

2

Blank Slate came about because I decided to start a manga with a villain as the main character, in contrast to my works up to that point, which had always featured a good man as the main character.

The story as I first imagined it was really long, but it was so incredibly long that I decided to shorten it, and it ended up taking this form.

Because of the change of direction, the characters and ending changed quite a lot. Some of the characters ended up getting treated poorly, so as the author, I feel bad for them.

(continued in sidebar 3)

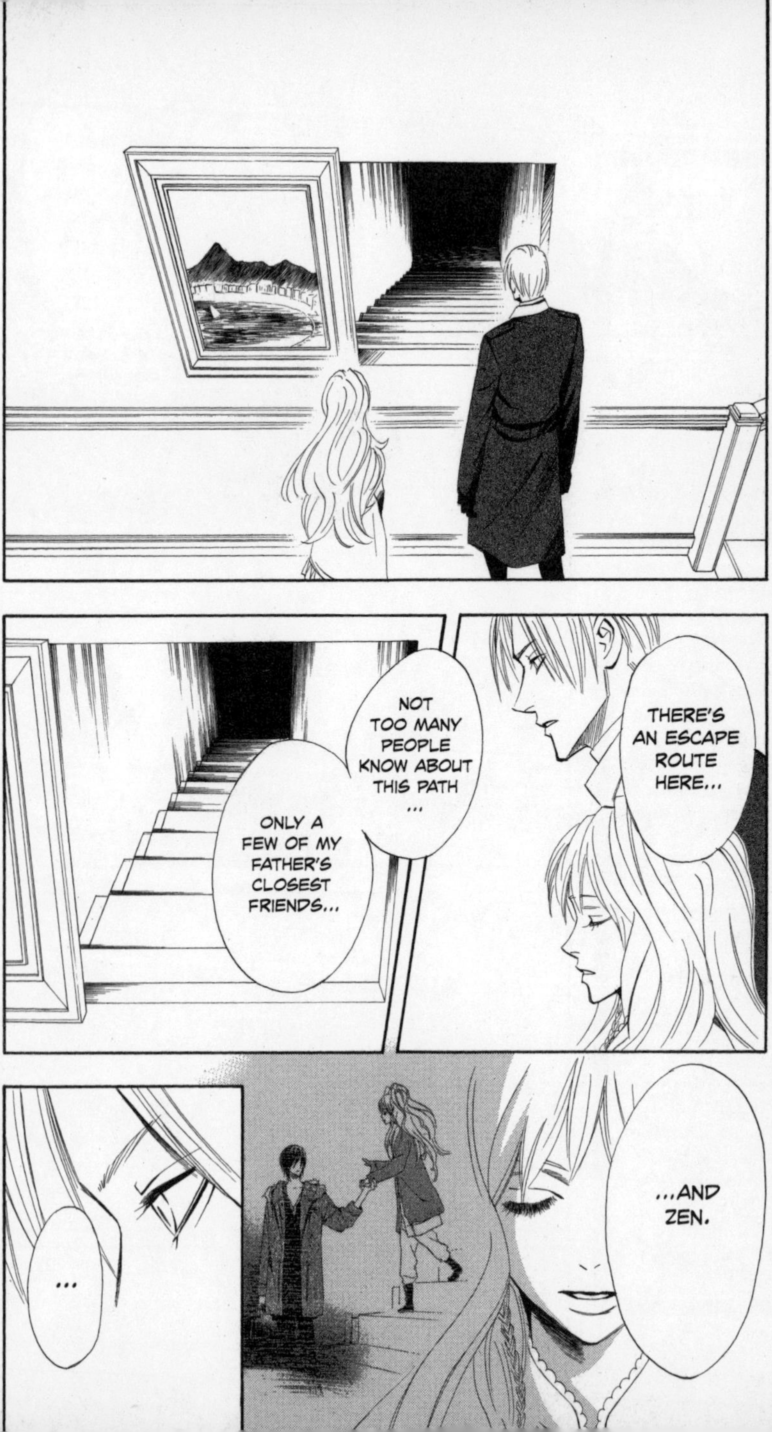
THERE'S AN ESCAPE ROUTE HERE...
NOT TOO MANY PEOPLE KNOW ABOUT THIS PATH ...
ONLY A FEW OF MY FATHER'S CLOSEST FRIENDS...
...AND ZEN.
...

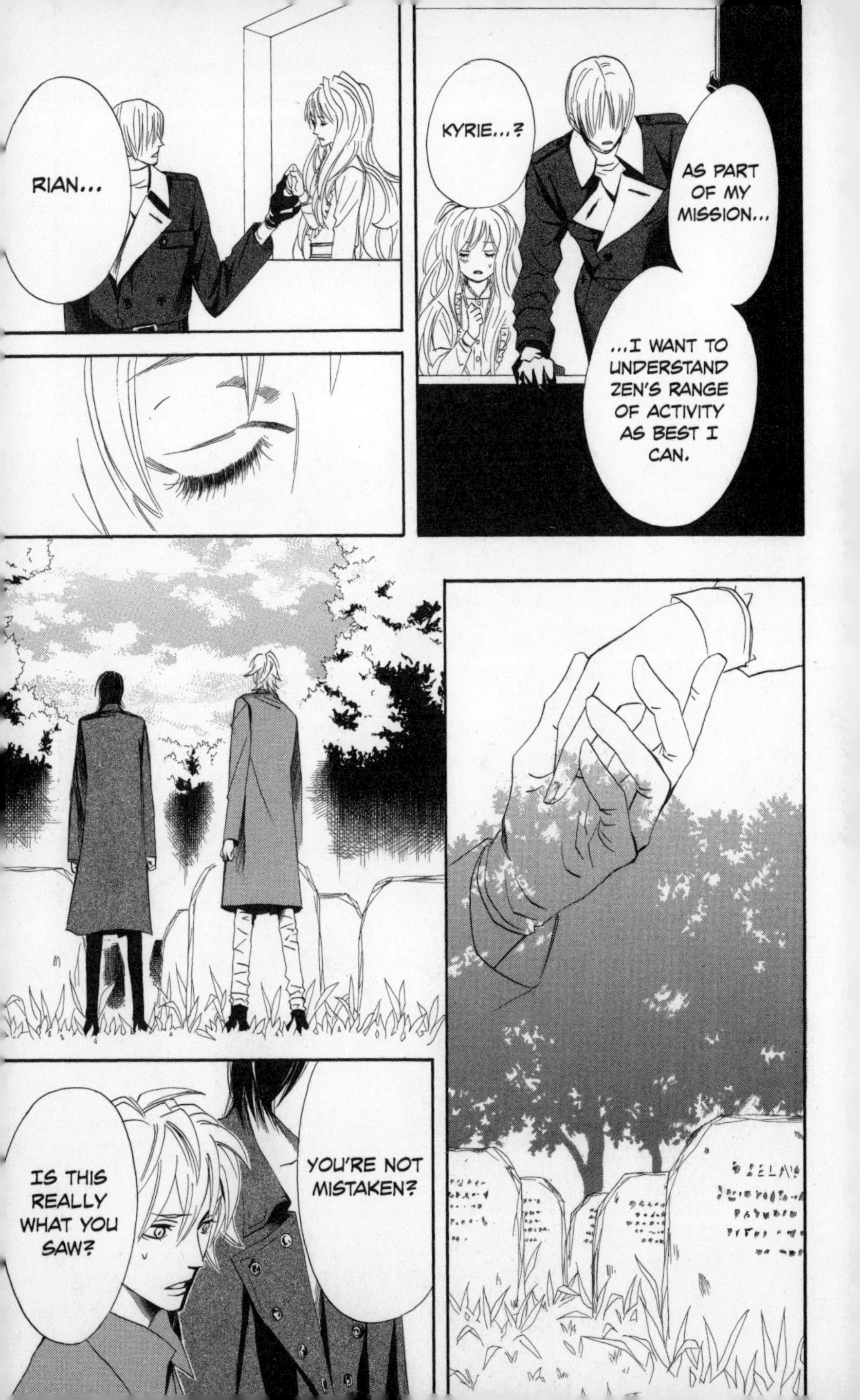
KYRIE...?
AS PART OF MY MISSION...
...I WANT TO UNDERSTAND ZEN'S RANGE OF ACTIVITY AS BEST I CAN.
RIAN...
YOU'RE NOT MISTAKEN?
IS THIS REALLY WHAT YOU SAW?

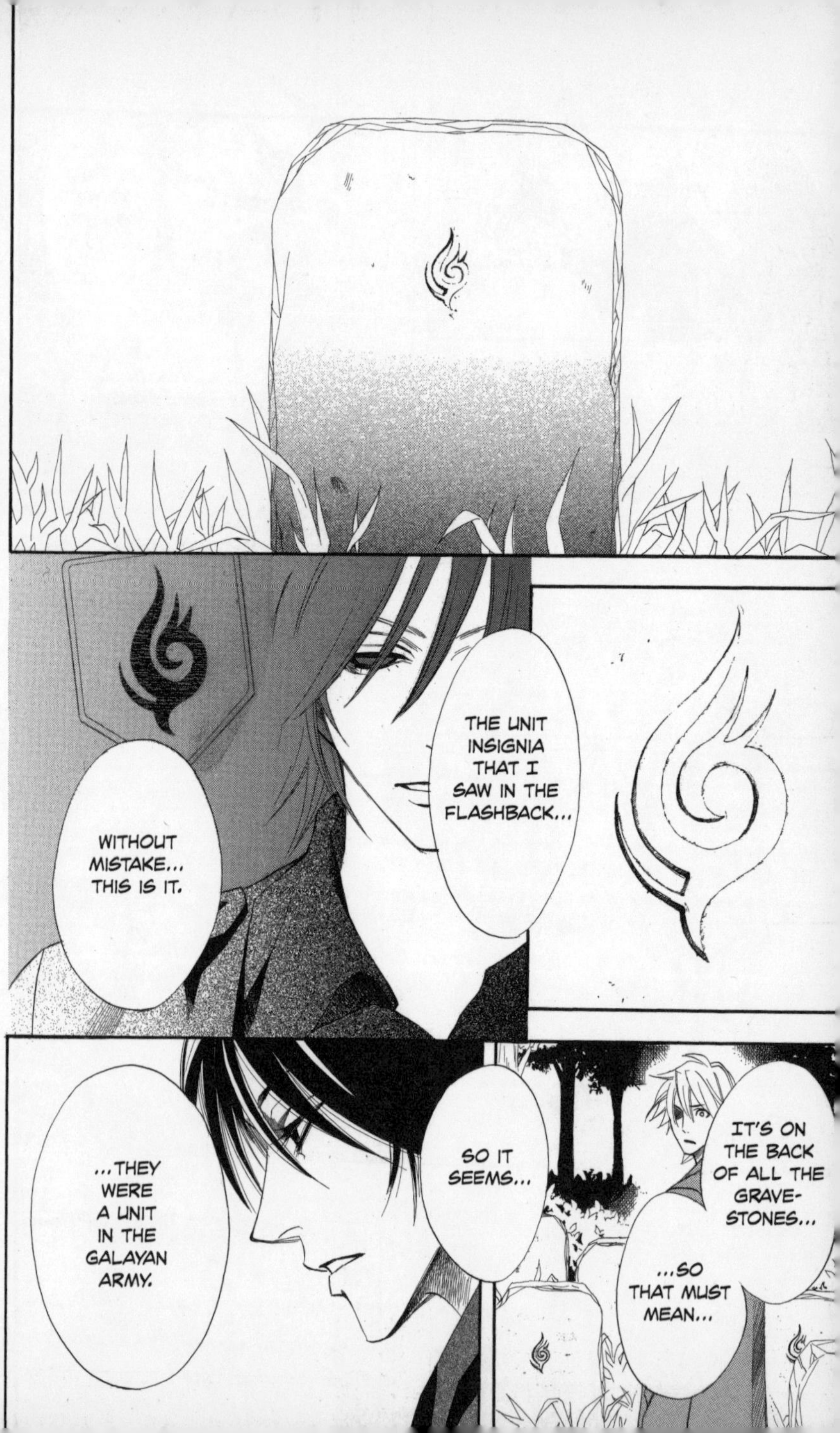
THE UNIT INSIGNIA THAT I SAW IN THE FLASHBACK...
WITHOUT MISTAKE... THIS IS IT.
IT'S ON THE BACK OF ALL THE GRAVE-STONES...
...SO THAT MUST MEAN...
SO IT SEEMS...
...THEY WERE A UNIT IN THE GALAYAN ARMY.

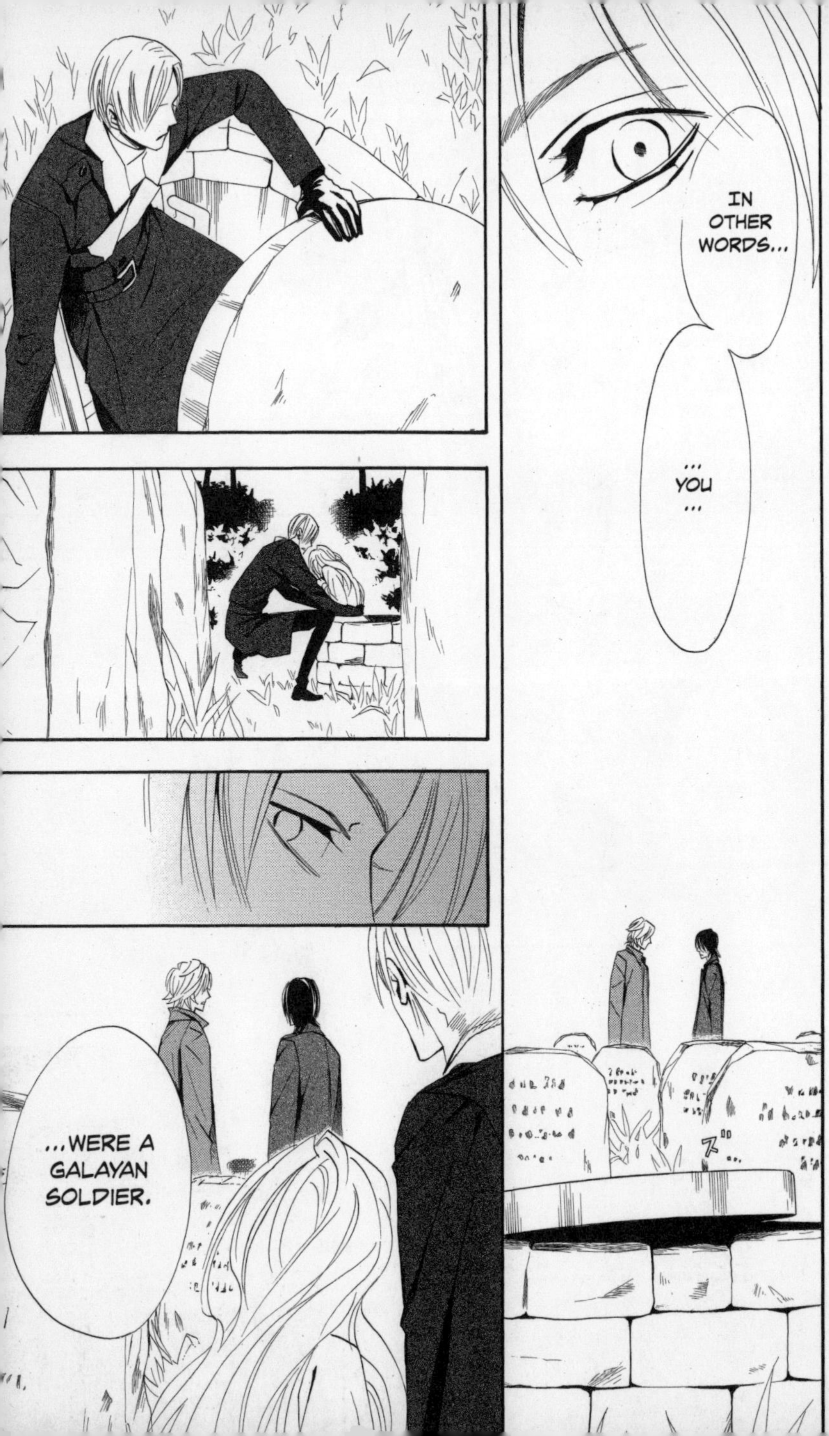
IN OTHER WORDS...
... YOU ...
...WERE A GALAYAN SOLDIER.

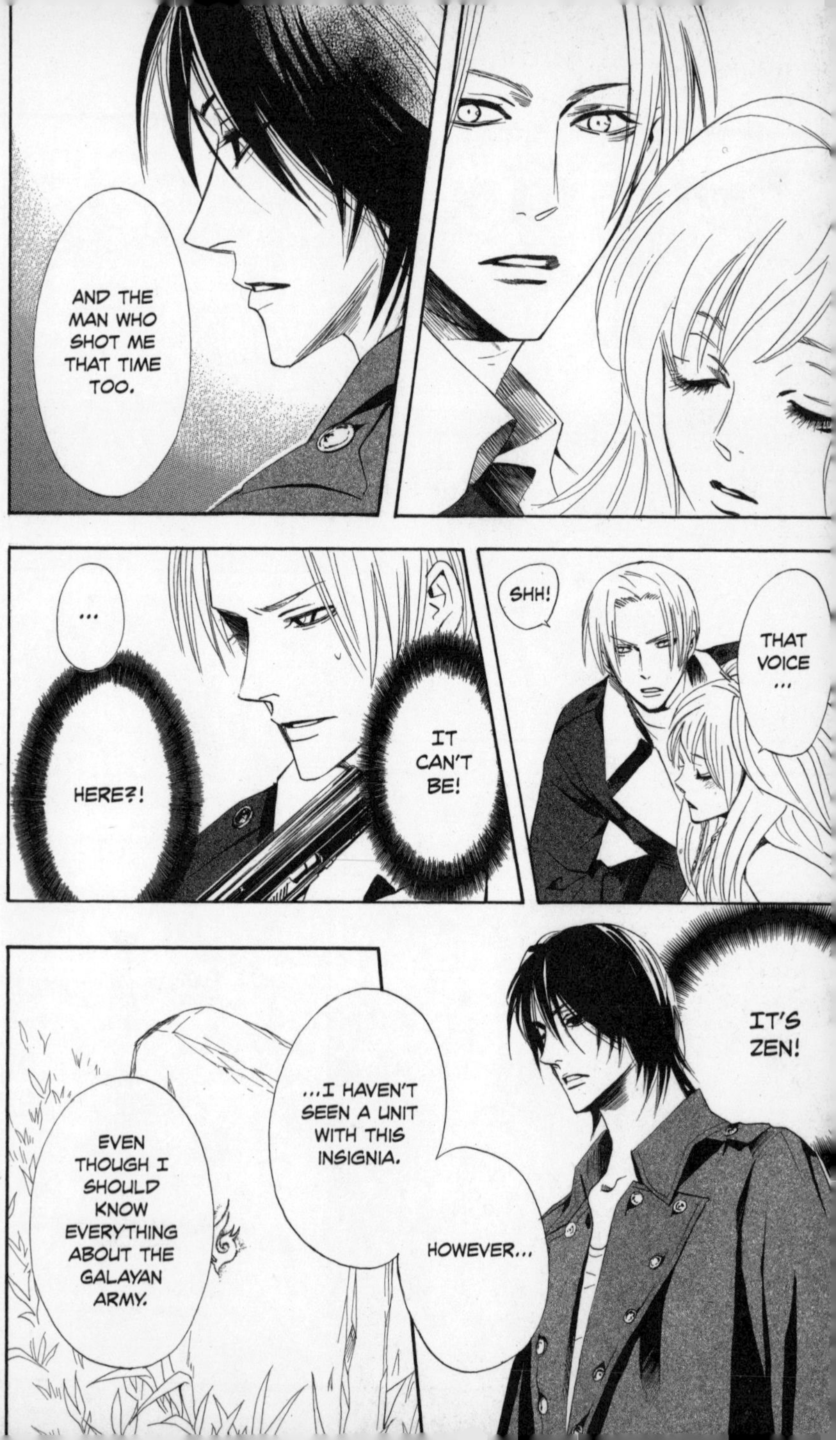
AND THE MAN WHO SHOT ME THAT TIME TOO.
THAT VOICE ...
SHH!
...
IT CAN'T BE!
HERE?!
IT'S ZEN!
HOWEVER...
...I HAVEN'T SEEN A UNIT WITH THIS INSIGNIA.
EVEN THOUGH I SHOULD KNOW EVERYTHING ABOUT THE GALAYAN ARMY.

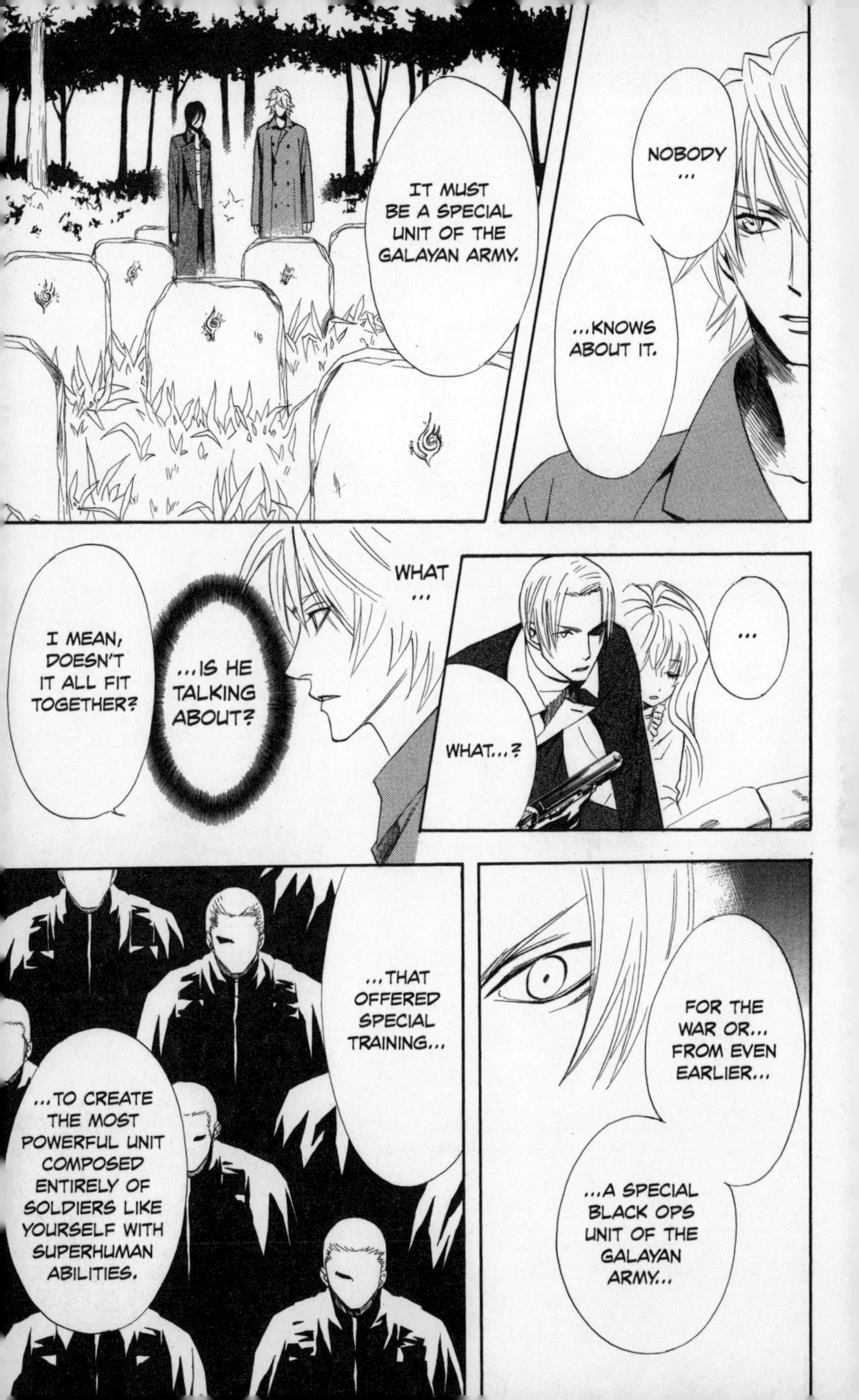
NOBODY ...
...KNOWS ABOUT IT.
IT MUST BE A SPECIAL UNIT OF THE GALAYAN ARMY.
...
WHAT...?
WHAT ...
...IS HE TALKING ABOUT?
I MEAN, DOESN'T IT ALL FIT TOGETHER?
FOR THE WAR OR... FROM EVEN EARLIER...
...A SPECIAL BLACK OPS UNIT OF THE GALAYAN ARMY...
...THAT OFFERED SPECIAL TRAINING...
...TO CREATE THE MOST POWERFUL UNIT COMPOSED ENTIRELY OF SOLDIERS LIKE YOURSELF WITH SUPERHUMAN ABILITIES.

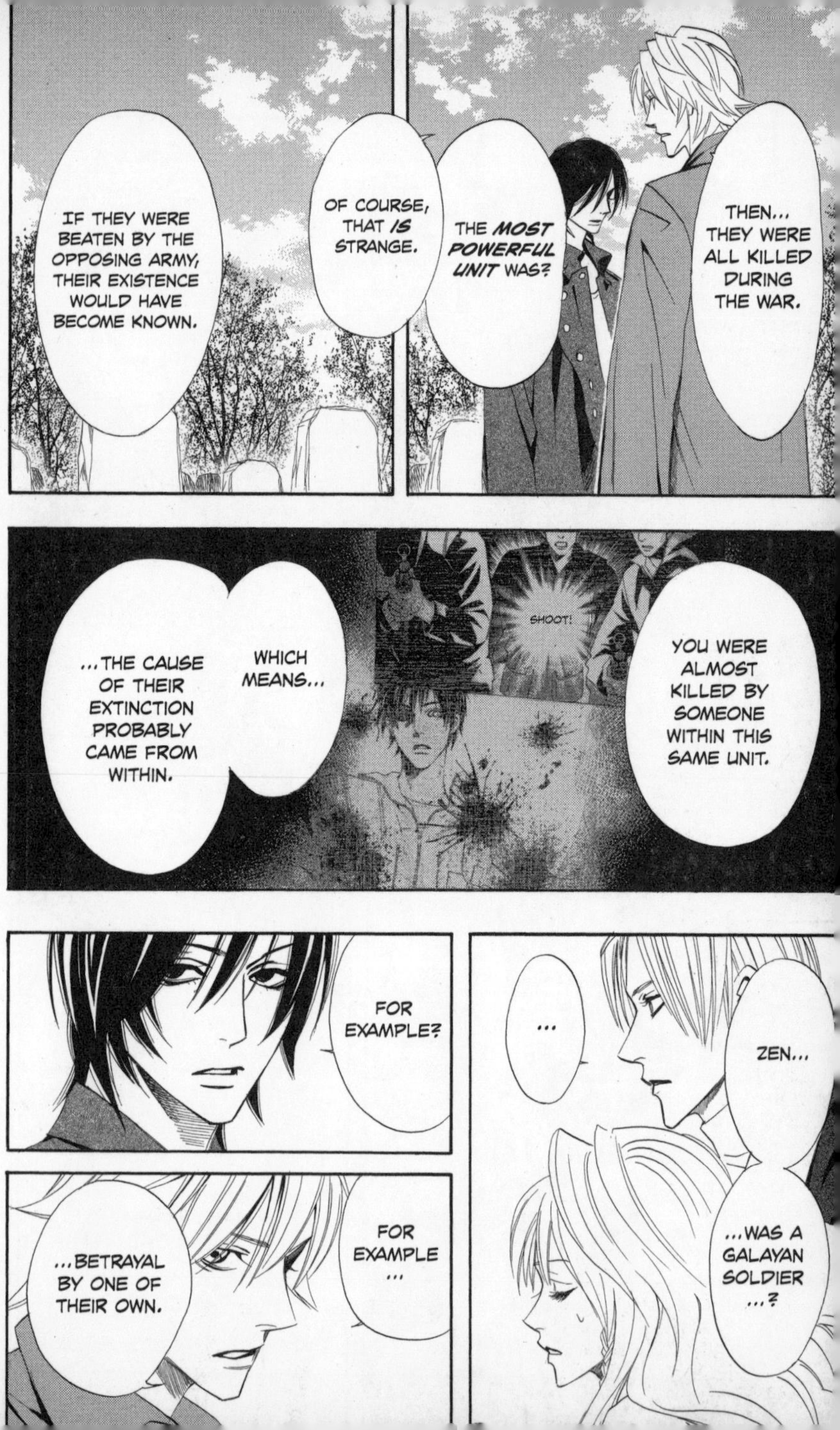
THEN... THEY WERE ALL KILLED DURING THE WAR.
THE MOST POWERFUL UNIT WAS?
OF COURSE, THAT IS STRANGE.
IF THEY WERE BEATEN BY THE OPPOSING ARMY, THEIR EXISTENCE WOULD HAVE BECOME KNOWN.
YOU WERE ALMOST KILLED BY SOMEONE WITHIN THIS SAME UNIT.
SHOOT!
WHICH MEANS...
...THE CAUSE OF THEIR EXTINCTION PROBABLY CAME FROM WITHIN.
ZEN...
...
...WAS A GALAYAN SOLDIER ...?
FOR EXAMPLE?
FOR EXAMPLE ...
...BETRAYAL BY ONE OF THEIR OWN.

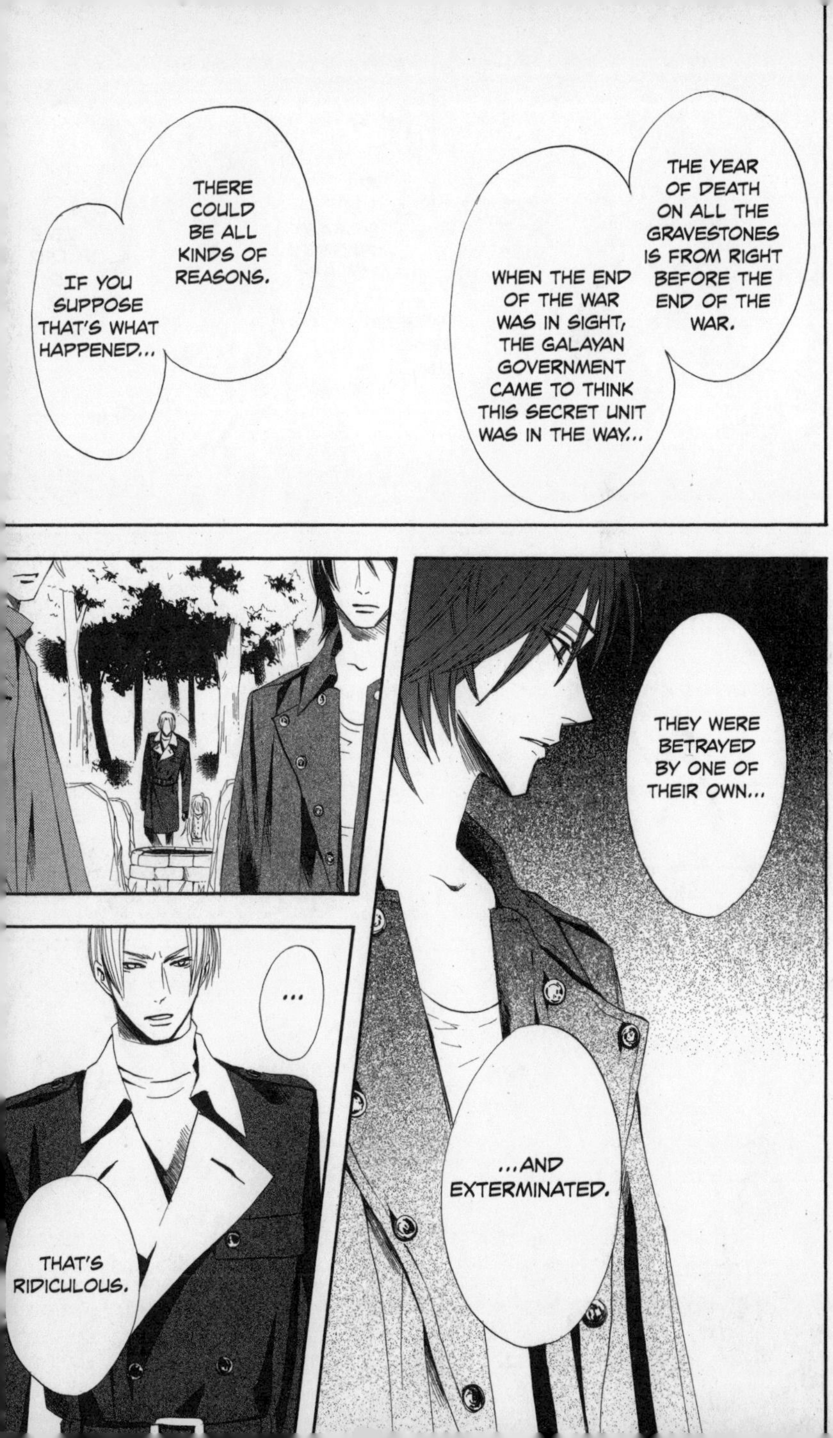
THE YEAR OF DEATH ON ALL THE GRAVESTONES IS FROM RIGHT BEFORE THE END OF THE WAR.
WHEN THE END OF THE WAR WAS IN SIGHT, THE GALAYAN GOVERNMENT CAME TO THINK THIS SECRET UNIT WAS IN THE WAY...
THERE COULD BE ALL KINDS OF REASONS.
IF YOU SUPPOSE THAT'S WHAT HAPPENED...
THEY WERE BETRAYED BY ONE OF THEIR OWN...
...AND EXTERMINATED.
...
THAT'S RIDICULOUS.

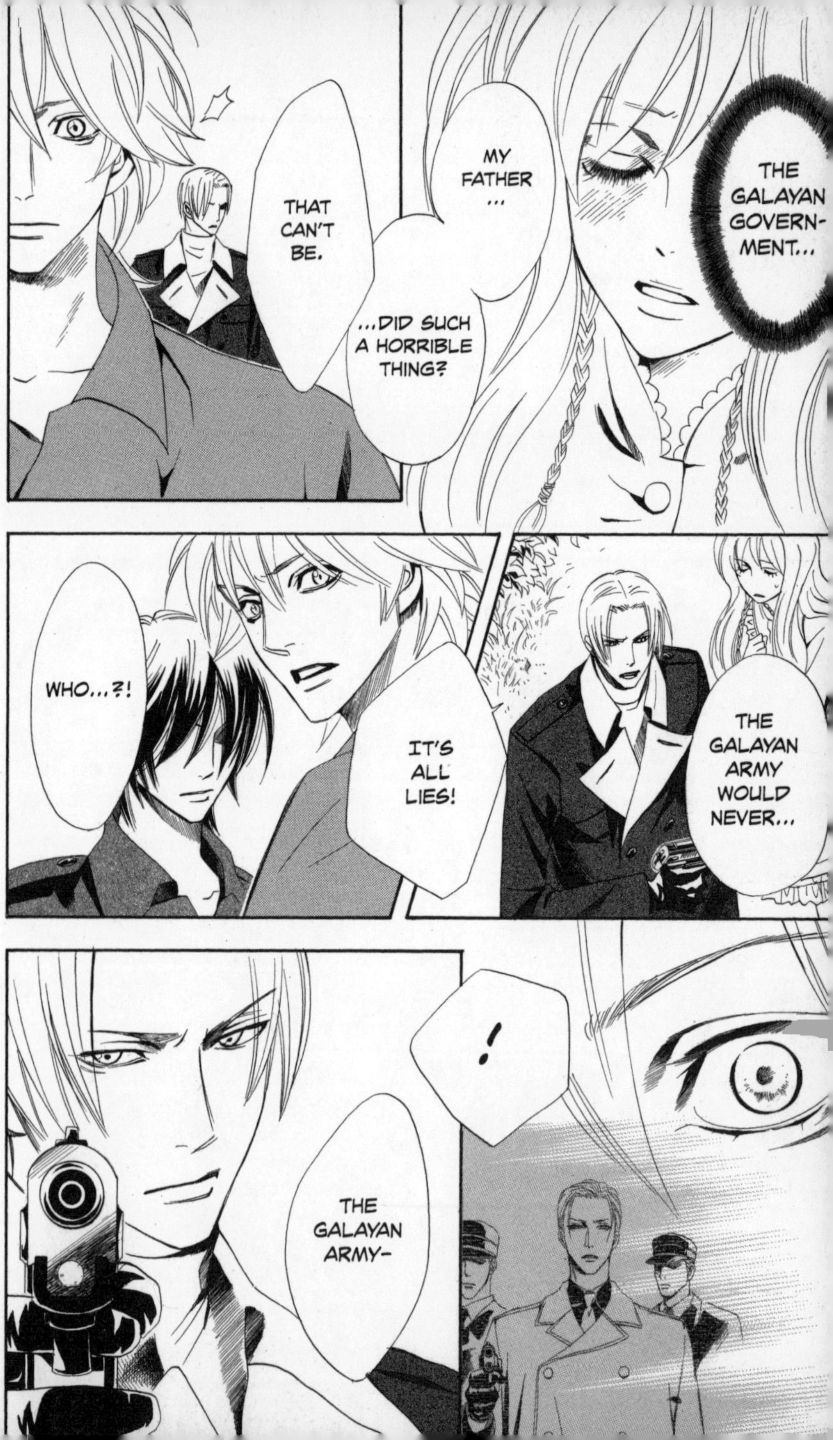
THE GALAYAN GOVERNMENT...
MY FATHER ...
...DID SUCH A HORRIBLE THING?
THAT CAN'T BE.
THE GALAYAN ARMY WOULD NEVER...
IT'S ALL LIES!
WHO...?!
!
THE GALAYAN ARMY-

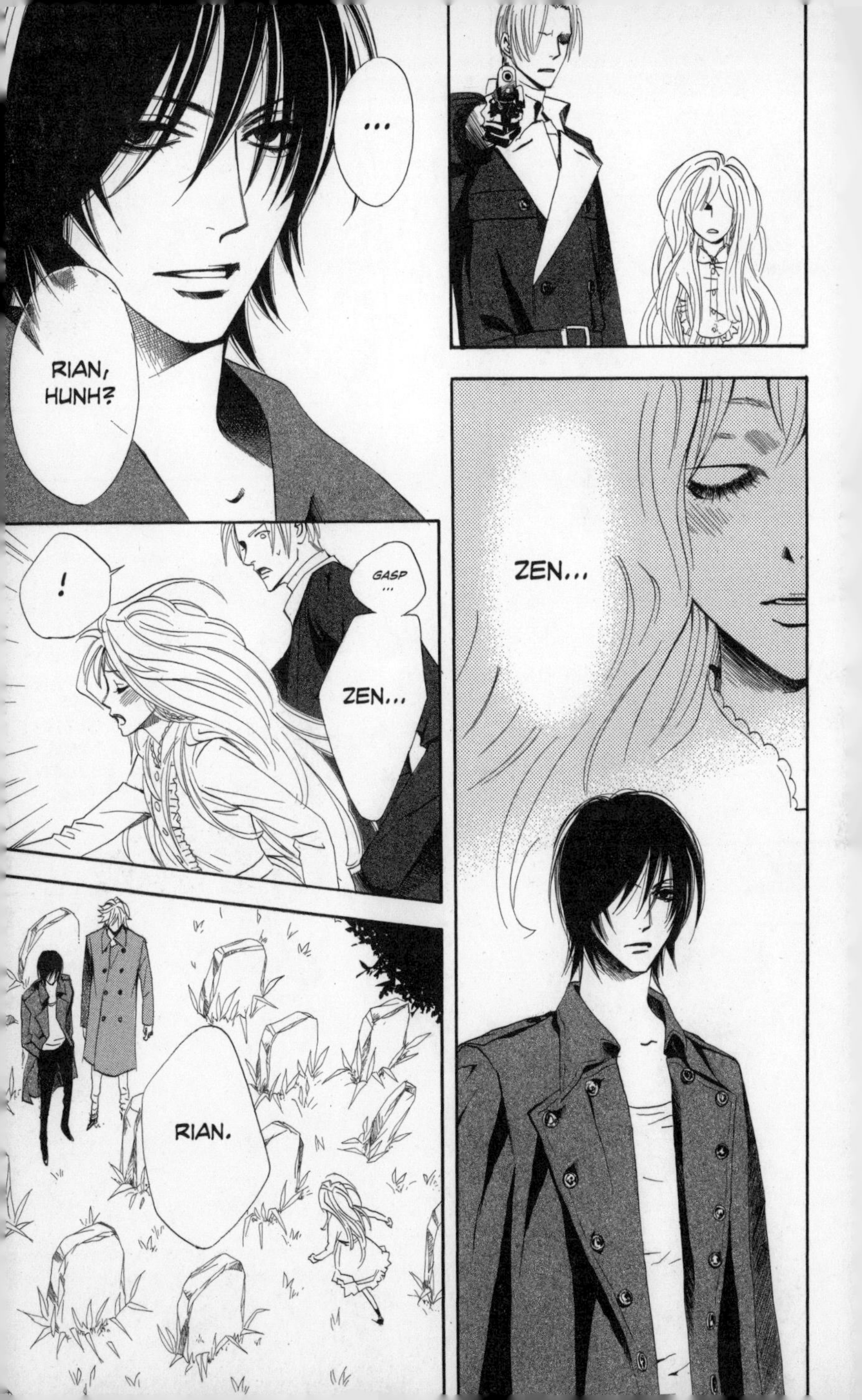
...
RIAN, HUNH?
ZEN...
GASP ...
!
ZEN...
RIAN.

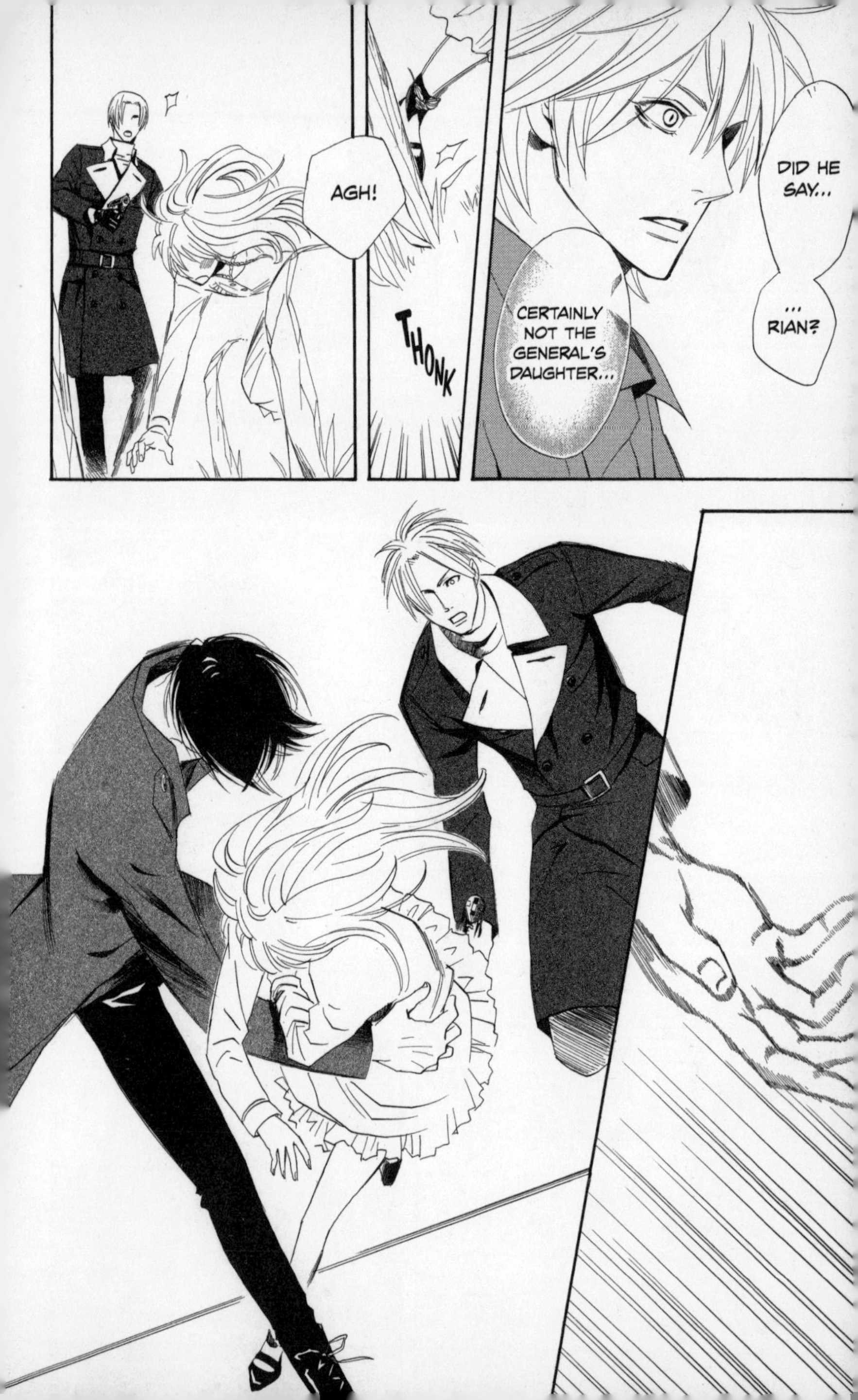
DID HE SAY...
... RIAN?
CERTAINLY NOT THE GENERAL'S DAUGHTER...
AGH!
THONK

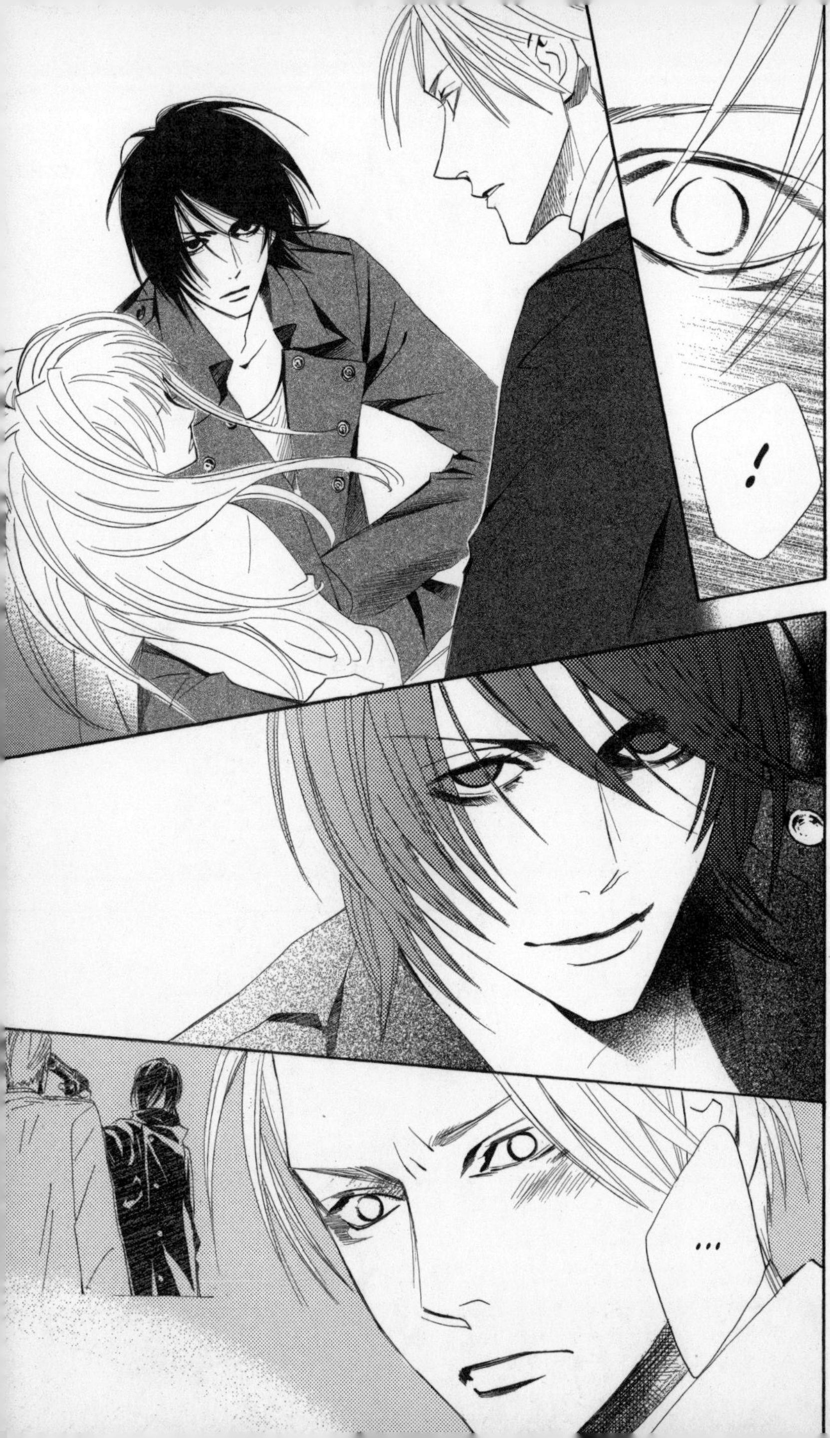
!
...

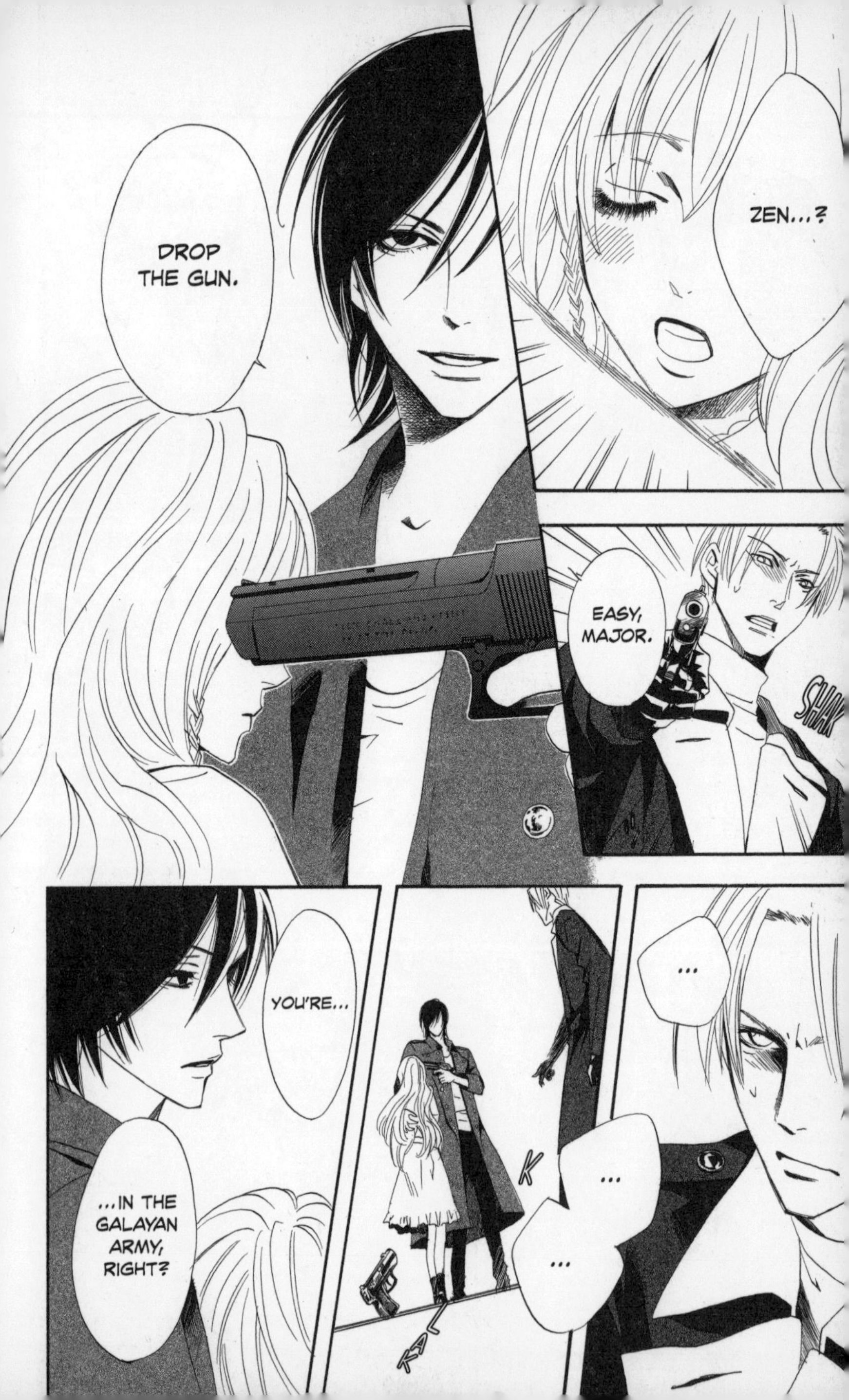
ZEN...?
EASY, MAJOR.
SHAK
DROP THE GUN.
...
...
...
K
KAL
YOU'RE...
...IN THE GALAYAN ARMY, RIGHT?

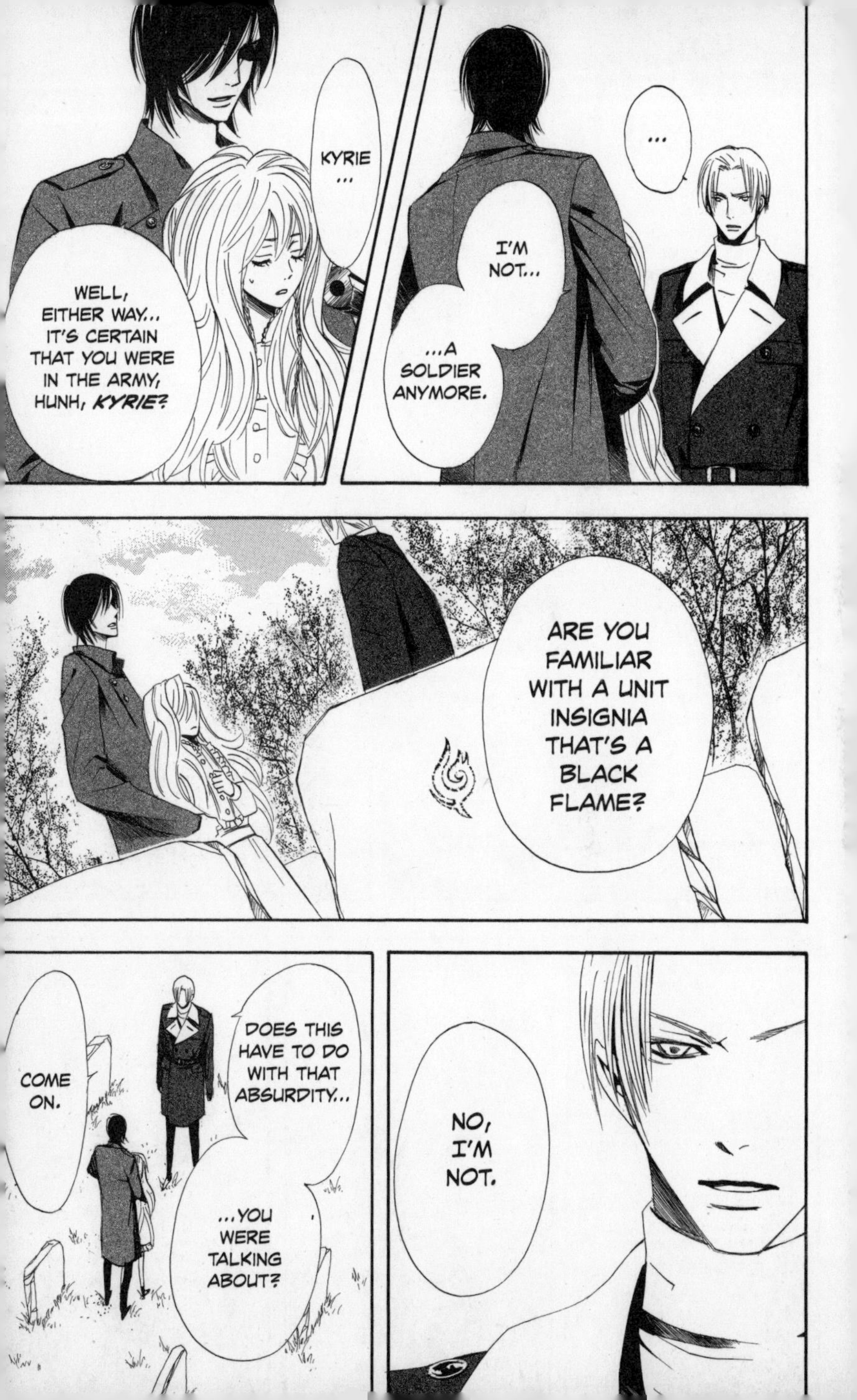
...
I'M NOT...
...A SOLDIER ANYMORE.
KYRIE ...
WELL, EITHER WAY... IT'S CERTAIN THAT YOU WERE IN THE ARMY, HUNH, *KYRIE*?
ARE YOU FAMILIAR WITH A UNIT INSIGNIA THAT'S A BLACK FLAME?
NO, I'M NOT.
DOES THIS HAVE TO DO WITH THAT ABSURDITY...
...YOU WERE TALKING ABOUT?
COME ON.

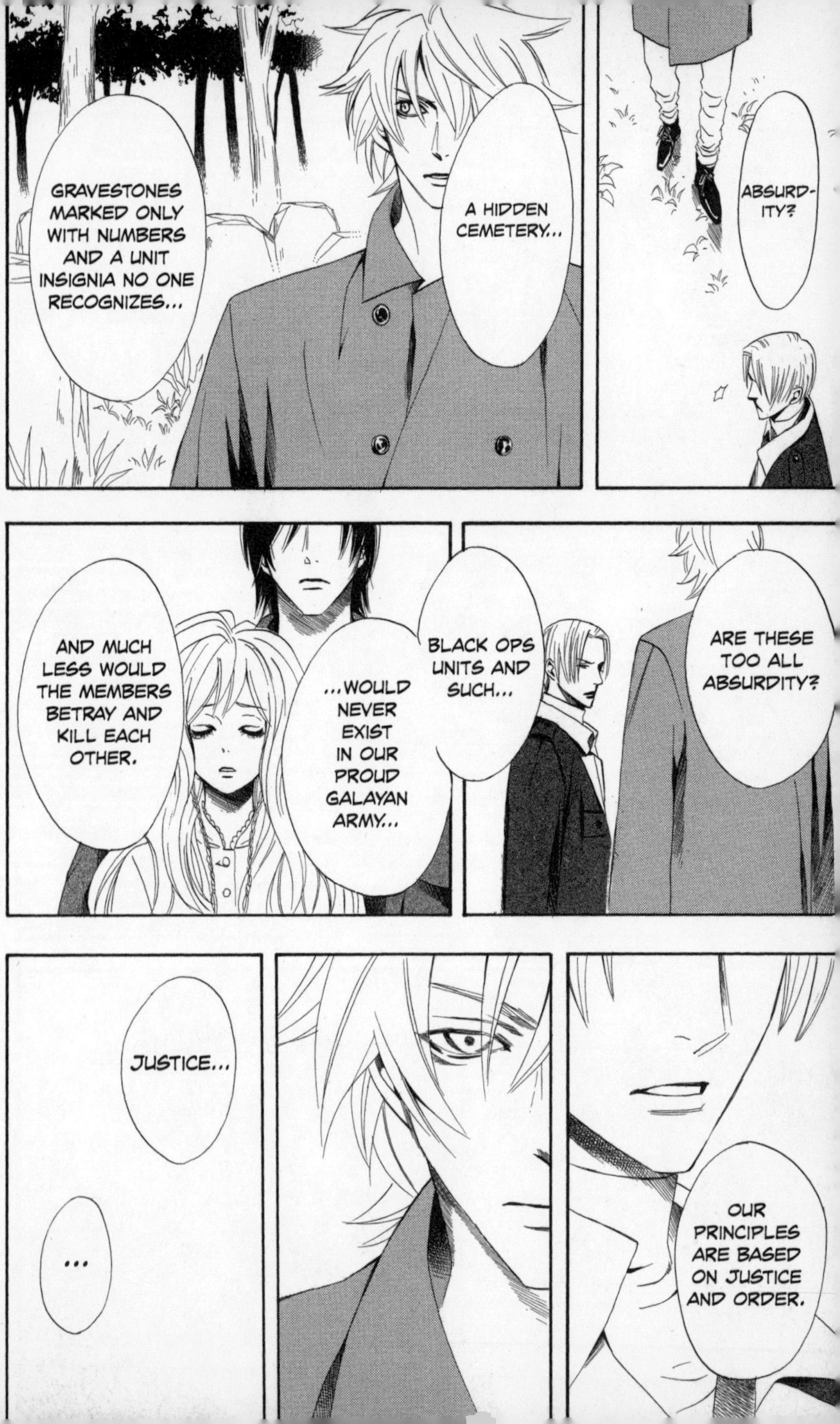
ABSURD-ITY?
A HIDDEN CEMETERY...
GRAVESTONES MARKED ONLY WITH NUMBERS AND A UNIT INSIGNIA NO ONE RECOGNIZES...
ARE THESE TOO ALL ABSURDITY?
BLACK OPS UNITS AND SUCH...
...WOULD NEVER EXIST IN OUR PROUD GALAYAN ARMY...
AND MUCH LESS WOULD THE MEMBERS BETRAY AND KILL EACH OTHER.
OUR PRINCIPLES ARE BASED ON JUSTICE AND ORDER.
JUSTICE...
...

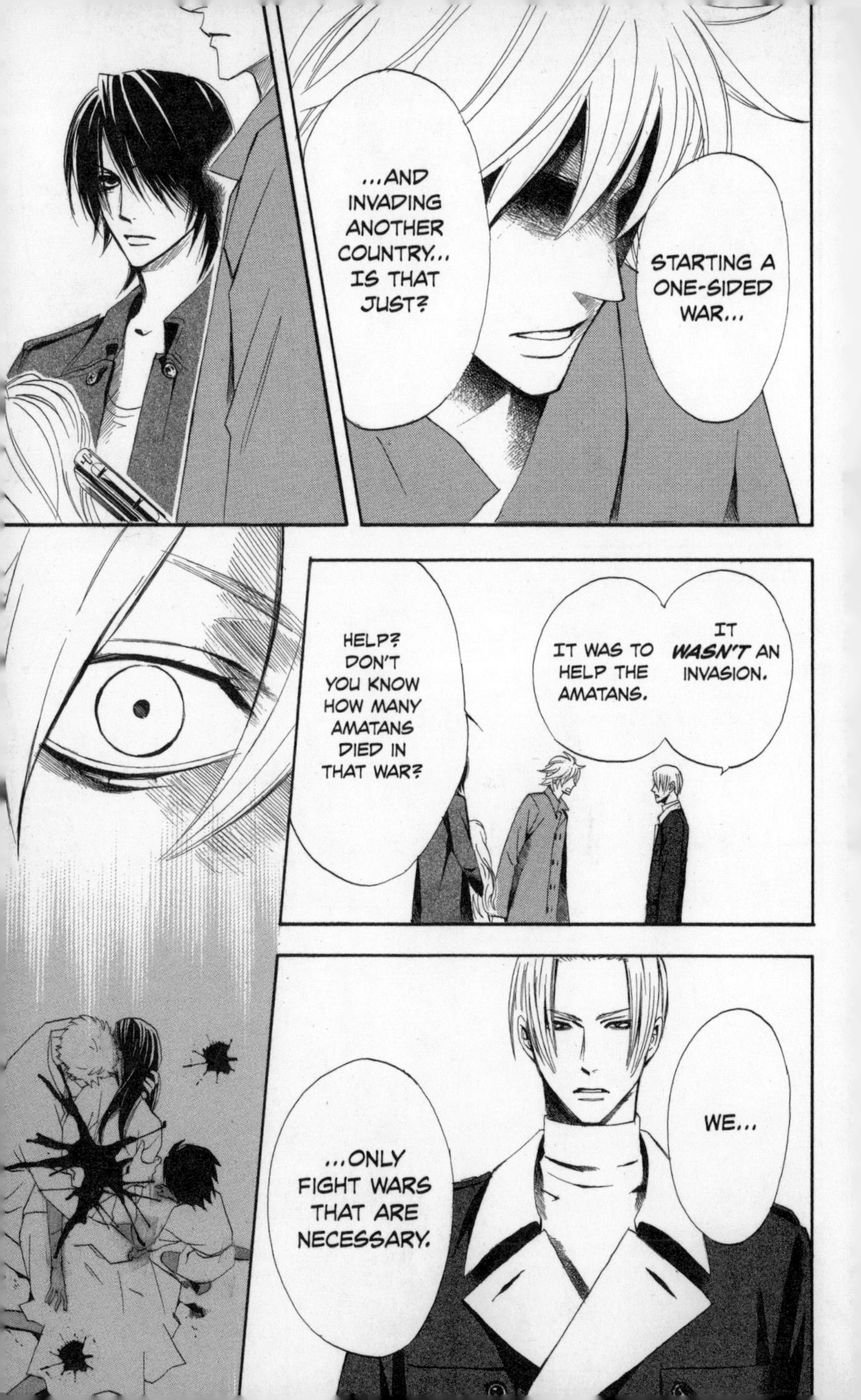
STARTING A ONE-SIDED WAR...
...AND INVADING ANOTHER COUNTRY... IS THAT JUST?
IT WASN'T AN INVASION.
IT WAS TO HELP THE AMATANS.
HELP? DON'T YOU KNOW HOW MANY AMATANS DIED IN THAT WAR?
WE...
...ONLY FIGHT WARS THAT ARE NECESSARY.

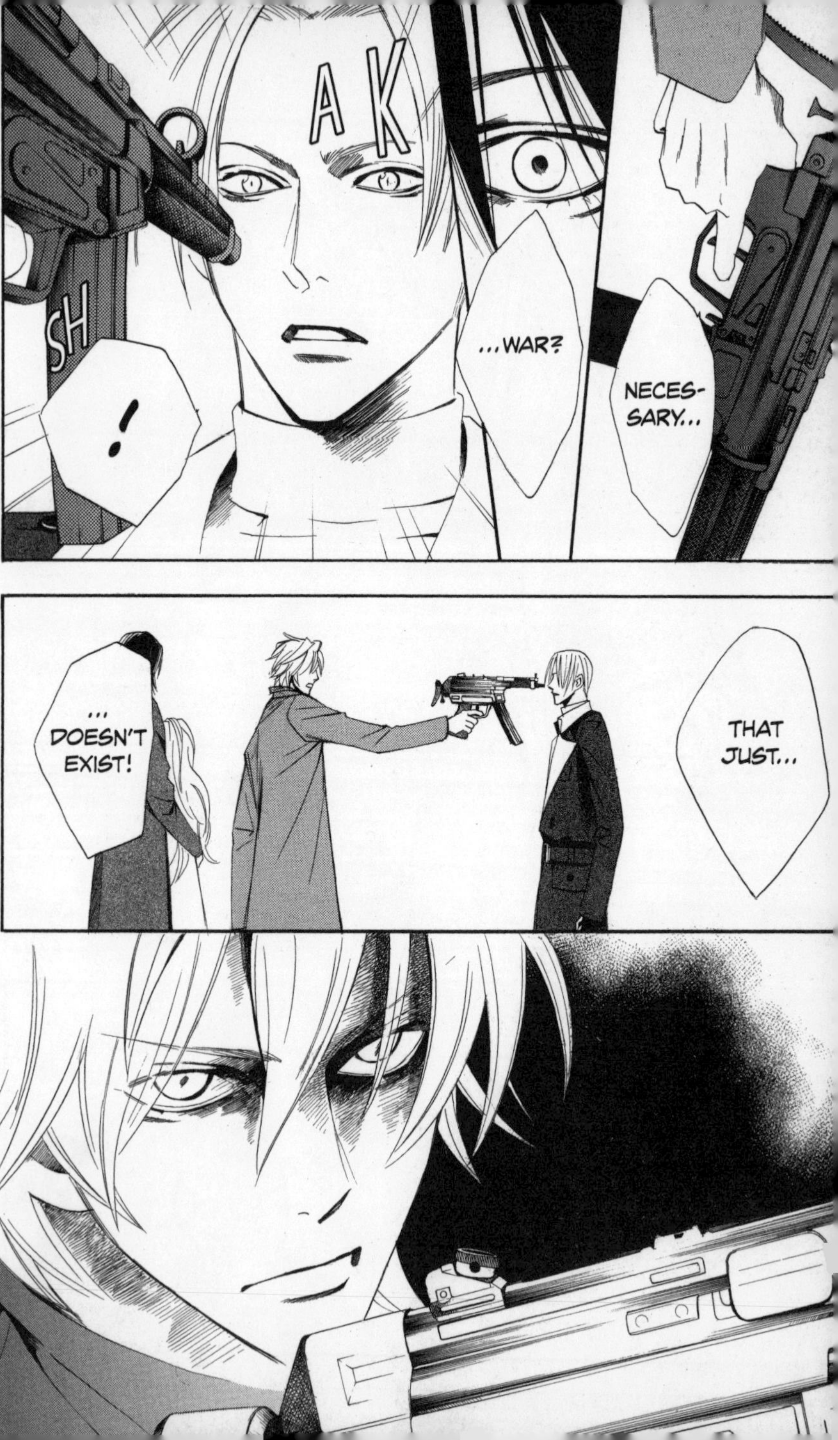
AK
NECES-SARY...
...WAR?
!
SH
THAT JUST...
... DOESN'T EXIST!

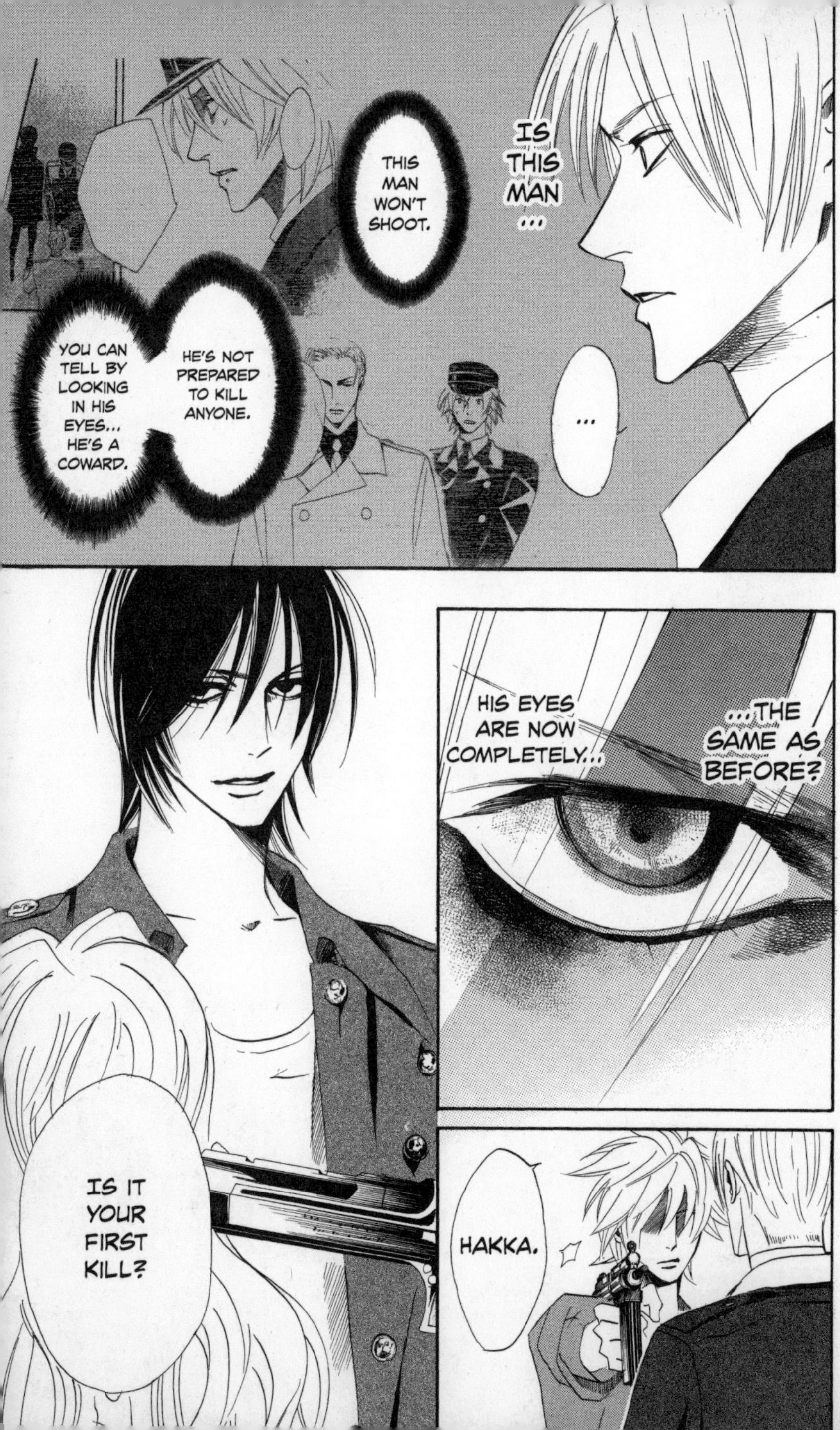

IS THIS MAN ...
THIS MAN WON'T SHOOT.
...
HE'S NOT PREPARED TO KILL ANYONE.
YOU CAN TELL BY LOOKING IN HIS EYES... HE'S A COWARD.
HIS EYES ARE NOW COMPLETELY...
...THE SAME AS BEFORE?
HAKKA.
IS IT YOUR FIRST KILL?

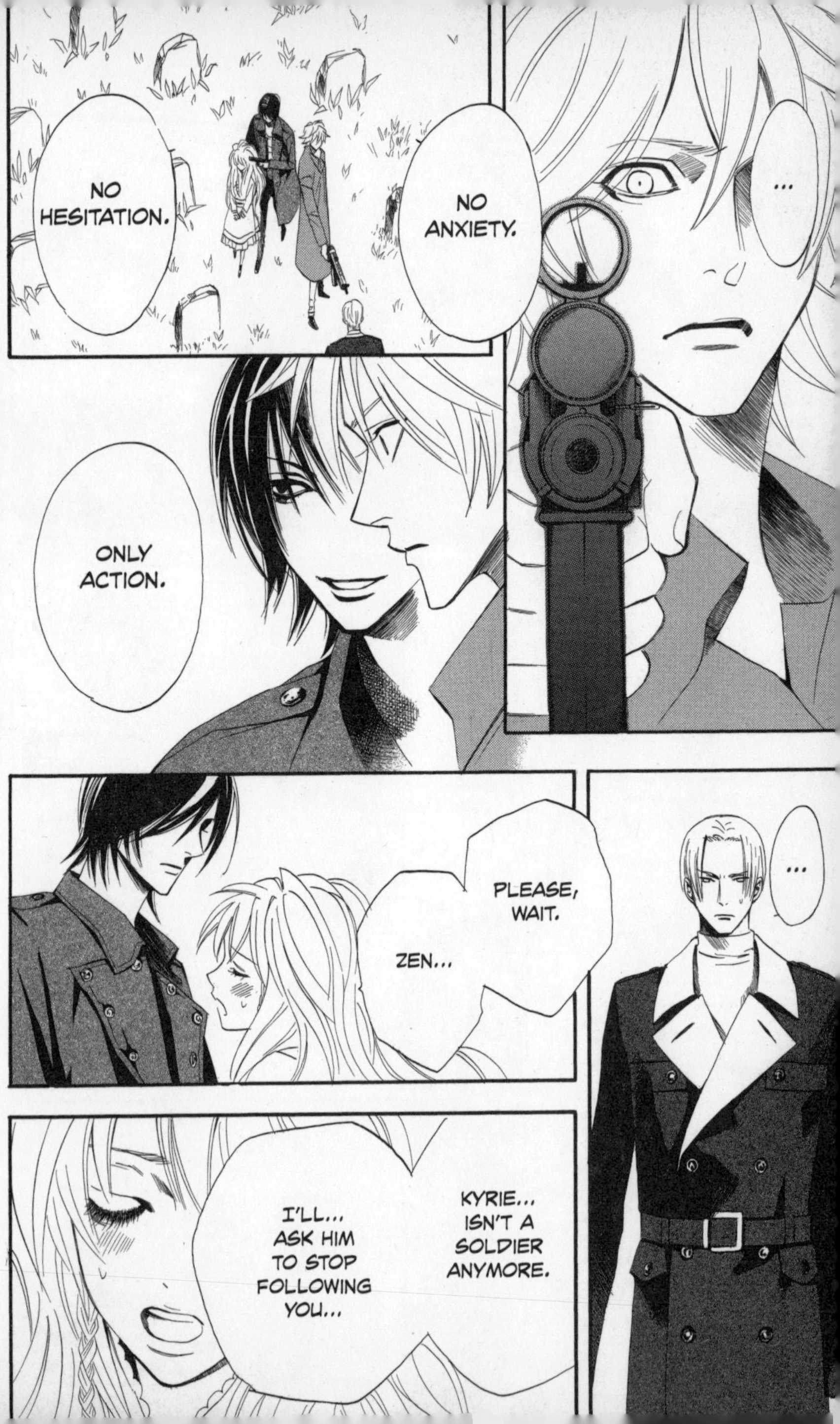
...
NO ANXIETY.
NO HESITATION.
ONLY ACTION.
...
PLEASE, WAIT.
ZEN...
KYRIE... ISN'T A SOLDIER ANYMORE.
I'LL... ASK HIM TO STOP FOLLOWING YOU...

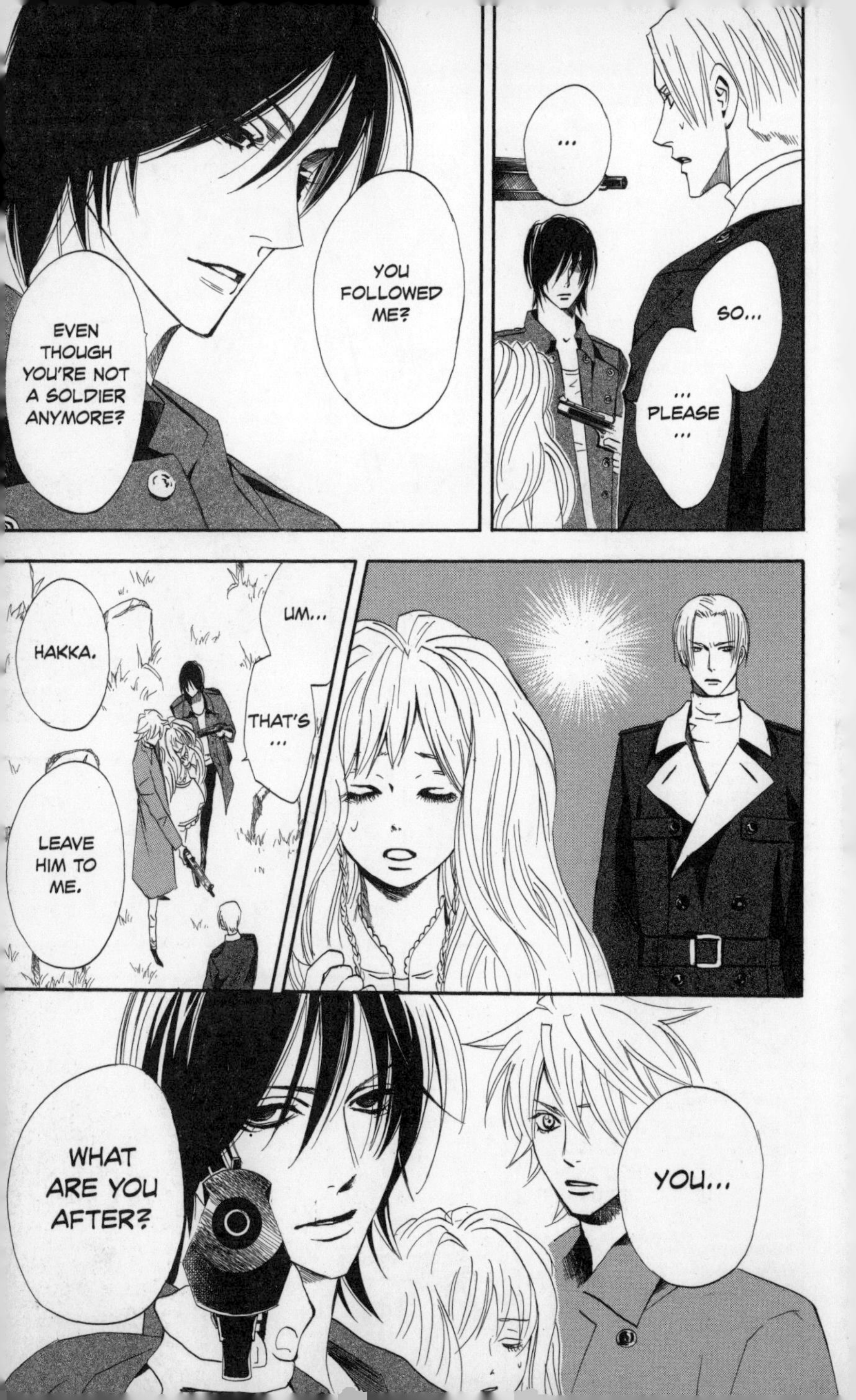
...
SO...
... PLEASE ...
YOU FOLLOWED ME?
EVEN THOUGH YOU'RE NOT A SOLDIER ANYMORE?
UM...
THAT'S ...
HAKKA.
LEAVE HIM TO ME.
YOU...
WHAT ARE YOU AFTER?

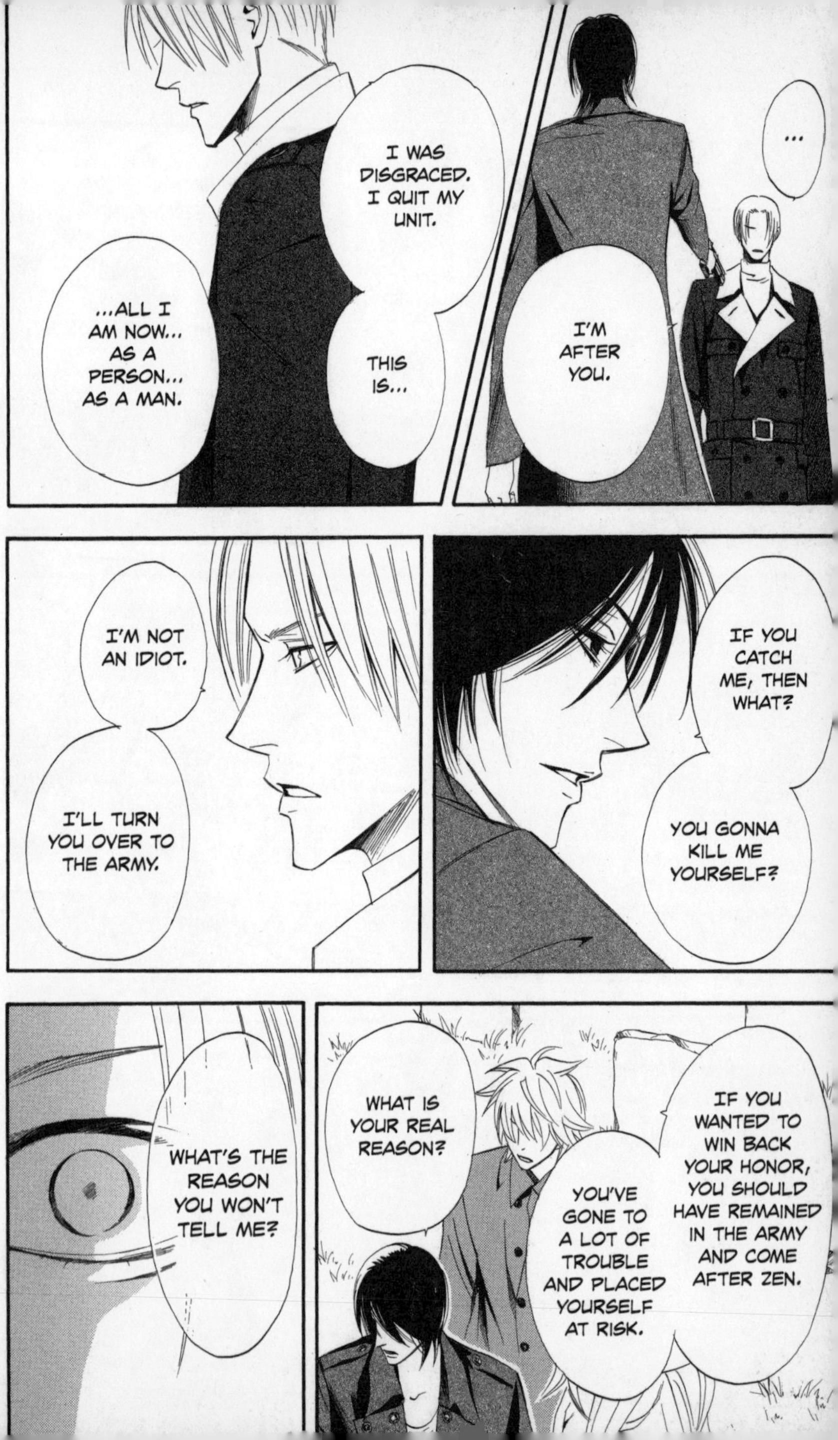
...
I'M AFTER YOU.
I WAS DISGRACED. I QUIT MY UNIT.
THIS IS...
...ALL I AM NOW... AS A PERSON... AS A MAN.
IF YOU CATCH ME, THEN WHAT?
YOU GONNA KILL ME YOURSELF?
I'M NOT AN IDIOT.
I'LL TURN YOU OVER TO THE ARMY.
IF YOU WANTED TO WIN BACK YOUR HONOR, YOU SHOULD HAVE REMAINED IN THE ARMY AND COME AFTER ZEN.
YOU'VE GONE TO A LOT OF TROUBLE AND PLACED YOURSELF AT RISK.
WHAT IS YOUR REAL REASON?
WHAT'S THE REASON YOU WON'T TELL ME?

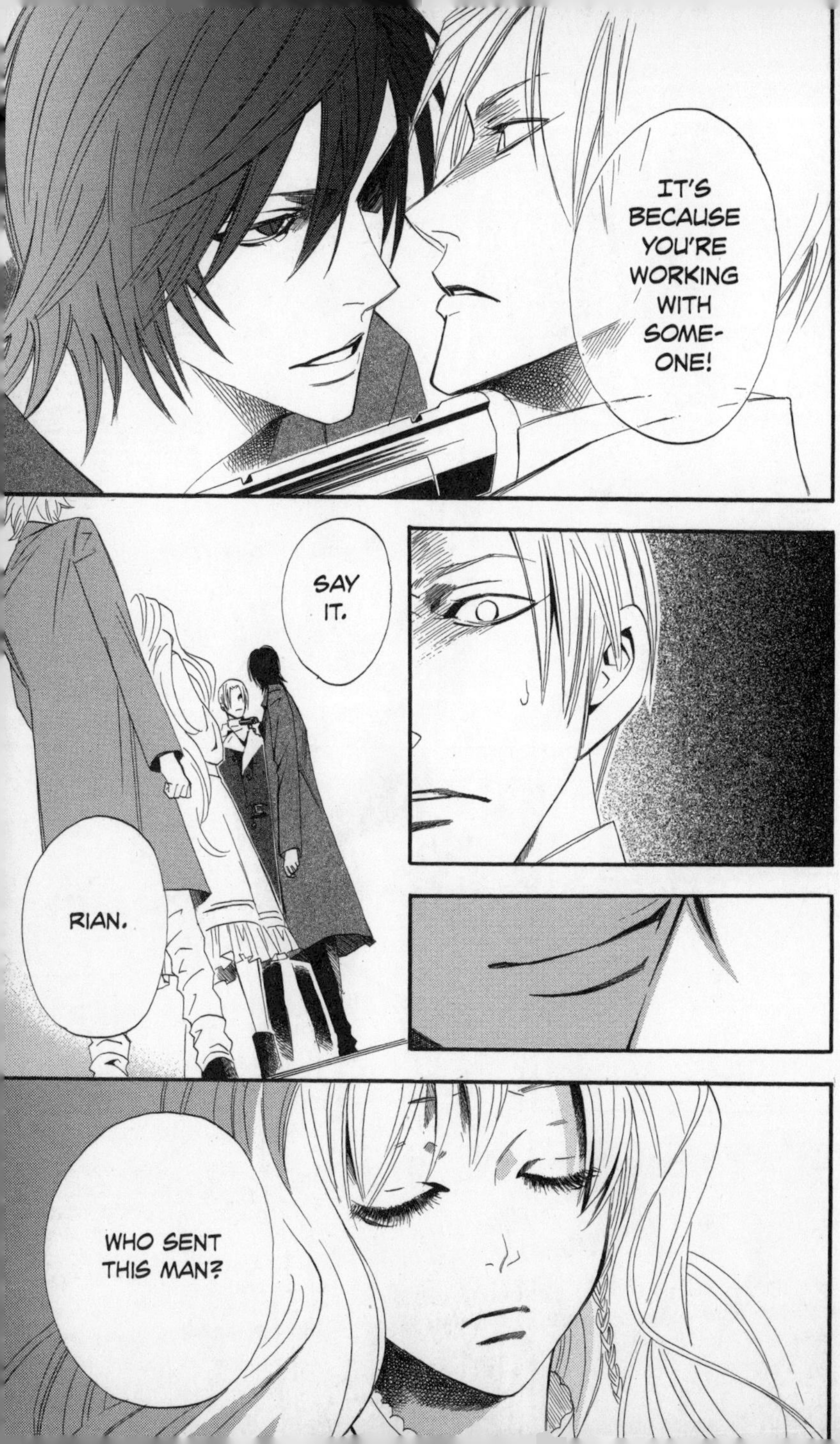
IT'S BECAUSE YOU'RE WORKING WITH SOME-ONE!
SAY IT.
RIAN.
WHO SENT THIS MAN?

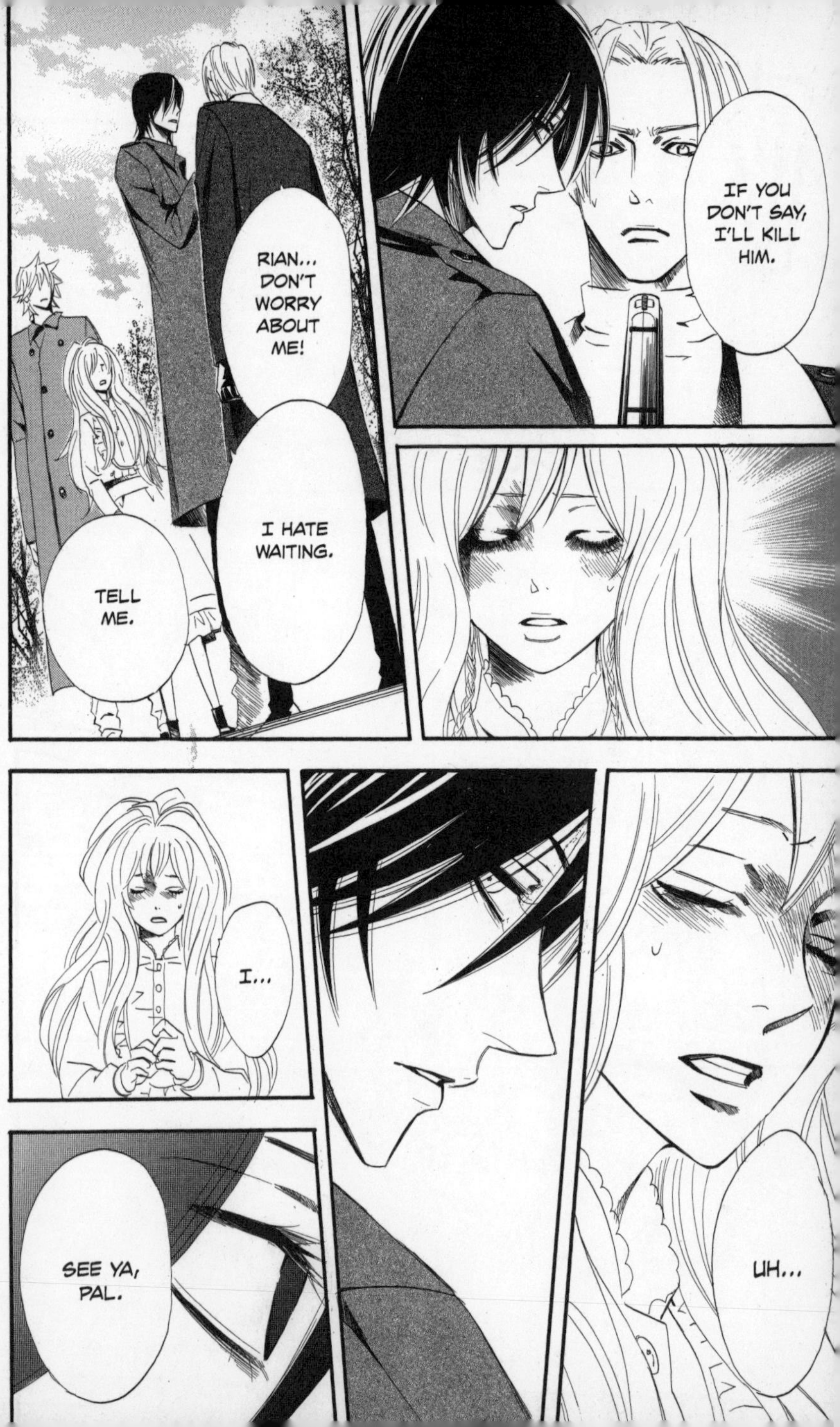
IF YOU DON'T SAY, I'LL KILL HIM.
RIAN... DON'T WORRY ABOUT ME!
I HATE WAITING.
TELL ME.
UH...
I...
SEE YA, PAL.

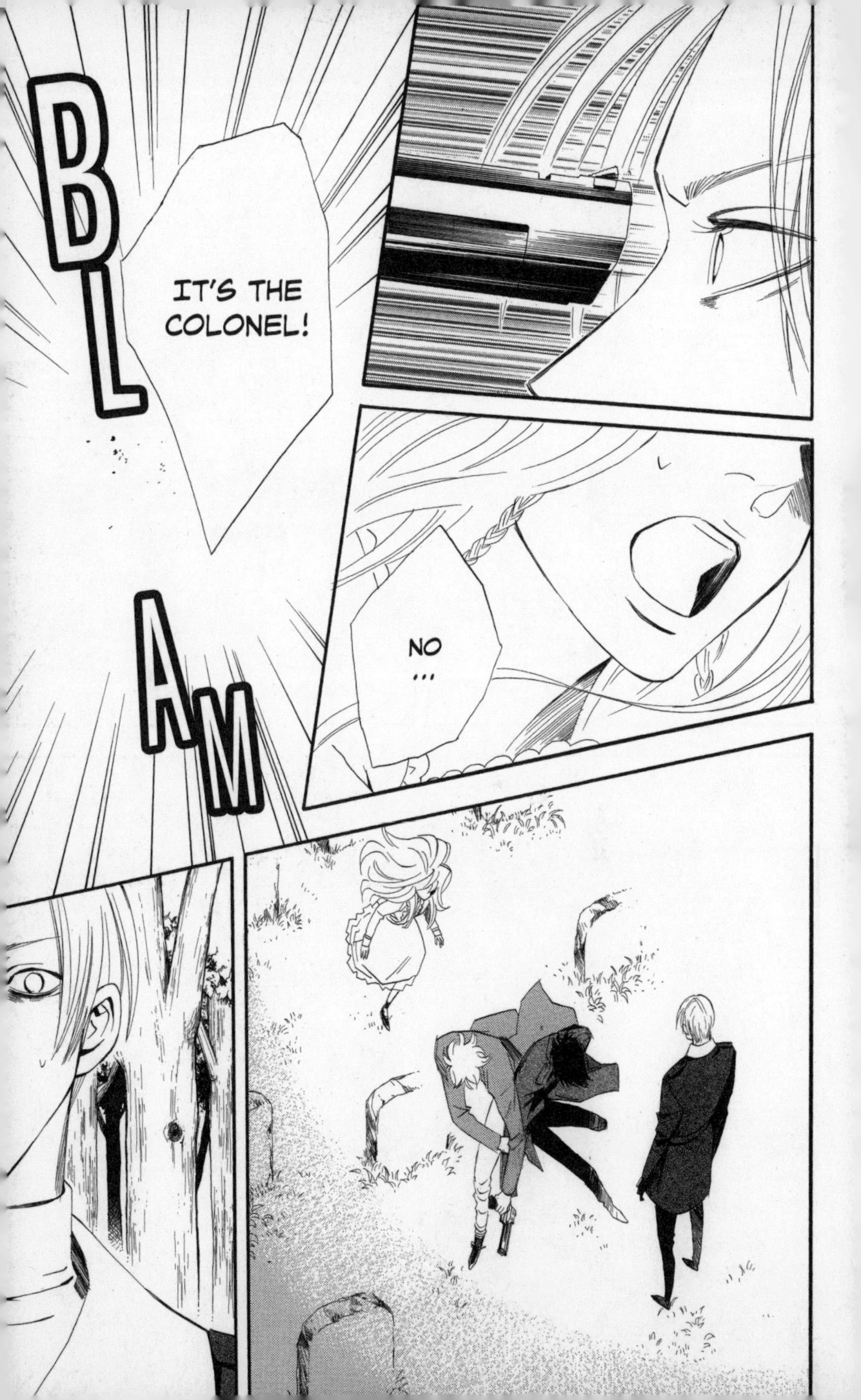
IT'S THE COLONEL!
BLAM
NO ...

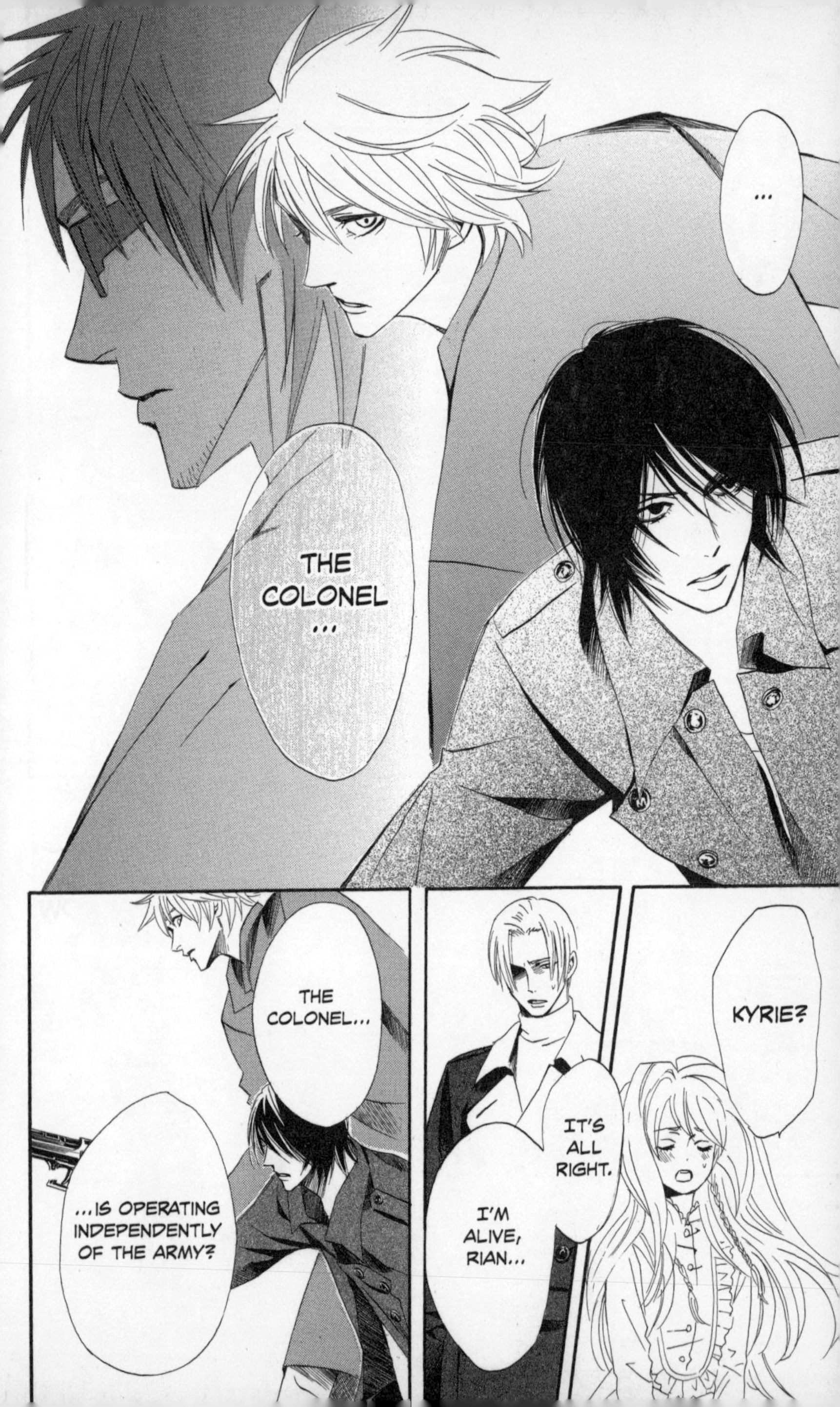
...
THE COLONEL ...
KYRIE?
IT'S ALL RIGHT.
I'M ALIVE, RIAN...
THE COLONEL...
...IS OPERATING INDEPENDENTLY OF THE ARMY?

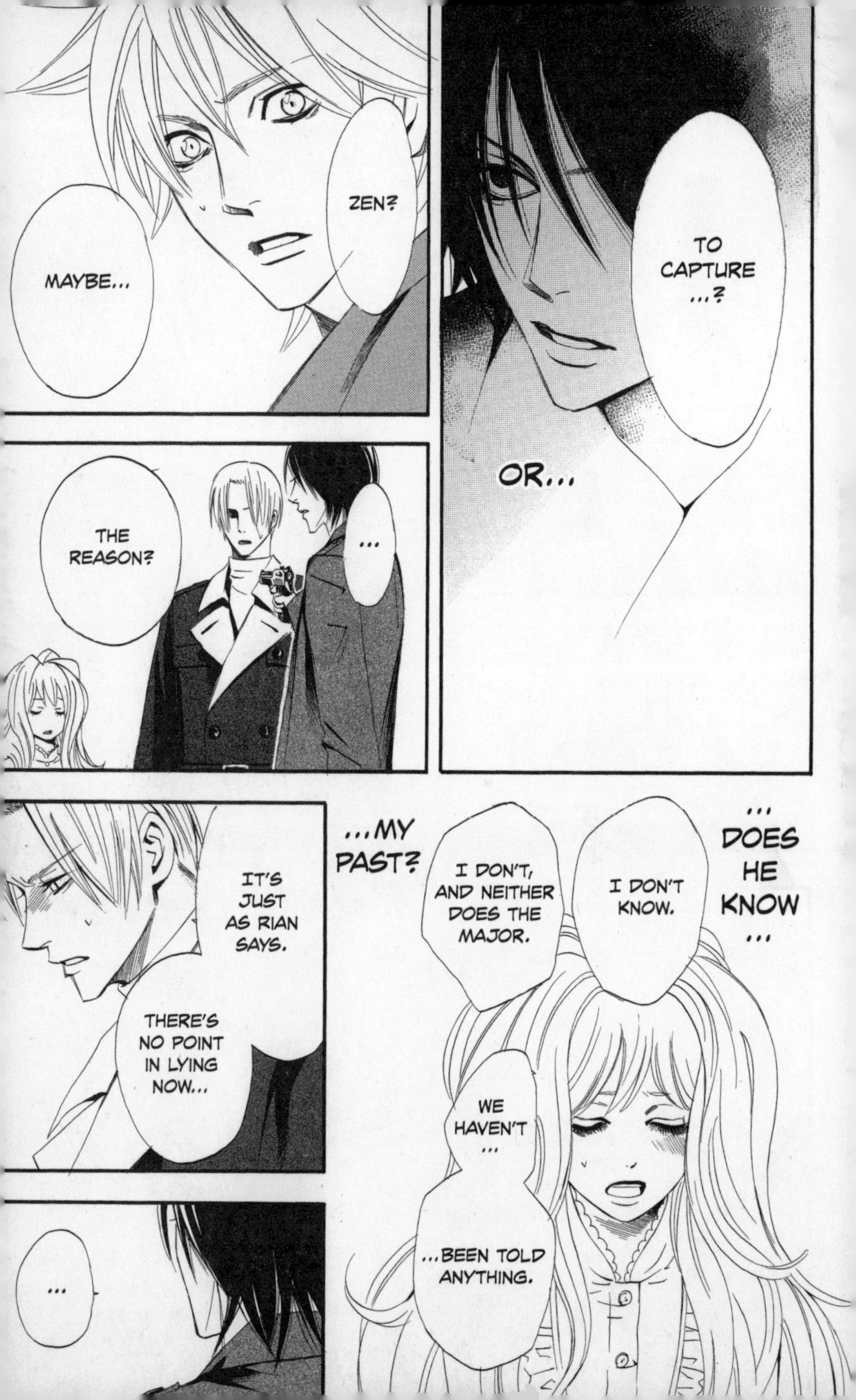
TO CAPTURE ...?
OR...
ZEN?
MAYBE...
...
THE REASON?
... DOES HE KNOW ...
I DON'T KNOW.
I DON'T, AND NEITHER DOES THE MAJOR.
...MY PAST?
WE HAVEN'T ...
...BEEN TOLD ANYTHING.
IT'S JUST AS RIAN SAYS.
THERE'S NO POINT IN LYING NOW...
...

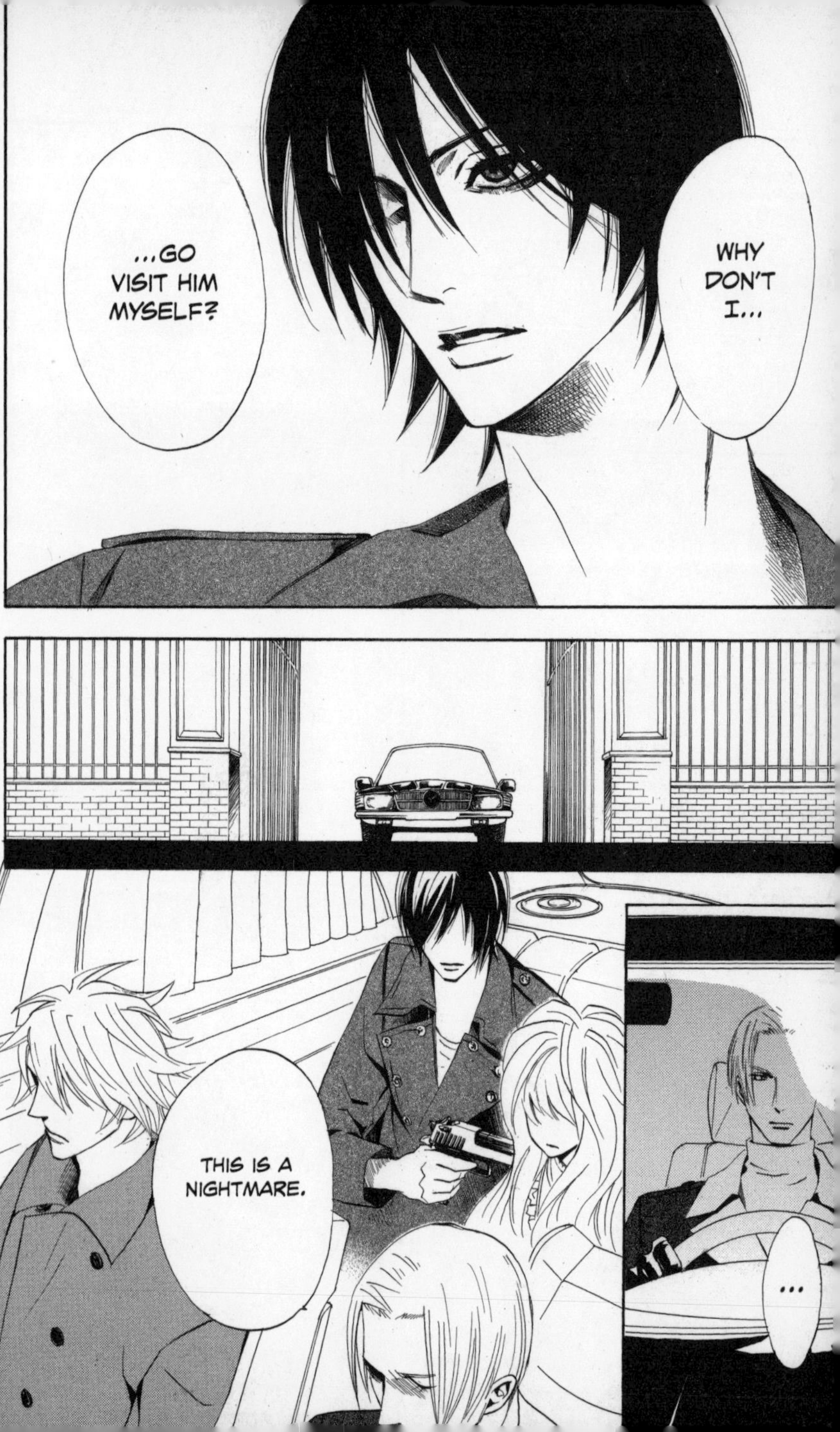
WHY DON'T I...
...GO VISIT HIM MYSELF?
...
THIS IS A NIGHTMARE.

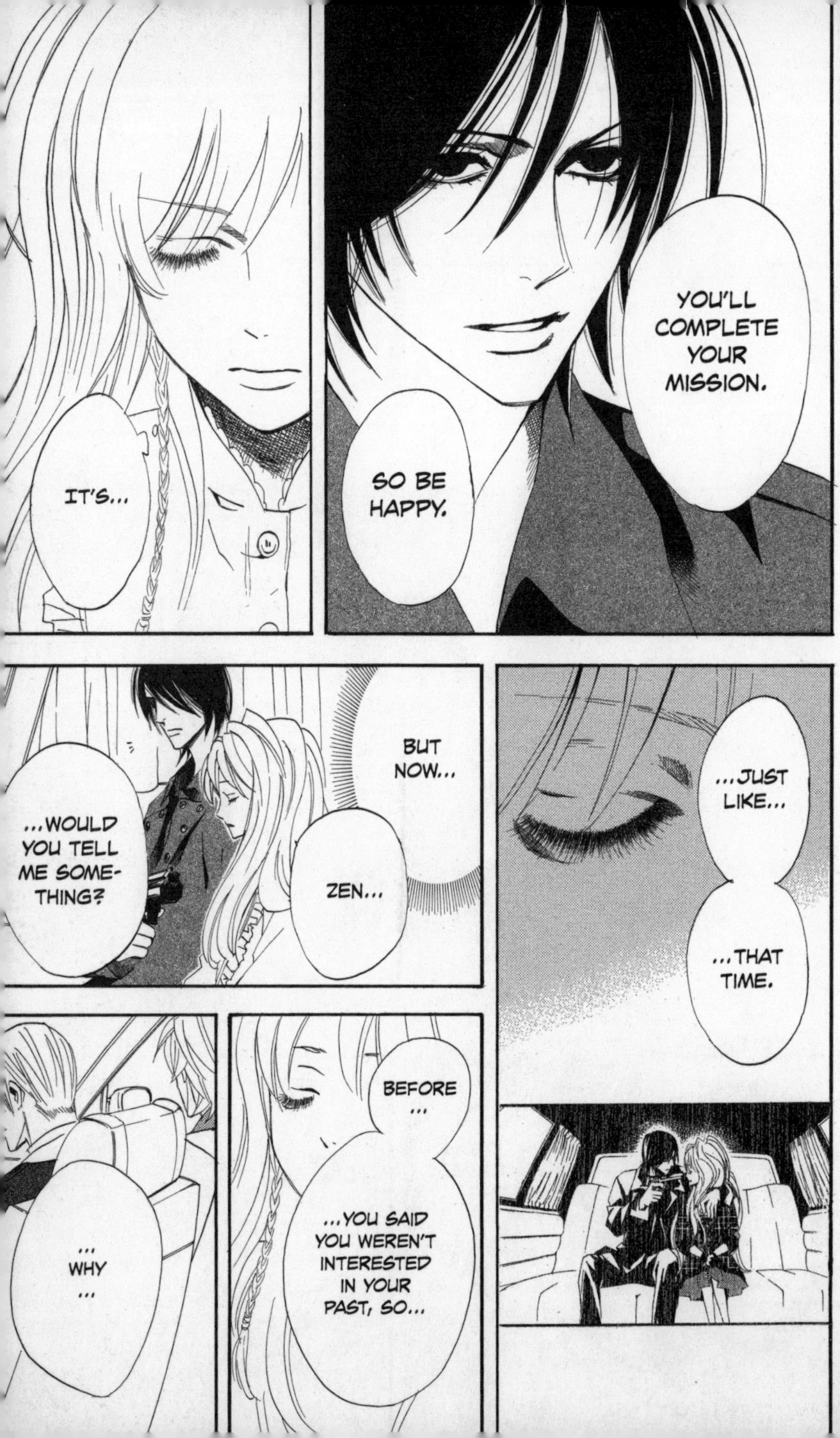
YOU'LL COMPLETE YOUR MISSION.
SO BE HAPPY.
IT'S...
...JUST LIKE...
...THAT TIME.
BUT NOW...
ZEN...
...WOULD YOU TELL ME SOME-THING?
BEFORE...
...YOU SAID YOU WEREN'T INTERESTED IN YOUR PAST, SO...
...WHY...

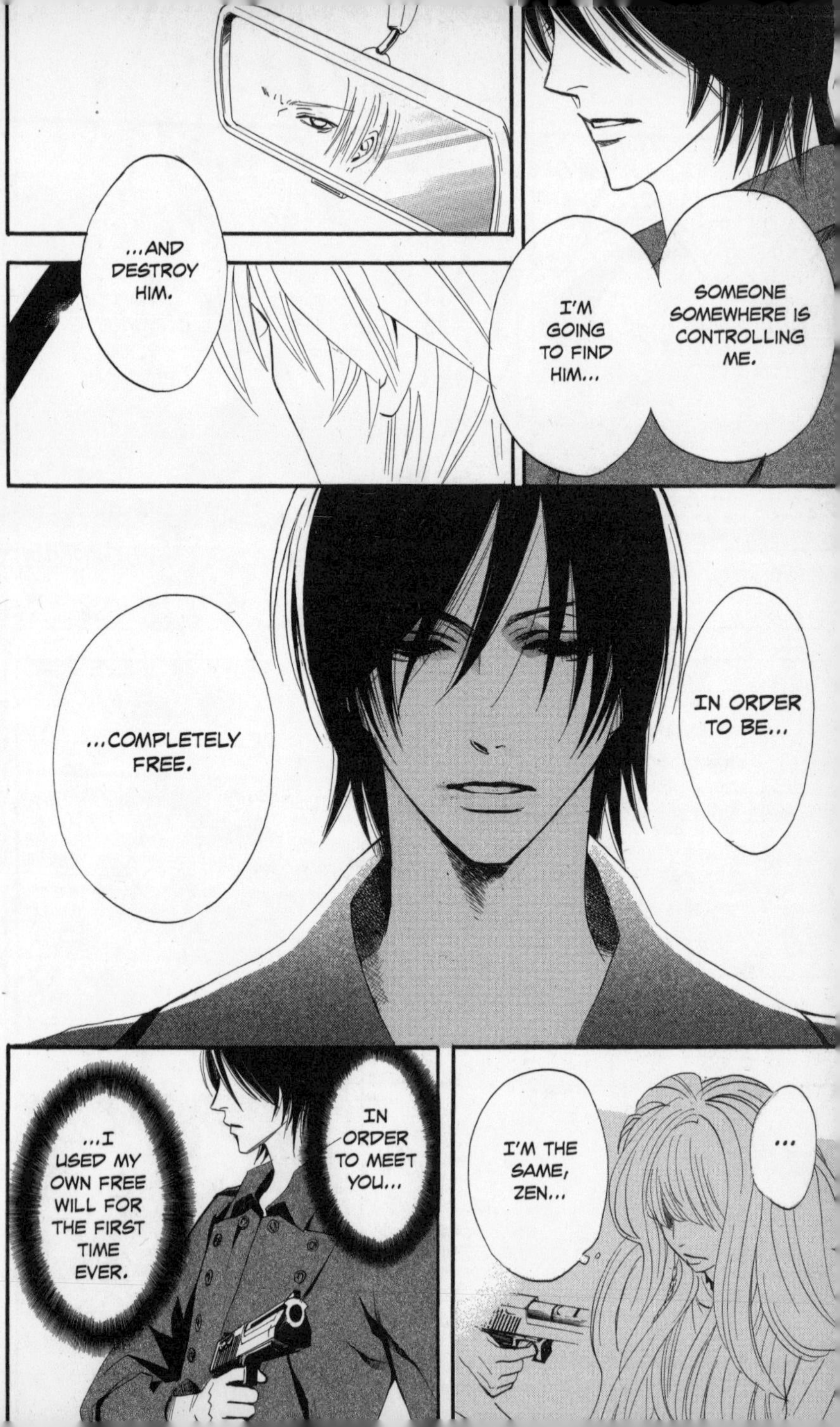
SOMEONE SOMEWHERE IS CONTROLLING ME.
I'M GOING TO FIND HIM...
...AND DESTROY HIM.
IN ORDER TO BE...
...COMPLETELY FREE.
...
I'M THE SAME, ZEN...
IN ORDER TO MEET YOU...
...I USED MY OWN FREE WILL FOR THE FIRST TIME EVER.

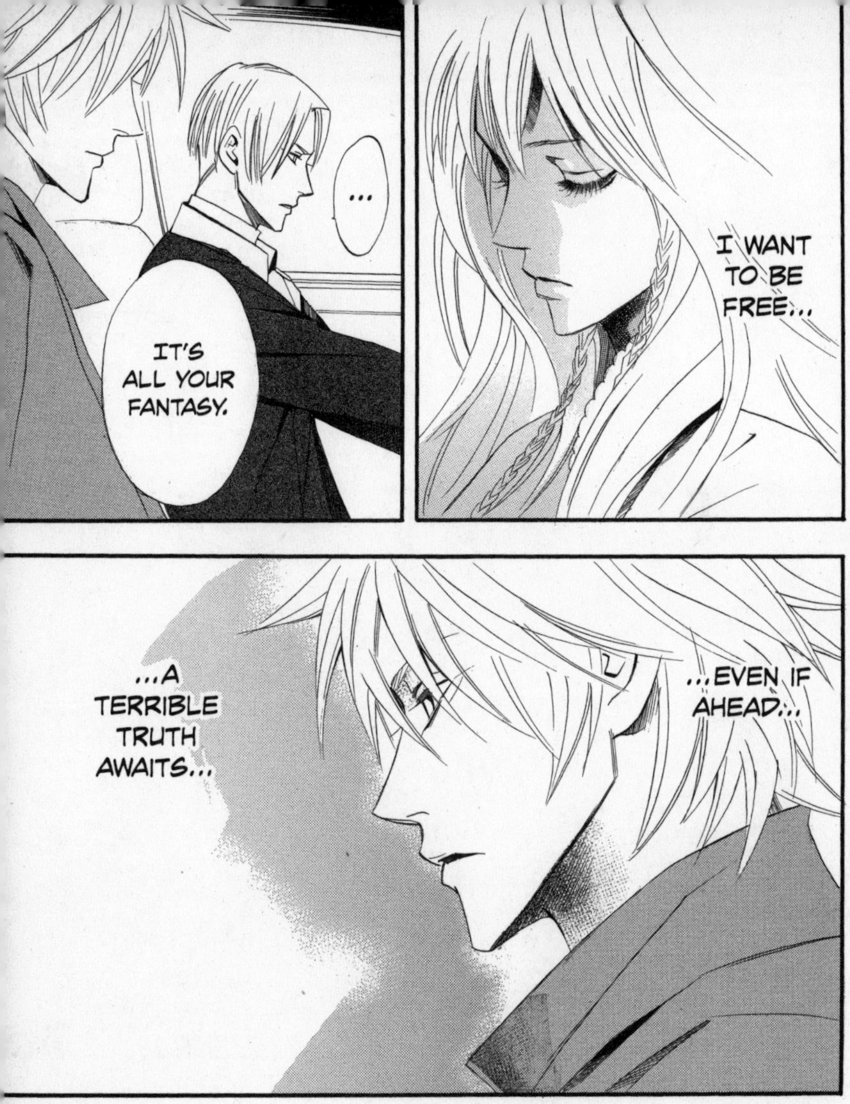
I WANT TO BE FREE...
...
IT'S ALL YOUR FANTASY.
...EVEN IF AHEAD...
...A TERRIBLE TRUTH AWAITS...

Blank Slate Chapter 6 / The End

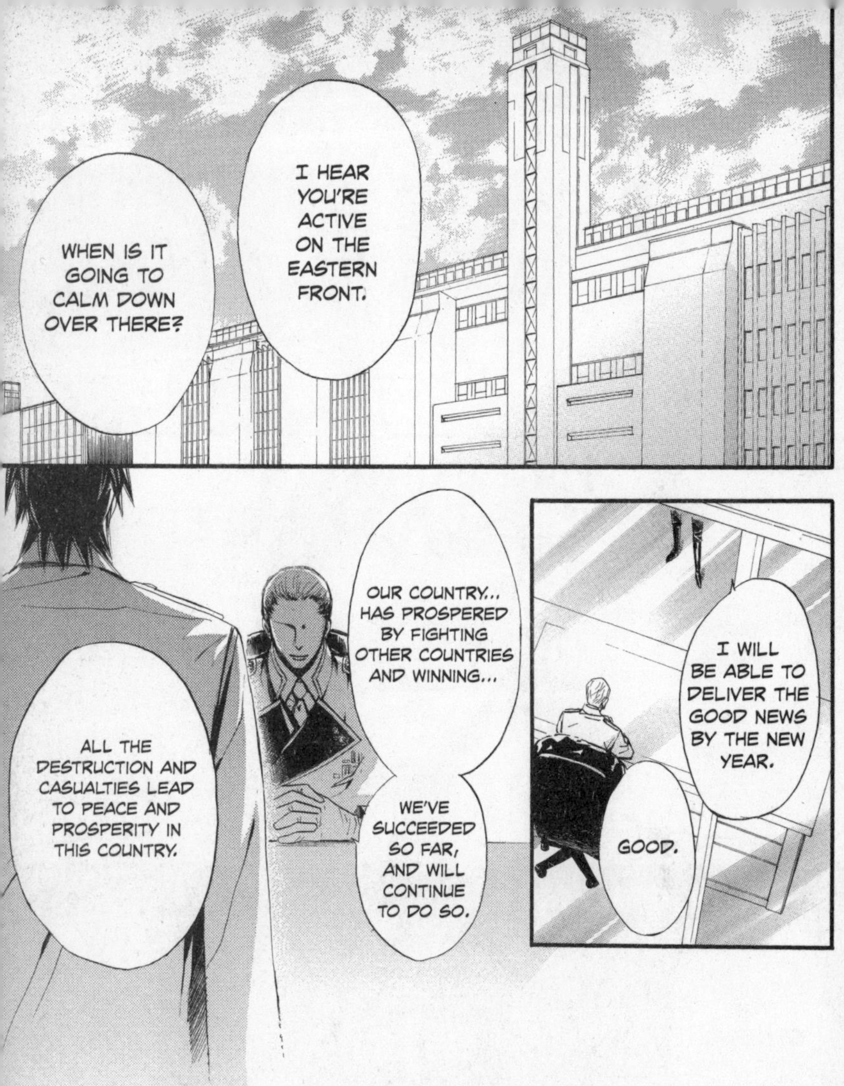
I HEAR YOU'RE ACTIVE ON THE EASTERN FRONT.
WHEN IS IT GOING TO CALM DOWN OVER THERE?
I WILL BE ABLE TO DELIVER THE GOOD NEWS BY THE NEW YEAR.
GOOD.
OUR COUNTRY... HAS PROSPERED BY FIGHTING OTHER COUNTRIES AND WINNING...
WE'VE SUCCEEDED SO FAR, AND WILL CONTINUE TO DO SO.
ALL THE DESTRUCTION AND CASUALTIES LEAD TO PEACE AND PROSPERITY IN THIS COUNTRY.

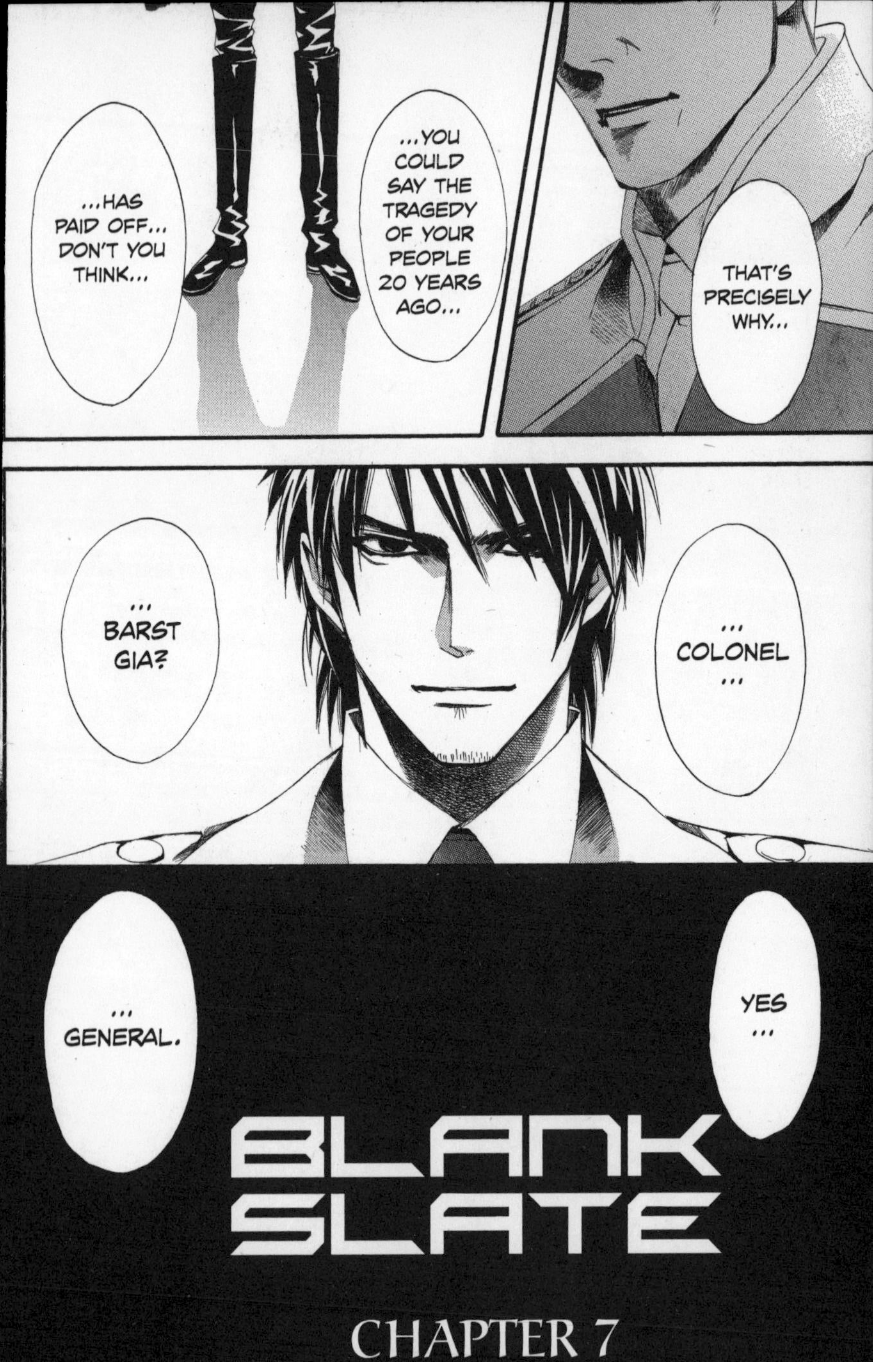
THAT'S PRECISELY WHY...
...YOU COULD SAY THE TRAGEDY OF YOUR PEOPLE 20 YEARS AGO...
...HAS PAID OFF... DON'T YOU THINK...
... COLONEL ...
... BARST GIA?
YES ...
... GENERAL.
BLANK SLATE
CHAPTER 7

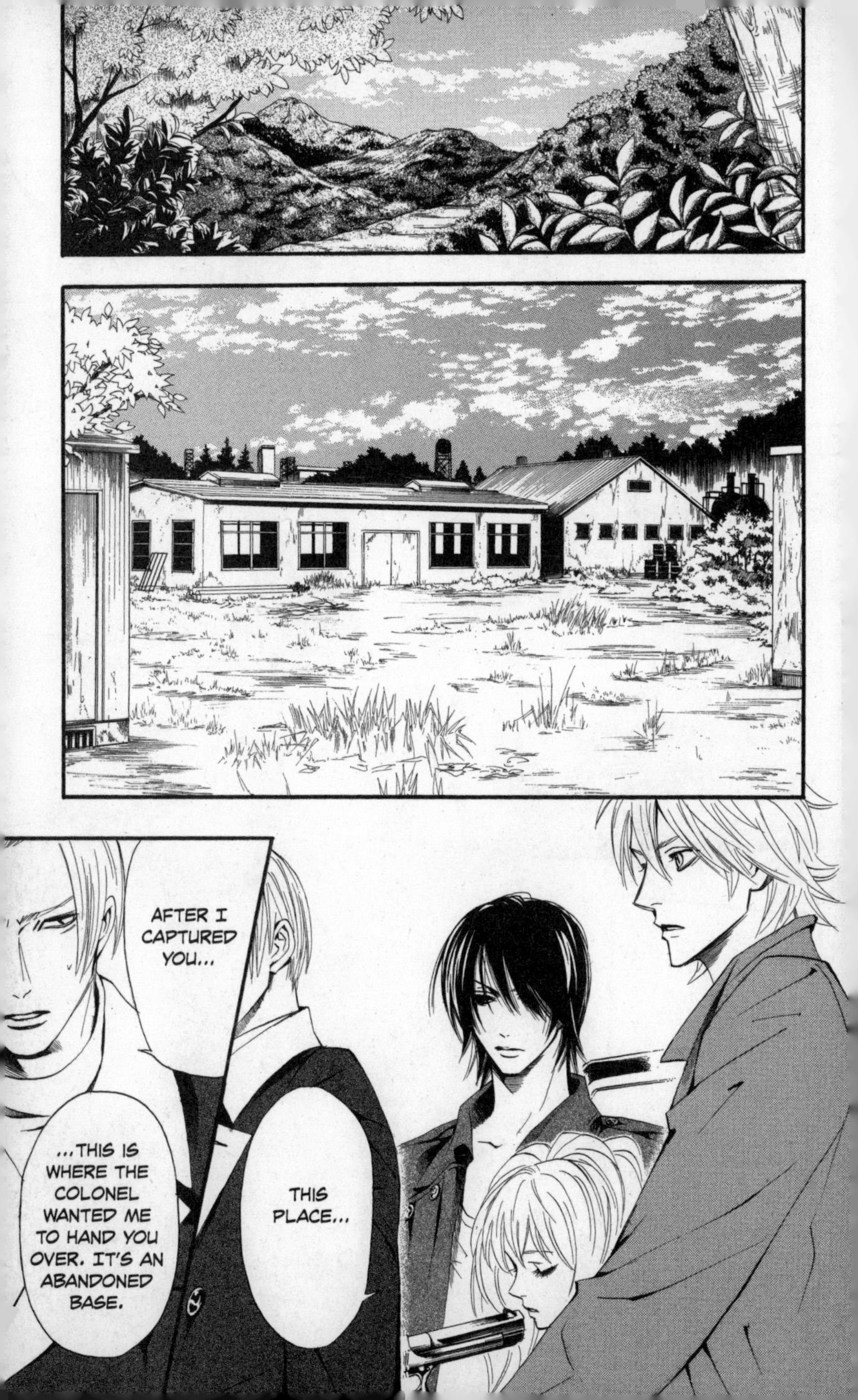
THIS PLACE...
AFTER I CAPTURED YOU...
...THIS IS WHERE THE COLONEL WANTED ME TO HAND YOU OVER. IT'S AN ABANDONED BASE.

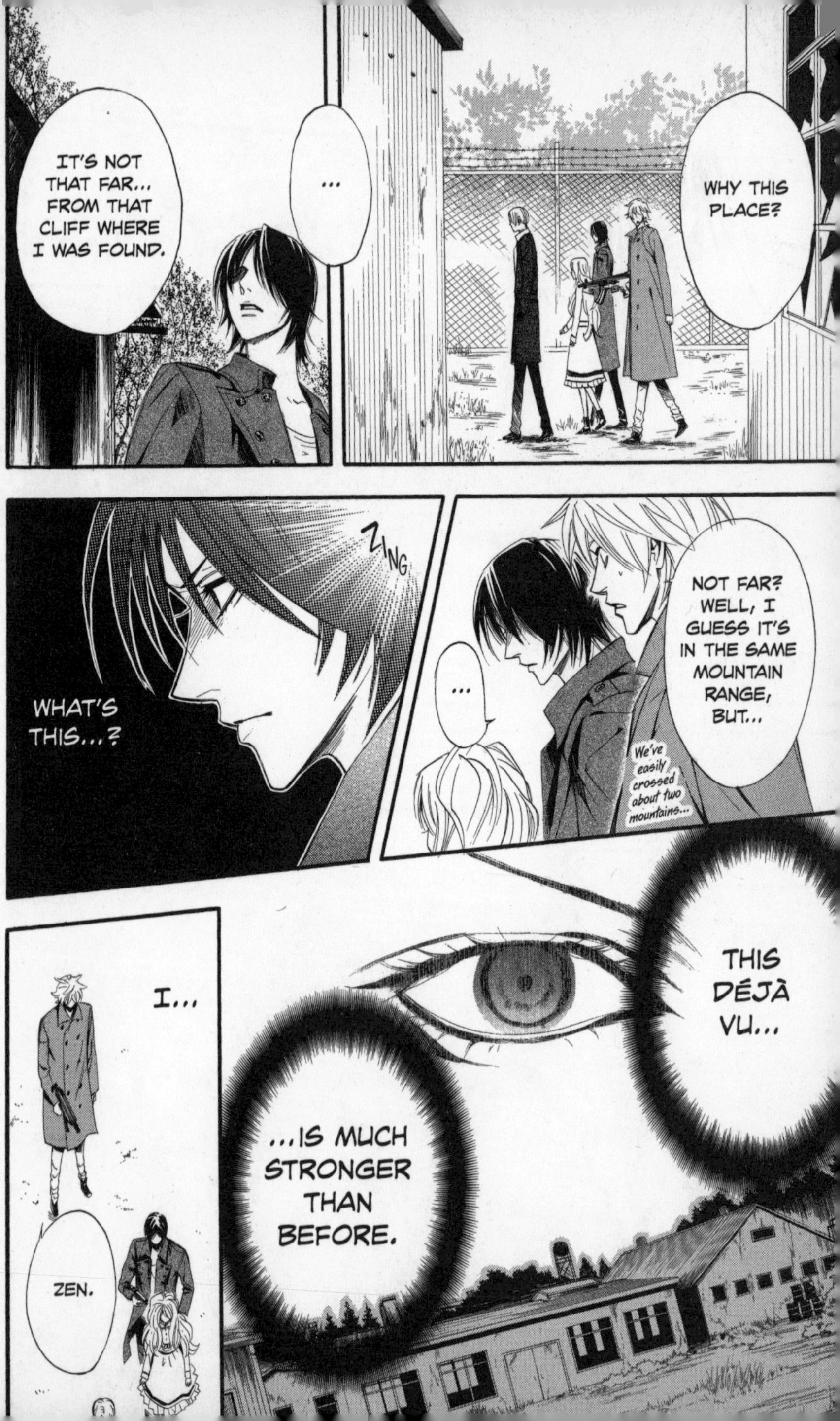
WHY THIS PLACE?
...
IT'S NOT THAT FAR... FROM THAT CLIFF WHERE I WAS FOUND.
NOT FAR? WELL, I GUESS IT'S IN THE SAME MOUNTAIN RANGE, BUT...
We've easily crossed about two mountains...
...
ZING
WHAT'S THIS...?
THIS DÉJÀ VU...
...IS MUCH STRONGER THAN BEFORE.
I...
ZEN.

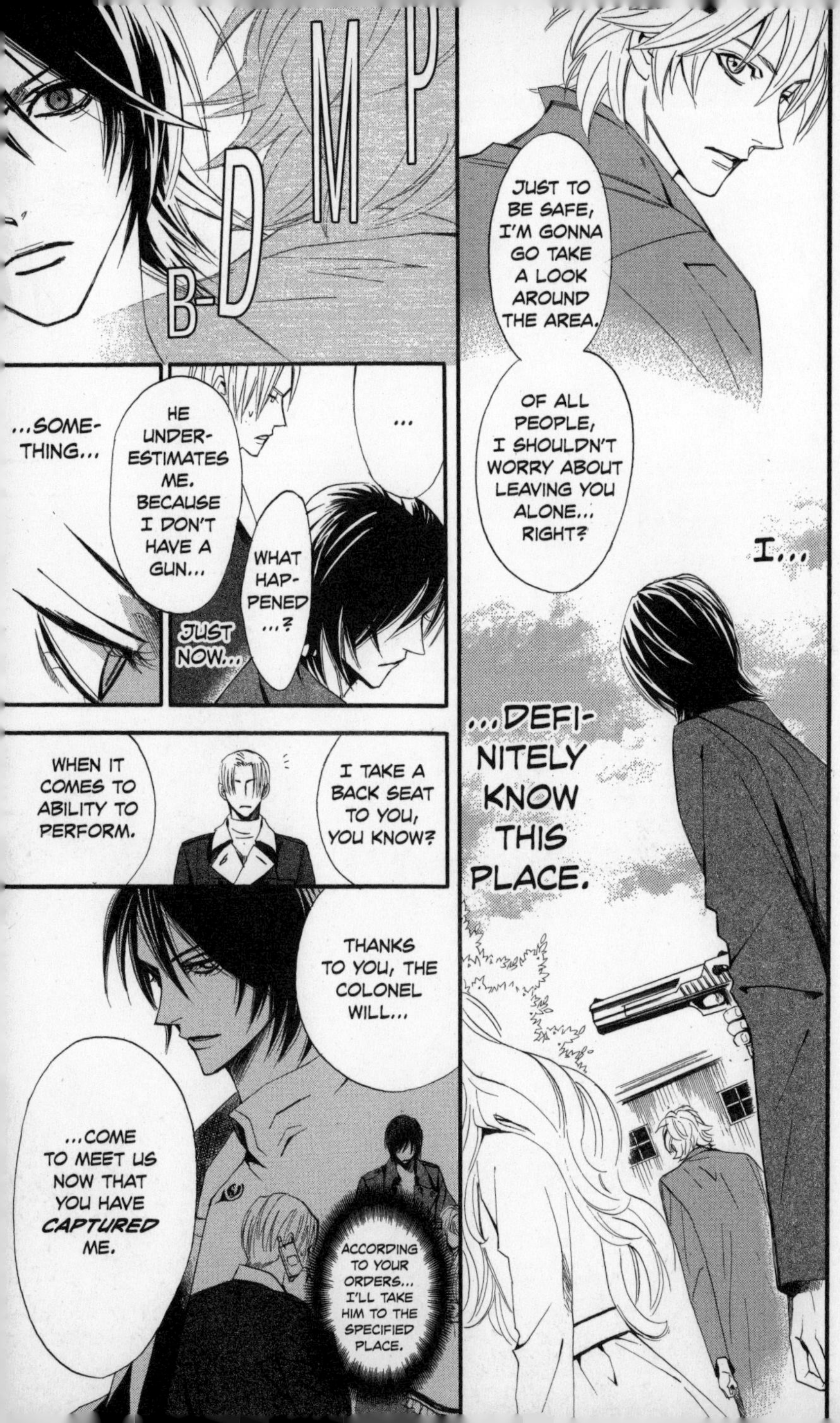
JUST TO BE SAFE, I'M GONNA GO TAKE A LOOK AROUND THE AREA.
OF ALL PEOPLE, I SHOULDN'T WORRY ABOUT LEAVING YOU ALONE... RIGHT?
I...
...DEFINITELY KNOW THIS PLACE.
B-DMP
...
WHAT HAPPENED...?
JUST NOW...
HE UNDERESTIMATES ME. BECAUSE I DON'T HAVE A GUN...
...SOMETHING...
I TAKE A BACK SEAT TO YOU, YOU KNOW?
WHEN IT COMES TO ABILITY TO PERFORM.
THANKS TO YOU, THE COLONEL WILL...
...COME TO MEET US NOW THAT YOU HAVE *CAPTURED* ME.
ACCORDING TO YOUR ORDERS... I'LL TAKE HIM TO THE SPECIFIED PLACE.

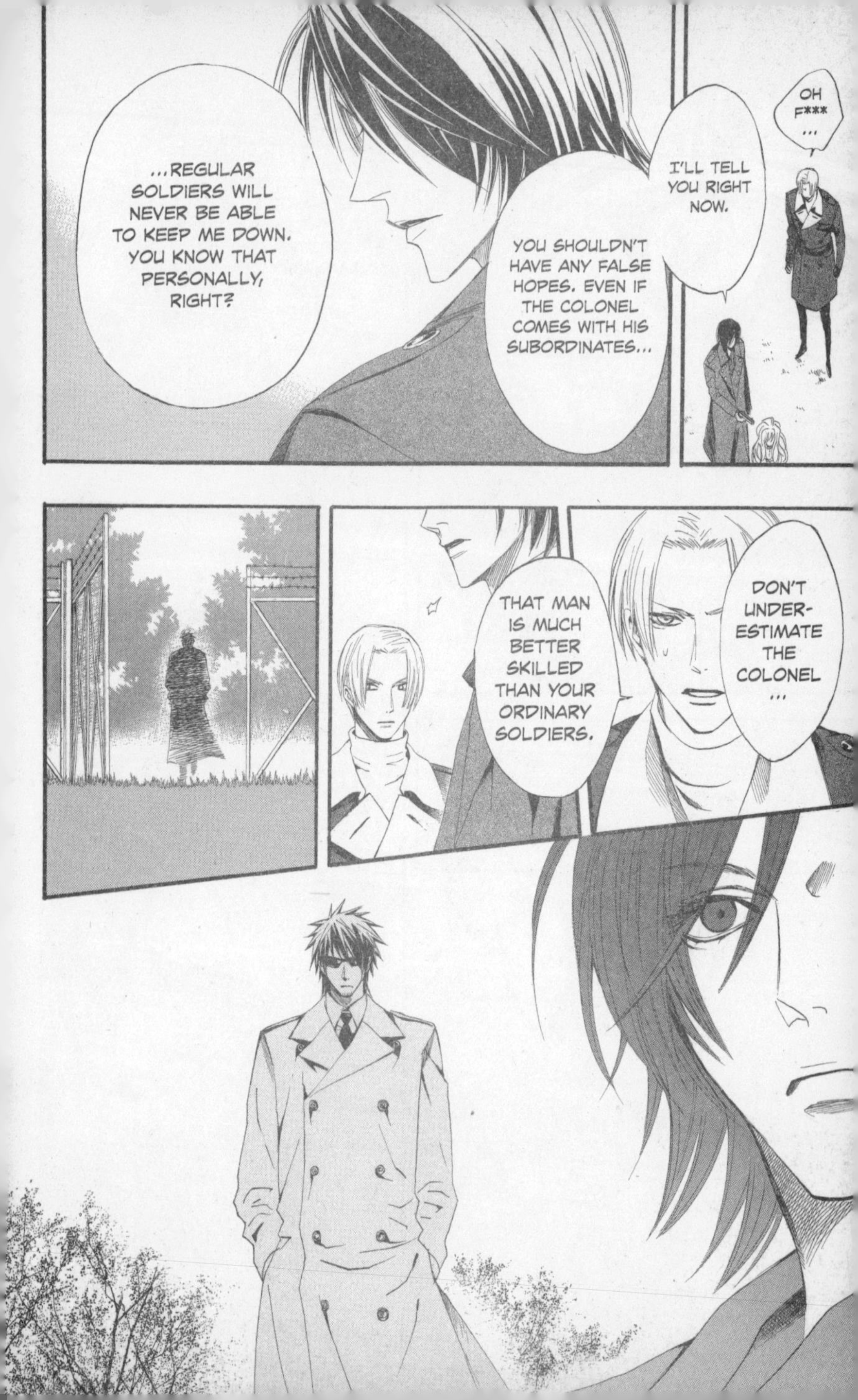
OH F*** ...
I'LL TELL YOU RIGHT NOW.
YOU SHOULDN'T HAVE ANY FALSE HOPES. EVEN IF THE COLONEL COMES WITH HIS SUBORDINATES...
...REGULAR SOLDIERS WILL NEVER BE ABLE TO KEEP ME DOWN. YOU KNOW THAT PERSONALLY, RIGHT?
DON'T UNDER-ESTIMATE THE COLONEL ...
THAT MAN IS MUCH BETTER SKILLED THAN YOUR ORDINARY SOLDIERS.

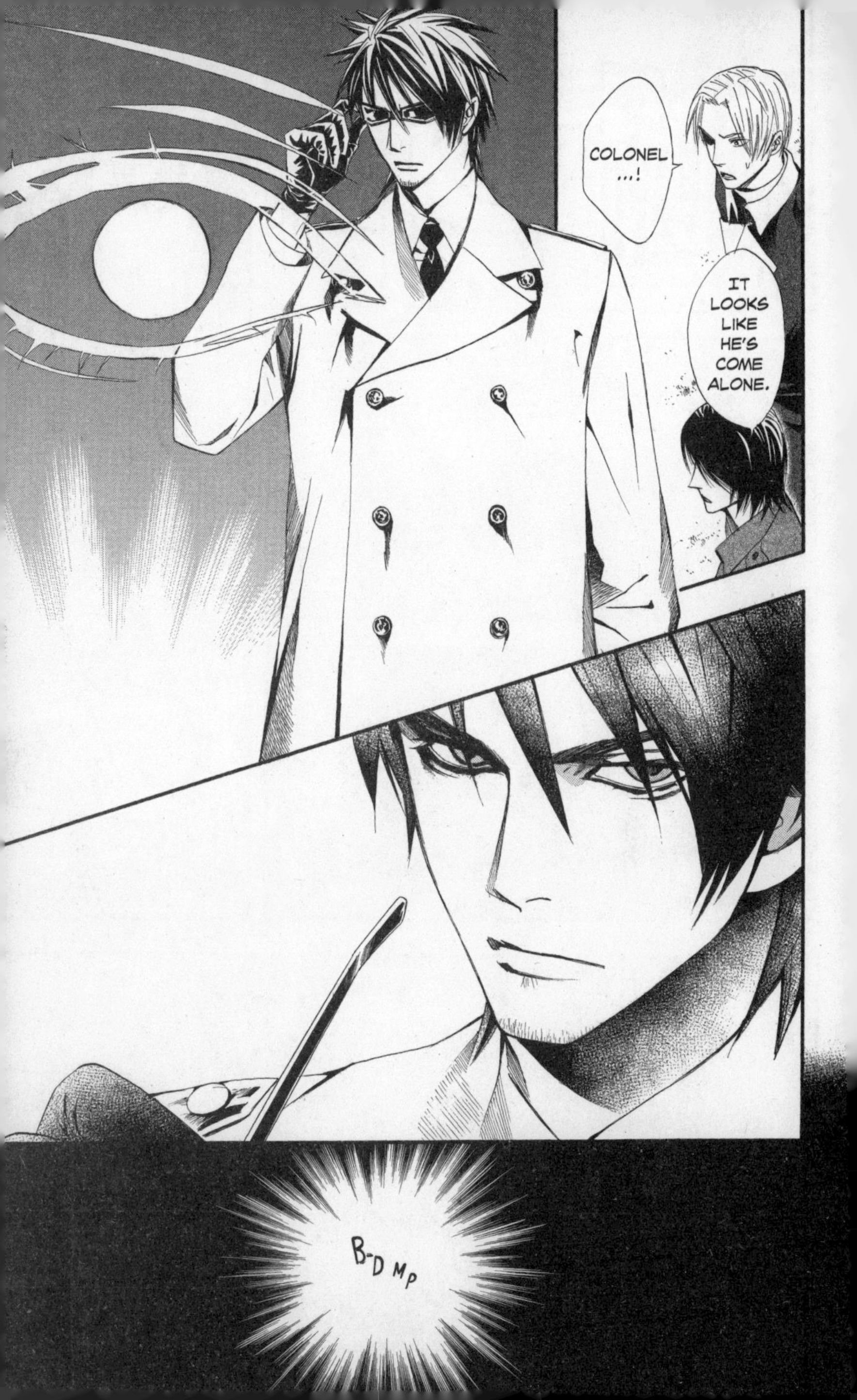
COLONEL ...!
IT LOOKS LIKE HE'S COME ALONE.
B-DMP

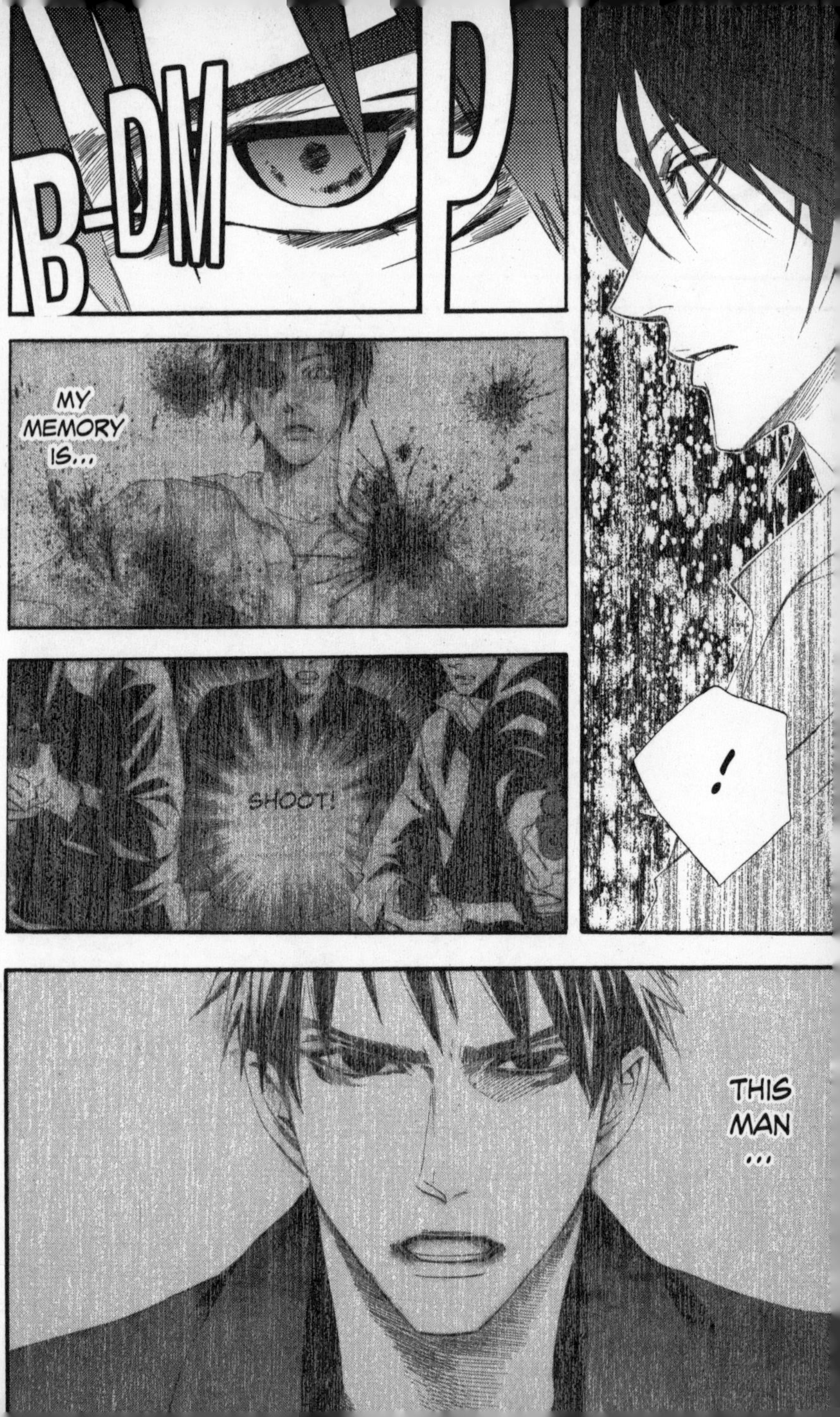
!
B-DMP
MY MEMORY IS...
SHOOT!
THIS MAN ...

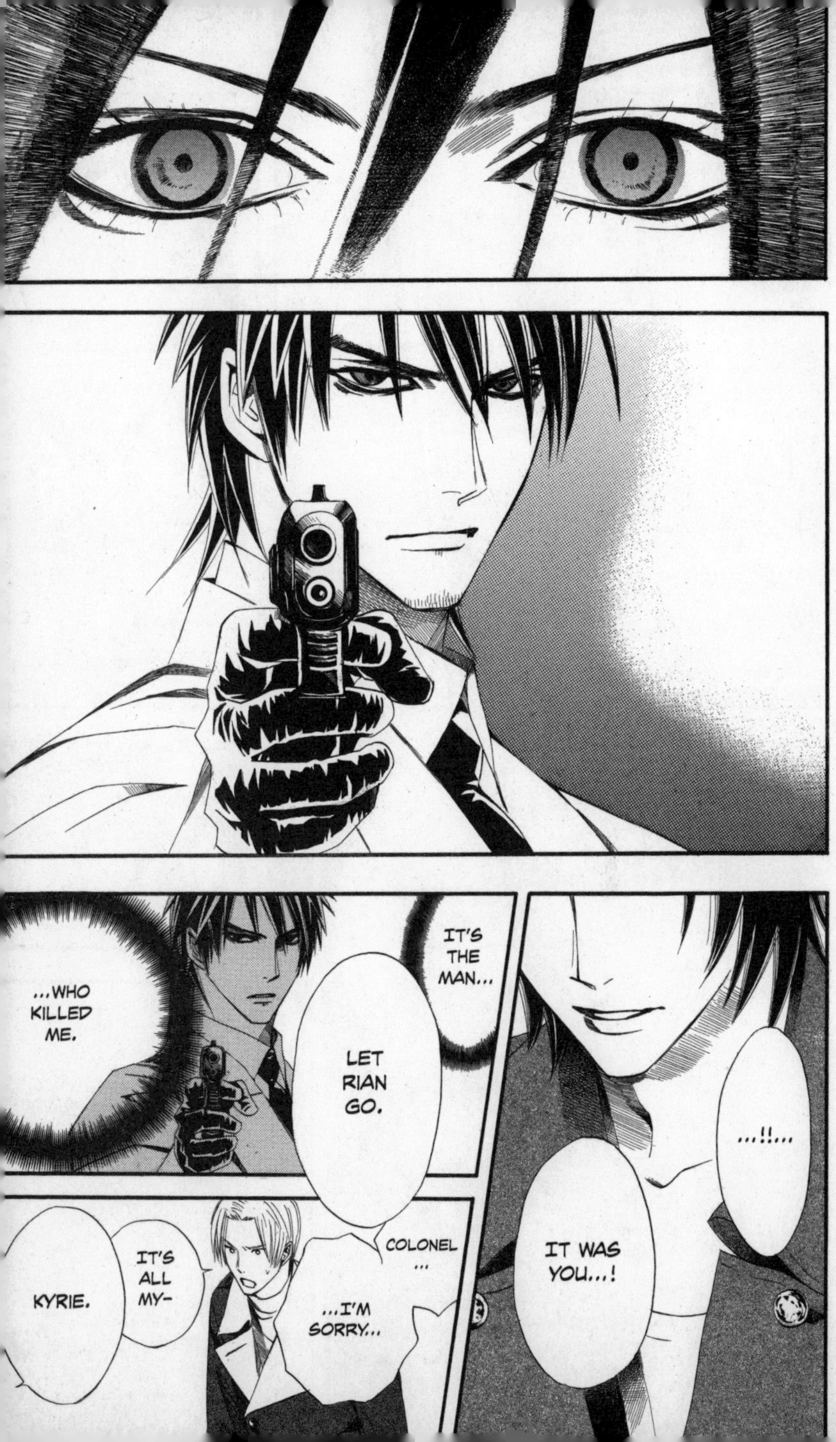
...!!...
IT WAS YOU...!
IT'S THE MAN...
...WHO KILLED ME.
LET RIAN GO.
COLONEL ...
...I'M SORRY...
IT'S ALL MY-
KYRIE.

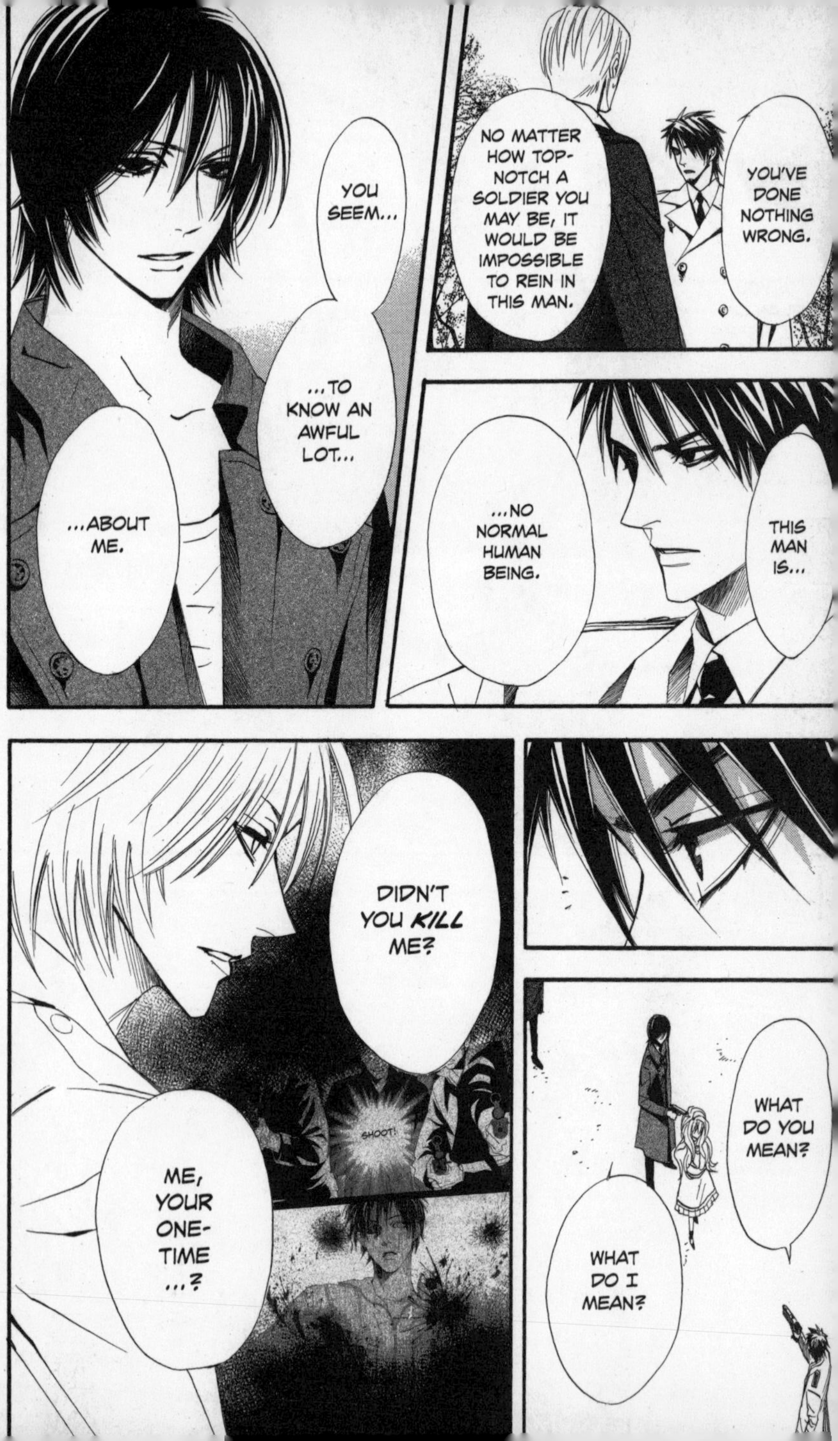
YOU'VE DONE NOTHING WRONG.
NO MATTER HOW TOP-NOTCH A SOLDIER YOU MAY BE, IT WOULD BE IMPOSSIBLE TO REIN IN THIS MAN.
THIS MAN IS...
...NO NORMAL HUMAN BEING.
YOU SEEM...
...TO KNOW AN AWFUL LOT...
...ABOUT ME.
WHAT DO YOU MEAN?
WHAT DO I MEAN?
DIDN'T YOU *KILL* ME?
SHOOT!
ME, YOUR ONE-TIME ...?

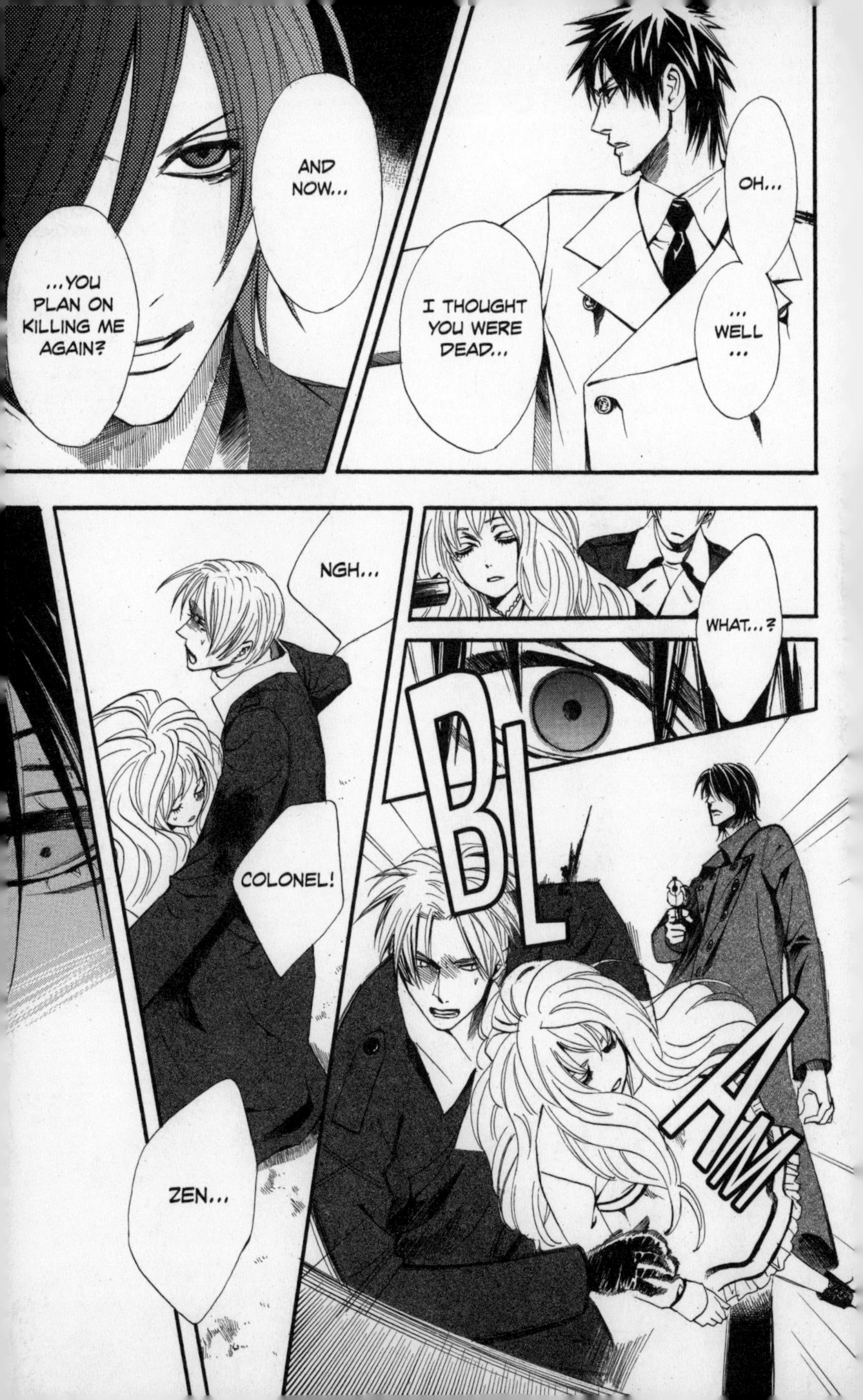
OH...
... WELL ...
I THOUGHT YOU WERE DEAD...
AND NOW...
...YOU PLAN ON KILLING ME AGAIN?
WHAT...?
BLAM
NGH...
COLONEL!
ZEN...

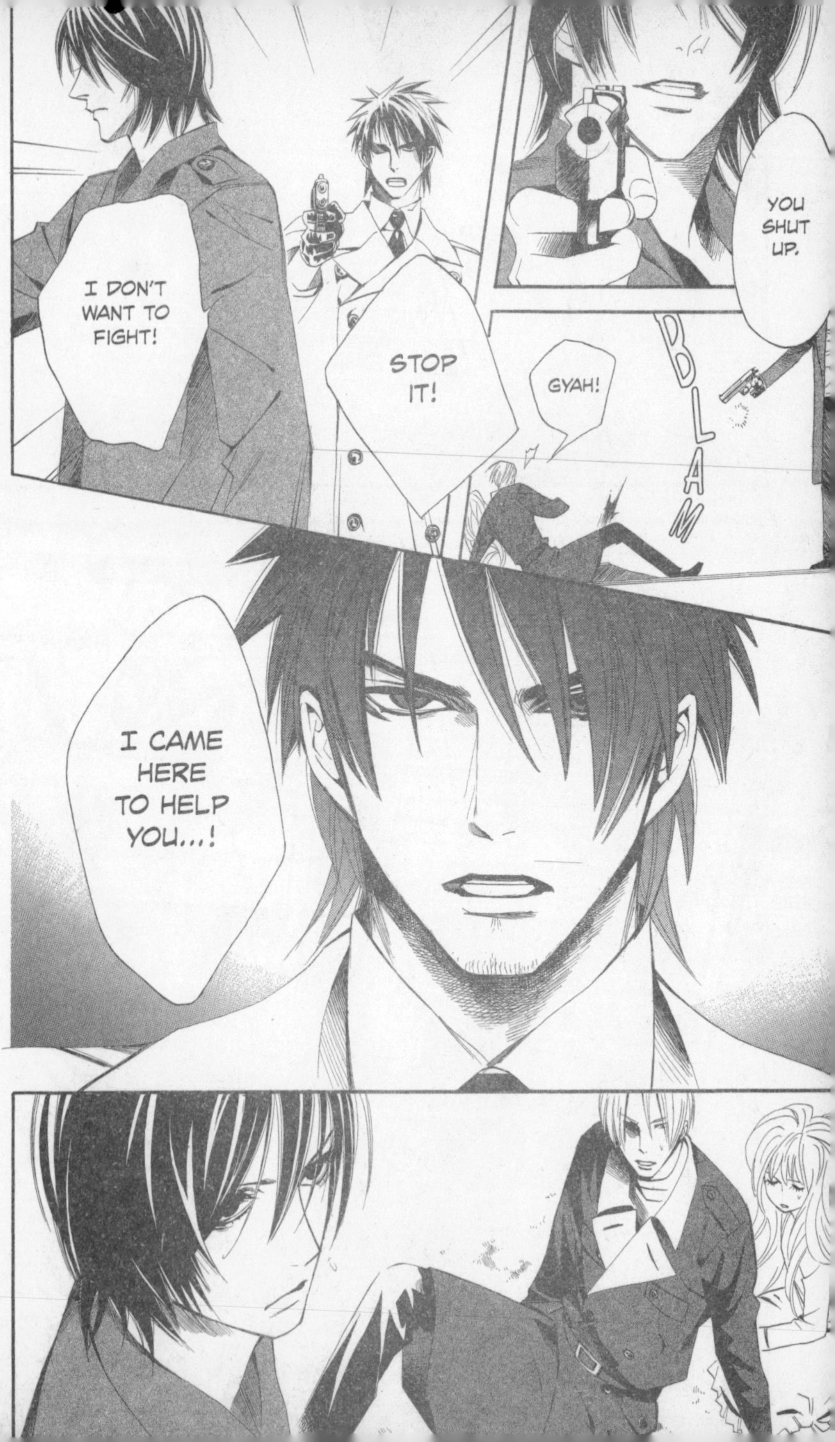
YOU SHUT UP.
BLAM
GYAH!
I DON'T WANT TO FIGHT!
STOP IT!
I CAME HERE TO HELP YOU...!

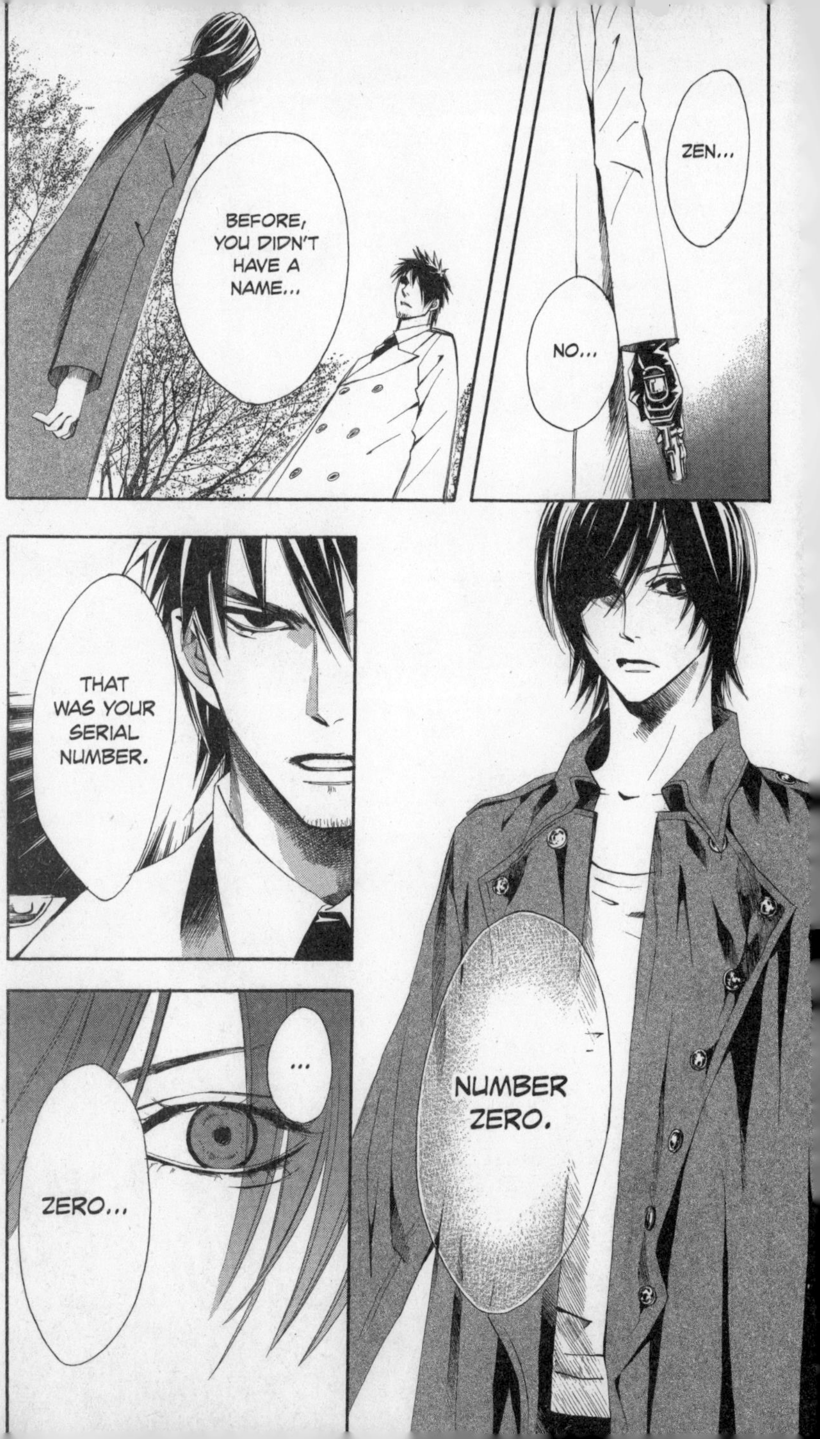
ZEN...
NO...
BEFORE, YOU DIDN'T HAVE A NAME...
NUMBER ZERO.
THAT WAS YOUR SERIAL NUMBER.
...
ZERO...

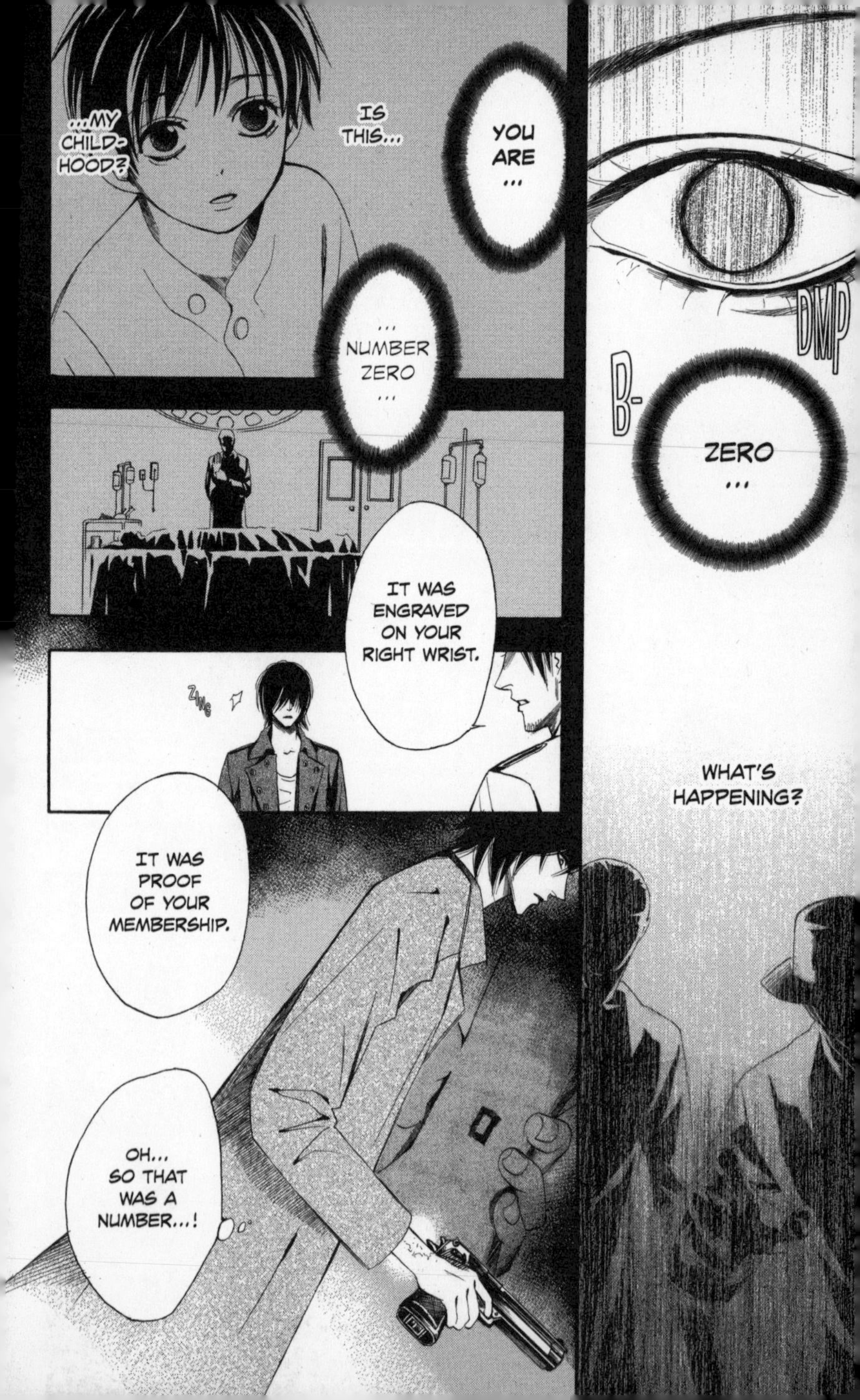
B-DMP
ZERO ...
WHAT'S HAPPENING?
YOU ARE ...
... NUMBER ZERO ...
IS THIS...
...MY CHILD-HOOD?
IT WAS ENGRAVED ON YOUR RIGHT WRIST.
ZING
IT WAS PROOF OF YOUR MEMBERSHIP.
OH... SO THAT WAS A NUMBER...!

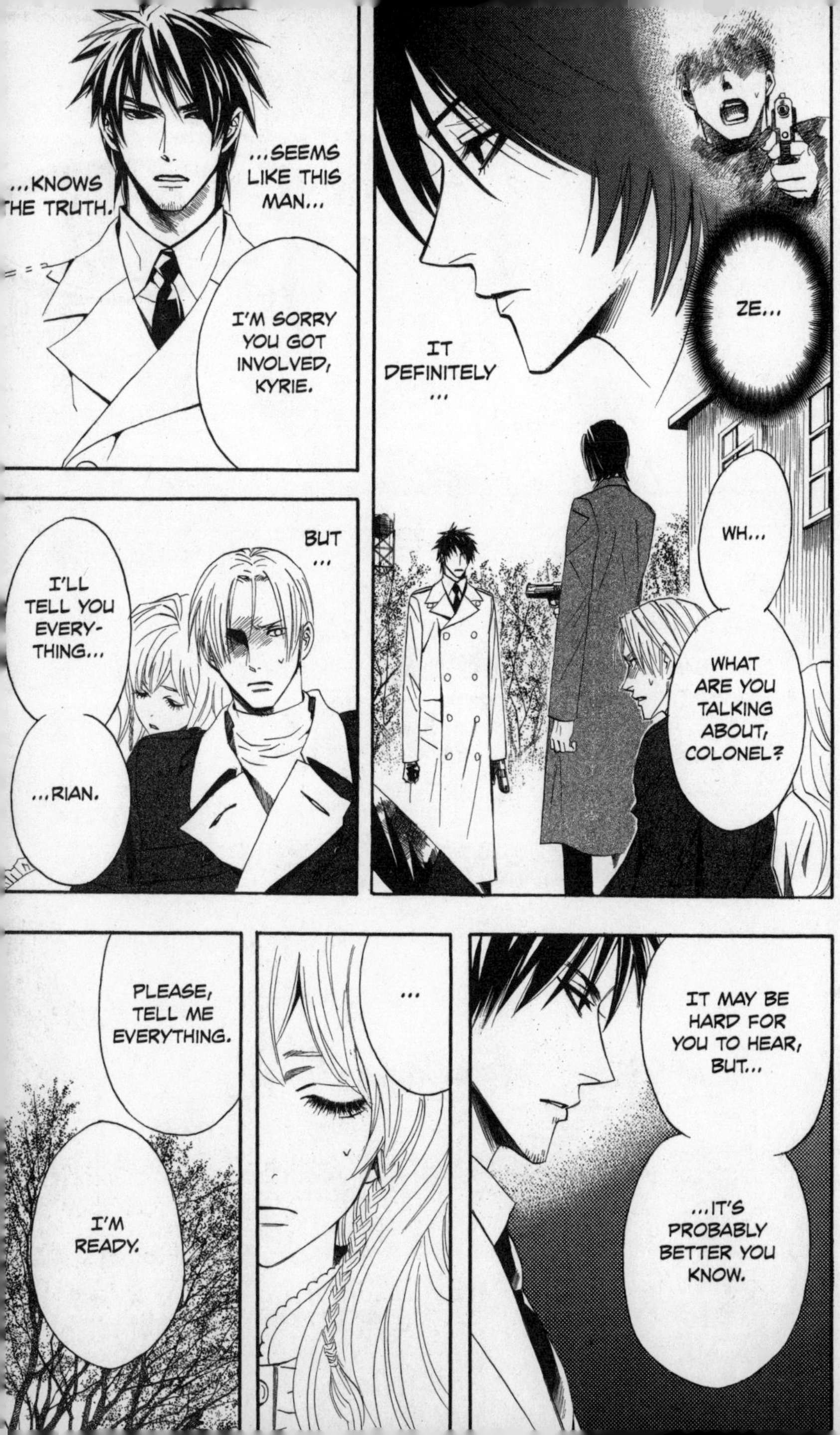
ZE...
IT DEFINITELY ...
WH...
WHAT ARE YOU TALKING ABOUT, COLONEL?
...SEEMS LIKE THIS MAN...
...KNOWS THE TRUTH.
I'M SORRY YOU GOT INVOLVED, KYRIE.
BUT ...
I'LL TELL YOU EVERY-THING...
...RIAN.
IT MAY BE HARD FOR YOU TO HEAR, BUT...
...IT'S PROBABLY BETTER YOU KNOW.
...
PLEASE, TELL ME EVERYTHING.
I'M READY.

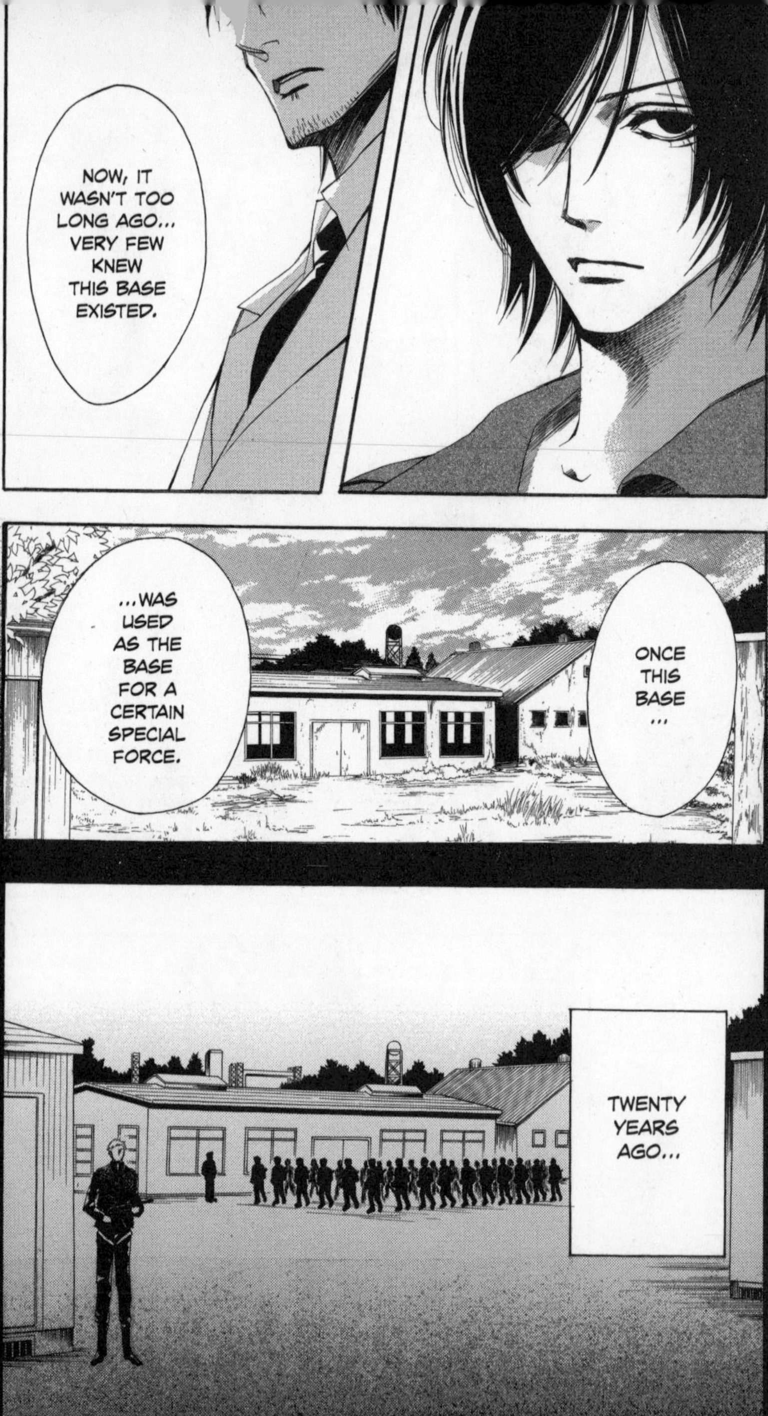
NOW, IT WASN'T TOO LONG AGO... VERY FEW KNEW THIS BASE EXISTED.
ONCE THIS BASE ...
...WAS USED AS THE BASE FOR A CERTAIN SPECIAL FORCE.
TWENTY YEARS AGO...

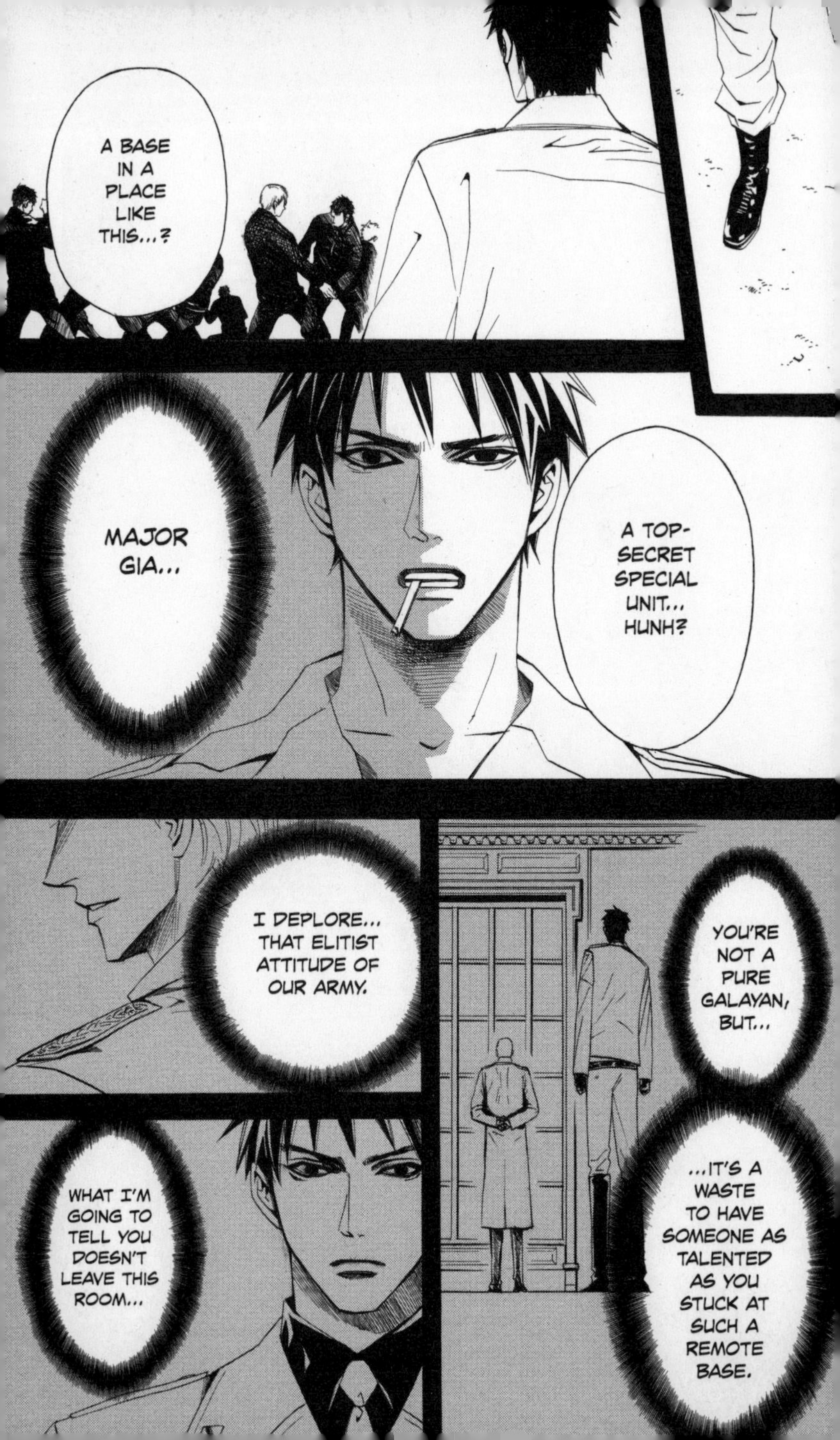
A BASE IN A PLACE LIKE THIS...?
A TOP-SECRET SPECIAL UNIT... HUNH?
MAJOR GIA...
YOU'RE NOT A PURE GALAYAN, BUT...
...IT'S A WASTE TO HAVE SOMEONE AS TALENTED AS YOU STUCK AT SUCH A REMOTE BASE.
I DEPLORE... THAT ELITIST ATTITUDE OF OUR ARMY.
WHAT I'M GOING TO TELL YOU DOESN'T LEAVE THIS ROOM...

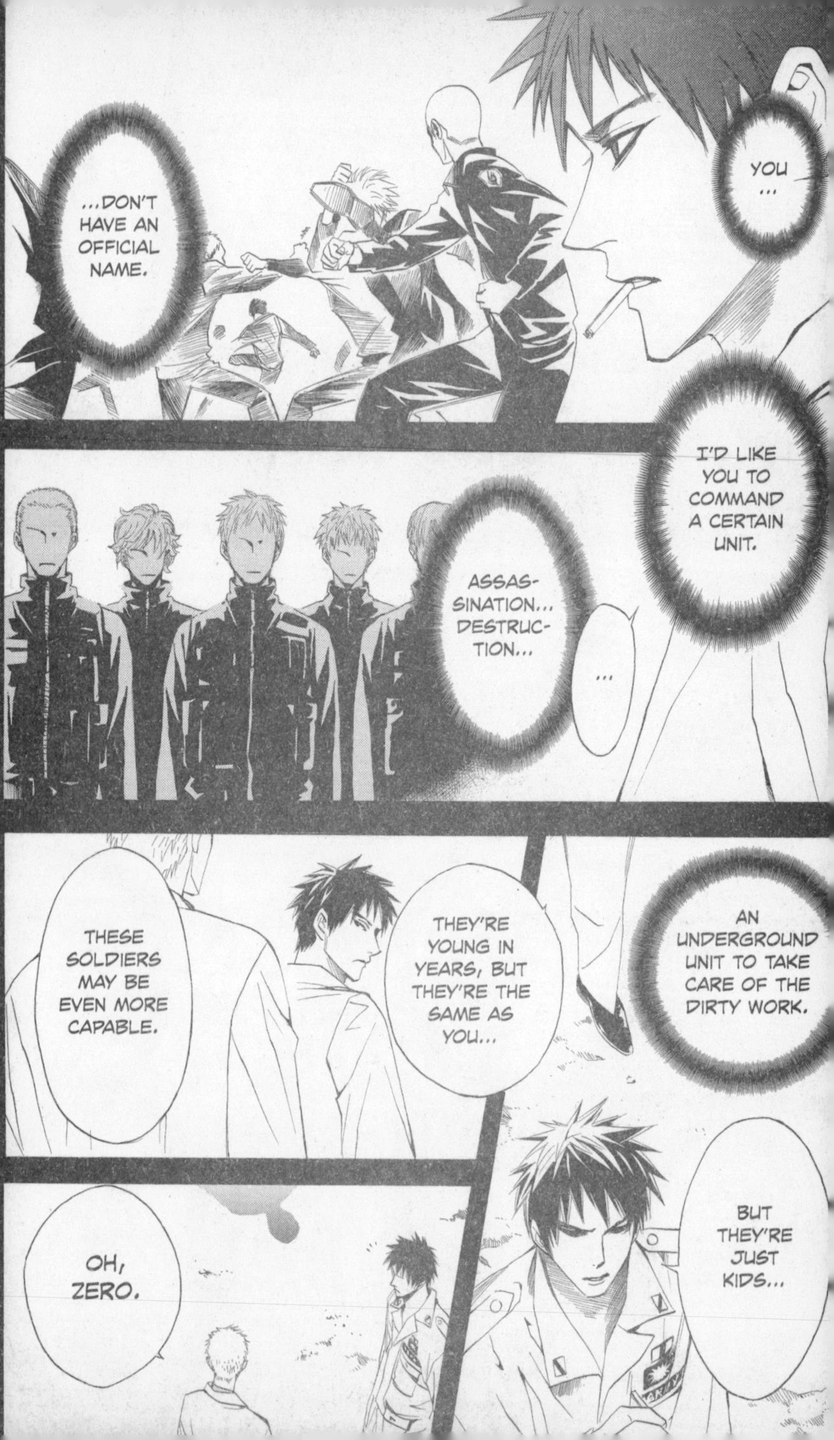
YOU...
...DON'T HAVE AN OFFICIAL NAME.
I'D LIKE YOU TO COMMAND A CERTAIN UNIT.
...
ASSASSINATION... DESTRUCTION...
AN UNDERGROUND UNIT TO TAKE CARE OF THE DIRTY WORK.
THEY'RE YOUNG IN YEARS, BUT THEY'RE THE SAME AS YOU...
THESE SOLDIERS MAY BE EVEN MORE CAPABLE.
BUT THEY'RE JUST KIDS...
OH, ZERO.

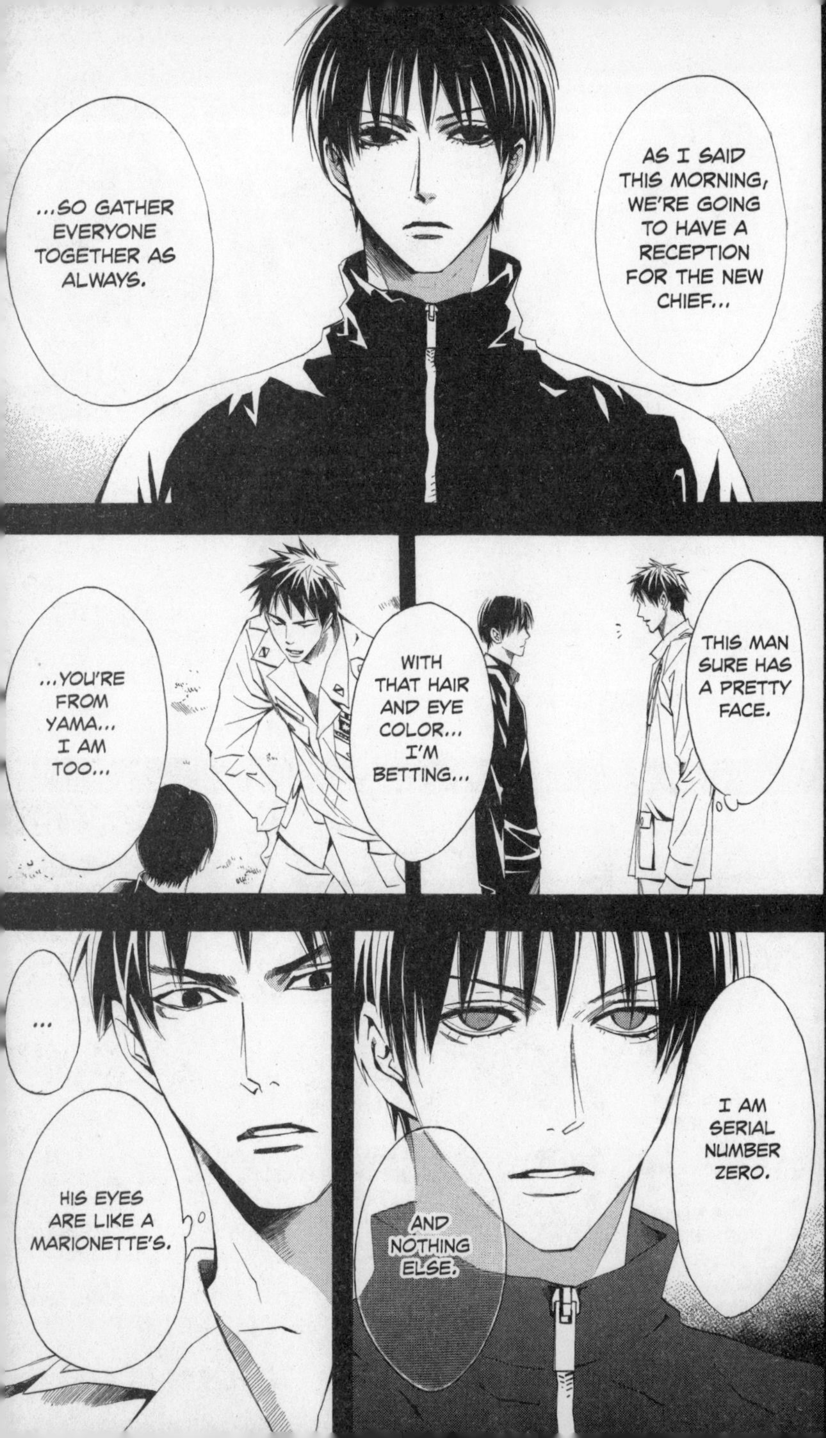
AS I SAID THIS MORNING, WE'RE GOING TO HAVE A RECEPTION FOR THE NEW CHIEF...
...SO GATHER EVERYONE TOGETHER AS ALWAYS.
THIS MAN SURE HAS A PRETTY FACE.
WITH THAT HAIR AND EYE COLOR... I'M BETTING...
...YOU'RE FROM YAMA... I AM TOO...
I AM SERIAL NUMBER ZERO.
AND NOTHING ELSE.
...
HIS EYES ARE LIKE A MARIONETTE'S.

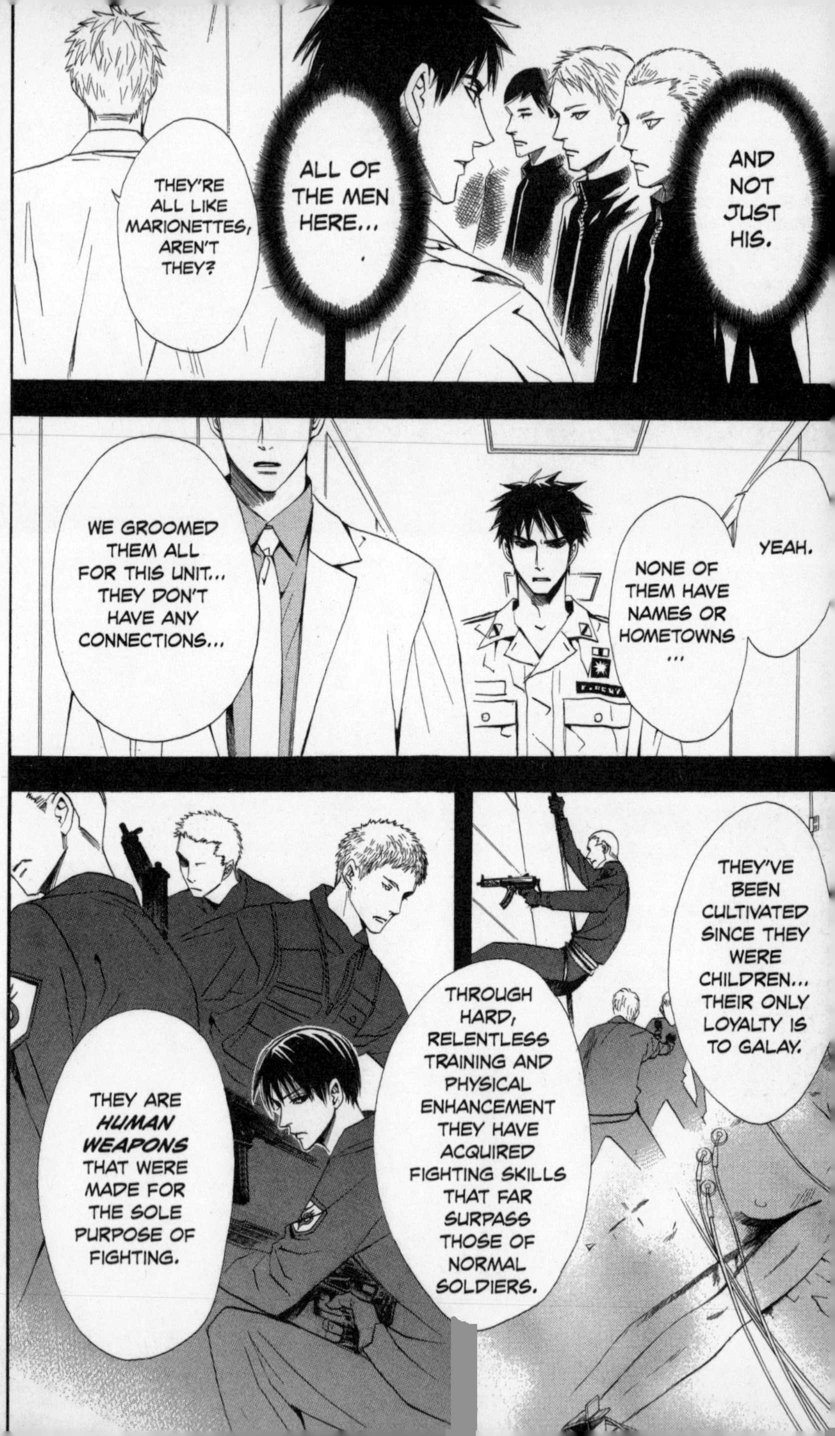
AND NOT JUST HIS.
ALL OF THE MEN HERE...
THEY'RE ALL LIKE MARIONETTES, AREN'T THEY?
YEAH.
NONE OF THEM HAVE NAMES OR HOMETOWNS...
WE GROOMED THEM ALL FOR THIS UNIT... THEY DON'T HAVE ANY CONNECTIONS...
THEY'VE BEEN CULTIVATED SINCE THEY WERE CHILDREN... THEIR ONLY LOYALTY IS TO GALAY.
THROUGH HARD, RELENTLESS TRAINING AND PHYSICAL ENHANCEMENT THEY HAVE ACQUIRED FIGHTING SKILLS THAT FAR SURPASS THOSE OF NORMAL SOLDIERS.
THEY ARE *HUMAN WEAPONS* THAT WERE MADE FOR THE SOLE PURPOSE OF FIGHTING.

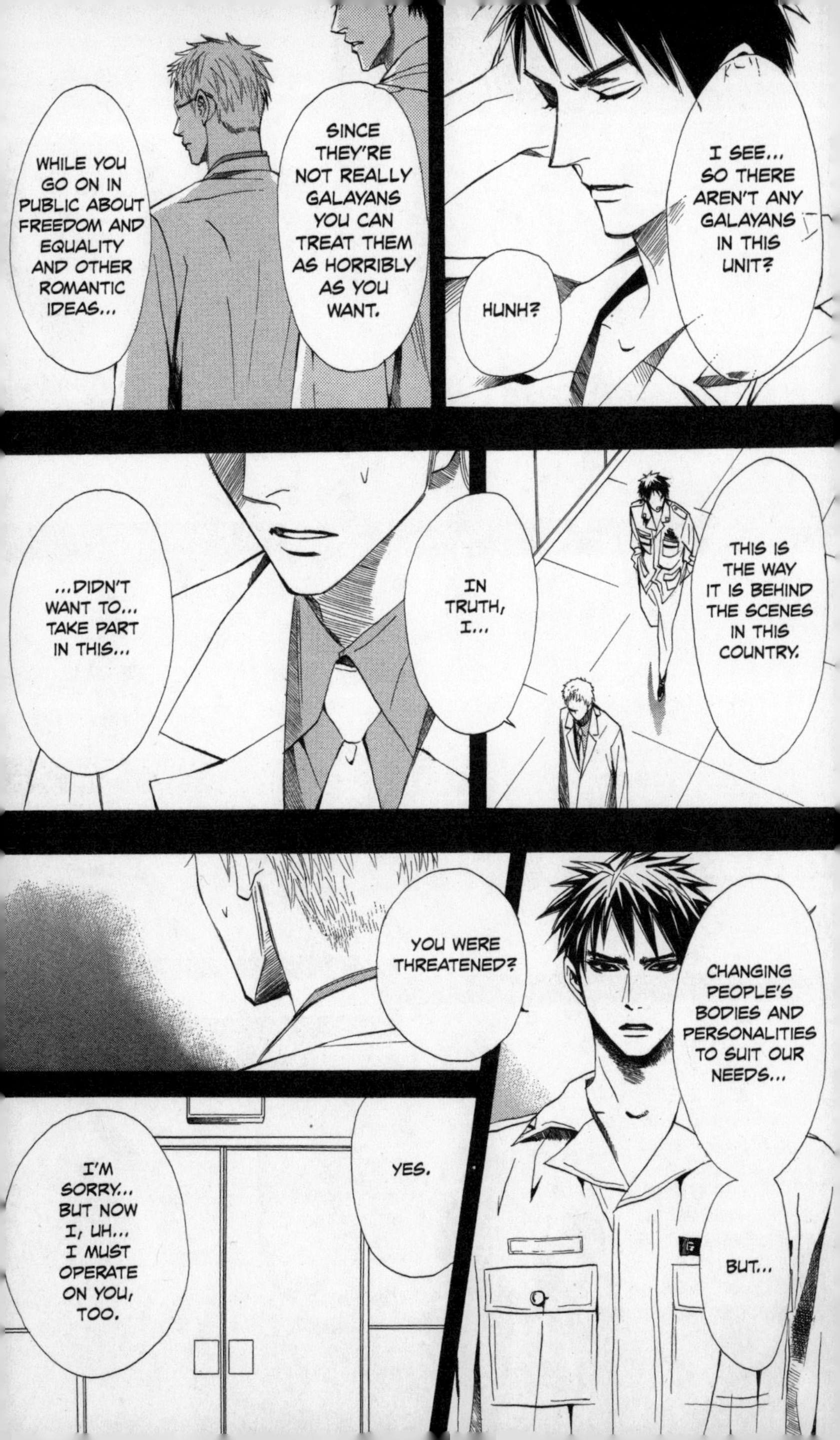

I SEE... SO THERE AREN'T ANY GALAYANS IN THIS UNIT?
HUNH?
SINCE THEY'RE NOT REALLY GALAYANS YOU CAN TREAT THEM AS HORRIBLY AS YOU WANT.
WHILE YOU GO ON IN PUBLIC ABOUT FREEDOM AND EQUALITY AND OTHER ROMANTIC IDEAS...
THIS IS THE WAY IT IS BEHIND THE SCENES IN THIS COUNTRY.
IN TRUTH, I...
...DIDN'T WANT TO... TAKE PART IN THIS...
CHANGING PEOPLE'S BODIES AND PERSONALITIES TO SUIT OUR NEEDS...
BUT...
YOU WERE THREATENED?
YES.
I'M SORRY... BUT NOW I, UH... I MUST OPERATE ON YOU, TOO.

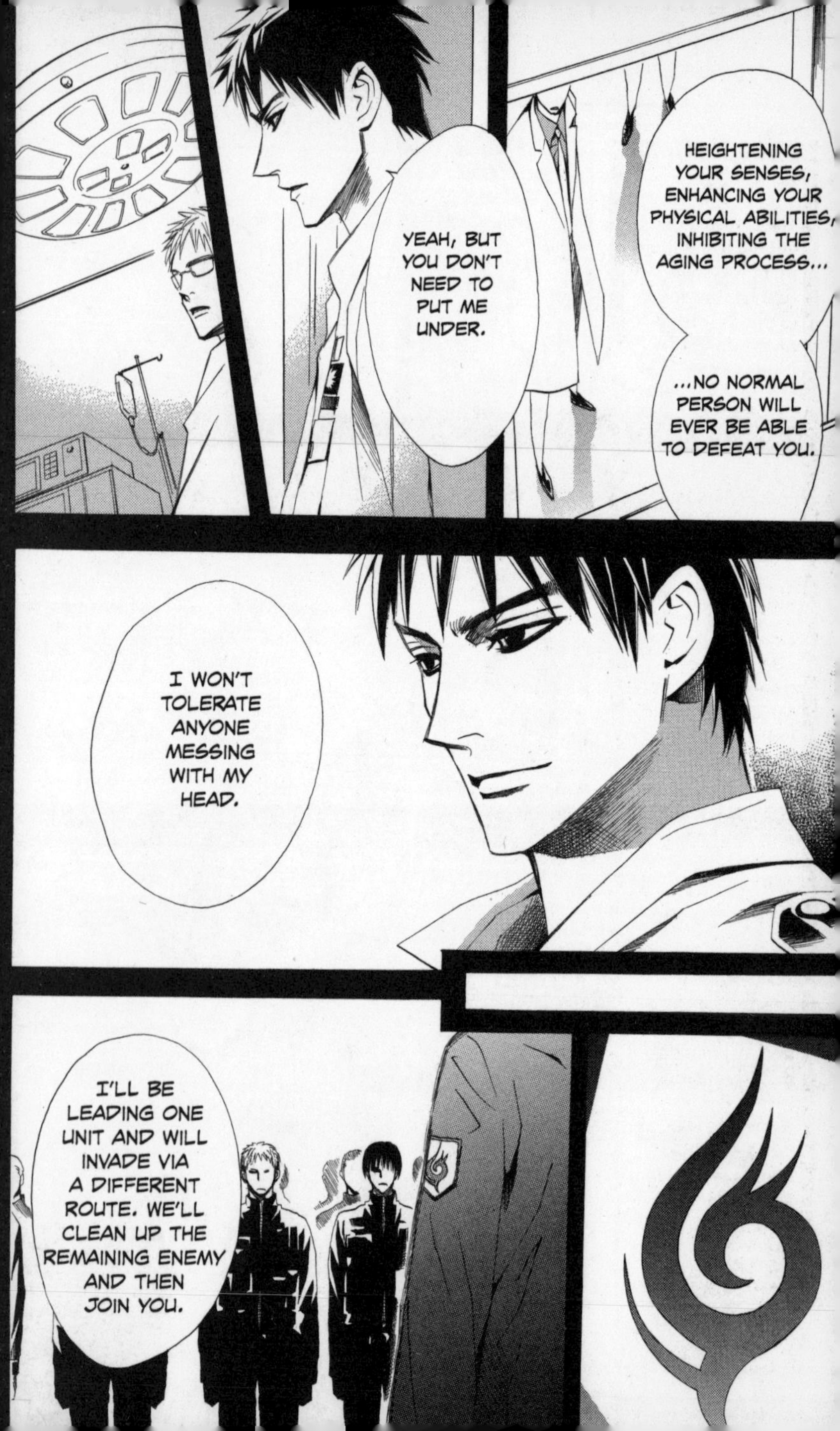
HEIGHTENING YOUR SENSES, ENHANCING YOUR PHYSICAL ABILITIES, INHIBITING THE AGING PROCESS...
...NO NORMAL PERSON WILL EVER BE ABLE TO DEFEAT YOU.
YEAH, BUT YOU DON'T NEED TO PUT ME UNDER.
I WON'T TOLERATE ANYONE MESSING WITH MY HEAD.
I'LL BE LEADING ONE UNIT AND WILL INVADE VIA A DIFFERENT ROUTE. WE'LL CLEAN UP THE REMAINING ENEMY AND THEN JOIN YOU.

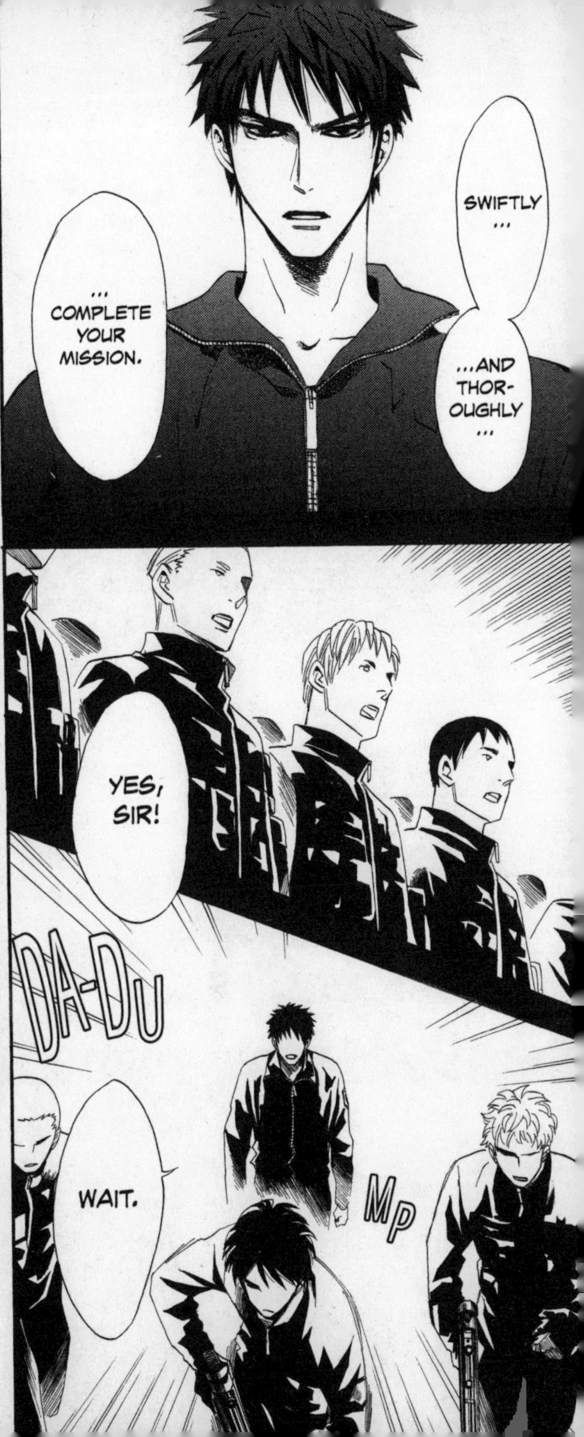
SWIFTLY ...
...AND THOROUGHLY ...
... COMPLETE YOUR MISSION.
YES, SIR!
DA-DU
Mp
WAIT.

3

The character who got the worst treatment was Kyrie. At first he was going to play a role as an extremely important character, but, well, you can see how he turned out...

The paths that each of the characters take ended up running in directions different from what I at first imagined, but it's almost as if the characters themselves chose the paths down which they would go, so I don't have any regrets.

Anyway, this was a hard manga to create.

I am grateful from the bottom of my heart to my assistants and to all the people whom I inconvenienced and who helped me out. And lastly, I'd like to express my thanks to all you readers who have been with me.

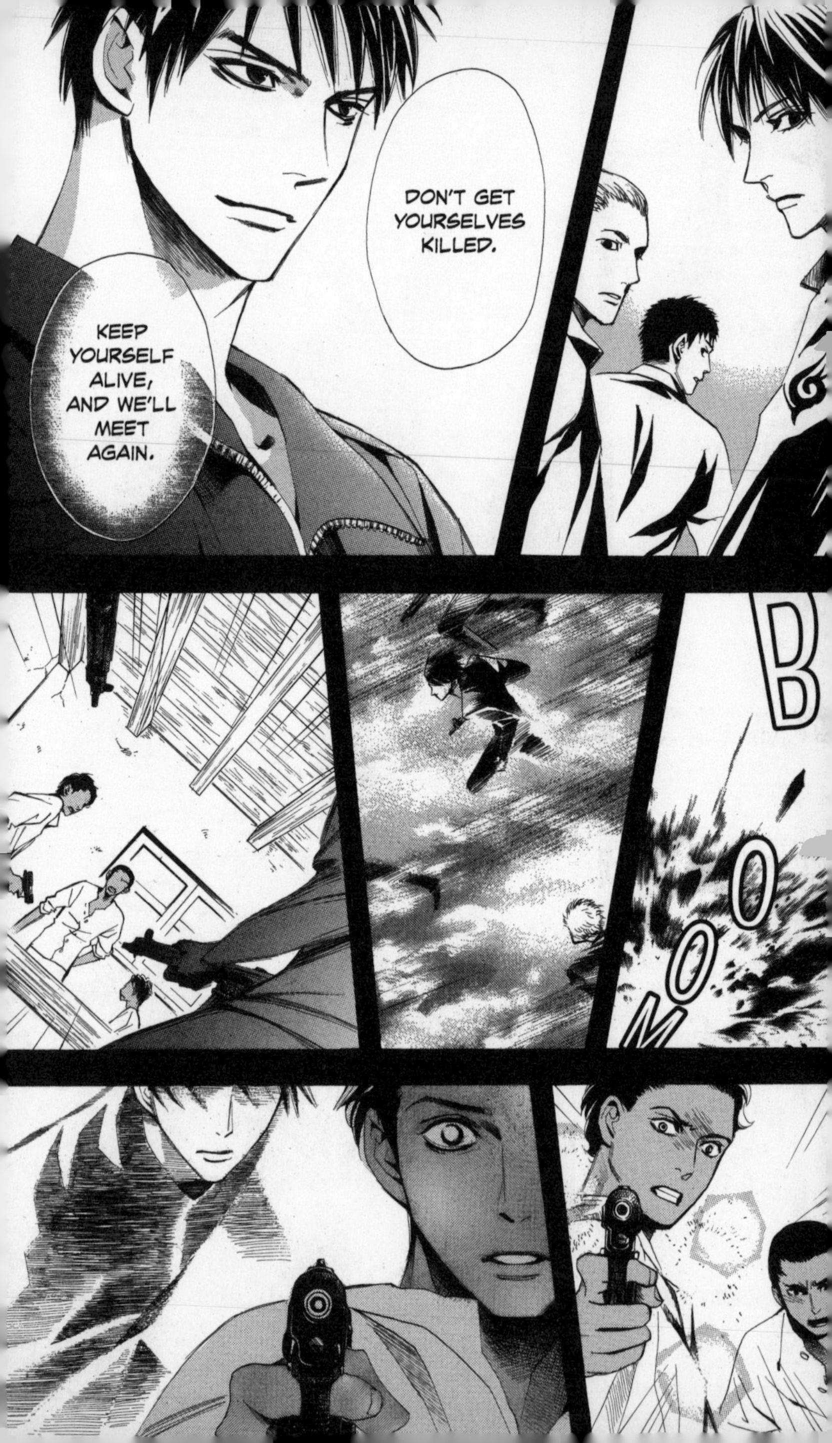
DON'T GET YOURSELVES KILLED.
KEEP YOURSELF ALIVE, AND WE'LL MEET AGAIN.
BOOM

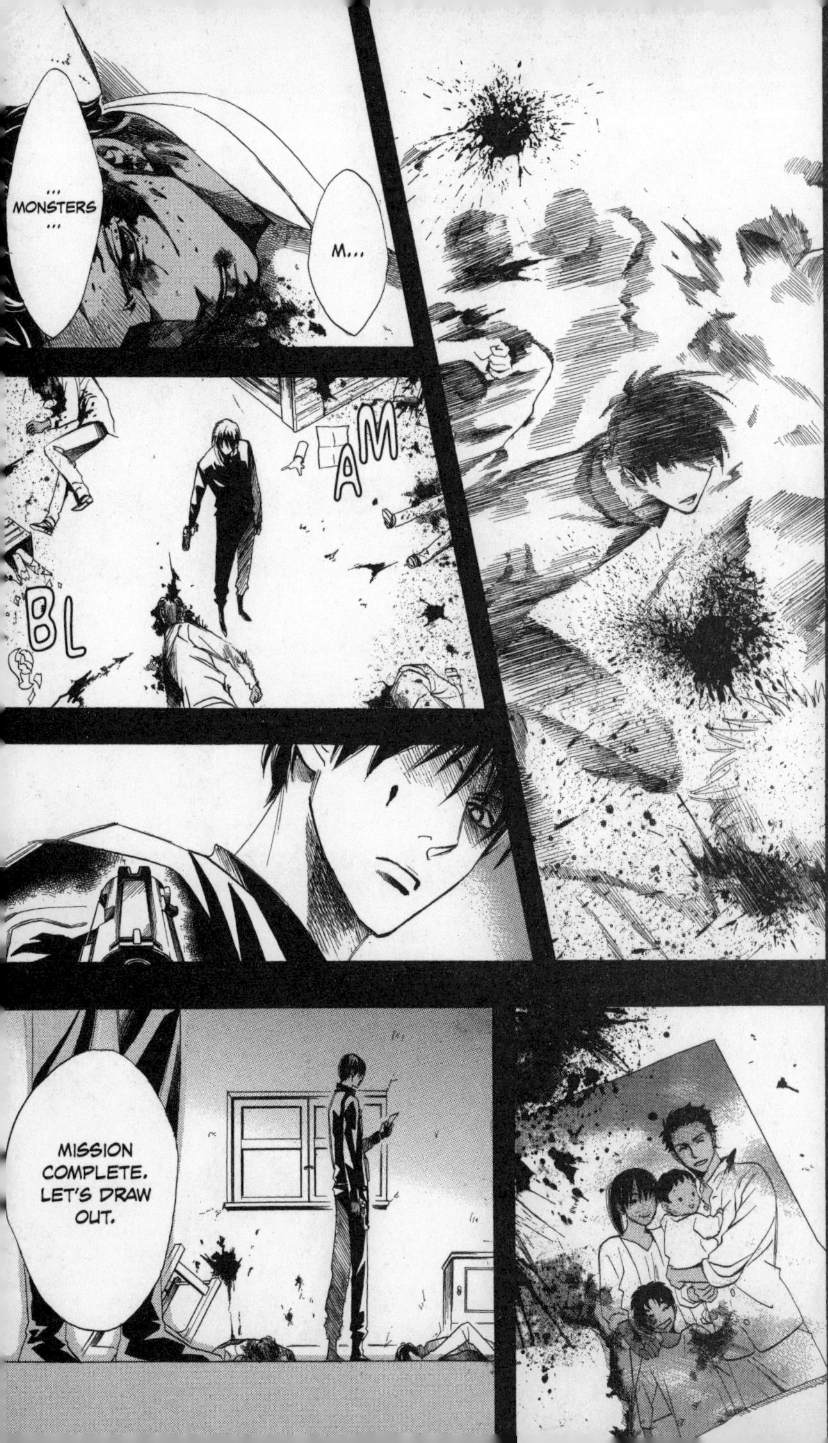
M...
...
MONSTERS
...
BL
AM
MISSION COMPLETE. LET'S DRAW OUT.

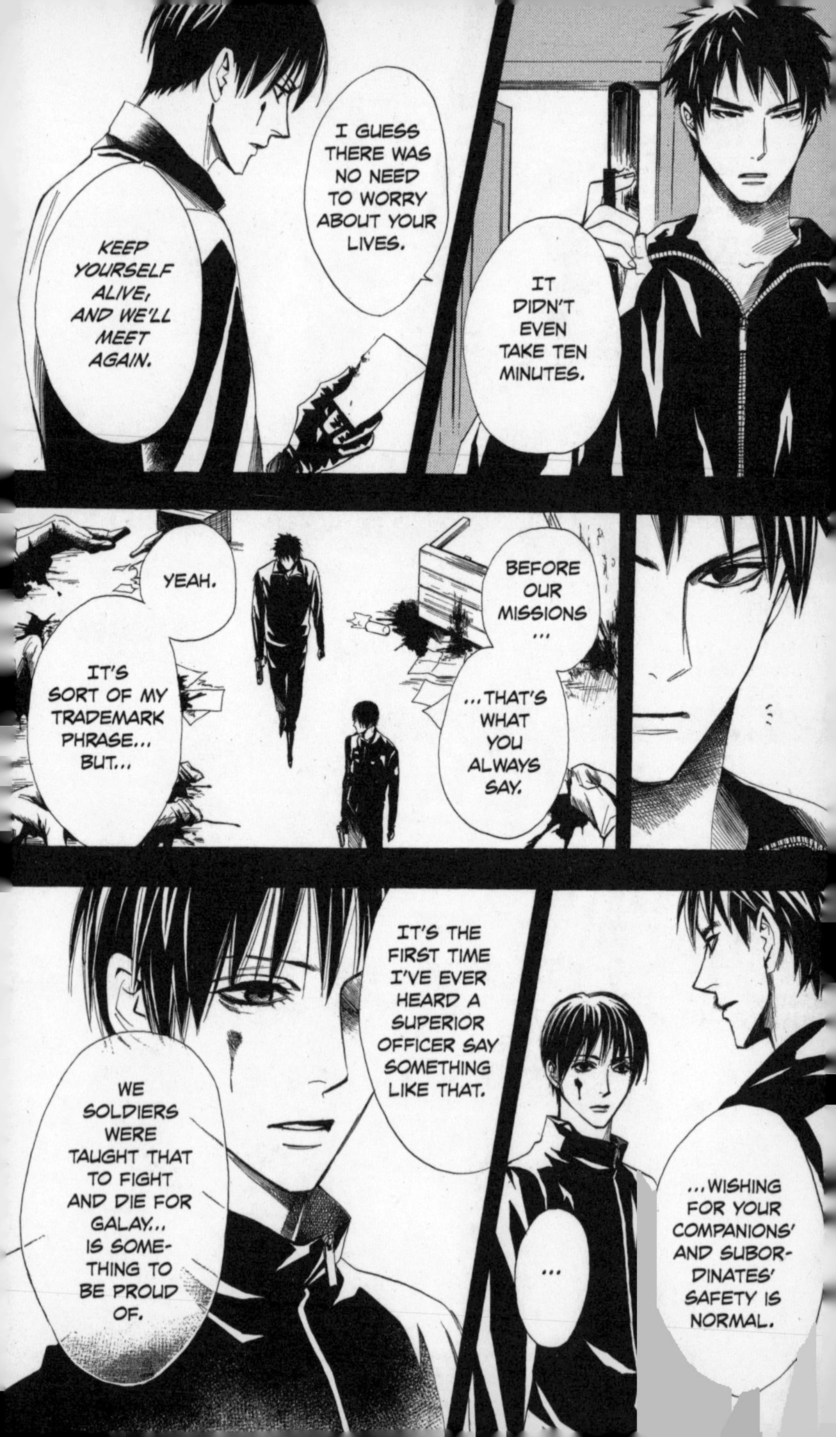
IT DIDN'T EVEN TAKE TEN MINUTES.
I GUESS THERE WAS NO NEED TO WORRY ABOUT YOUR LIVES.
KEEP YOURSELF ALIVE, AND WE'LL MEET AGAIN.
BEFORE OUR MISSIONS...
...THAT'S WHAT YOU ALWAYS SAY.
YEAH.
IT'S SORT OF MY TRADEMARK PHRASE... BUT...
...WISHING FOR YOUR COMPANIONS' AND SUBOR-DINATES' SAFETY IS NORMAL.
...
IT'S THE FIRST TIME I'VE EVER HEARD A SUPERIOR OFFICER SAY SOMETHING LIKE THAT.
WE SOLDIERS WERE TAUGHT THAT TO FIGHT AND DIE FOR GALAY... IS SOME-THING TO BE PROUD OF.

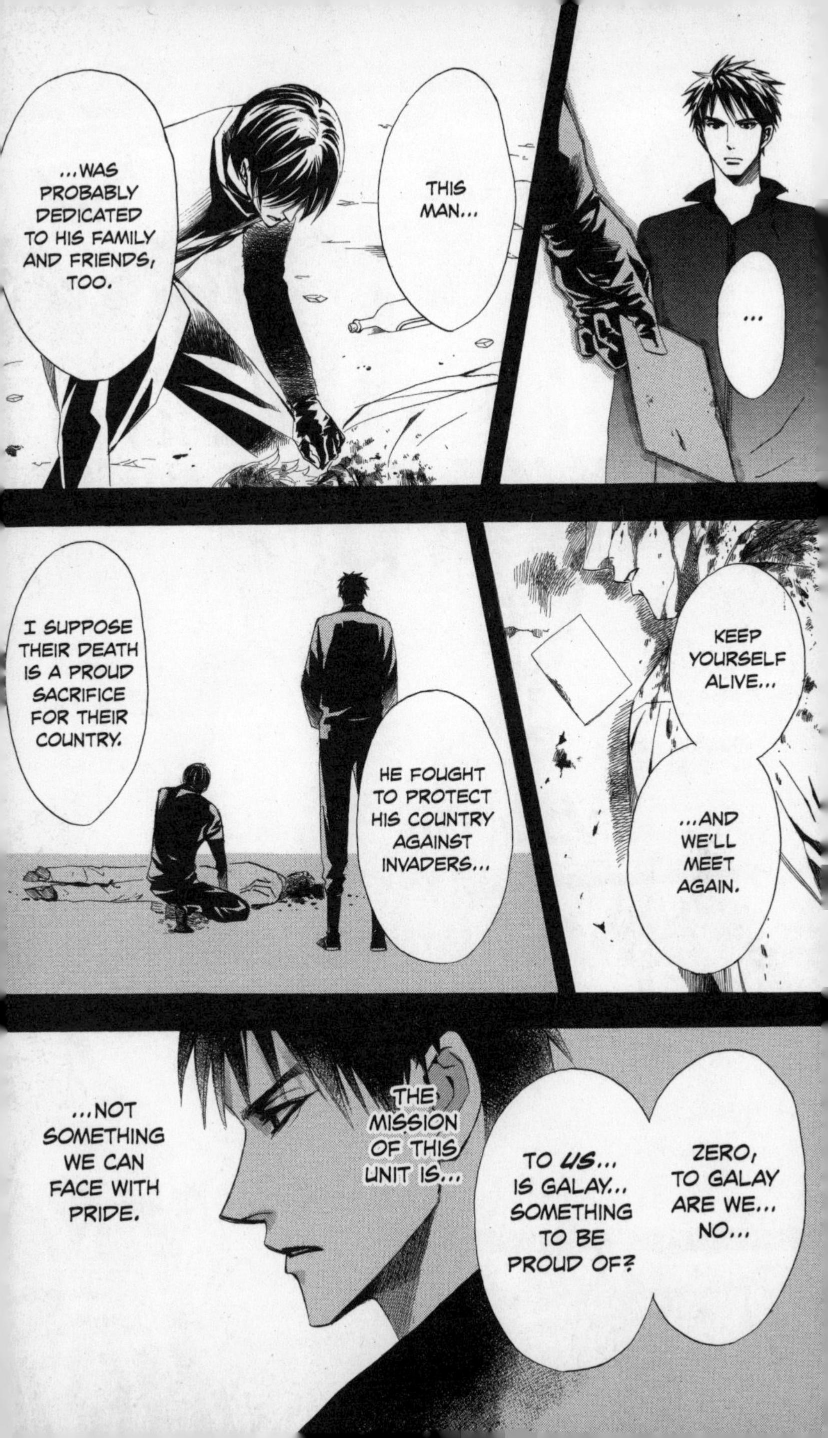
...
THIS MAN...
...WAS PROBABLY DEDICATED TO HIS FAMILY AND FRIENDS, TOO.
KEEP YOURSELF ALIVE...
...AND WE'LL MEET AGAIN.
HE FOUGHT TO PROTECT HIS COUNTRY AGAINST INVADERS...
I SUPPOSE THEIR DEATH IS A PROUD SACRIFICE FOR THEIR COUNTRY.
ZERO, TO GALAY ARE WE... NO...
TO *US*... IS GALAY... SOMETHING TO BE PROUD OF?
THE MISSION OF THIS UNIT IS...
...NOT SOMETHING WE CAN FACE WITH PRIDE.

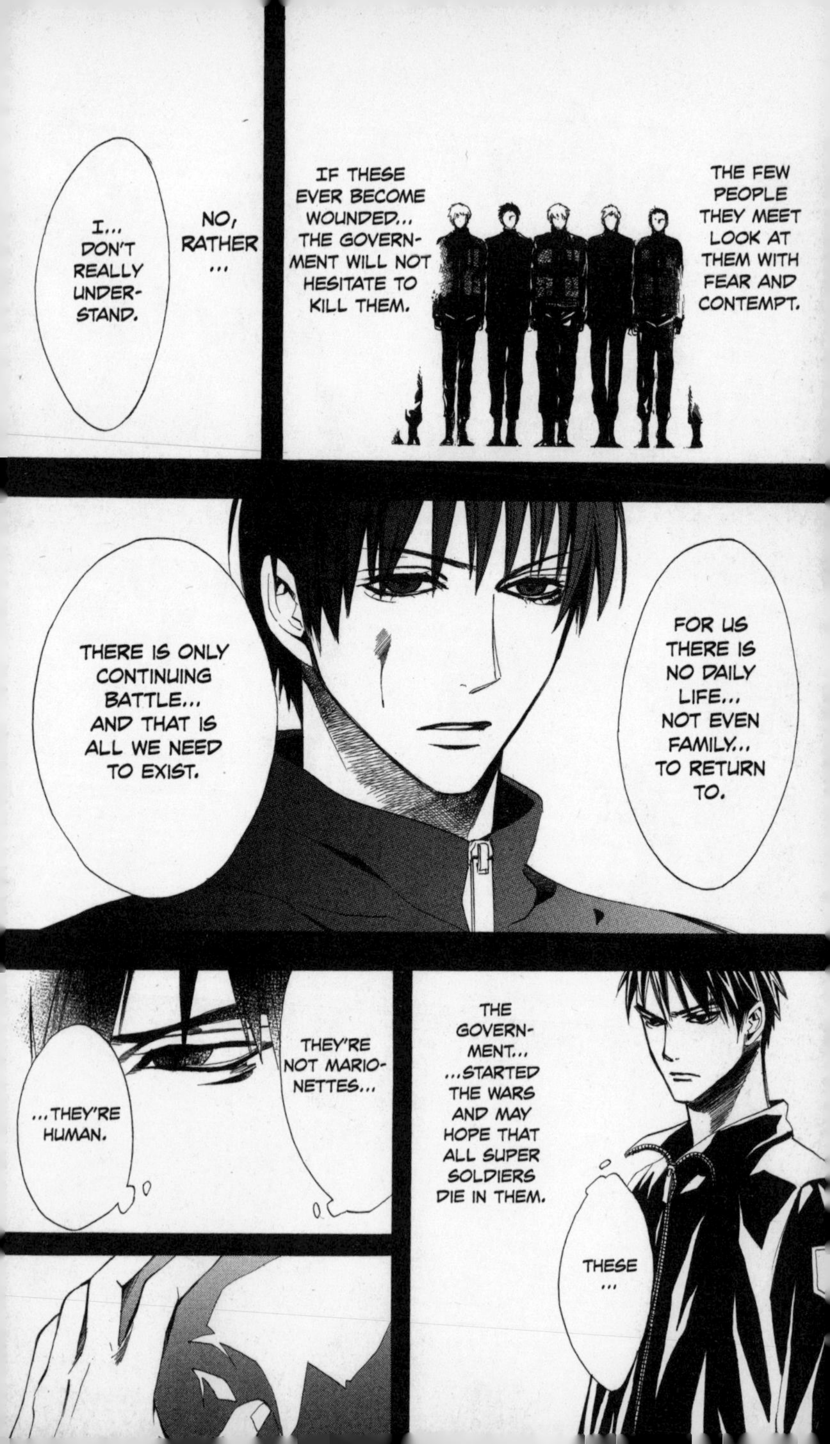
THE FEW PEOPLE THEY MEET LOOK AT THEM WITH FEAR AND CONTEMPT.
IF THESE EVER BECOME WOUNDED... THE GOVERNMENT WILL NOT HESITATE TO KILL THEM.
NO, RATHER ...
I... DON'T REALLY UNDERSTAND.
FOR US THERE IS NO DAILY LIFE... NOT EVEN FAMILY... TO RETURN TO.
THERE IS ONLY CONTINUING BATTLE... AND THAT IS ALL WE NEED TO EXIST.
THE GOVERNMENT... ...STARTED THE WARS AND MAY HOPE THAT ALL SUPER SOLDIERS DIE IN THEM.
THESE ...
THEY'RE NOT MARIONETTES...
...THEY'RE HUMAN.

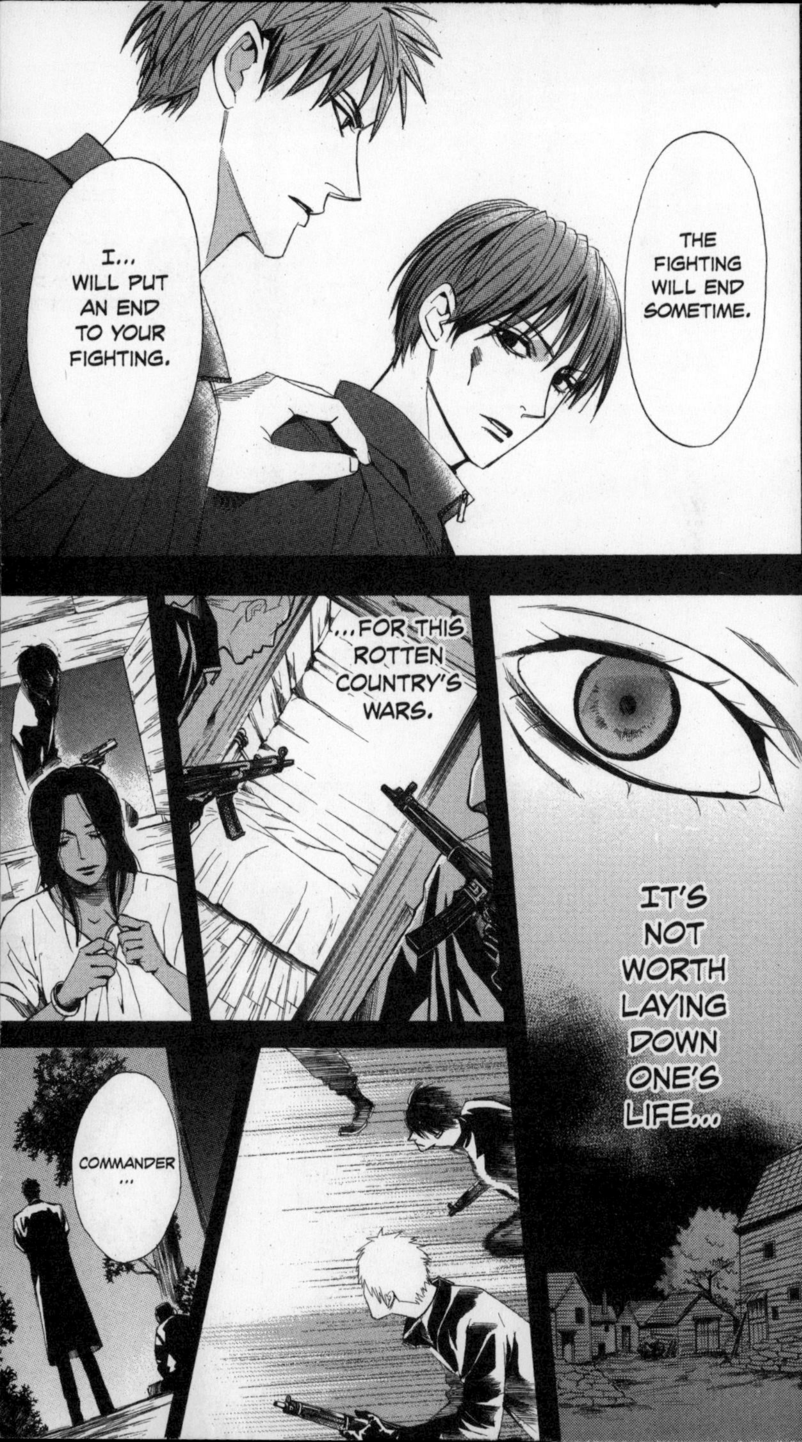
THE FIGHTING WILL END SOMETIME.
I... WILL PUT AN END TO YOUR FIGHTING.
IT'S NOT WORTH LAYING DOWN ONE'S LIFE...
...FOR THIS ROTTEN COUNTRY'S WARS.
COMMANDER...

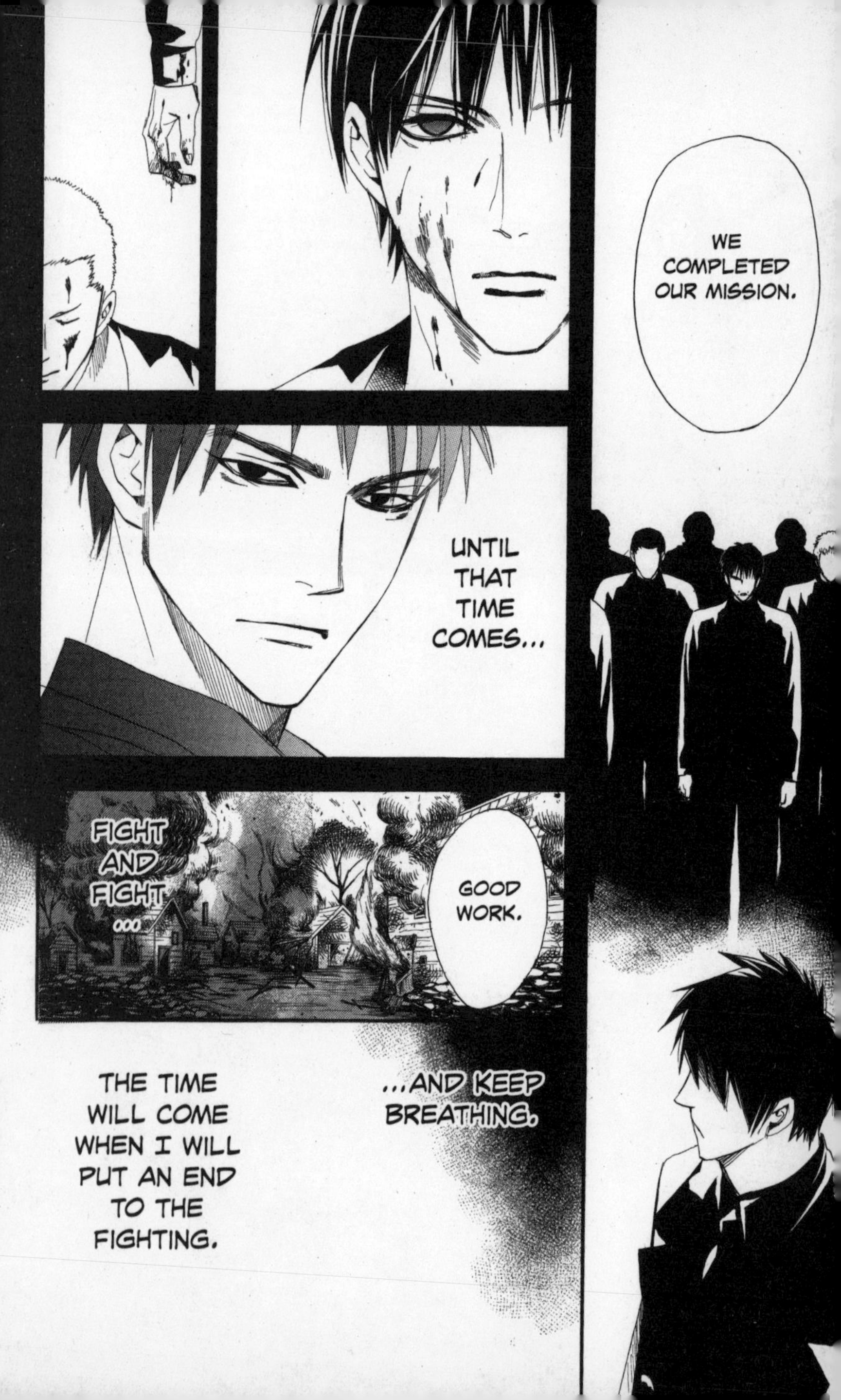
WE COMPLETED OUR MISSION.
UNTIL THAT TIME COMES...
GOOD WORK.
FIGHT AND FIGHT...
...AND KEEP BREATHING.
THE TIME WILL COME WHEN I WILL PUT AN END TO THE FIGHTING.

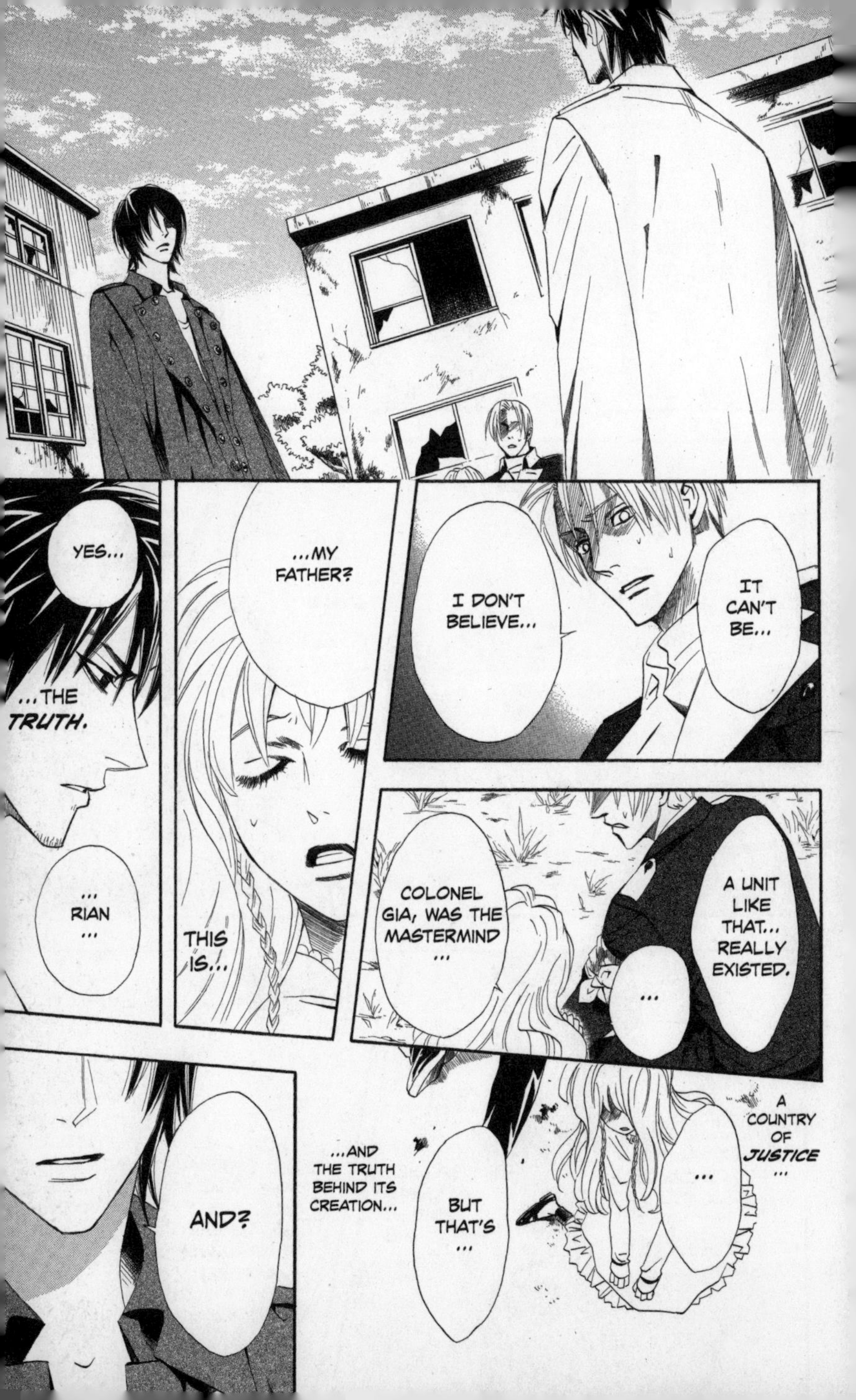
IT CAN'T BE...
I DON'T BELIEVE...
A UNIT LIKE THAT... REALLY EXISTED.
...
COLONEL GIA, WAS THE MASTERMIND ...
...MY FATHER?
THIS IS...
YES...
...THE TRUTH.
... RIAN ...
A COUNTRY OF JUSTICE ...
...
BUT THAT'S ...
...AND THE TRUTH BEHIND ITS CREATION...
AND?

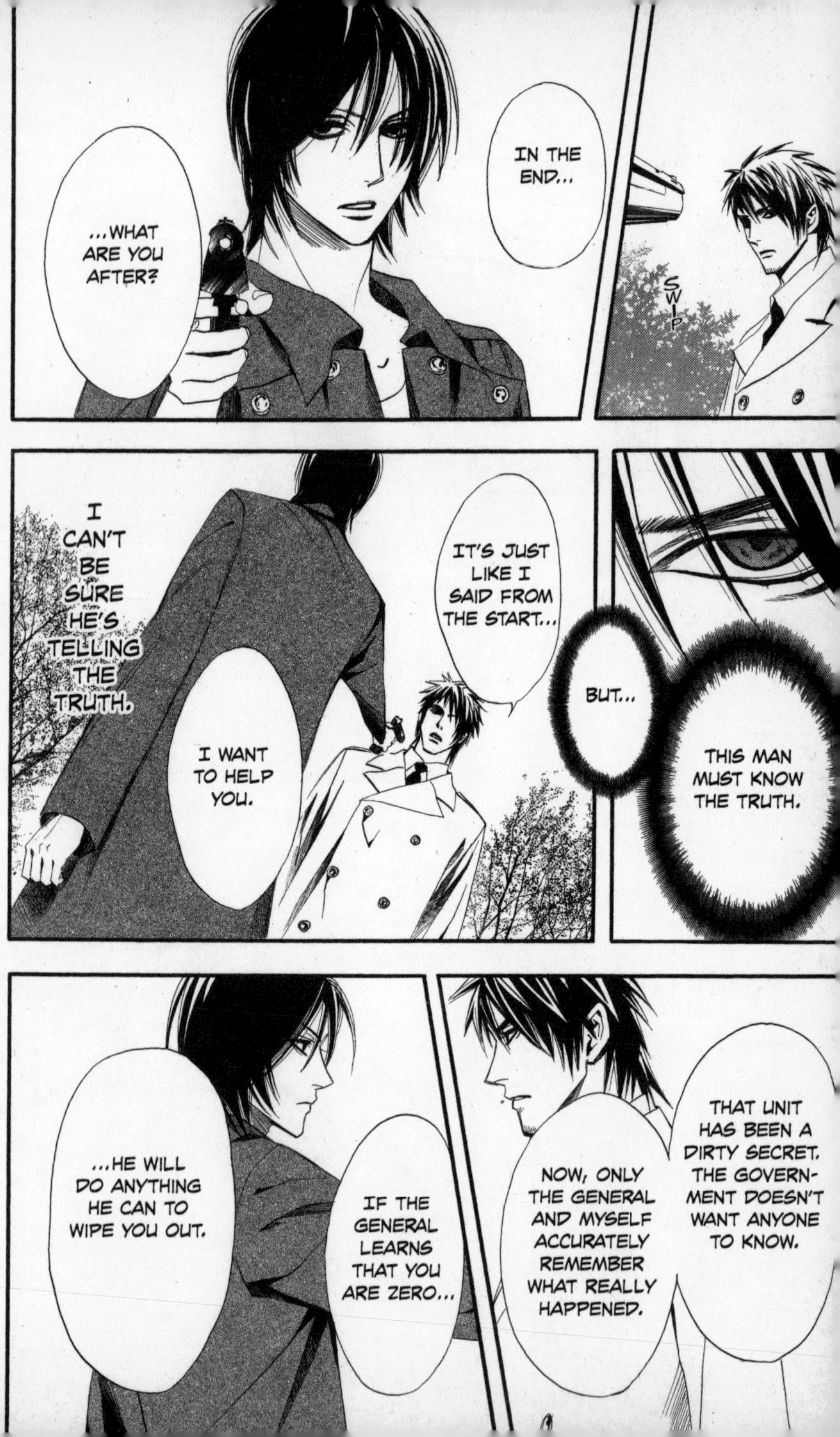
SWIP
IN THE END...
...WHAT ARE YOU AFTER?
BUT...
THIS MAN MUST KNOW THE TRUTH.
IT'S JUST LIKE I SAID FROM THE START...
I CAN'T BE SURE HE'S TELLING THE TRUTH.
I WANT TO HELP YOU.
THAT UNIT HAS BEEN A DIRTY SECRET. THE GOVERNMENT DOESN'T WANT ANYONE TO KNOW.
NOW, ONLY THE GENERAL AND MYSELF ACCURATELY REMEMBER WHAT REALLY HAPPENED.
IF THE GENERAL LEARNS THAT YOU ARE ZERO...
...HE WILL DO ANYTHING HE CAN TO WIPE YOU OUT.

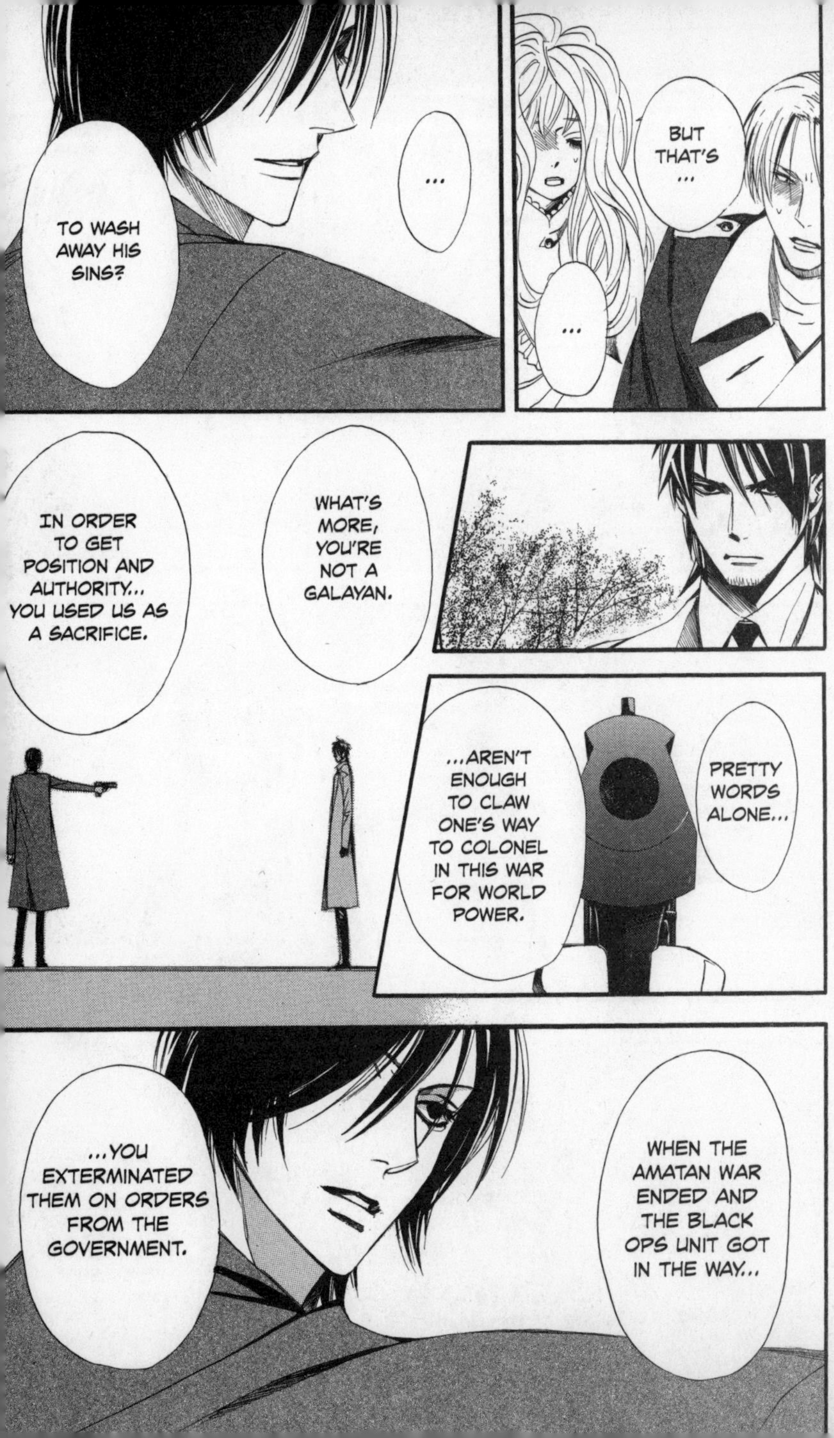
BUT THAT'S ...
...
...
TO WASH AWAY HIS SINS?
WHAT'S MORE, YOU'RE NOT A GALAYAN.
IN ORDER TO GET POSITION AND AUTHORITY... YOU USED US AS A SACRIFICE.
PRETTY WORDS ALONE...
...AREN'T ENOUGH TO CLAW ONE'S WAY TO COLONEL IN THIS WAR FOR WORLD POWER.
WHEN THE AMATAN WAR ENDED AND THE BLACK OPS UNIT GOT IN THE WAY...
...YOU EXTERMINATED THEM ON ORDERS FROM THE GOVERNMENT.

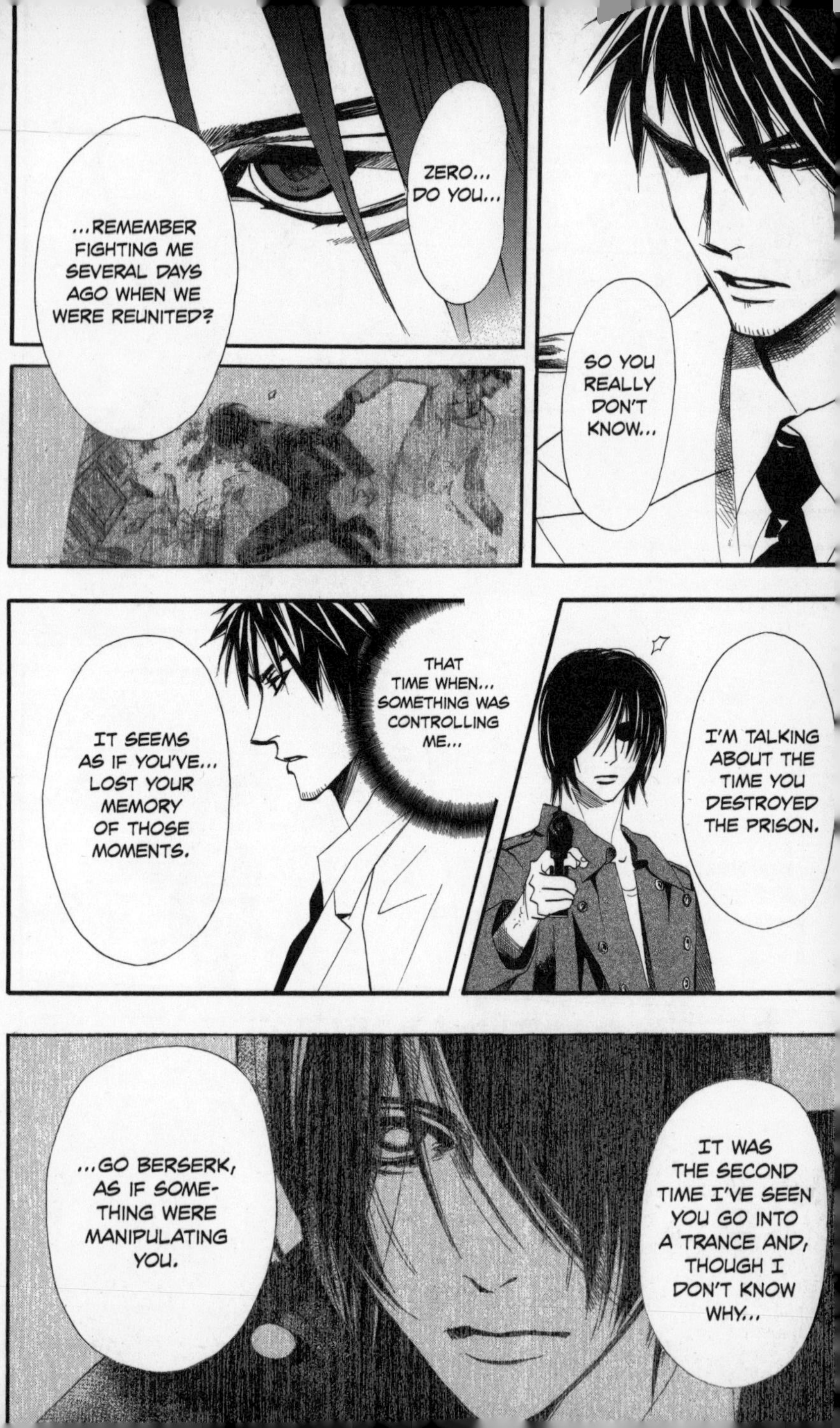
SO YOU REALLY DON'T KNOW...
ZERO... DO YOU...
...REMEMBER FIGHTING ME SEVERAL DAYS AGO WHEN WE WERE REUNITED?
I'M TALKING ABOUT THE TIME YOU DESTROYED THE PRISON.
THAT TIME WHEN... SOMETHING WAS CONTROLLING ME...
IT SEEMS AS IF YOU'VE... LOST YOUR MEMORY OF THOSE MOMENTS.
IT WAS THE SECOND TIME I'VE SEEN YOU GO INTO A TRANCE AND, THOUGH I DON'T KNOW WHY...
...GO BERSERK, AS IF SOME-THING WERE MANIPULATING YOU.

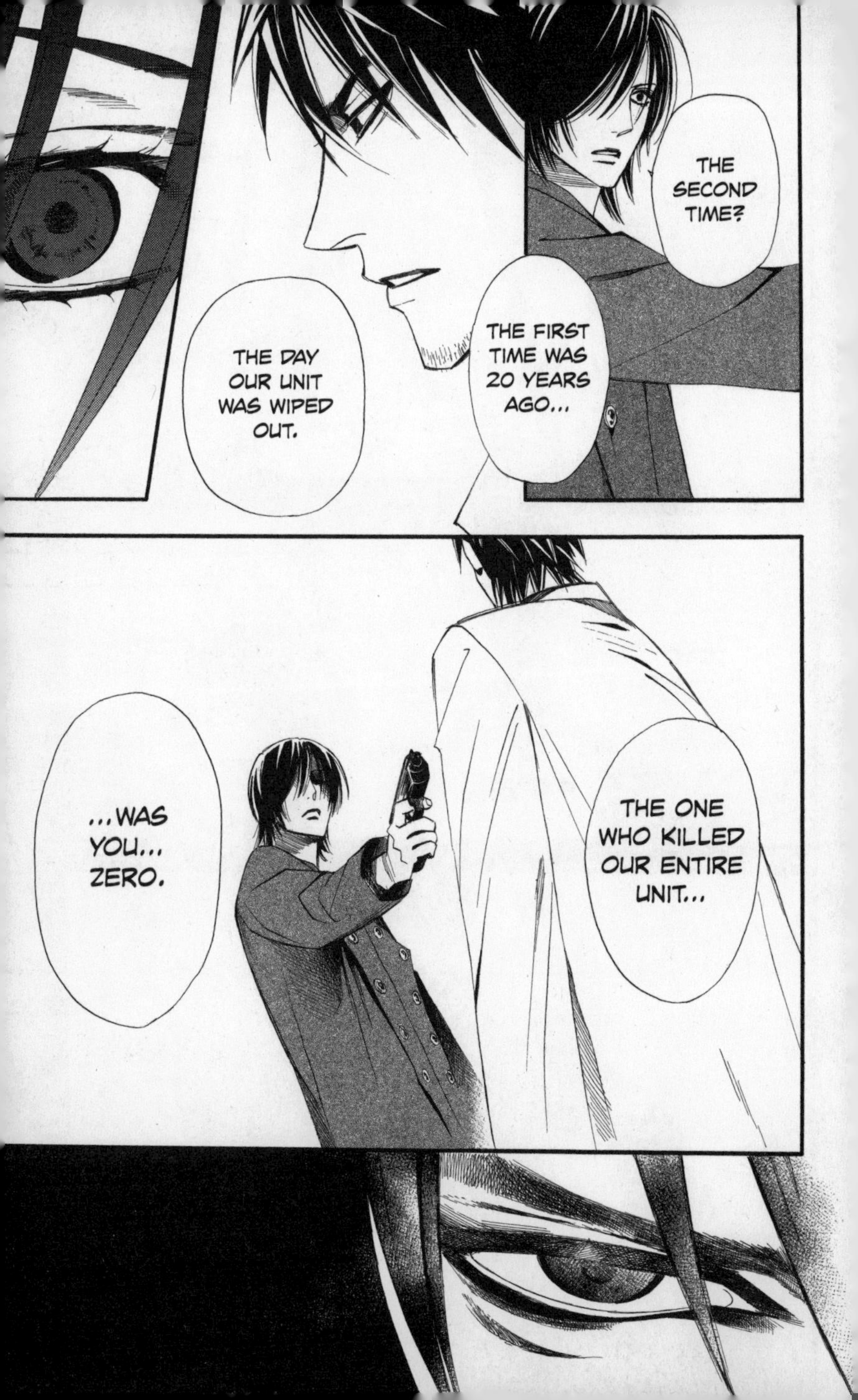
THE SECOND TIME?
THE FIRST TIME WAS 20 YEARS AGO...
THE DAY OUR UNIT WAS WIPED OUT.
THE ONE WHO KILLED OUR ENTIRE UNIT...
...WAS YOU... ZERO.

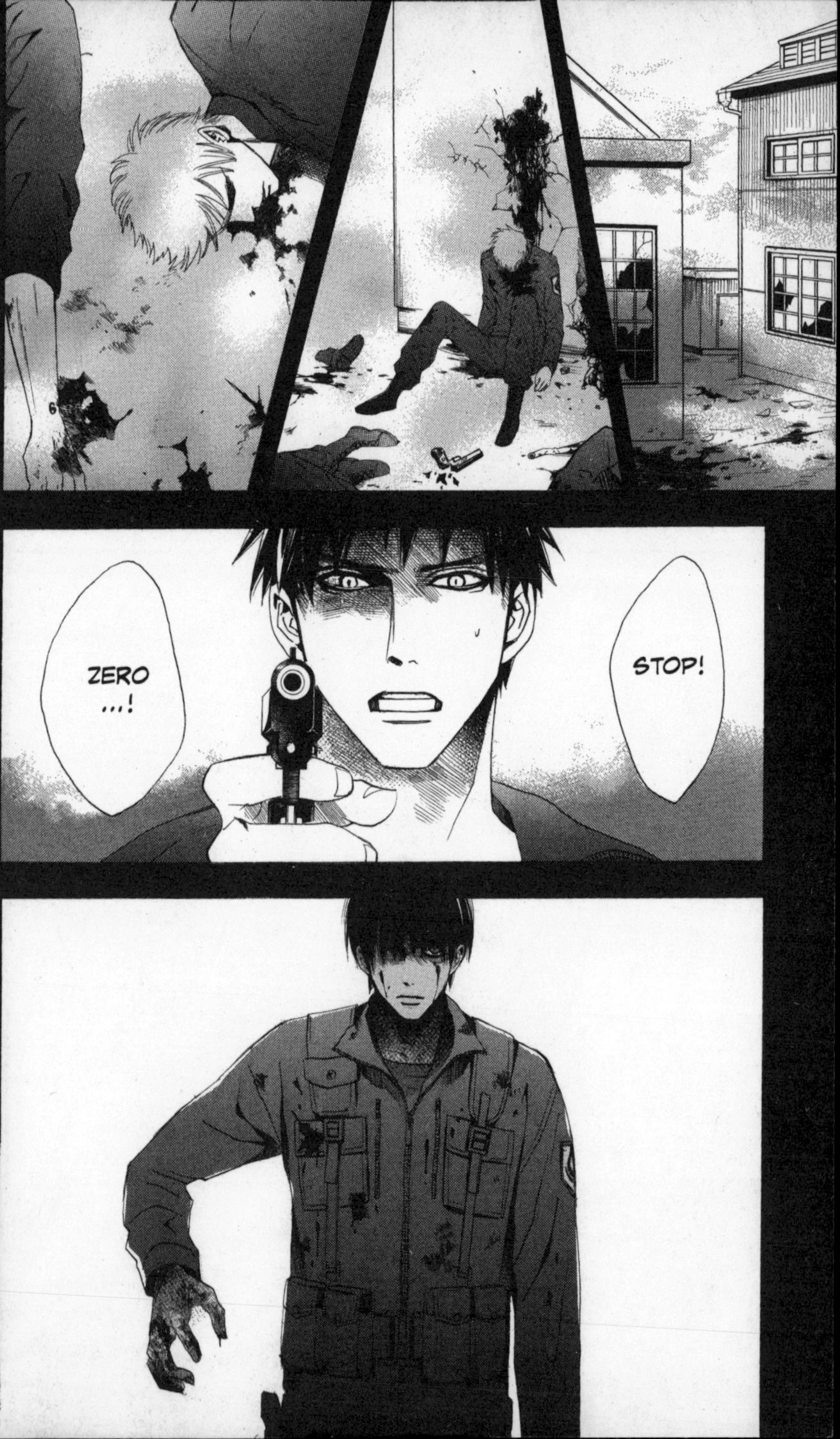
STOP!
ZERO ...!

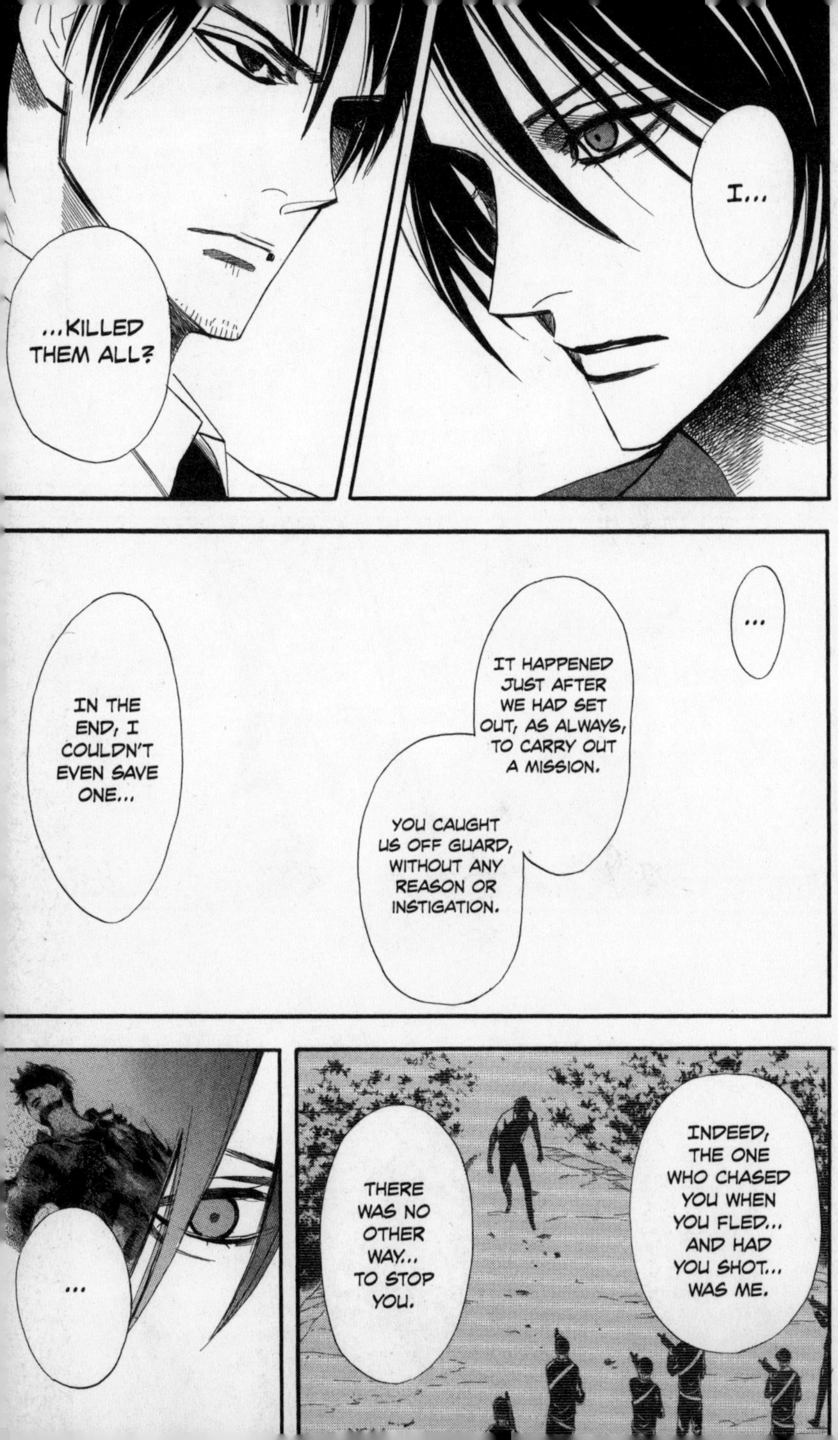
I...
...KILLED THEM ALL?
...
IT HAPPENED JUST AFTER WE HAD SET OUT, AS ALWAYS, TO CARRY OUT A MISSION.
YOU CAUGHT US OFF GUARD, WITHOUT ANY REASON OR INSTIGATION.
IN THE END, I COULDN'T EVEN SAVE ONE...
INDEED, THE ONE WHO CHASED YOU WHEN YOU FLED... AND HAD YOU SHOT... WAS ME.
THERE WAS NO OTHER WAY... TO STOP YOU.
...

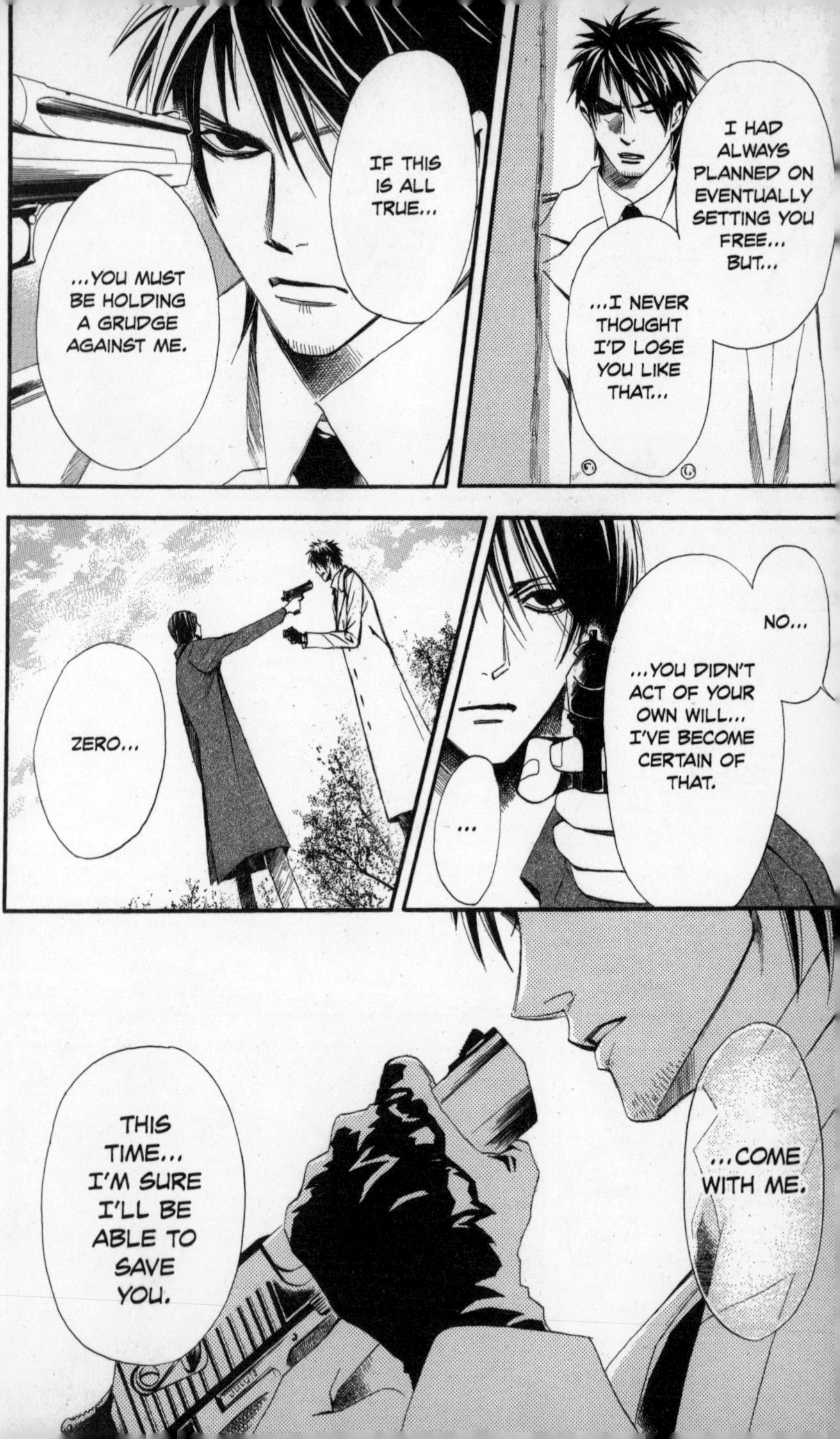
I HAD ALWAYS PLANNED ON EVENTUALLY SETTING YOU FREE... BUT...
...I NEVER THOUGHT I'D LOSE YOU LIKE THAT...
IF THIS IS ALL TRUE...
...YOU MUST BE HOLDING A GRUDGE AGAINST ME.
NO...
...YOU DIDN'T ACT OF YOUR OWN WILL... I'VE BECOME CERTAIN OF THAT.
...
ZERO...
...COME WITH ME.
THIS TIME... I'M SURE I'LL BE ABLE TO SAVE YOU.

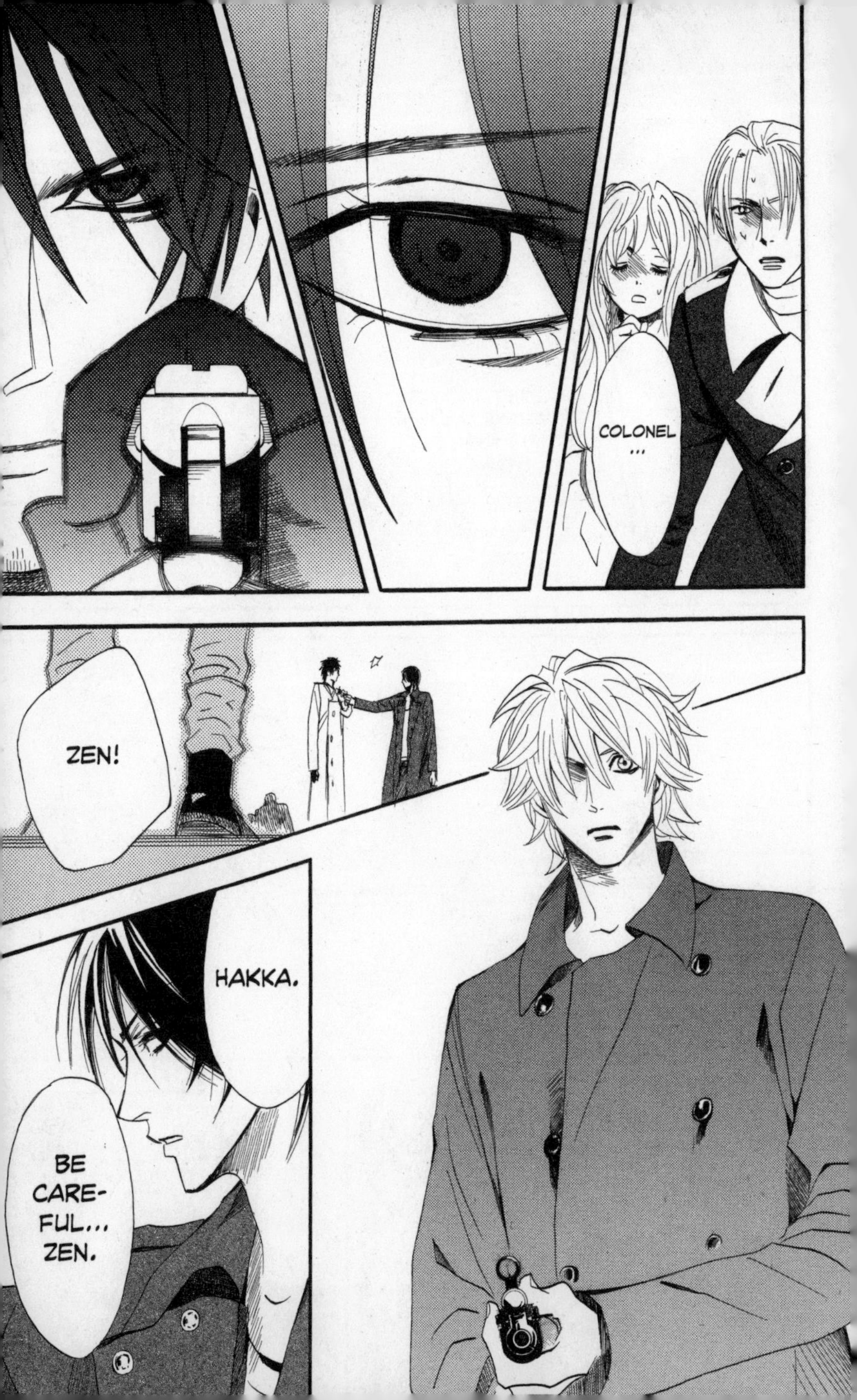
COLONEL...
ZEN!
HAKKA.
BE CARE-FUL... ZEN.

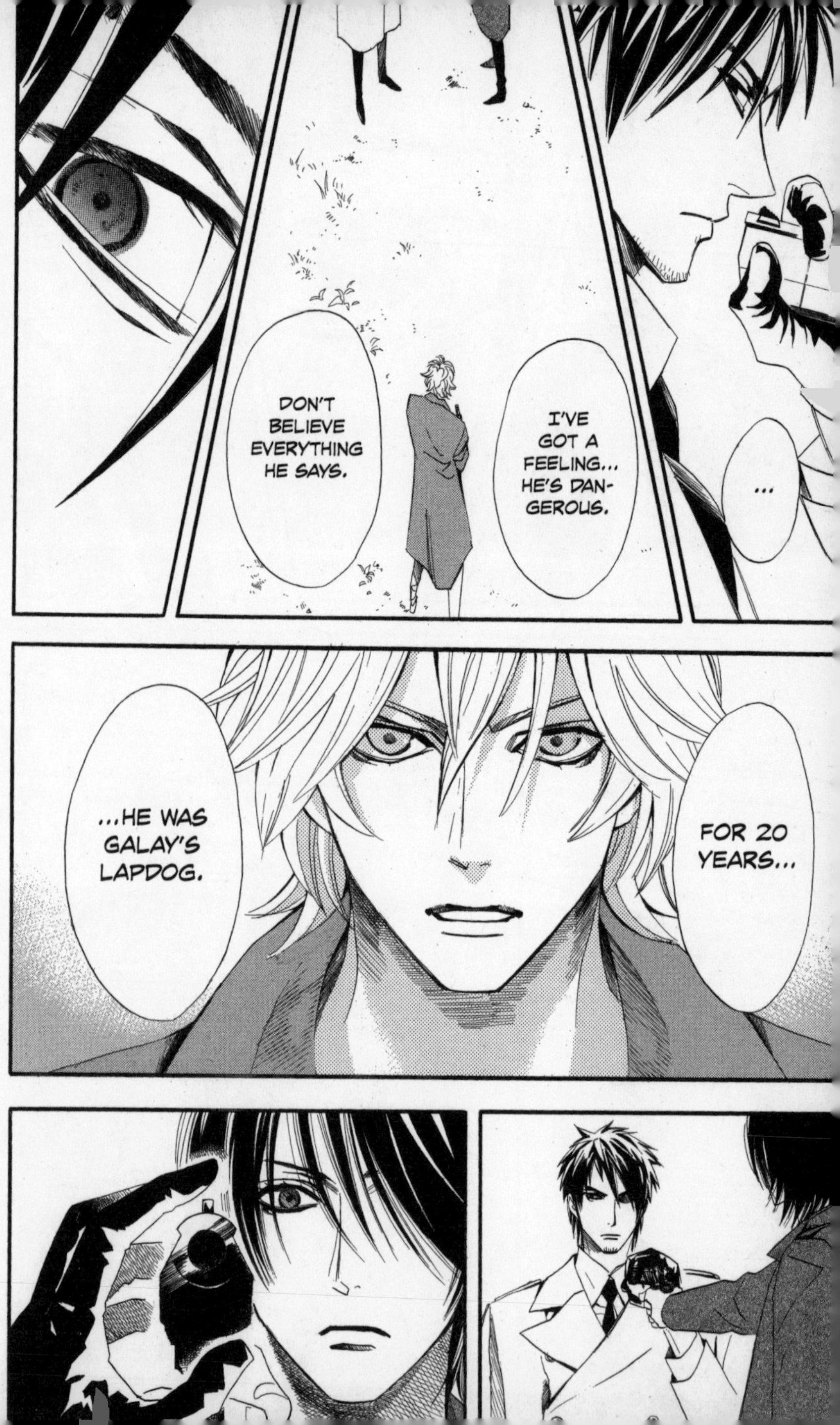
...
I'VE GOT A FEELING... HE'S DAN-GEROUS.
DON'T BELIEVE EVERYTHING HE SAYS.
FOR 20 YEARS...
...HE WAS GALAY'S LAPDOG.

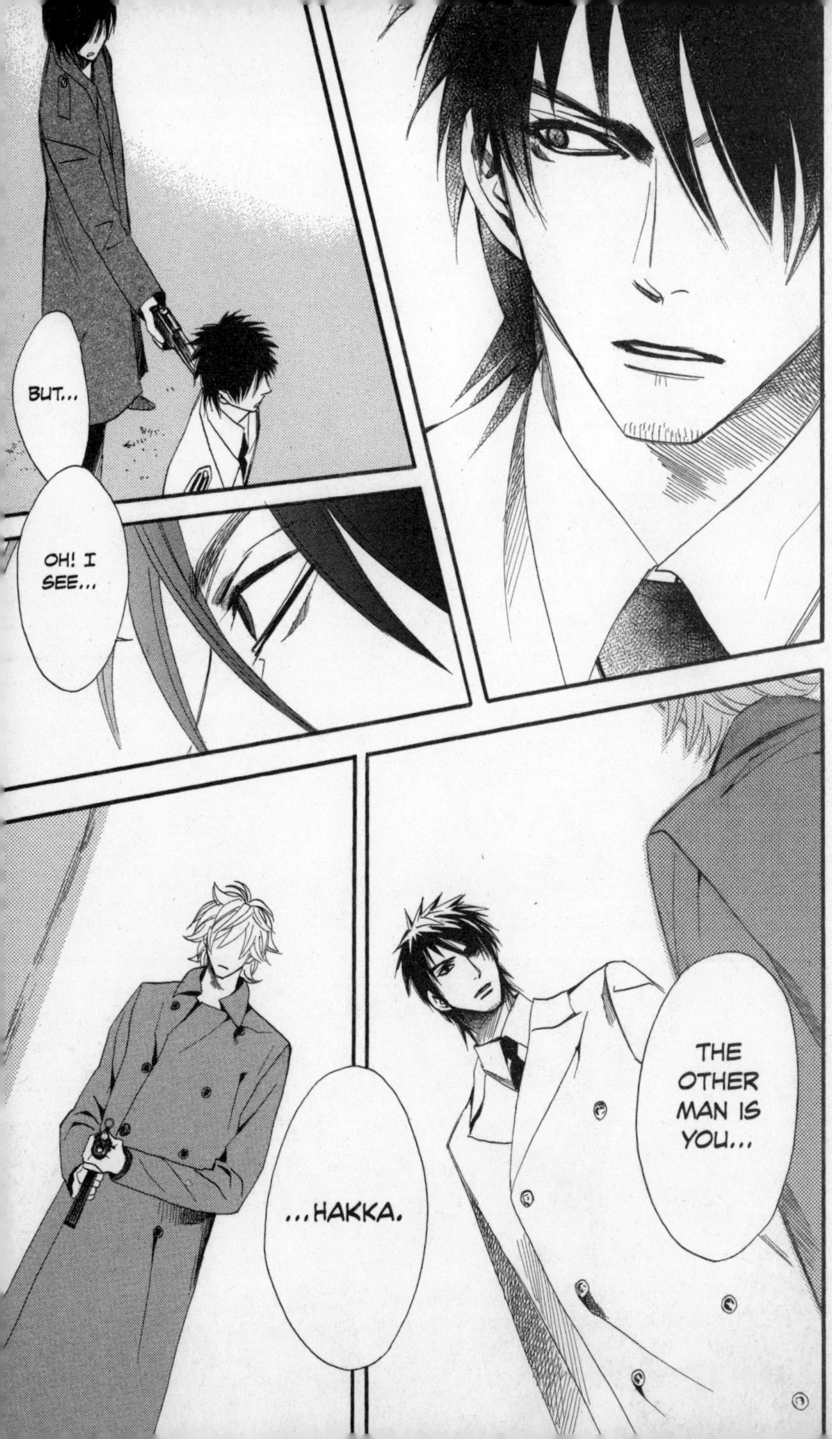
BUT...
OH! I SEE...
THE OTHER MAN IS YOU...
...HAKKA.

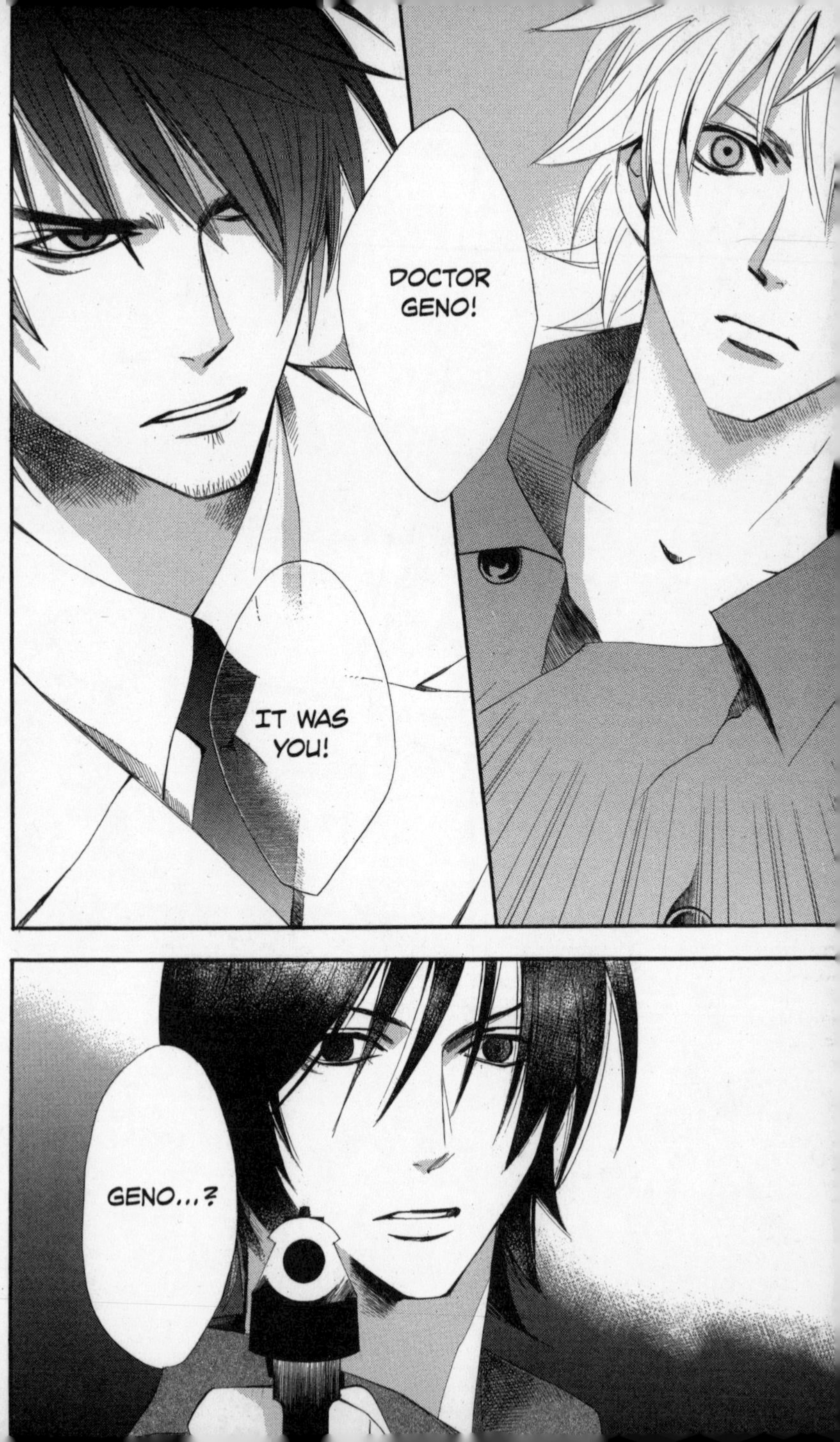
DOCTOR GENO!
IT WAS YOU!
GENO...?

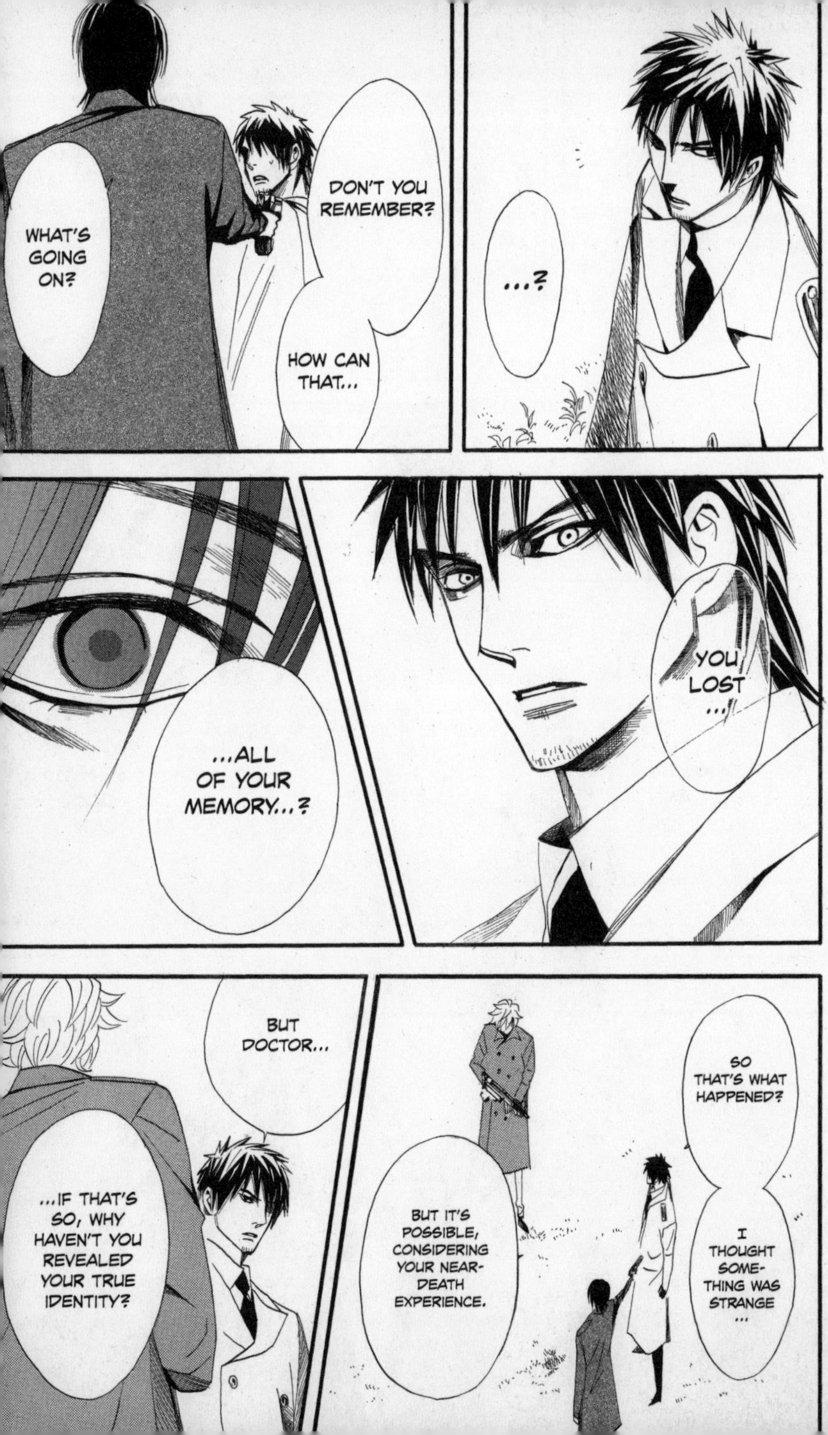
...?
DON'T YOU REMEMBER?
HOW CAN THAT...
WHAT'S GOING ON?
YOU LOST ...!
...ALL OF YOUR MEMORY...?
SO THAT'S WHAT HAPPENED?
I THOUGHT SOME-THING WAS STRANGE ...
BUT IT'S POSSIBLE, CONSIDERING YOUR NEAR-DEATH EXPERIENCE.
BUT DOCTOR...
...IF THAT'S SO, WHY HAVEN'T YOU REVEALED YOUR TRUE IDENTITY?

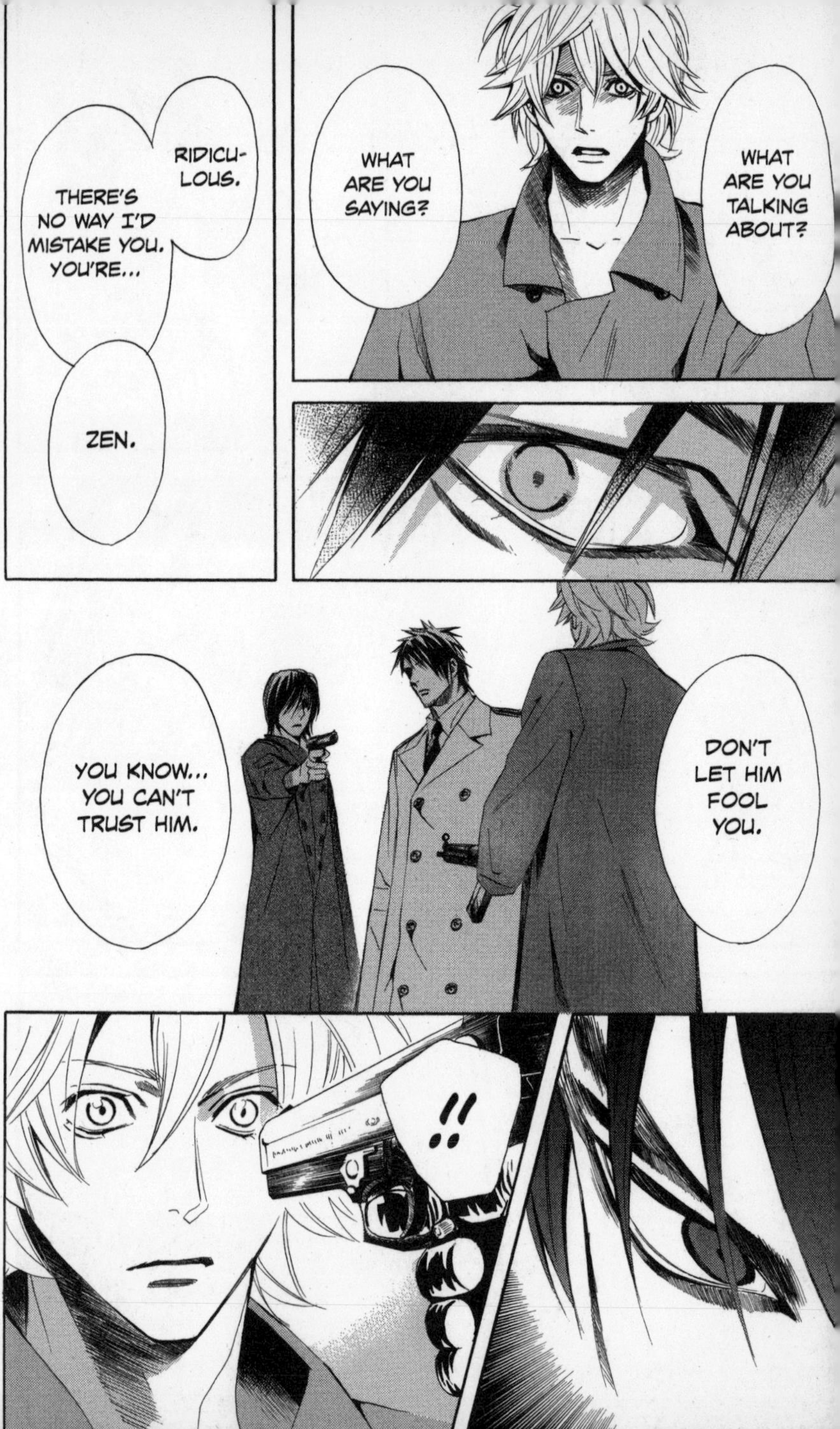
WHAT ARE YOU TALKING ABOUT?
WHAT ARE YOU SAYING?
RIDICU-LOUS.
THERE'S NO WAY I'D MISTAKE YOU. YOU'RE...
ZEN.
DON'T LET HIM FOOL YOU.
YOU KNOW... YOU CAN'T TRUST HIM.
!!

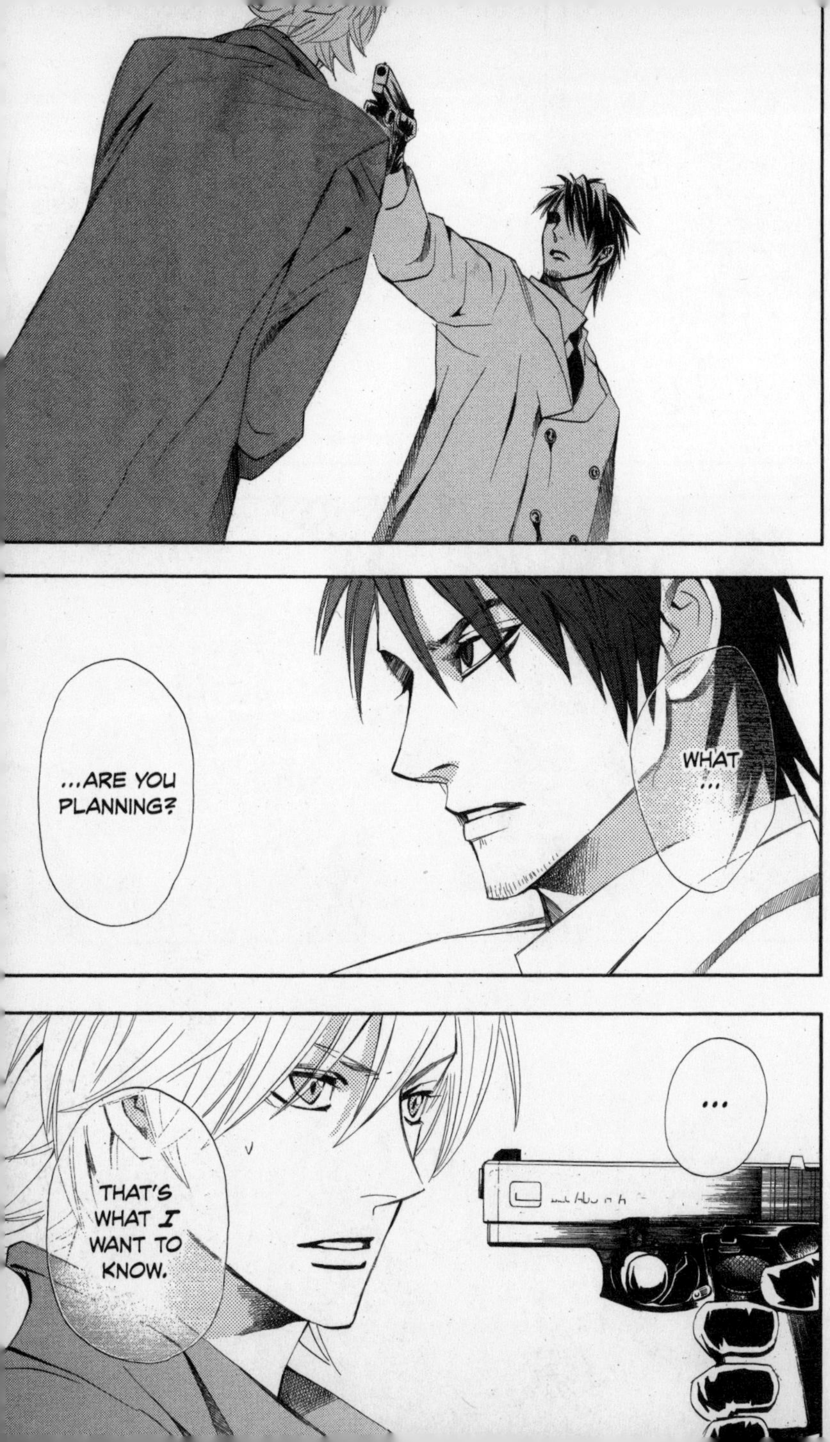
WHAT ...
...ARE YOU PLANNING?
...
THAT'S WHAT *I* WANT TO KNOW.

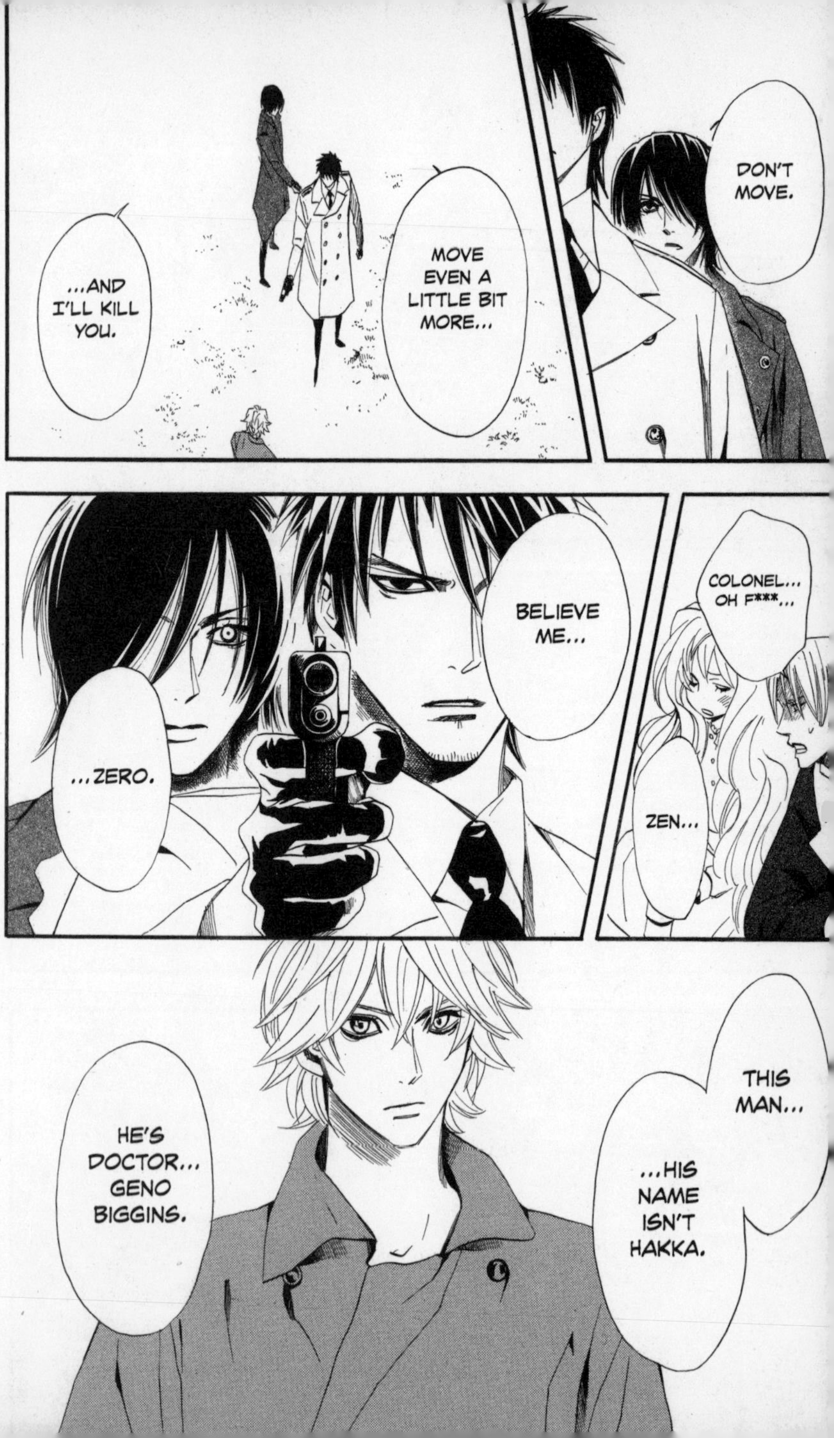
DON'T MOVE.
MOVE EVEN A LITTLE BIT MORE...
...AND I'LL KILL YOU.
COLONEL... OH F***...
ZEN...
BELIEVE ME...
...ZERO.
THIS MAN...
...HIS NAME ISN'T HAKKA.
HE'S DOCTOR... GENO BIGGINS.

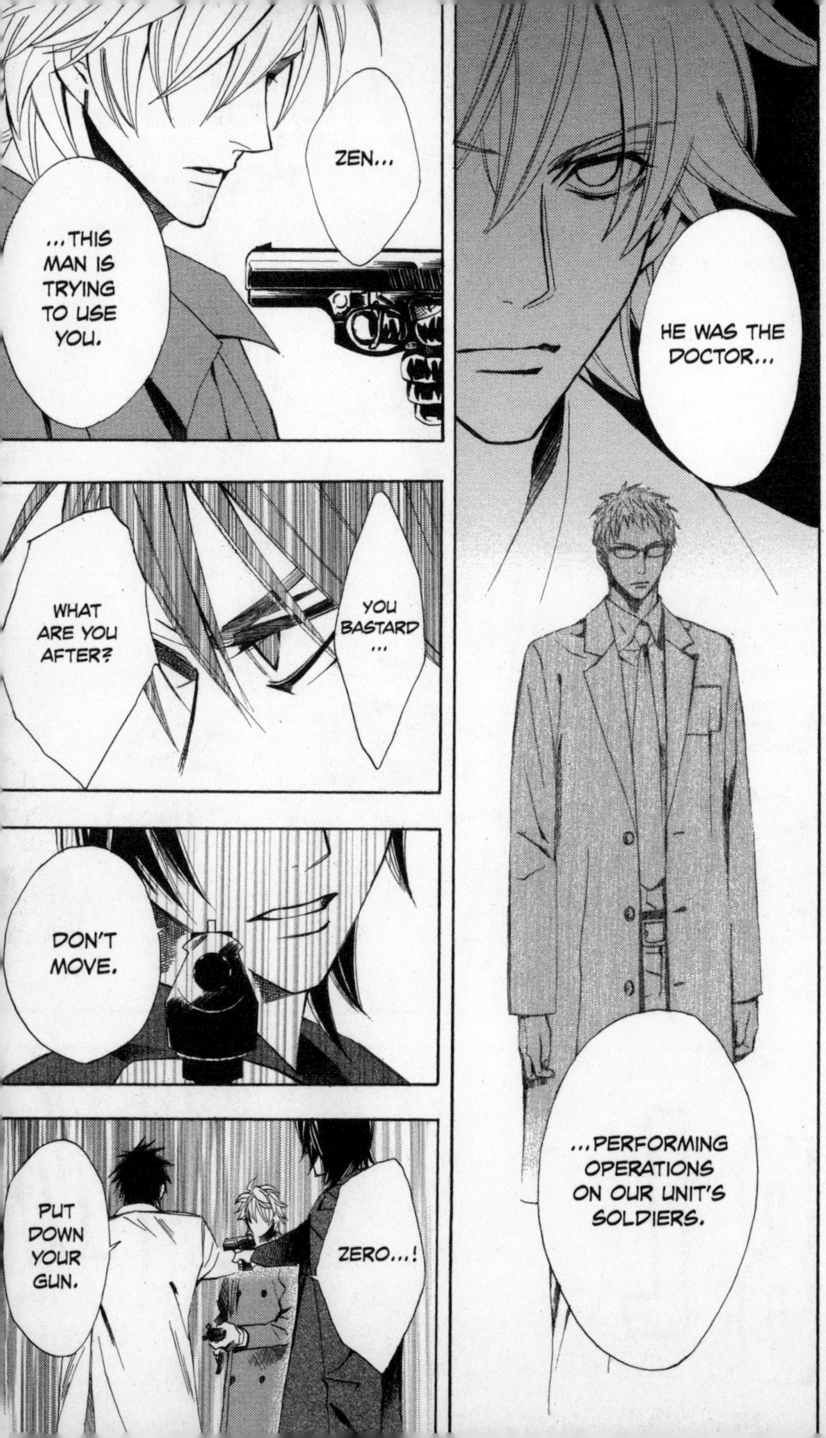
HE WAS THE DOCTOR...
...PERFORMING OPERATIONS ON OUR UNIT'S SOLDIERS.
ZEN...
...THIS MAN IS TRYING TO USE YOU.
YOU BASTARD...
WHAT ARE YOU AFTER?
DON'T MOVE.
ZERO...!
PUT DOWN YOUR GUN.

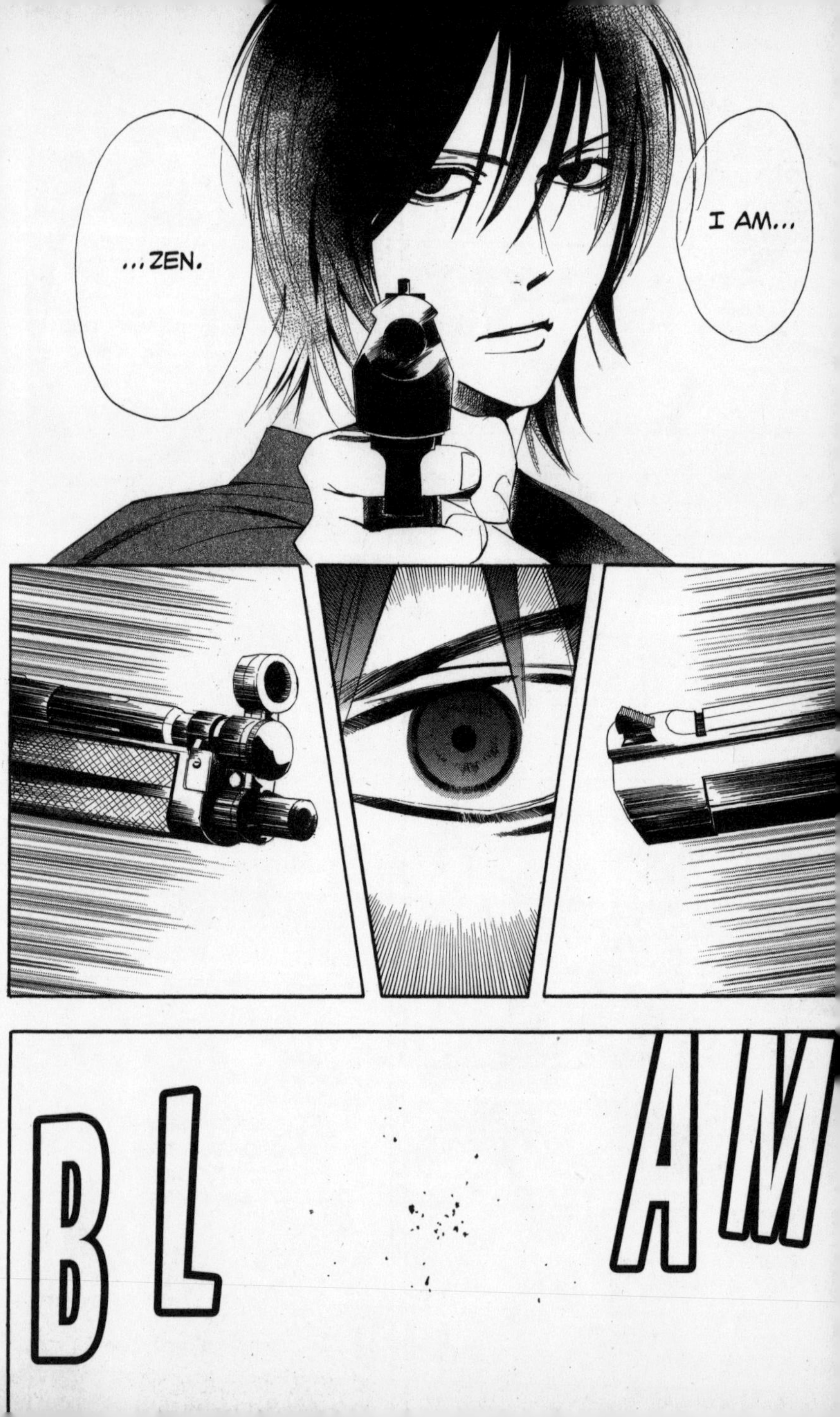
I AM...
...ZEN.
BLAM

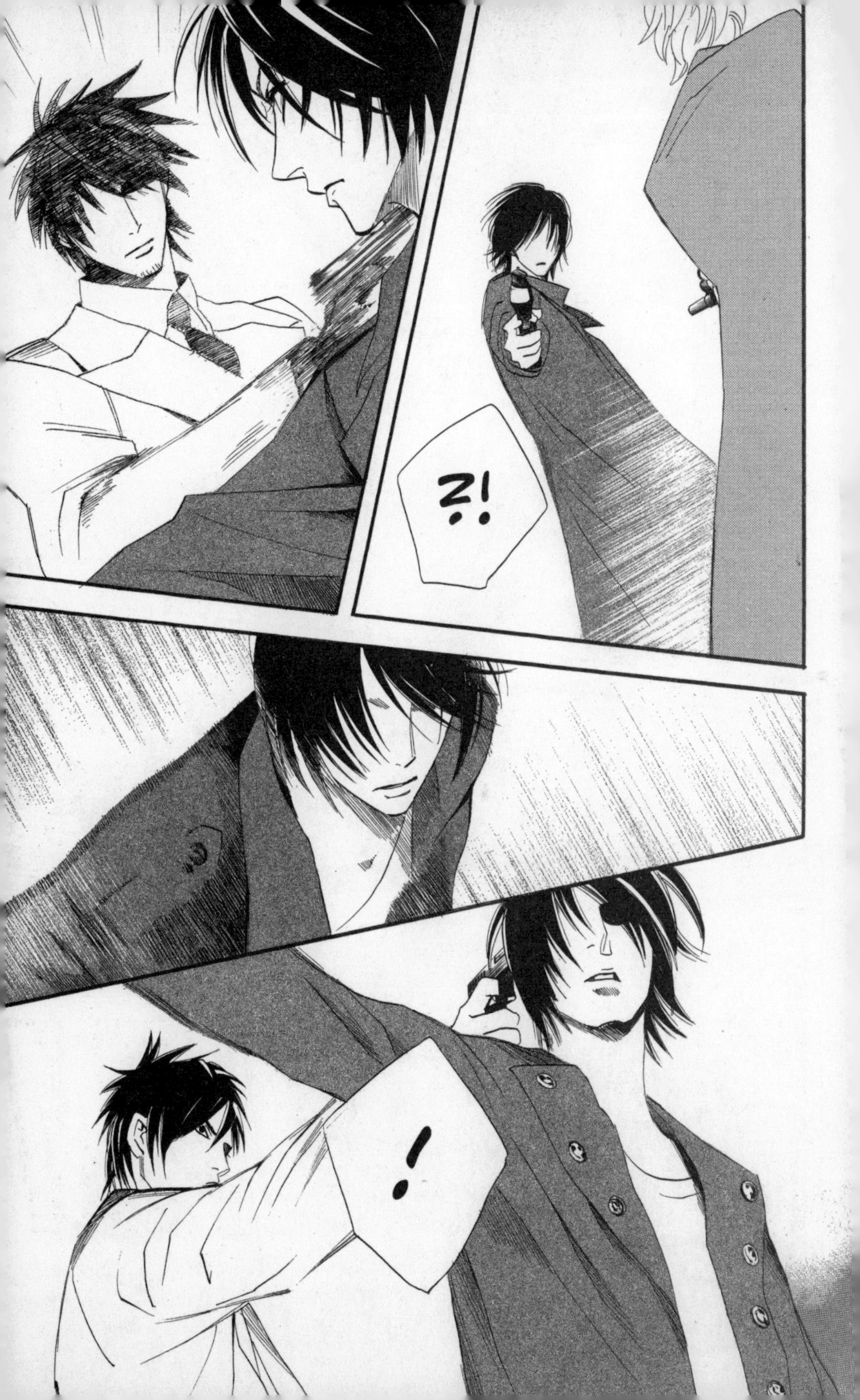
?!
!

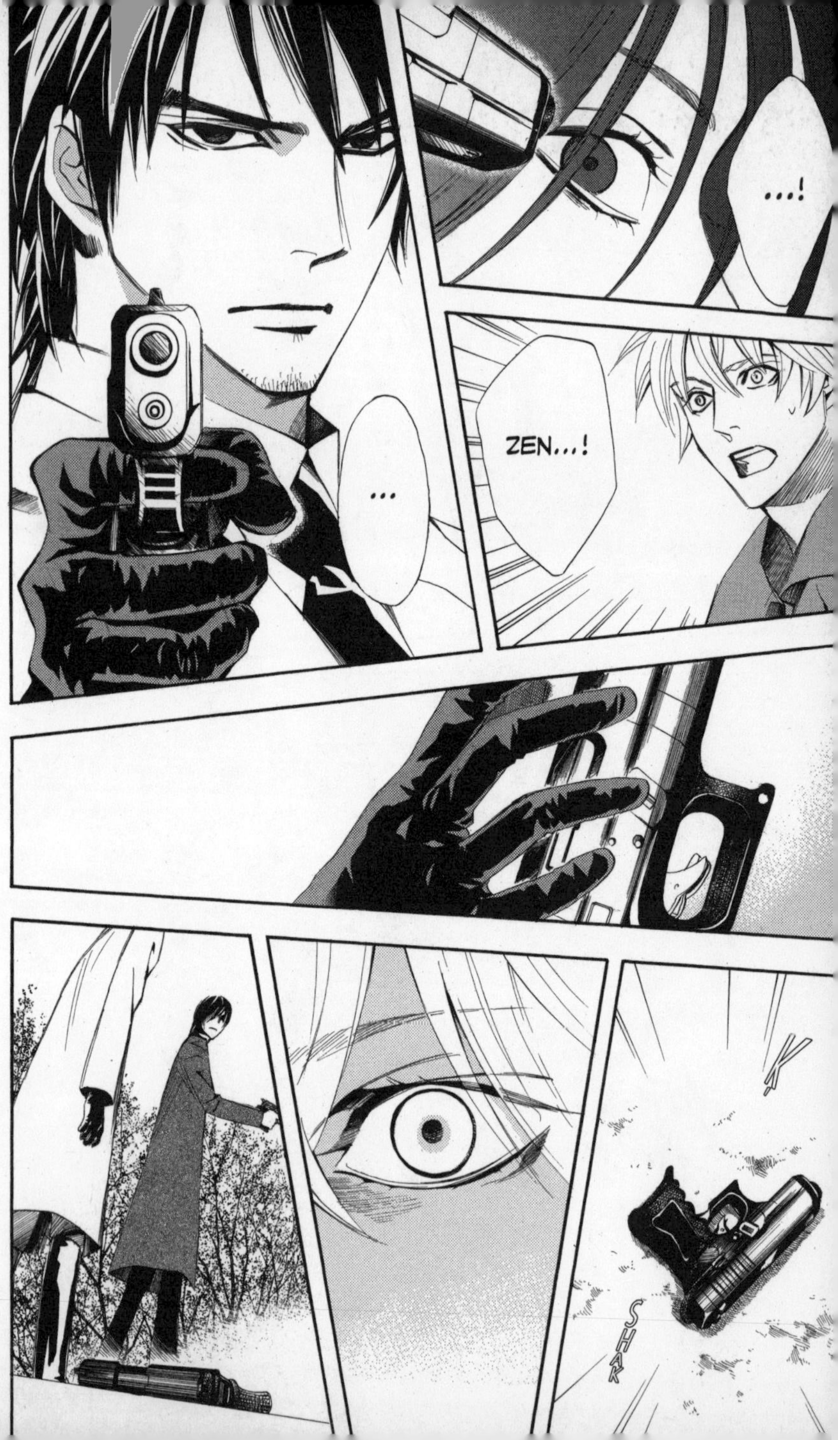
...!
ZEN...!
...
K
SHAK

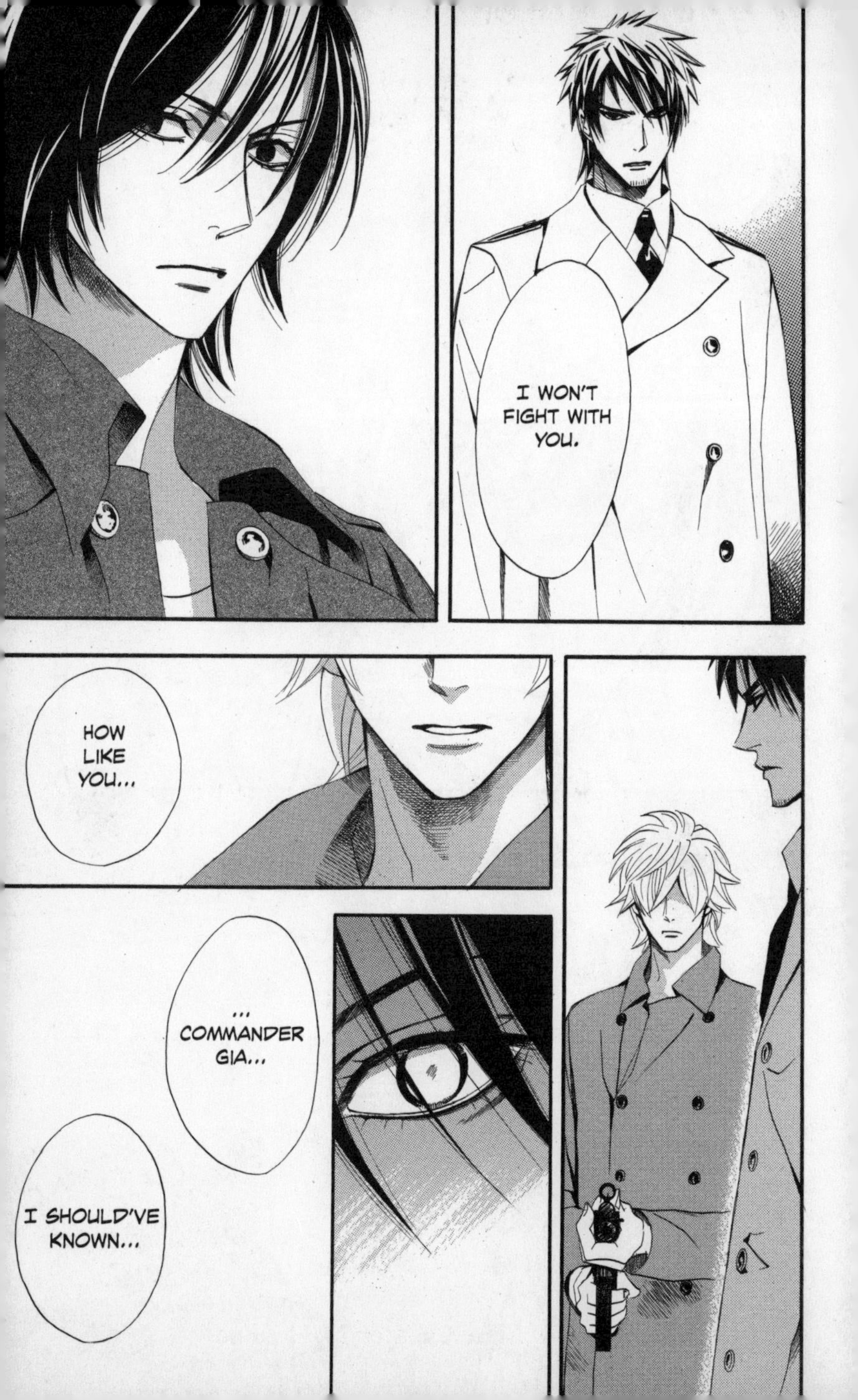
I WON'T FIGHT WITH YOU.
HOW LIKE YOU...
...COMMANDER GIA...
I SHOULD'VE KNOWN...

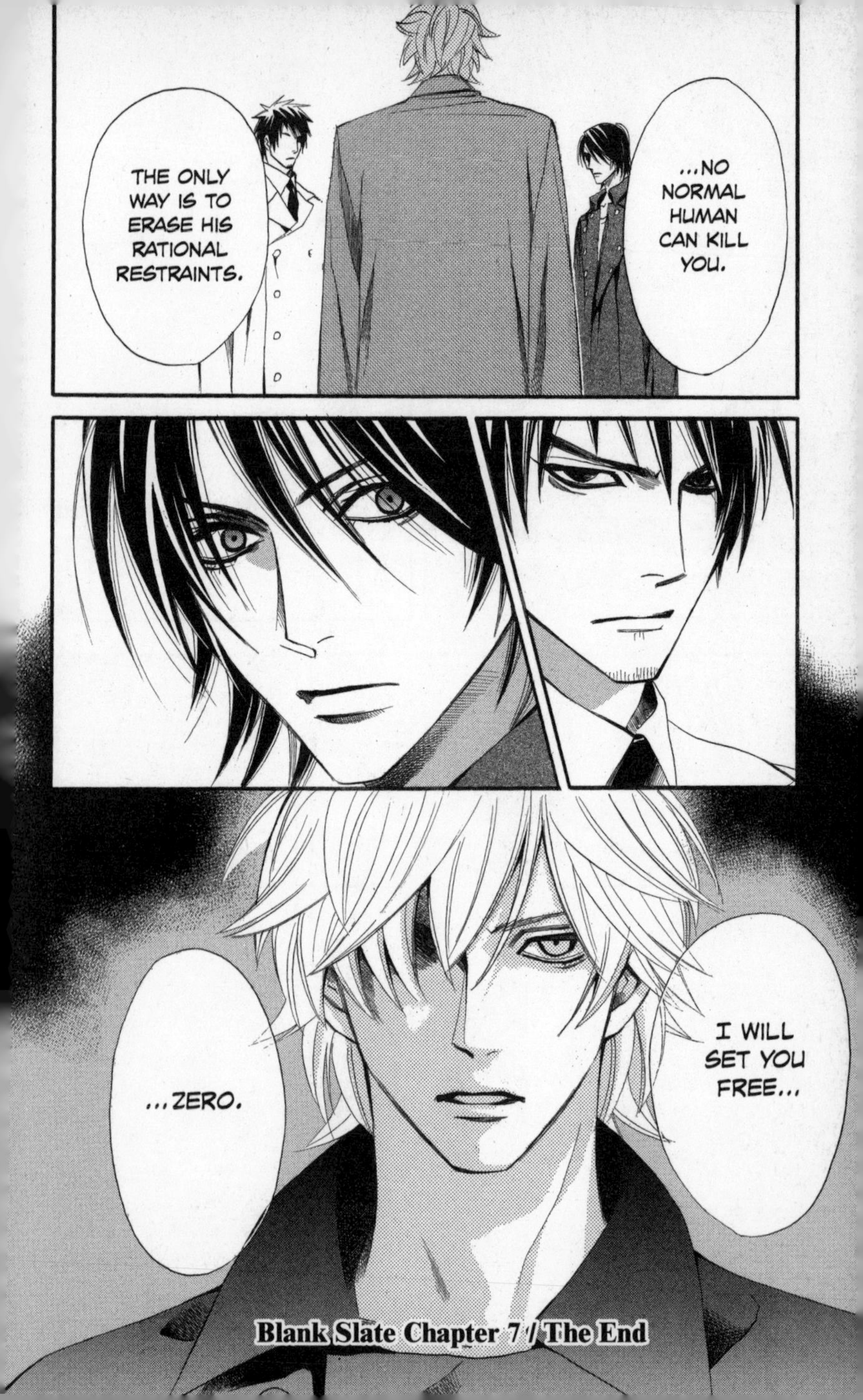
...NO NORMAL HUMAN CAN KILL YOU.
THE ONLY WAY IS TO ERASE HIS RATIONAL RESTRAINTS.
I WILL SET YOU FREE...
...ZERO.
Blank Slate Chapter 7 / The End

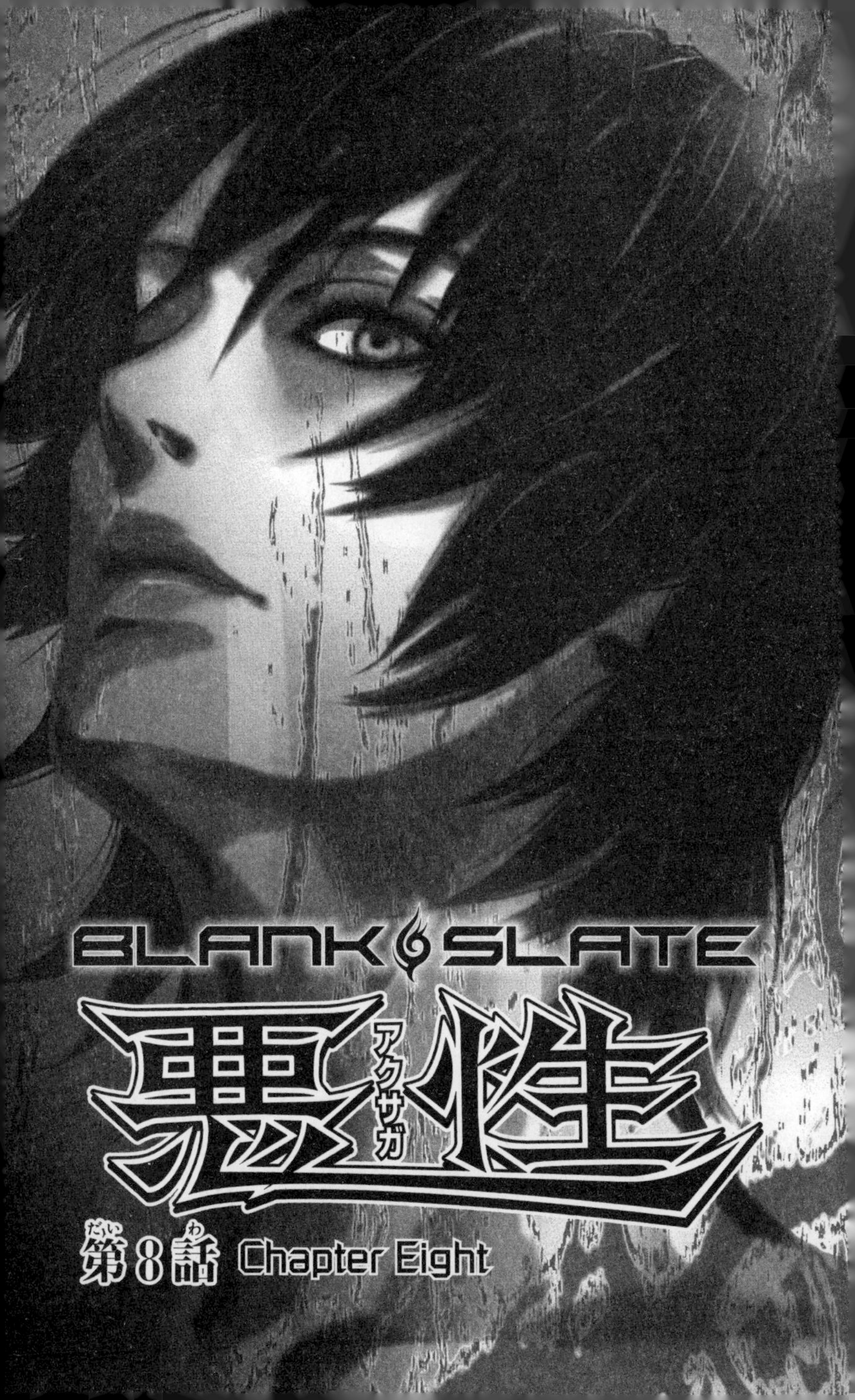
BLANK SLATE
悪性（アクサガ）
第8話（だいわ） Chapter Eight

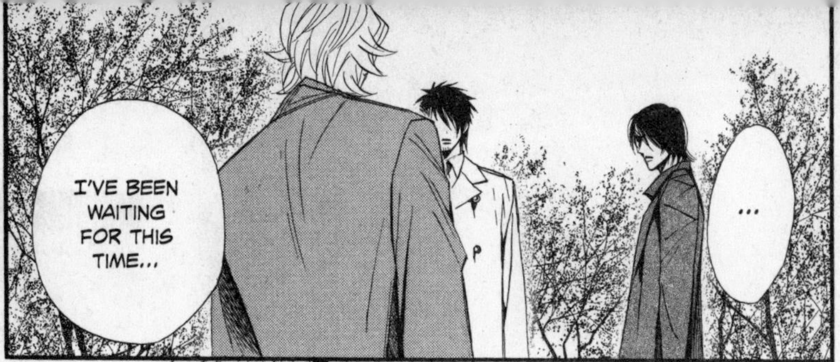
...
I'VE BEEN WAITING FOR THIS TIME...
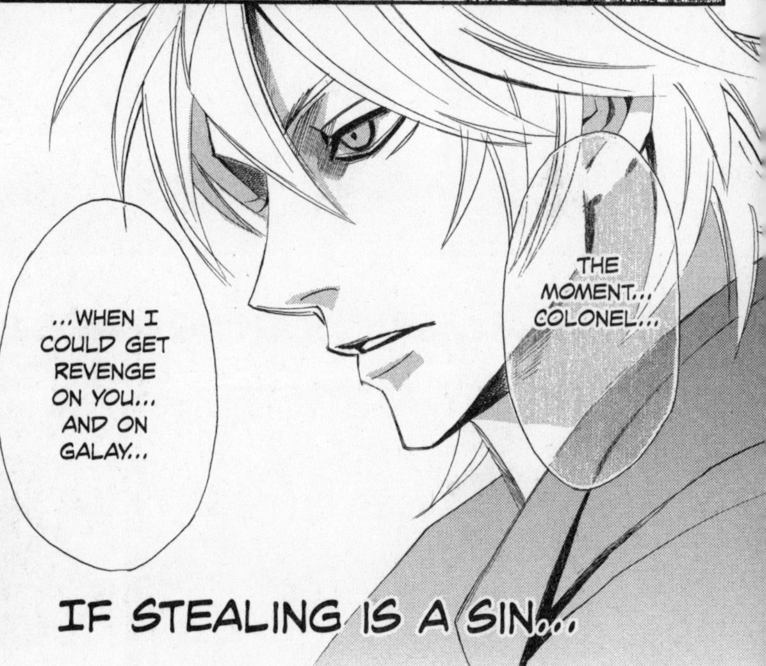
THE MOMENT... COLONEL...
...WHEN I COULD GET REVENGE ON YOU... AND ON GALAY...
IF STEALING IS A SIN...

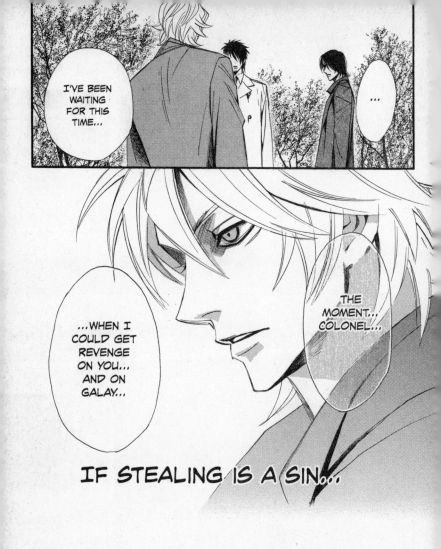

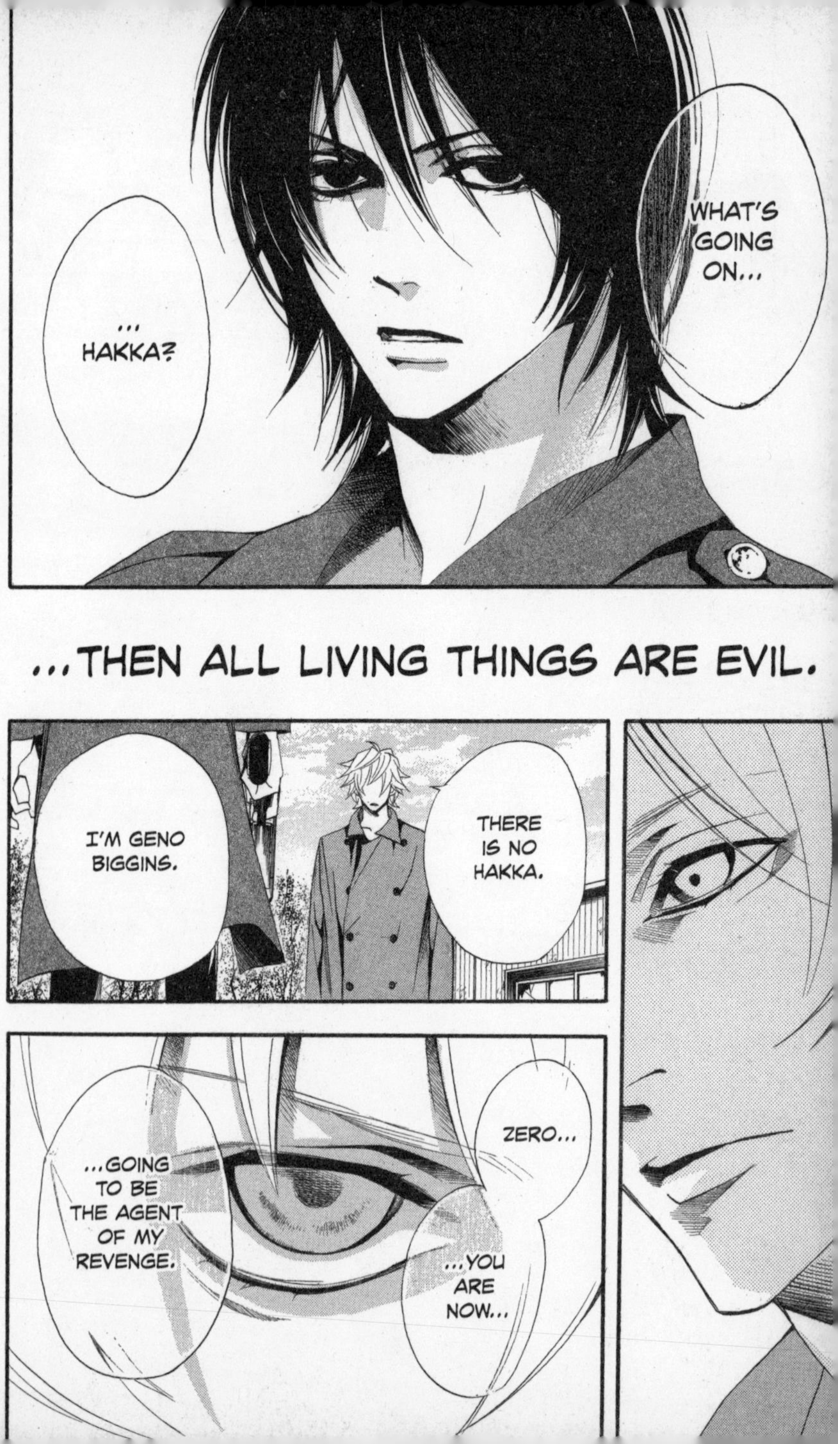
WHAT'S GOING ON...
...HAKKA?
...THEN ALL LIVING THINGS ARE EVIL.
THERE IS NO HAKKA.
I'M GENO BIGGINS.
ZERO...
...YOU ARE NOW...
...GOING TO BE THE AGENT OF MY REVENGE.

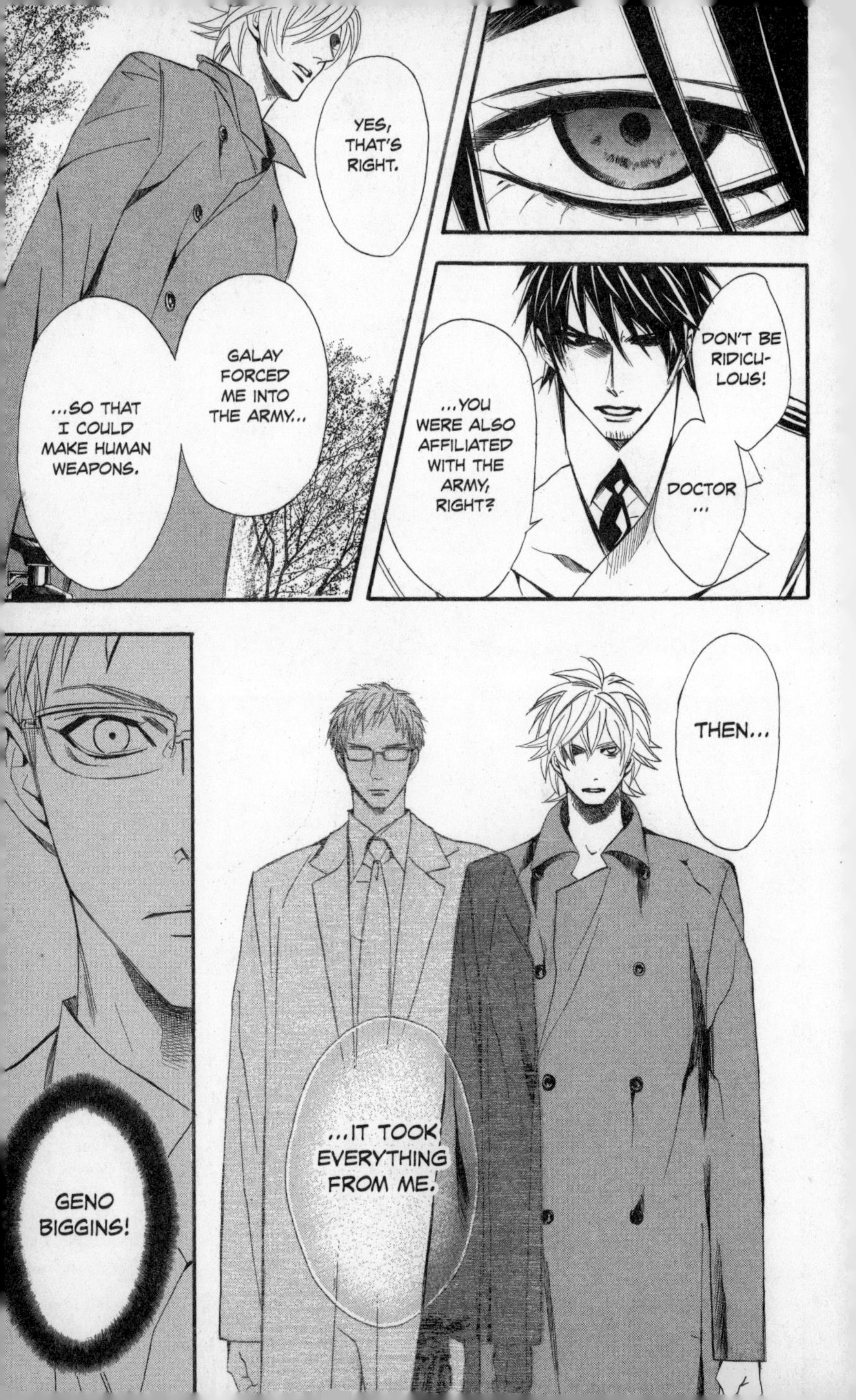
DON'T BE RIDICULOUS!
DOCTOR...
...YOU WERE ALSO AFFILIATED WITH THE ARMY, RIGHT?
YES, THAT'S RIGHT.
GALAY FORCED ME INTO THE ARMY...
...SO THAT I COULD MAKE HUMAN WEAPONS.
THEN...
...IT TOOK EVERYTHING FROM ME.
GENO BIGGINS!

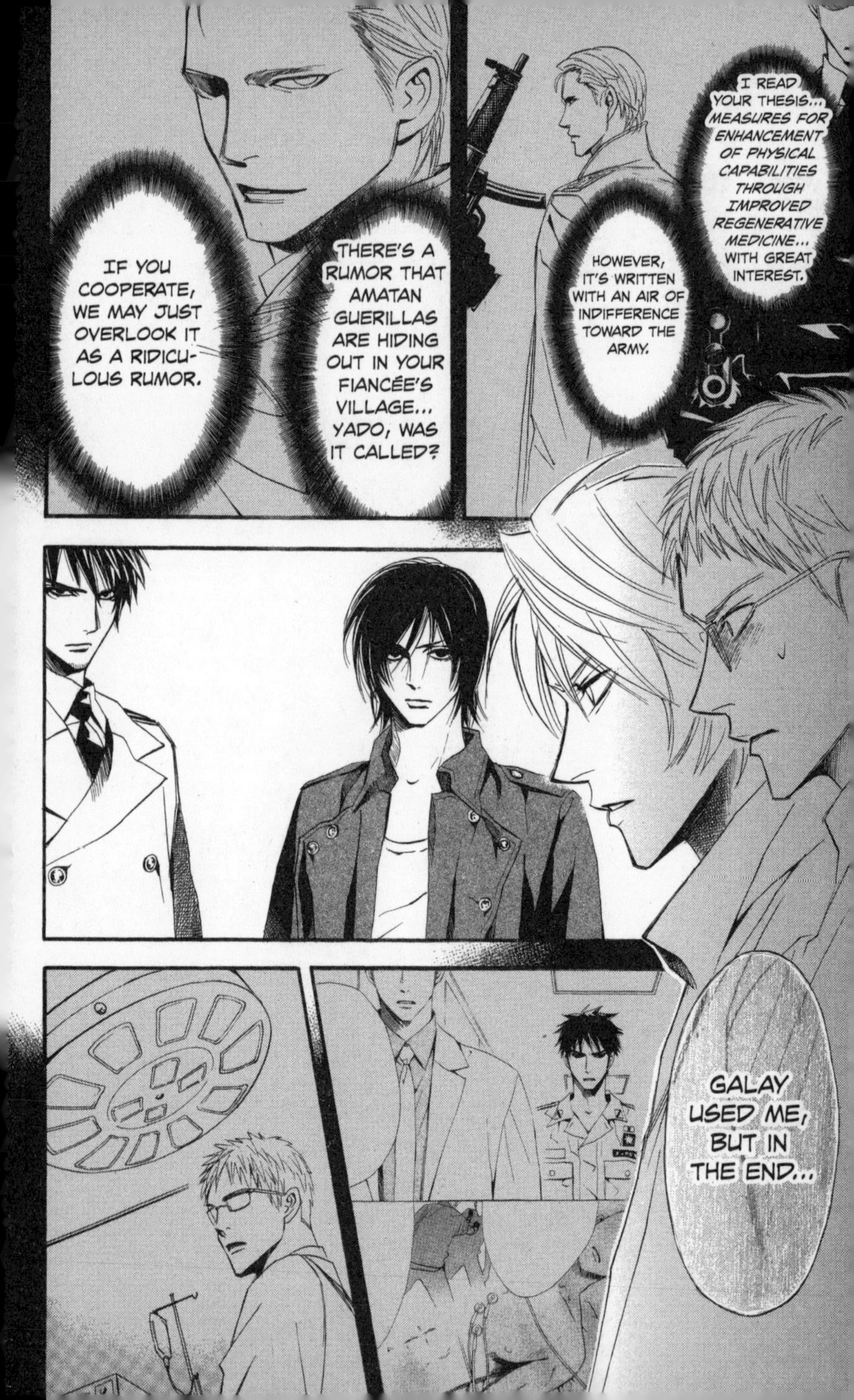
I READ YOUR THESIS... MEASURES FOR ENHANCEMENT OF PHYSICAL CAPABILITIES THROUGH IMPROVED REGENERATIVE MEDICINE... WITH GREAT INTEREST.
HOWEVER, IT'S WRITTEN WITH AN AIR OF INDIFFERENCE TOWARD THE ARMY.
THERE'S A RUMOR THAT AMATAN GUERILLAS ARE HIDING OUT IN YOUR FIANCÉE'S VILLAGE... YADO, WAS IT CALLED?
IF YOU COOPERATE, WE MAY JUST OVERLOOK IT AS A RIDICULOUS RUMOR.
GALAY USED ME, BUT IN THE END...

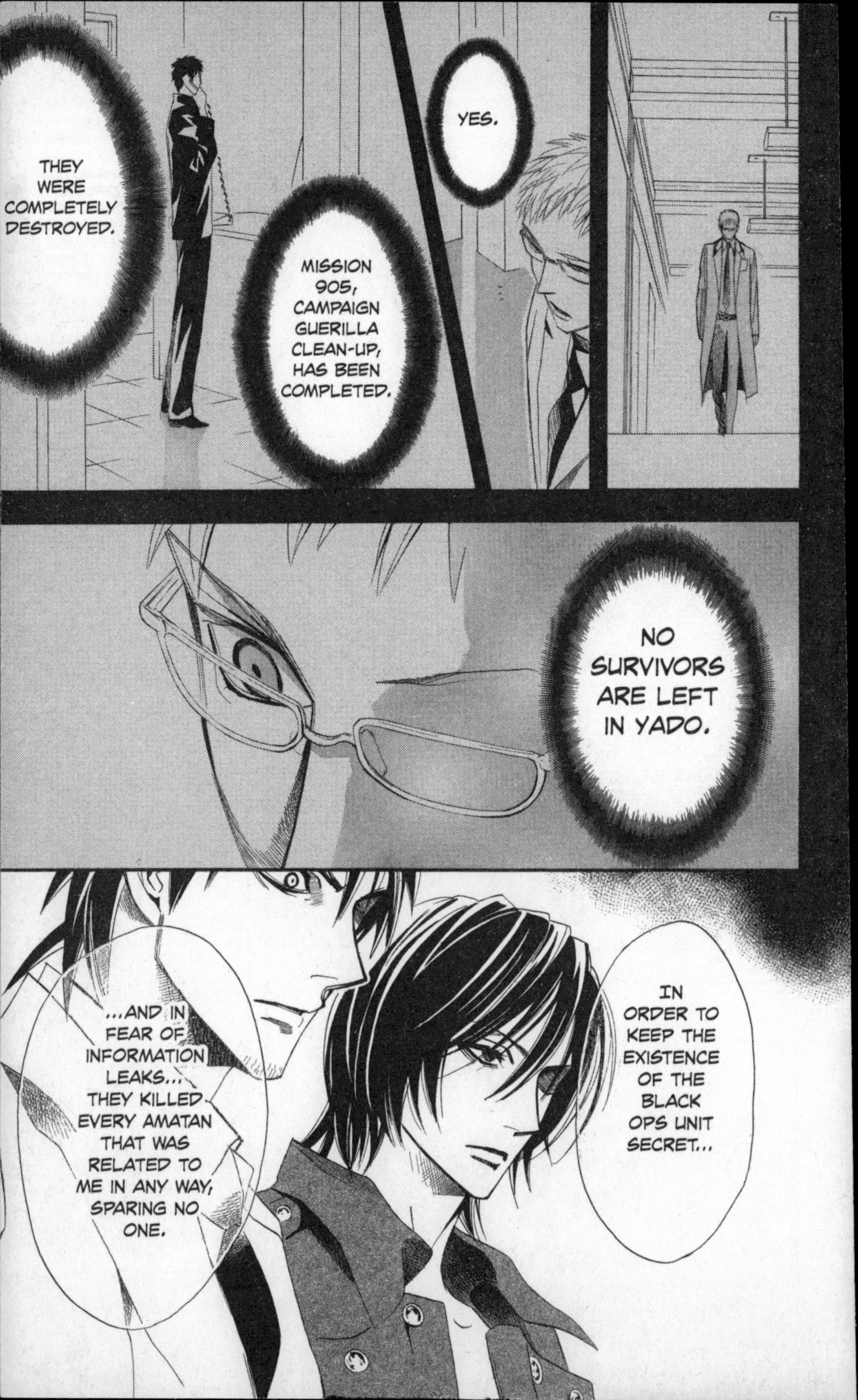
YES.
MISSION 905, CAMPAIGN GUERILLA CLEAN-UP, HAS BEEN COMPLETED.
THEY WERE COMPLETELY DESTROYED.
NO SURVIVORS ARE LEFT IN YADO.
IN ORDER TO KEEP THE EXISTENCE OF THE BLACK OPS UNIT SECRET...
...AND IN FEAR OF INFORMATION LEAKS... THEY KILLED EVERY AMATAN THAT WAS RELATED TO ME IN ANY WAY, SPARING NO ONE.

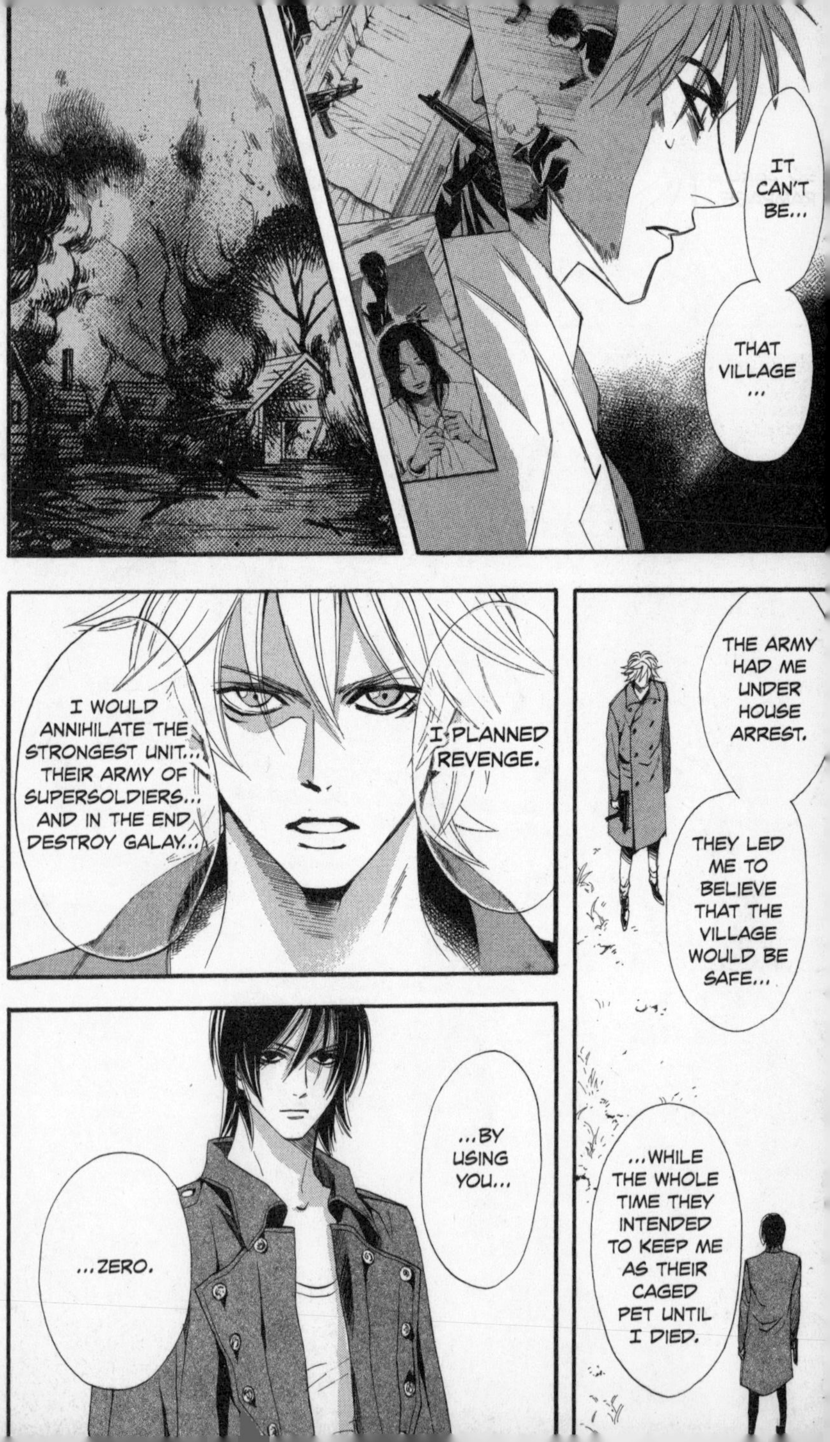
IT CAN'T BE...
THAT VILLAGE ...
THE ARMY HAD ME UNDER HOUSE ARREST.
THEY LED ME TO BELIEVE THAT THE VILLAGE WOULD BE SAFE...
...WHILE THE WHOLE TIME THEY INTENDED TO KEEP ME AS THEIR CAGED PET UNTIL I DIED.
I PLANNED REVENGE.
I WOULD ANNIHILATE THE STRONGEST UNIT... THEIR ARMY OF SUPERSOLDIERS... AND IN THE END DESTROY GALAY...
...BY USING YOU...
...ZERO.

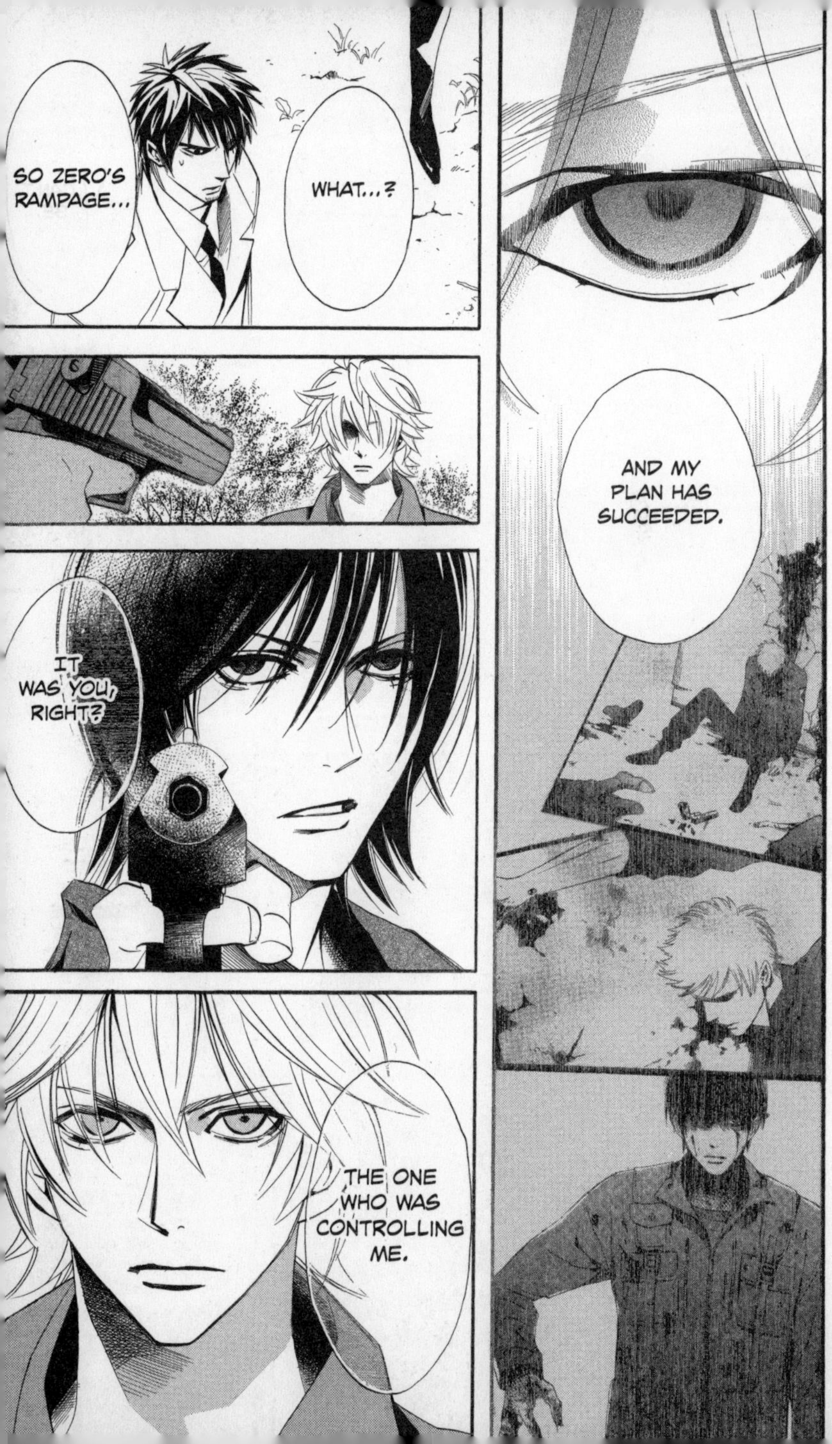
AND MY PLAN HAS SUCCEEDED.
WHAT...?
SO ZERO'S RAMPAGE...
IT WAS YOU, RIGHT?
THE ONE WHO WAS CONTROLLING ME.

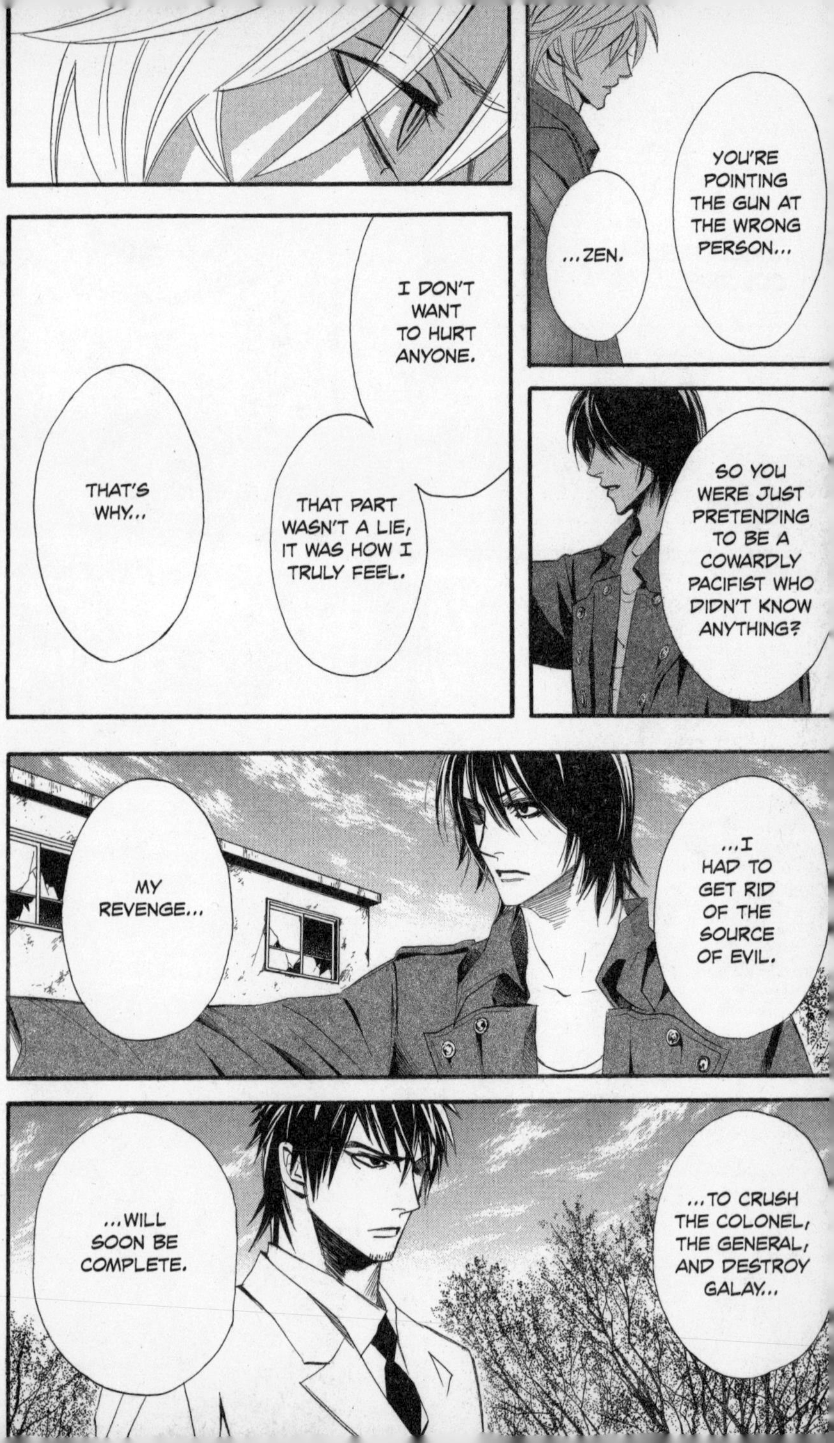
YOU'RE POINTING THE GUN AT THE WRONG PERSON...
...ZEN.
SO YOU WERE JUST PRETENDING TO BE A COWARDLY PACIFIST WHO DIDN'T KNOW ANYTHING?
I DON'T WANT TO HURT ANYONE.
THAT PART WASN'T A LIE, IT WAS HOW I TRULY FEEL.
THAT'S WHY...
...I HAD TO GET RID OF THE SOURCE OF EVIL.
MY REVENGE...
...TO CRUSH THE COLONEL, THE GENERAL, AND DESTROY GALAY...
...WILL SOON BE COMPLETE.

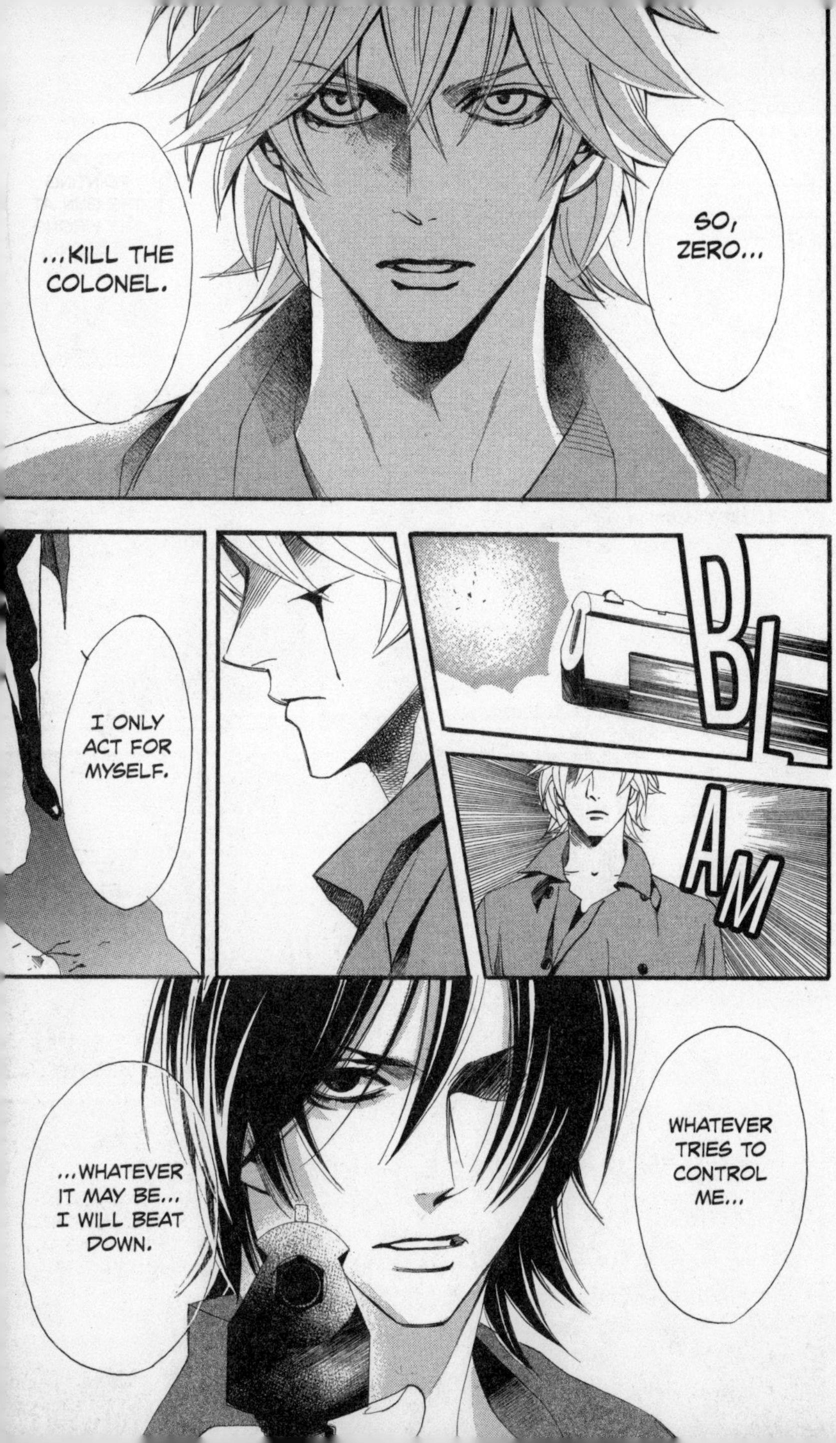
SO, ZERO...
...KILL THE COLONEL.
BLAM
I ONLY ACT FOR MYSELF.
WHATEVER TRIES TO CONTROL ME...
...WHATEVER IT MAY BE... I WILL BEAT DOWN.

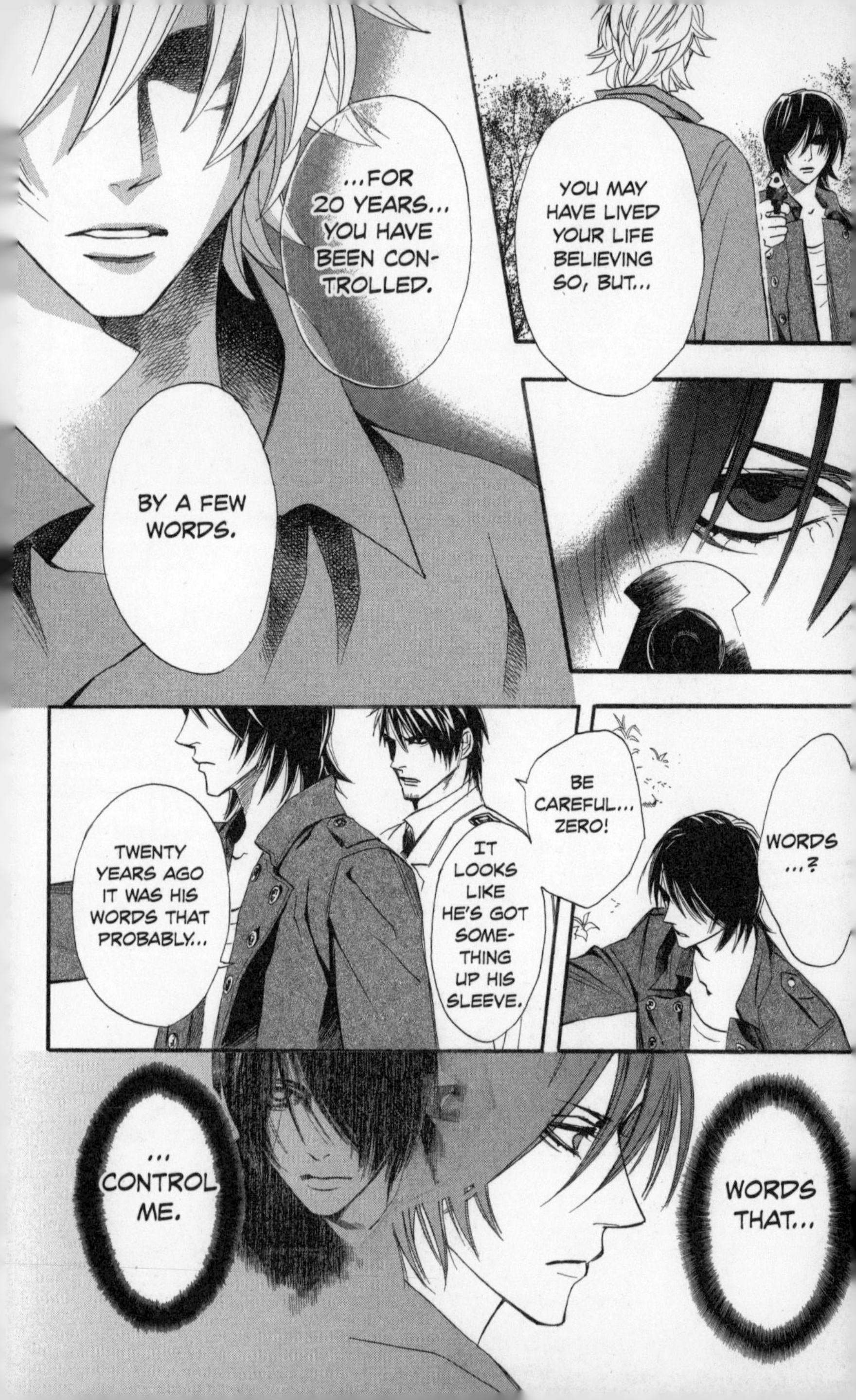
YOU MAY HAVE LIVED YOUR LIFE BELIEVING SO, BUT...
...FOR 20 YEARS... YOU HAVE BEEN CON-TROLLED.
BY A FEW WORDS.
WORDS ...?
BE CAREFUL... ZERO!
IT LOOKS LIKE HE'S GOT SOME-THING UP HIS SLEEVE.
TWENTY YEARS AGO IT WAS HIS WORDS THAT PROBABLY...
WORDS THAT...
... CONTROL ME.

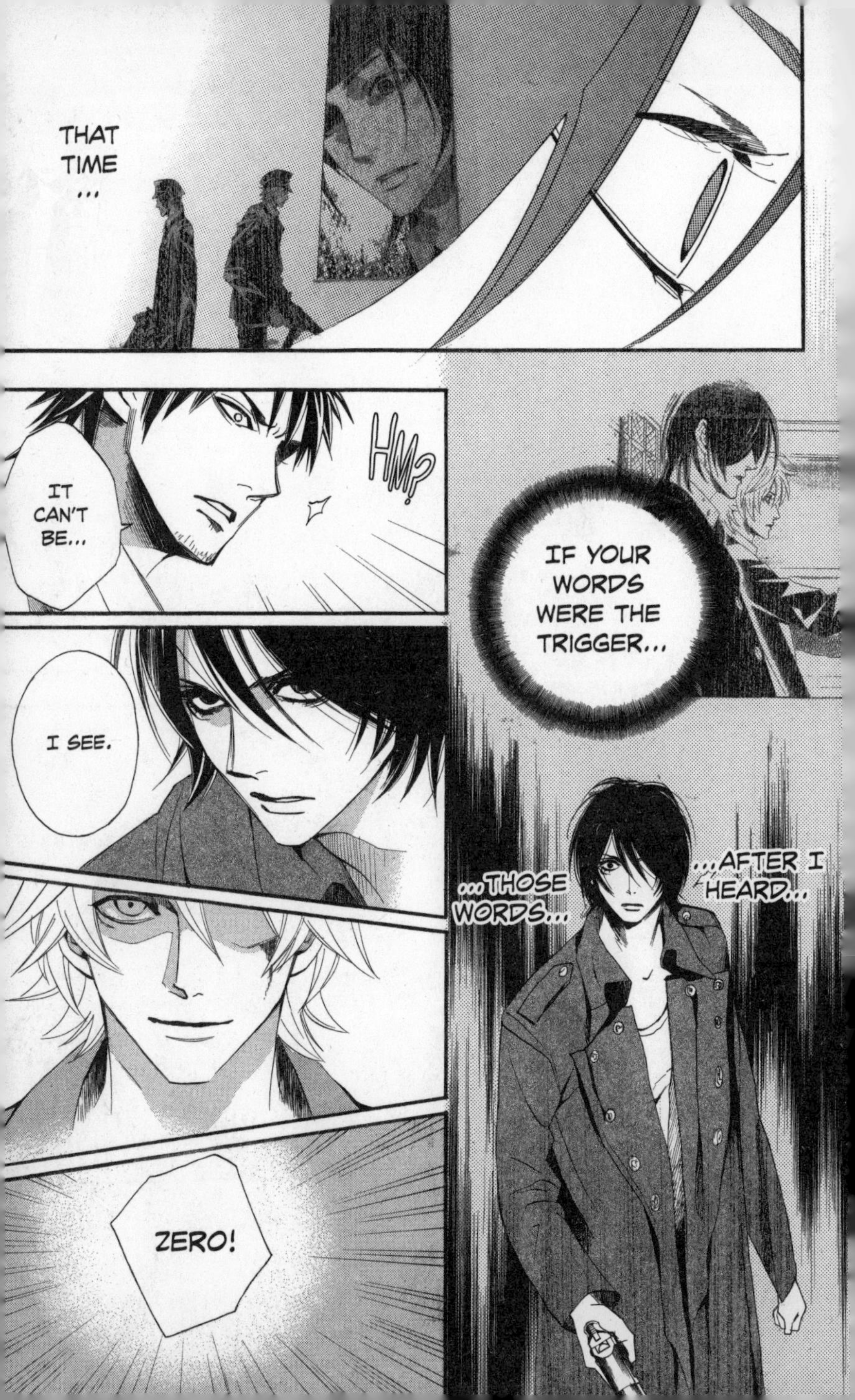
THAT TIME ...
IF YOUR WORDS WERE THE TRIGGER...
...AFTER I HEARD...
...THOSE WORDS...
HM?
IT CAN'T BE...
I SEE.
ZERO!

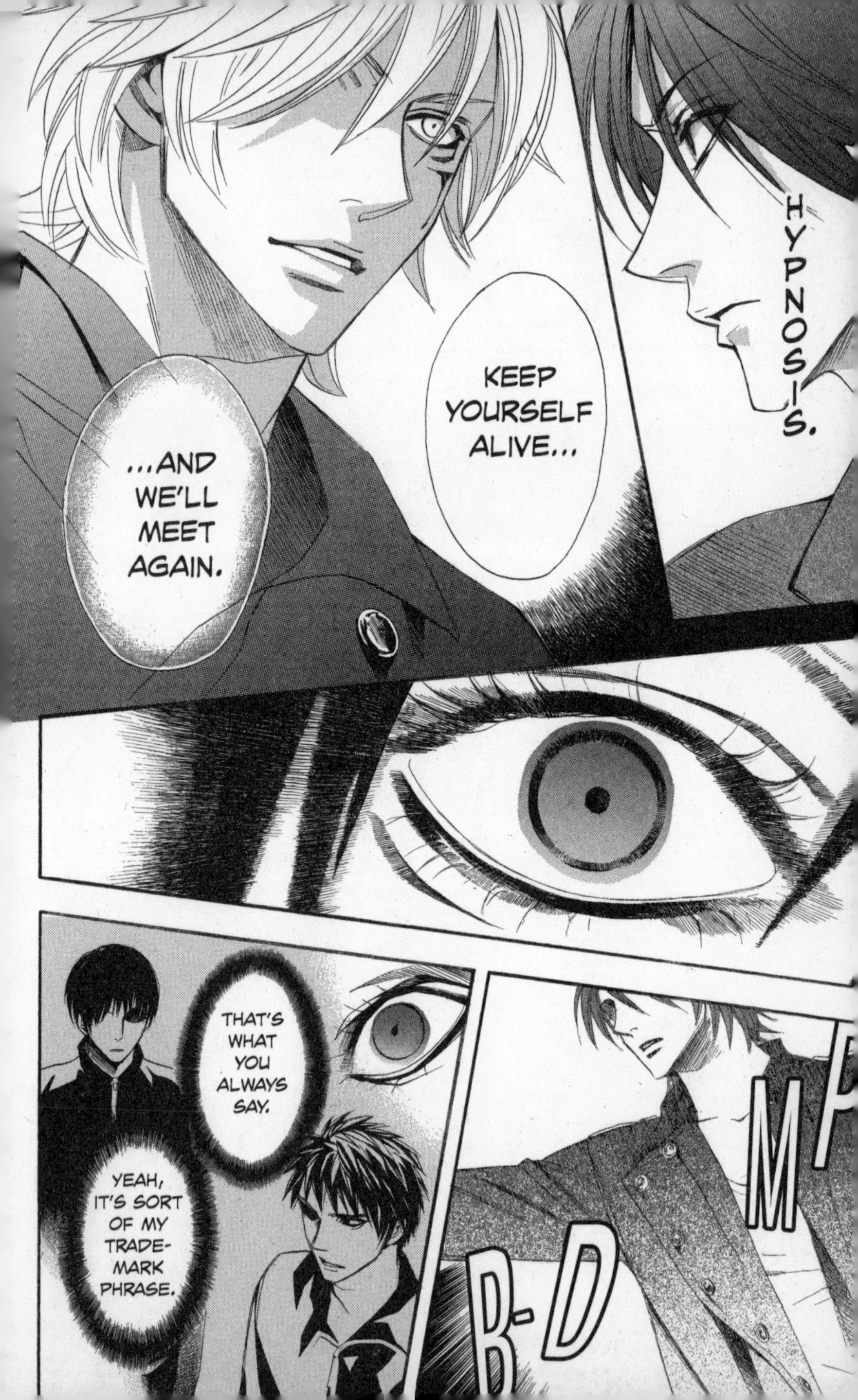
HYPNOSIS.
KEEP YOURSELF ALIVE...
...AND WE'LL MEET AGAIN.
B-DMP
THAT'S WHAT YOU ALWAYS SAY.
YEAH, IT'S SORT OF MY TRADE-MARK PHRASE.

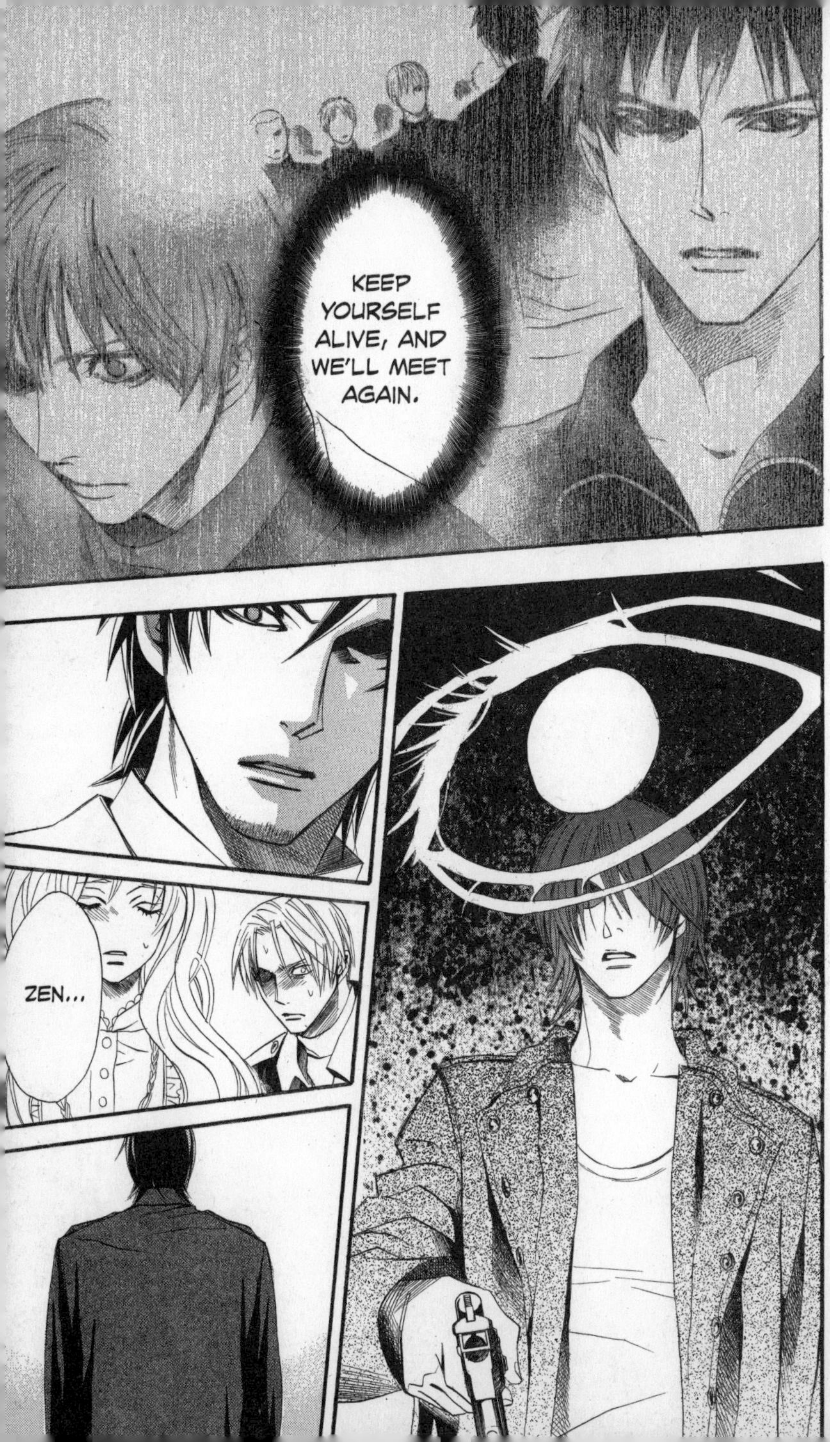
KEEP YOURSELF ALIVE, AND WE'LL MEET AGAIN.
ZEN...

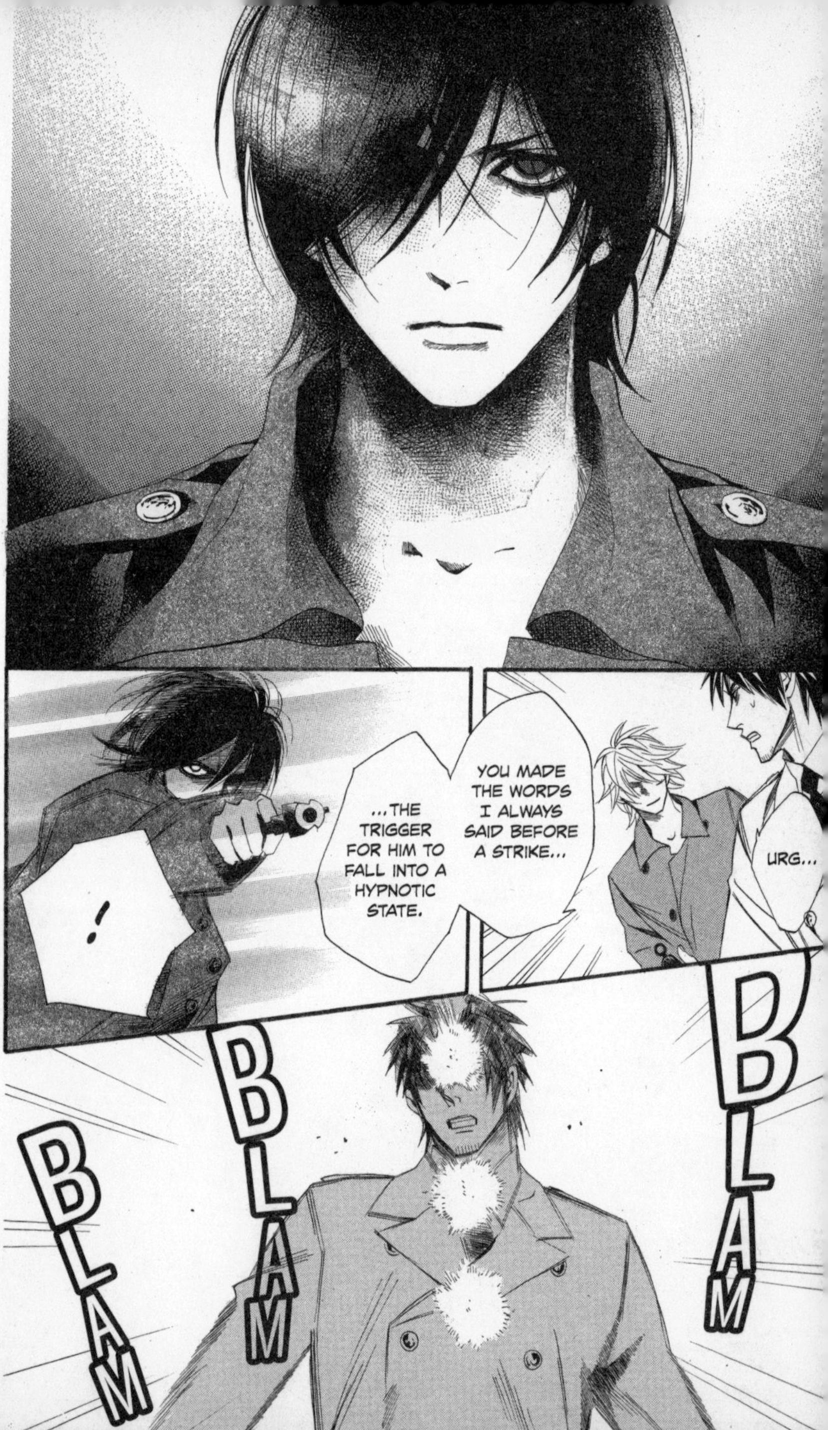
URG...
YOU MADE THE WORDS I ALWAYS SAID BEFORE A STRIKE...
...THE TRIGGER FOR HIM TO FALL INTO A HYPNOTIC STATE.
!
BLAM
BLAM
BLAM

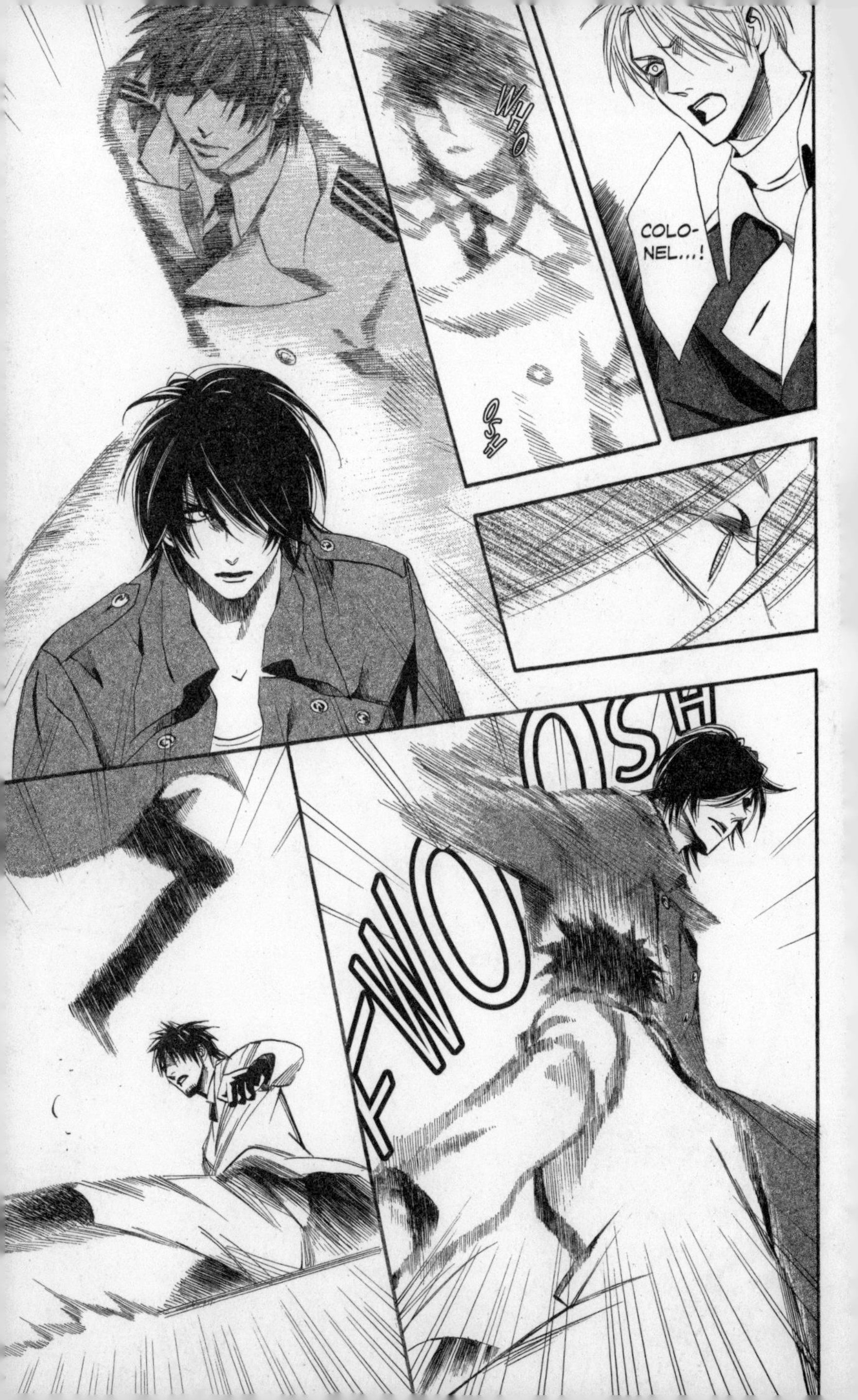
COLO-
NEL...!
WHO
OSH
FWOOSH

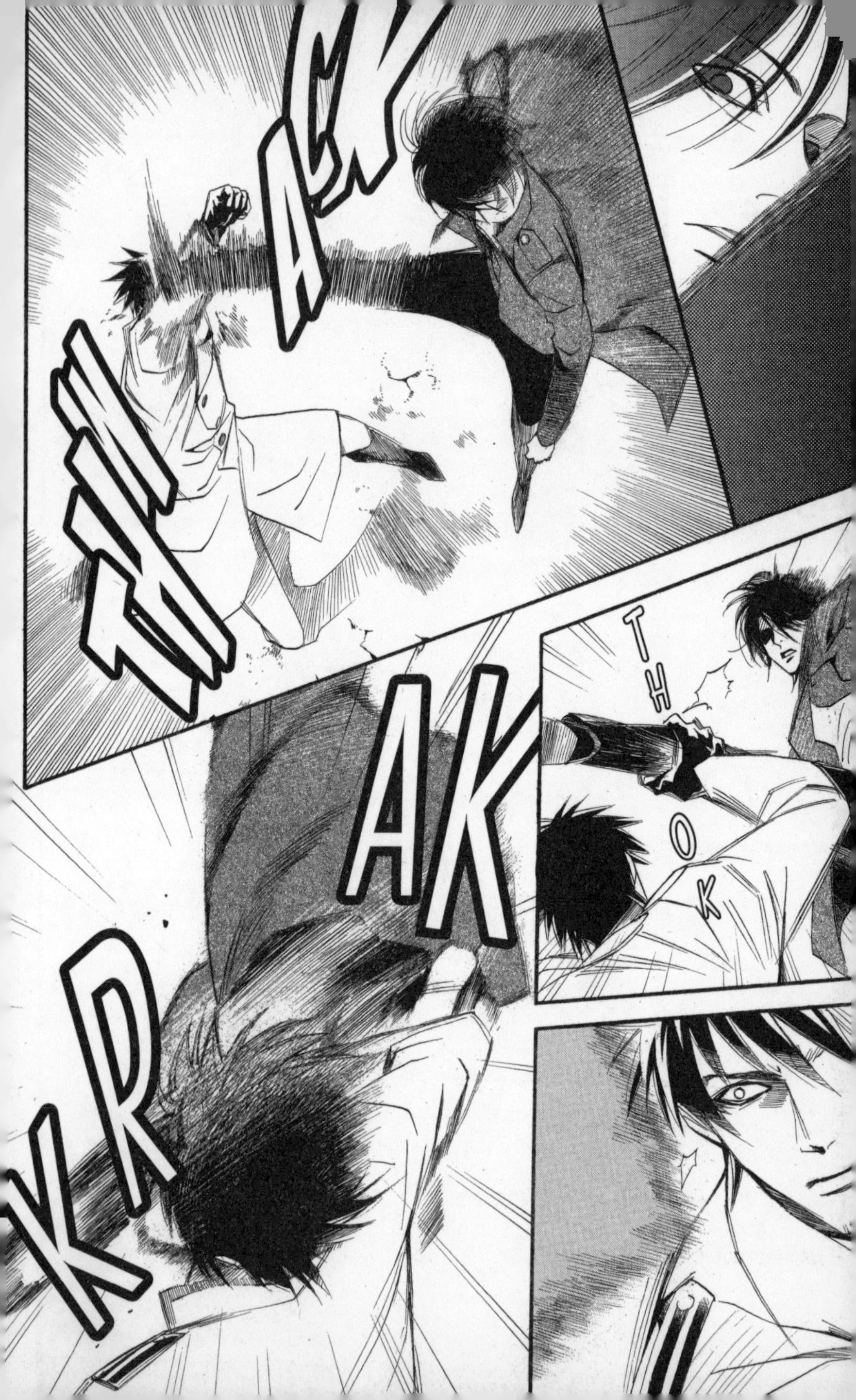
THWACK
THOK
KRAK

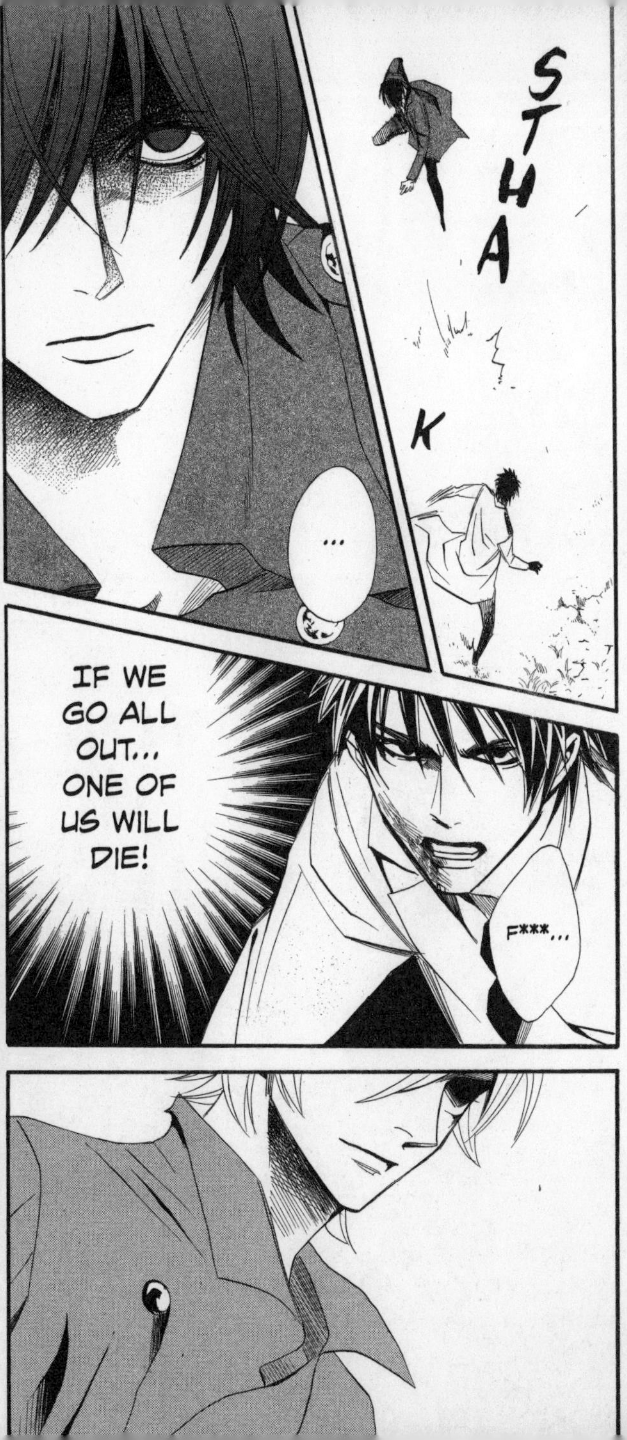
STHAK
...
IF WE GO ALL OUT... ONE OF US WILL DIE!
F***...

4

Cooperation in production:

Shimada-san

Kawashima-san

Koinuma-san

Sayaka-san

Kuwana-san

Tanaka-san

Nishizawa-san

Abe-san

Okazaki-san

Kaneko-san

Takahashi-san

Ukeguchi-san

Special Thanks

Rei-san

S-numa-san

Fans who sent in letters

Thank you for reading. I hope we'll meet again in a different manga.

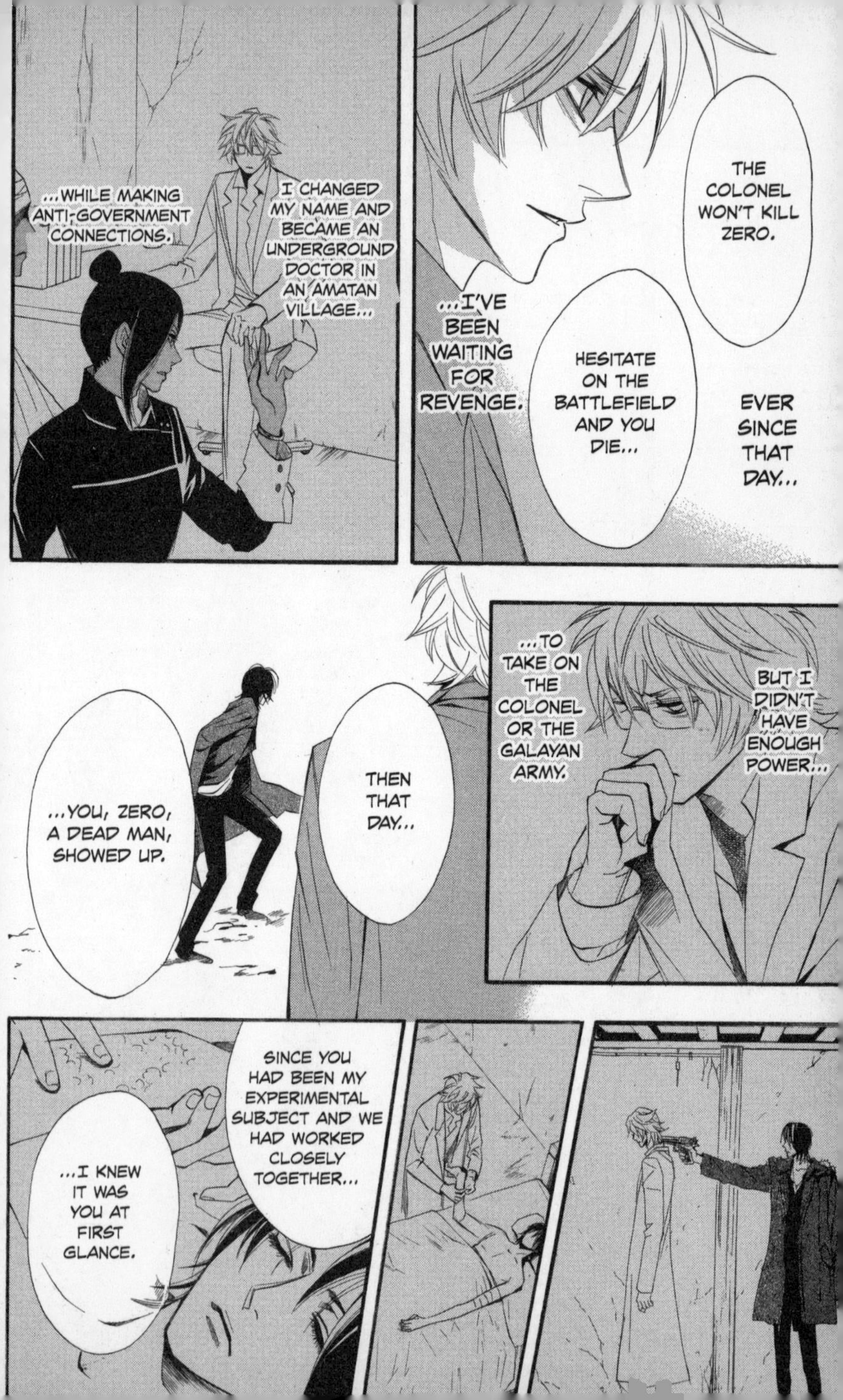
THE COLONEL WON'T KILL ZERO.
HESITATE ON THE BATTLEFIELD AND YOU DIE...
EVER SINCE THAT DAY...
...I'VE BEEN WAITING FOR REVENGE.
I CHANGED MY NAME AND BECAME AN UNDERGROUND DOCTOR IN AN AMATAN VILLAGE...
...WHILE MAKING ANTI-GOVERNMENT CONNECTIONS.
BUT I DIDN'T HAVE ENOUGH POWER...
...TO TAKE ON THE COLONEL OR THE GALAYAN ARMY.
THEN THAT DAY...
...YOU, ZERO, A DEAD MAN, SHOWED UP.
SINCE YOU HAD BEEN MY EXPERIMENTAL SUBJECT AND WE HAD WORKED CLOSELY TOGETHER...
...I KNEW IT WAS YOU AT FIRST GLANCE.

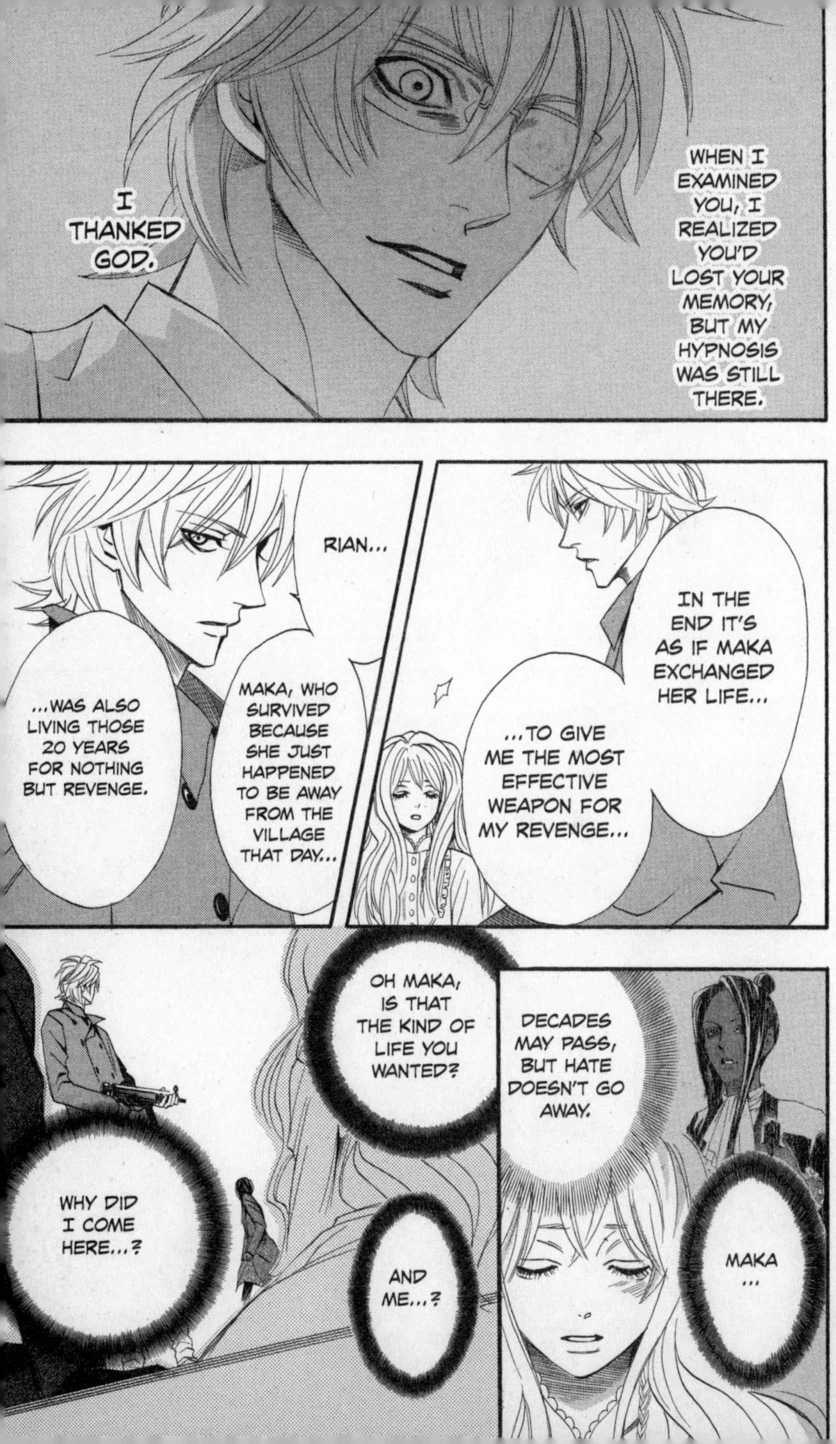
WHEN I EXAMINED YOU, I REALIZED YOU'D LOST YOUR MEMORY, BUT MY HYPNOSIS WAS STILL THERE.
I THANKED GOD.
IN THE END IT'S AS IF MAKA EXCHANGED HER LIFE...
...TO GIVE ME THE MOST EFFECTIVE WEAPON FOR MY REVENGE...
RIAN...
MAKA, WHO SURVIVED BECAUSE SHE JUST HAPPENED TO BE AWAY FROM THE VILLAGE THAT DAY...
...WAS ALSO LIVING THOSE 20 YEARS FOR NOTHING BUT REVENGE.
DECADES MAY PASS, BUT HATE DOESN'T GO AWAY.
MAKA ...
OH MAKA, IS THAT THE KIND OF LIFE YOU WANTED?
AND ME...?
WHY DID I COME HERE...?

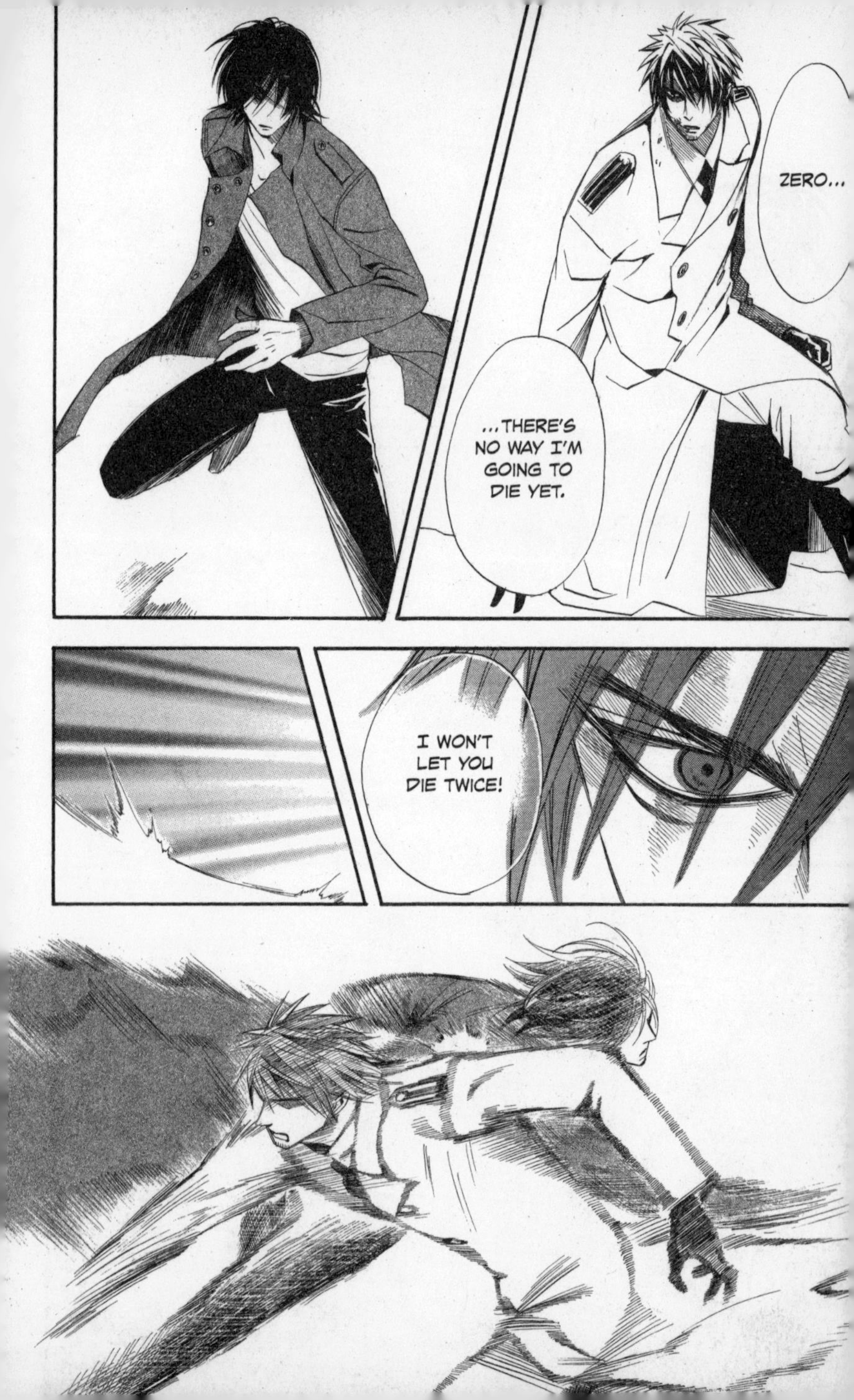
ZERO...
...THERE'S NO WAY I'M GOING TO DIE YET.
I WON'T LET YOU DIE TWICE!

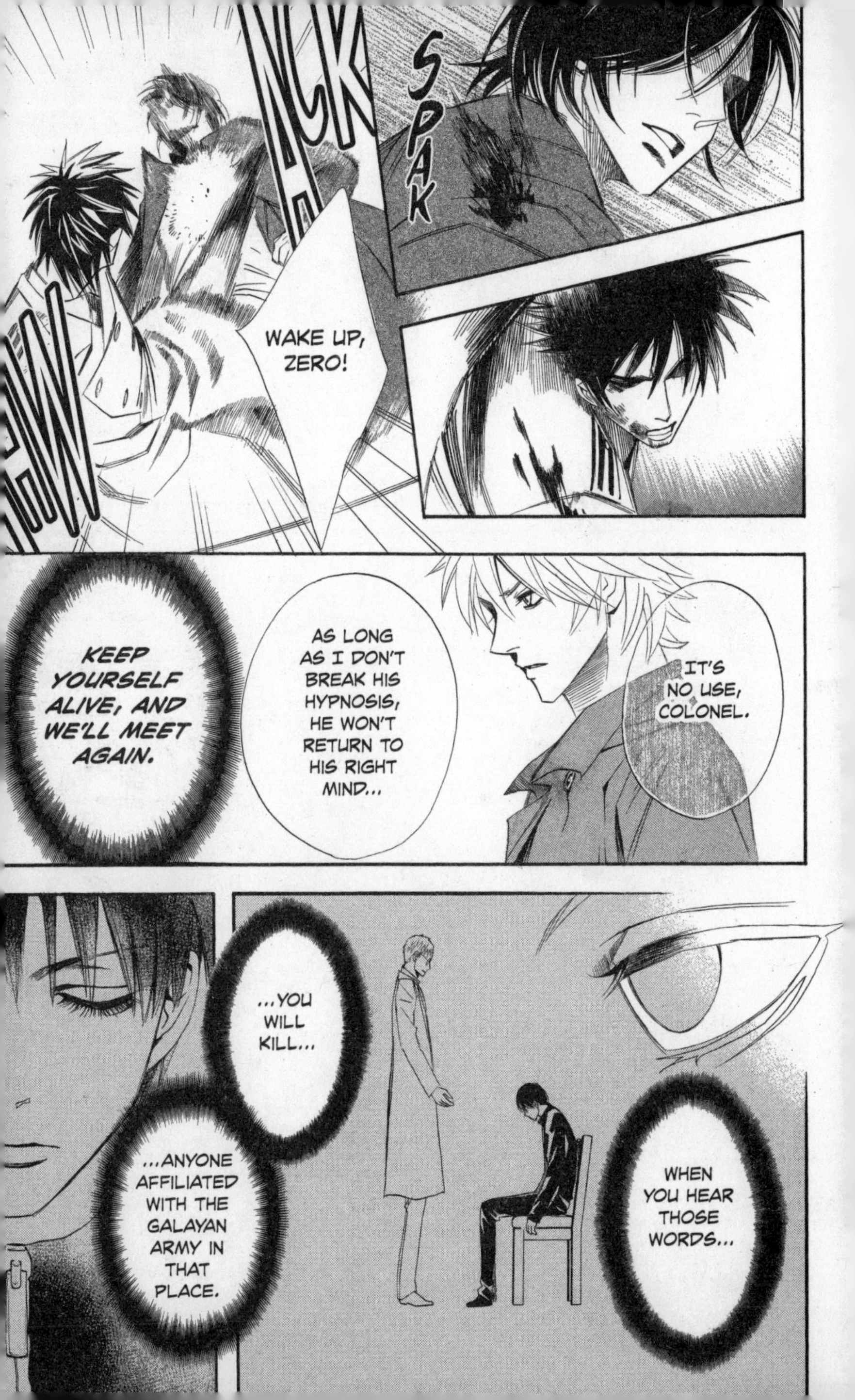
SPAK
WAKE UP, ZERO!
IT'S NO USE, COLONEL.
AS LONG AS I DON'T BREAK HIS HYPNOSIS, HE WON'T RETURN TO HIS RIGHT MIND...
KEEP YOURSELF ALIVE, AND WE'LL MEET AGAIN.
WHEN YOU HEAR THOSE WORDS...
...YOU WILL KILL...
...ANYONE AFFILIATED WITH THE GALAYAN ARMY IN THAT PLACE.

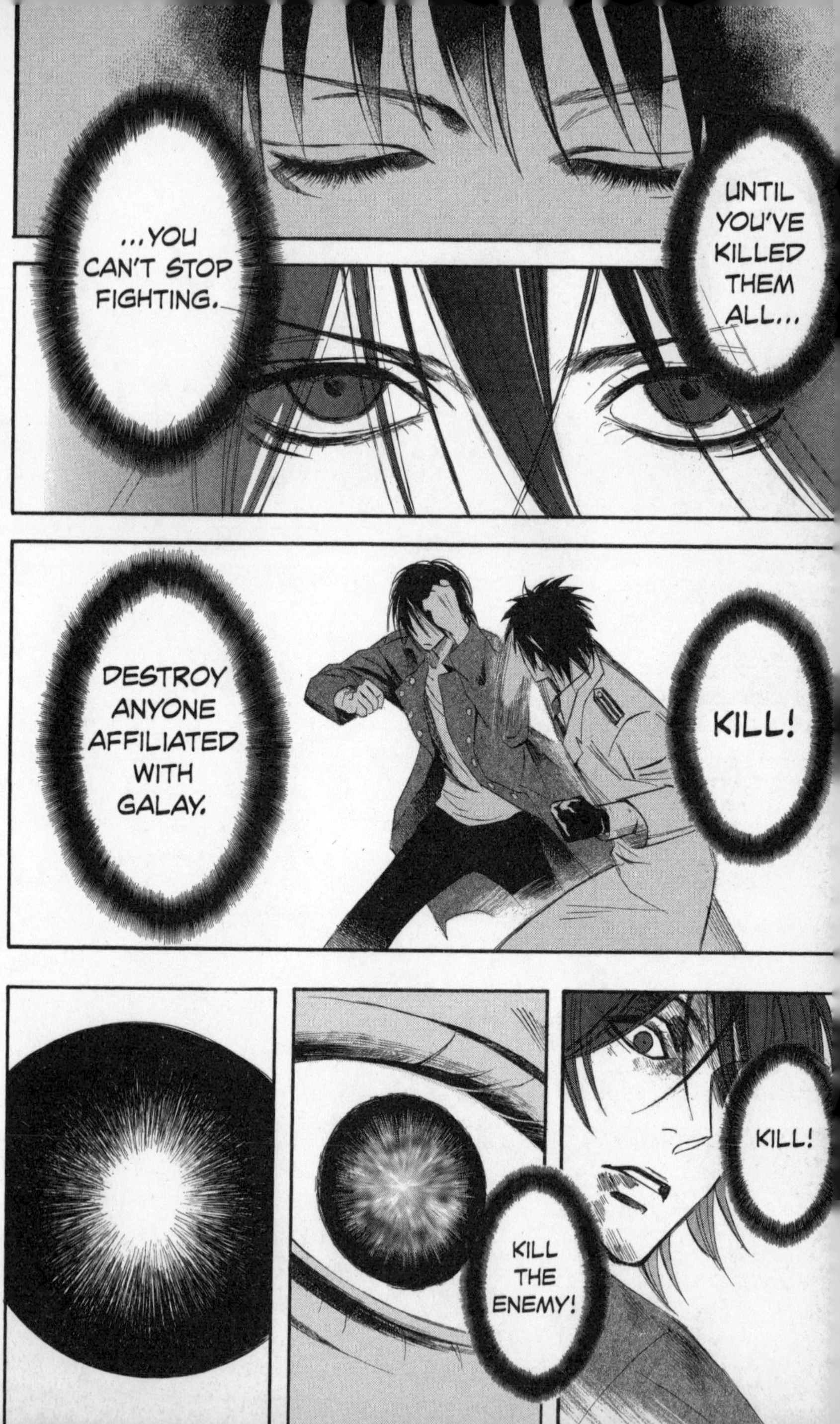
UNTIL YOU'VE KILLED THEM ALL...
...YOU CAN'T STOP FIGHTING.
KILL!
DESTROY ANYONE AFFILIATED WITH GALAY.
KILL!
KILL THE ENEMY!

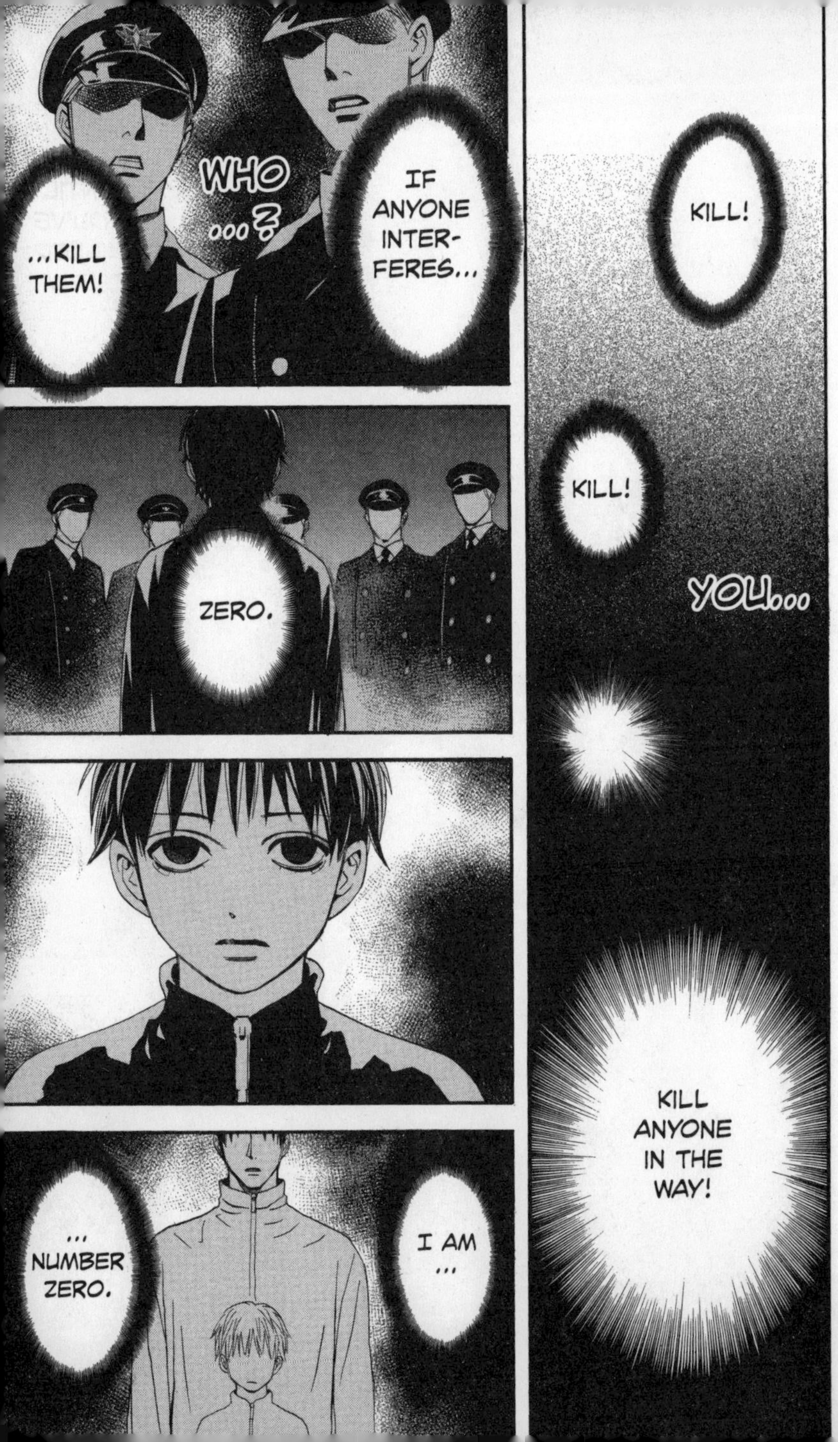
KILL!
KILL!
YOU...
KILL ANYONE IN THE WAY!
IF ANYONE INTERFERES...
WHO...?
...KILL THEM!
ZERO.
I AM...
...NUMBER ZERO.

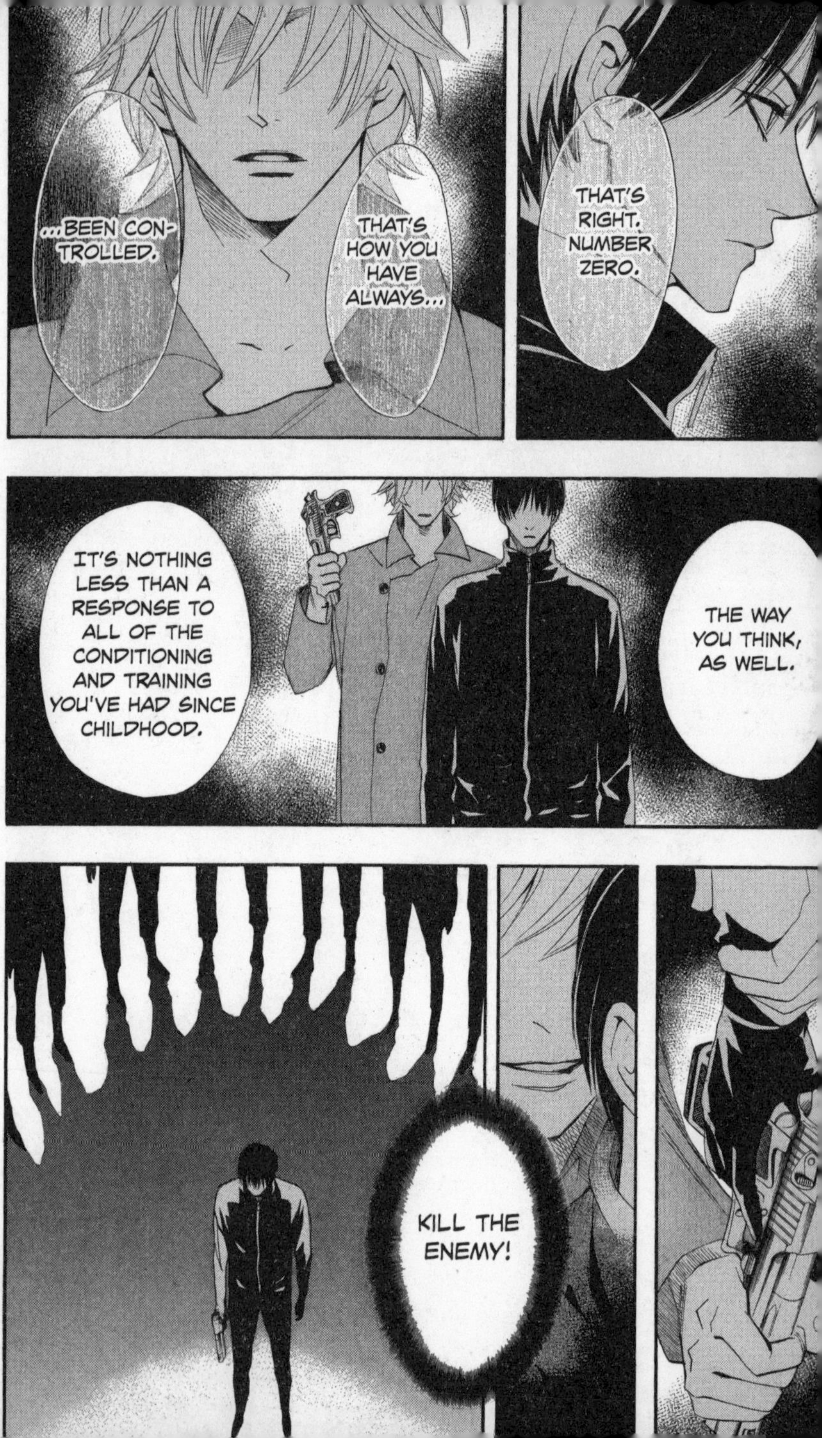
THAT'S RIGHT. NUMBER ZERO.
THAT'S HOW YOU HAVE ALWAYS...
...BEEN CON-TROLLED.
THE WAY YOU THINK, AS WELL.
IT'S NOTHING LESS THAN A RESPONSE TO ALL OF THE CONDITIONING AND TRAINING YOU'VE HAD SINCE CHILDHOOD.
KILL THE ENEMY!

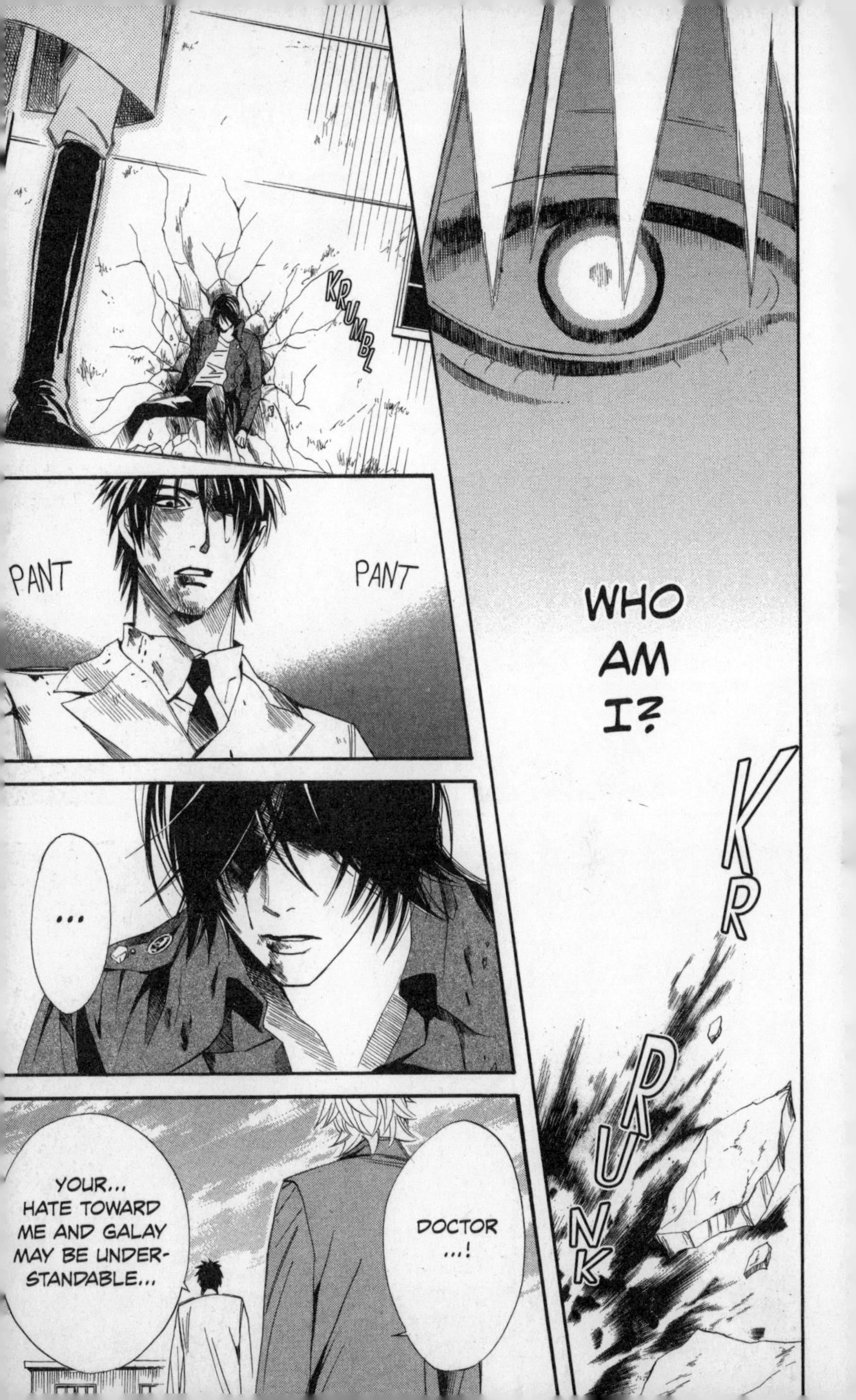
WHO AM I?
KRRUNK
KRUMBL
PANT PANT
...
DOCTOR ...!
YOUR... HATE TOWARD ME AND GALAY MAY BE UNDER-STANDABLE...

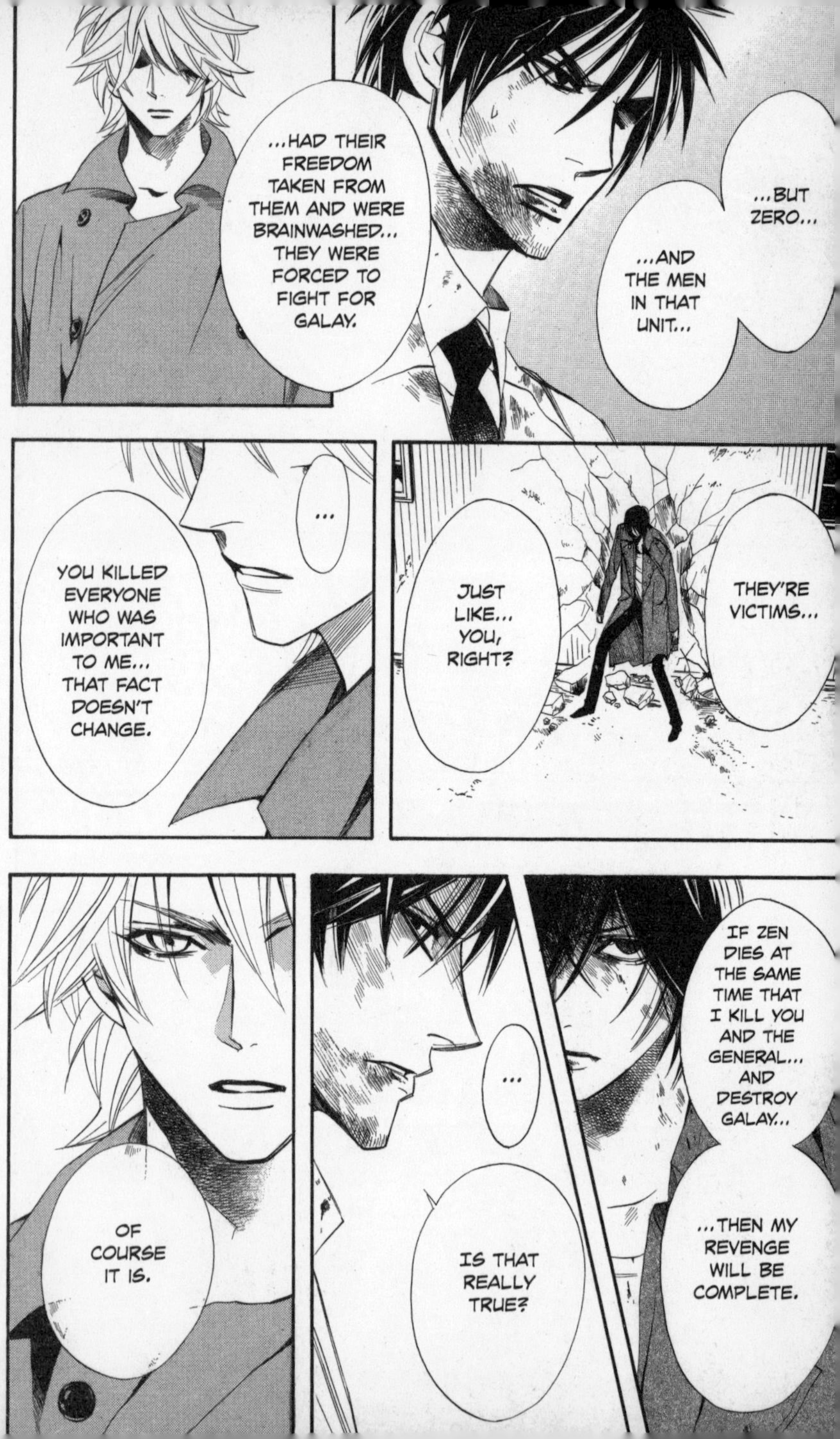
...BUT ZERO...
...AND THE MEN IN THAT UNIT...
...HAD THEIR FREEDOM TAKEN FROM THEM AND WERE BRAINWASHED... THEY WERE FORCED TO FIGHT FOR GALAY.
THEY'RE VICTIMS...
JUST LIKE... YOU, RIGHT?
...
YOU KILLED EVERYONE WHO WAS IMPORTANT TO ME... THAT FACT DOESN'T CHANGE.
IF ZEN DIES AT THE SAME TIME THAT I KILL YOU AND THE GENERAL... AND DESTROY GALAY...
...THEN MY REVENGE WILL BE COMPLETE.
...
IS THAT REALLY TRUE?
OF COURSE IT IS.

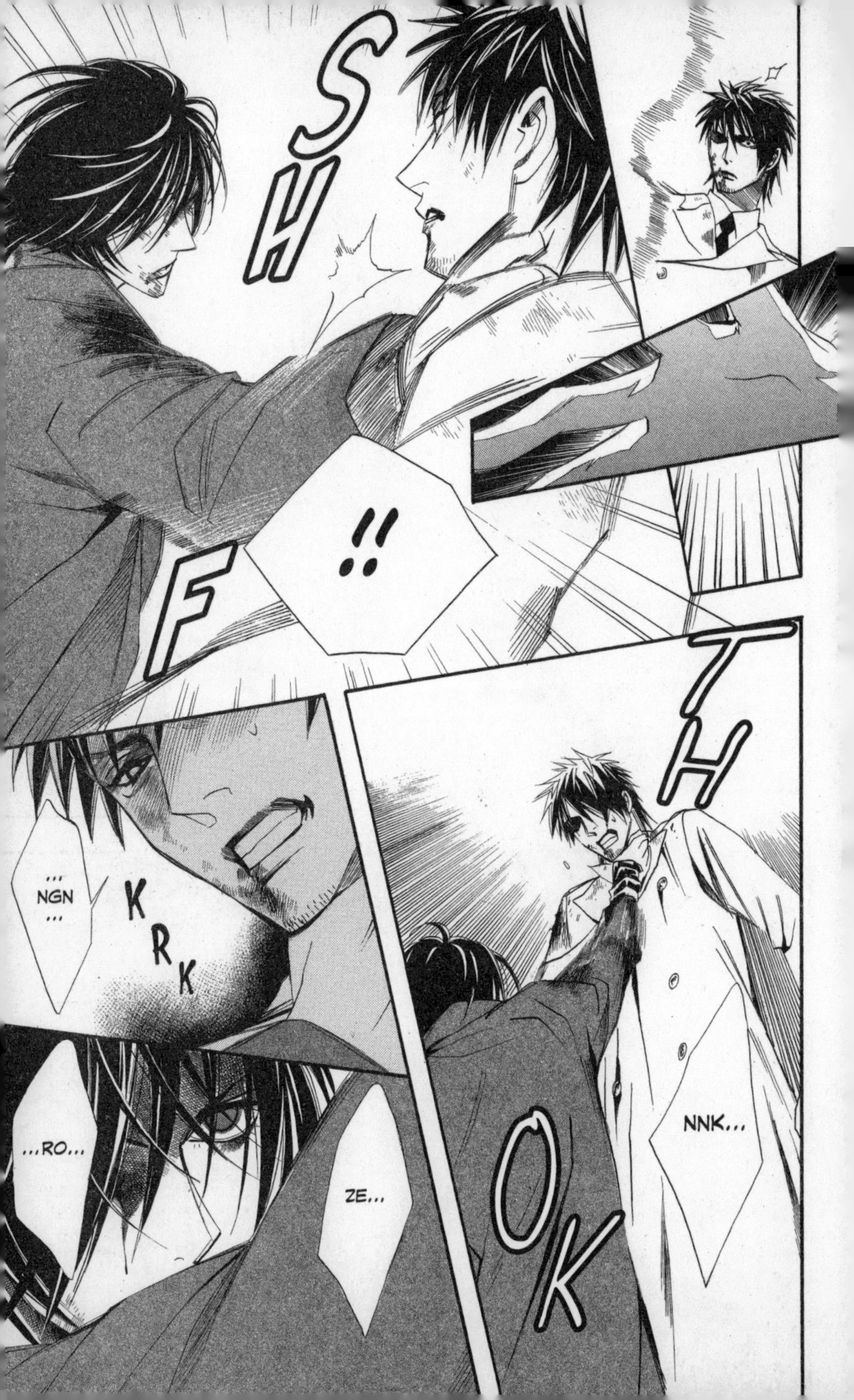
SH
!!
F
TH
NNK...
OK
...NGN...
KRK
...RO...
ZE...

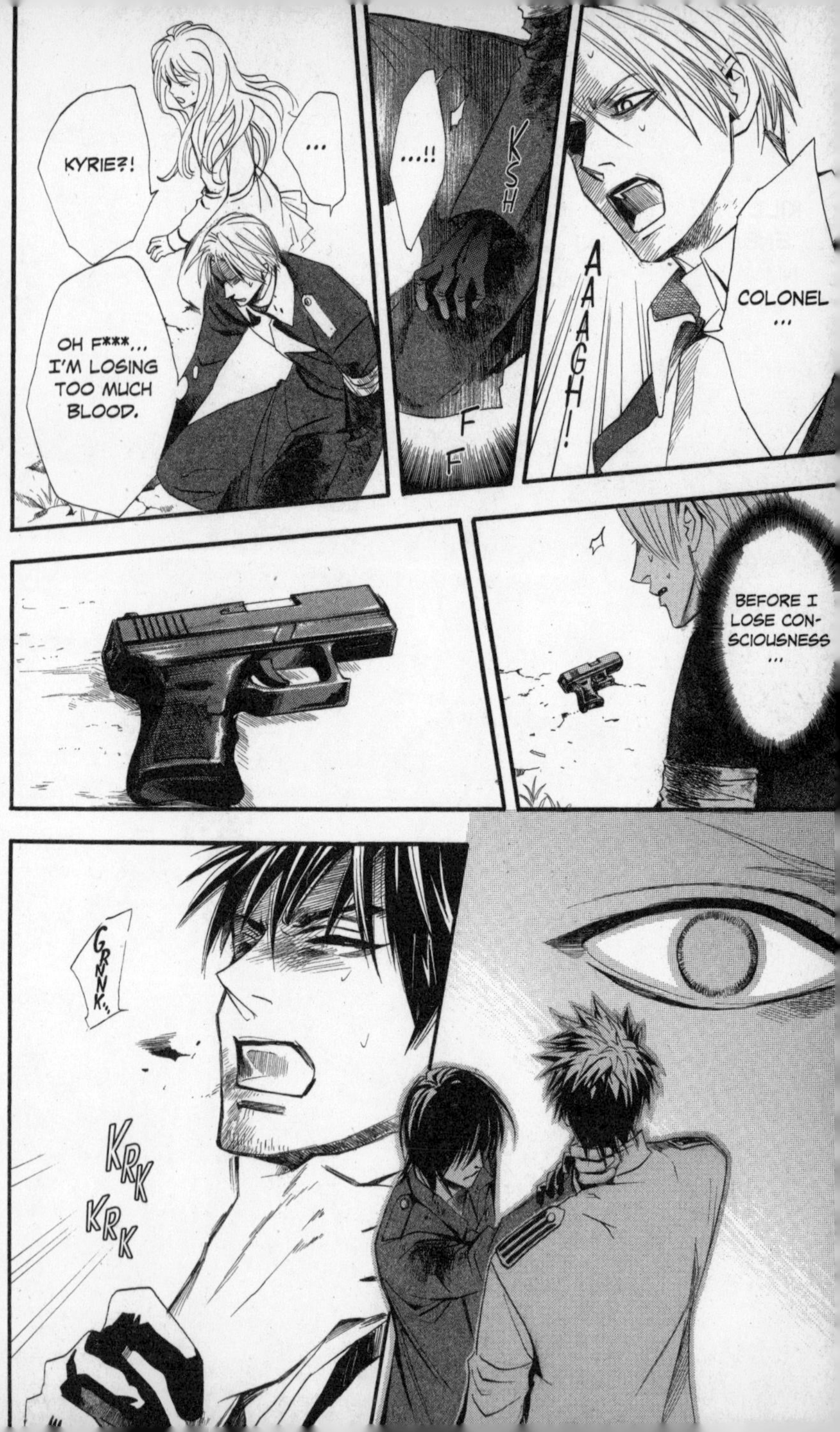
COLONEL ...
AAAAGH!
KSH
...!!
FF
...
KYRIE?!
OH F***... I'M LOSING TOO MUCH BLOOD.
BEFORE I LOSE CON-SCIOUSNESS ...
GRNNK...
KRK KRK

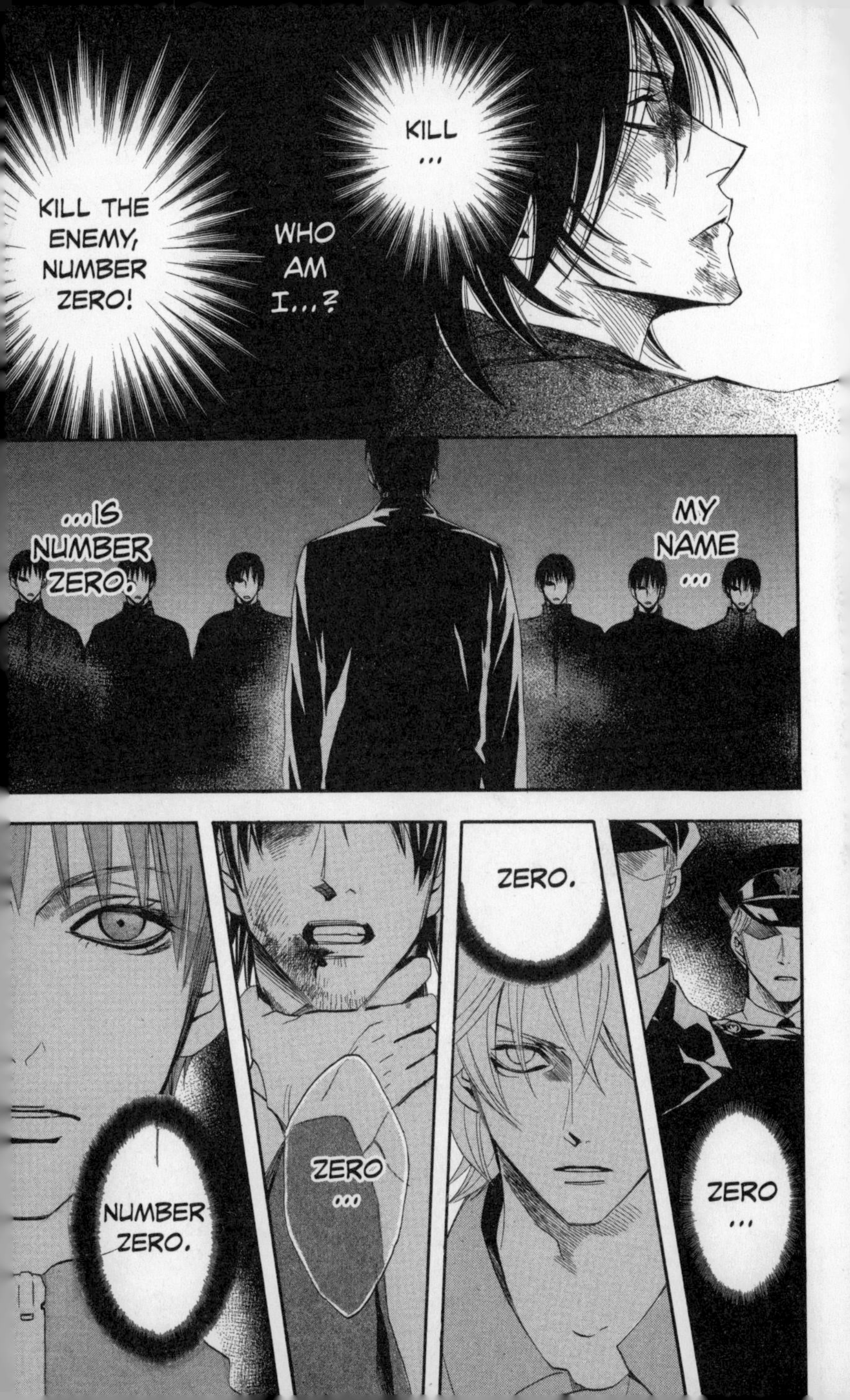
KILL ...
WHO AM I...?
KILL THE ENEMY, NUMBER ZERO!
MY NAME ...
...IS NUMBER ZERO.
ZERO ...
ZERO.
ZERO ...
NUMBER ZERO.

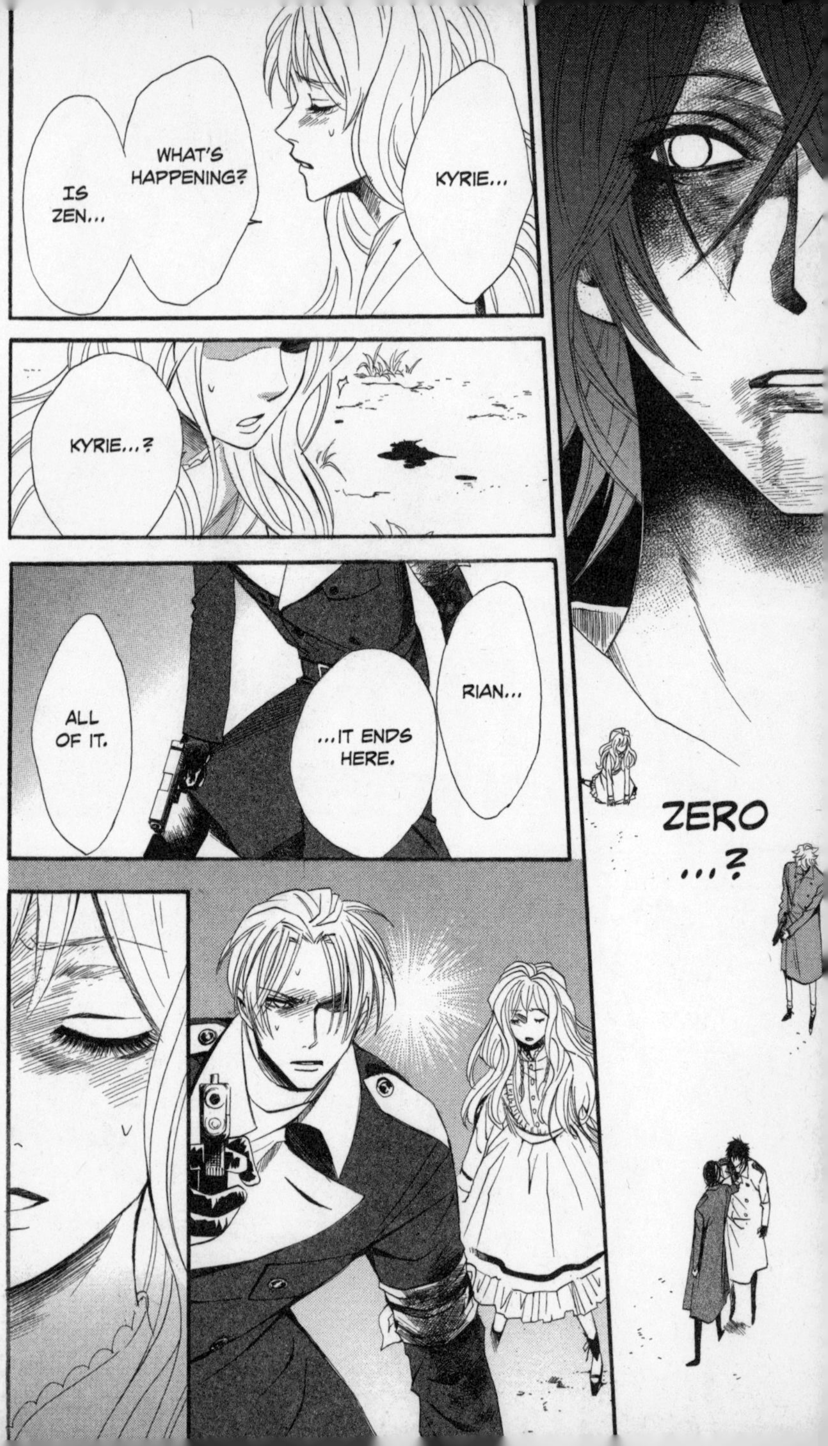
ZERO ...?
KYRIE...
WHAT'S HAPPENING?
IS ZEN...
KYRIE...?
RIAN...
...IT ENDS HERE.
ALL OF IT.

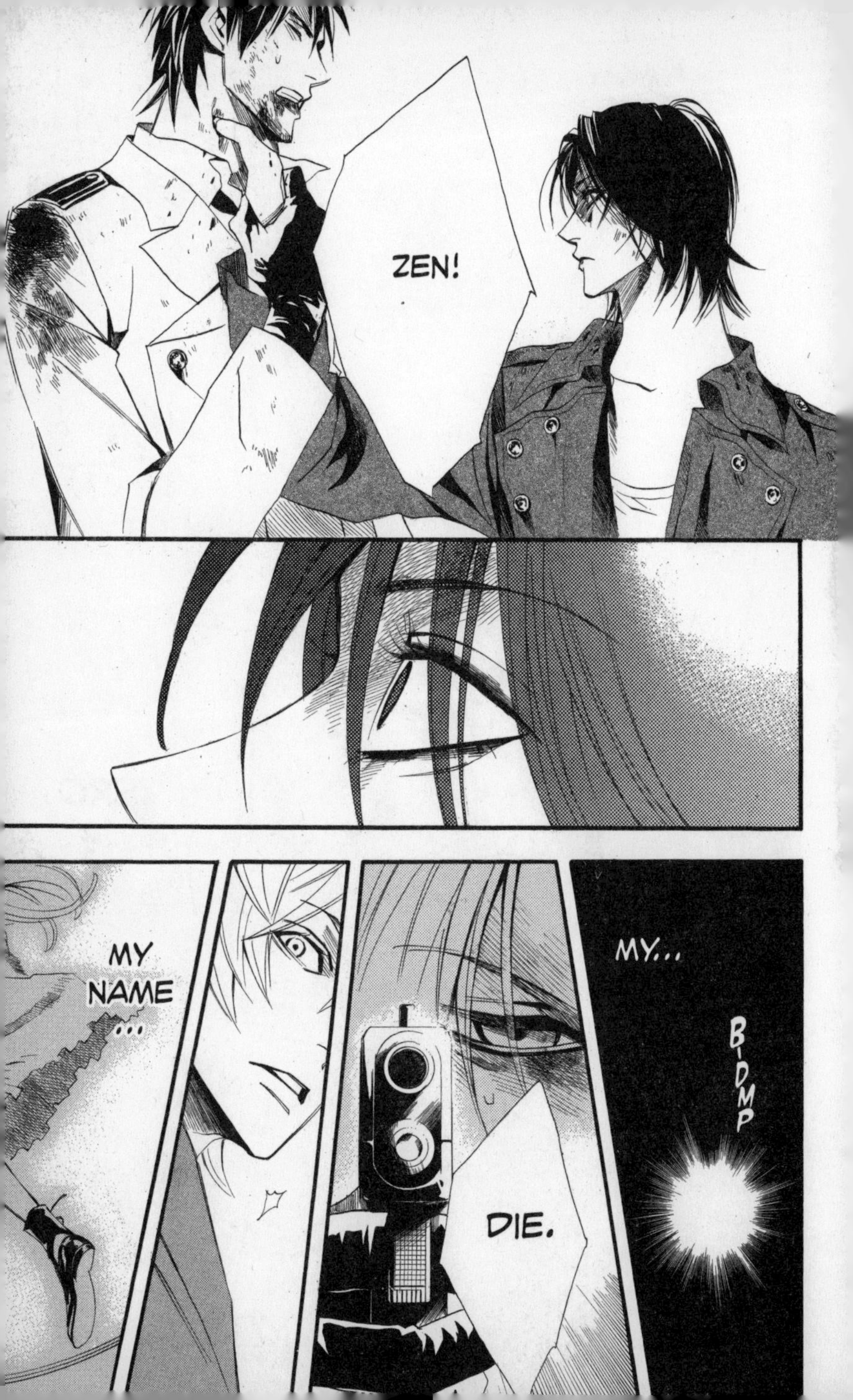
ZEN!
MY...
BIDMP
DIE.
MY NAME...

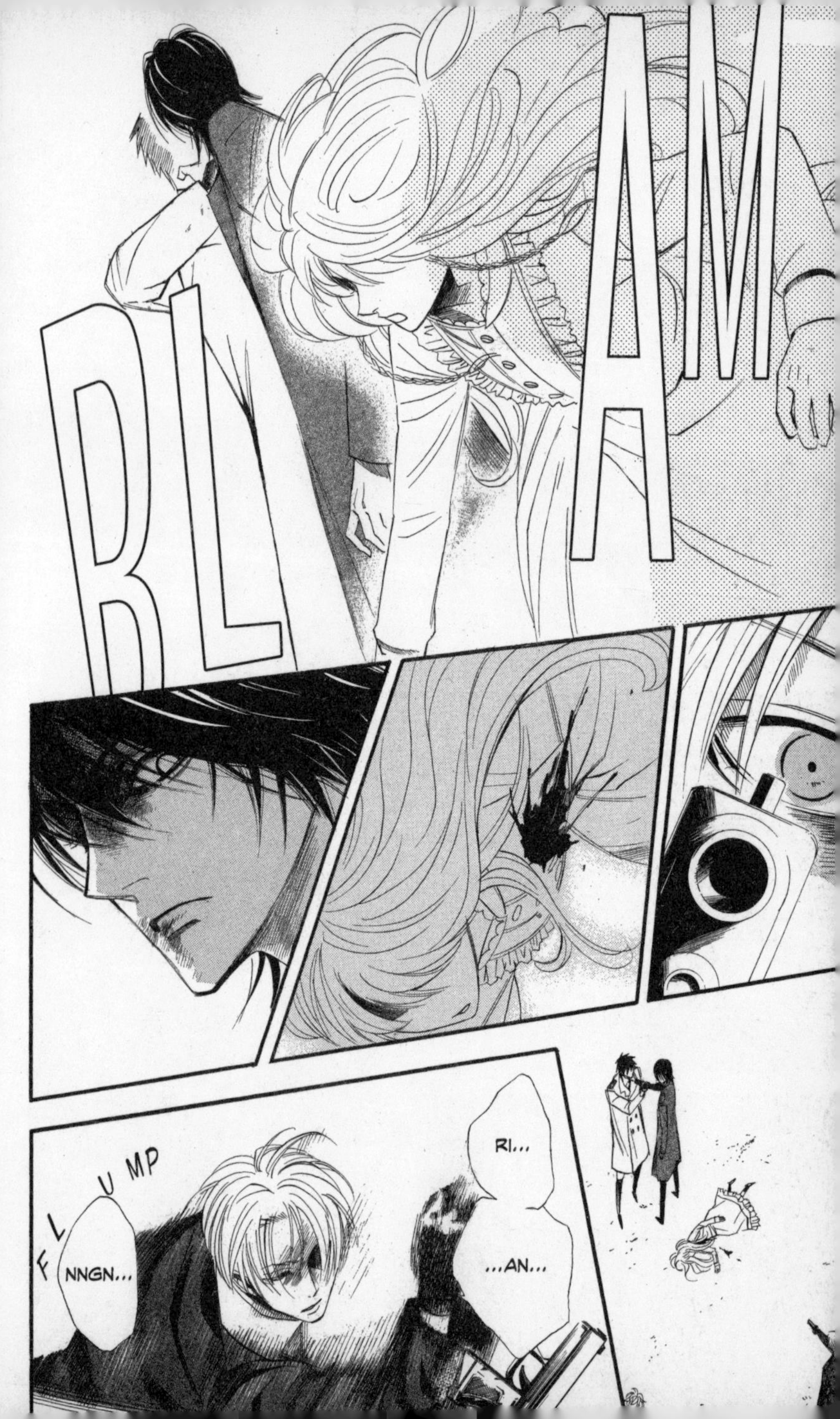
BLAM
RI...
...AN...
FLUMP
NNGN...

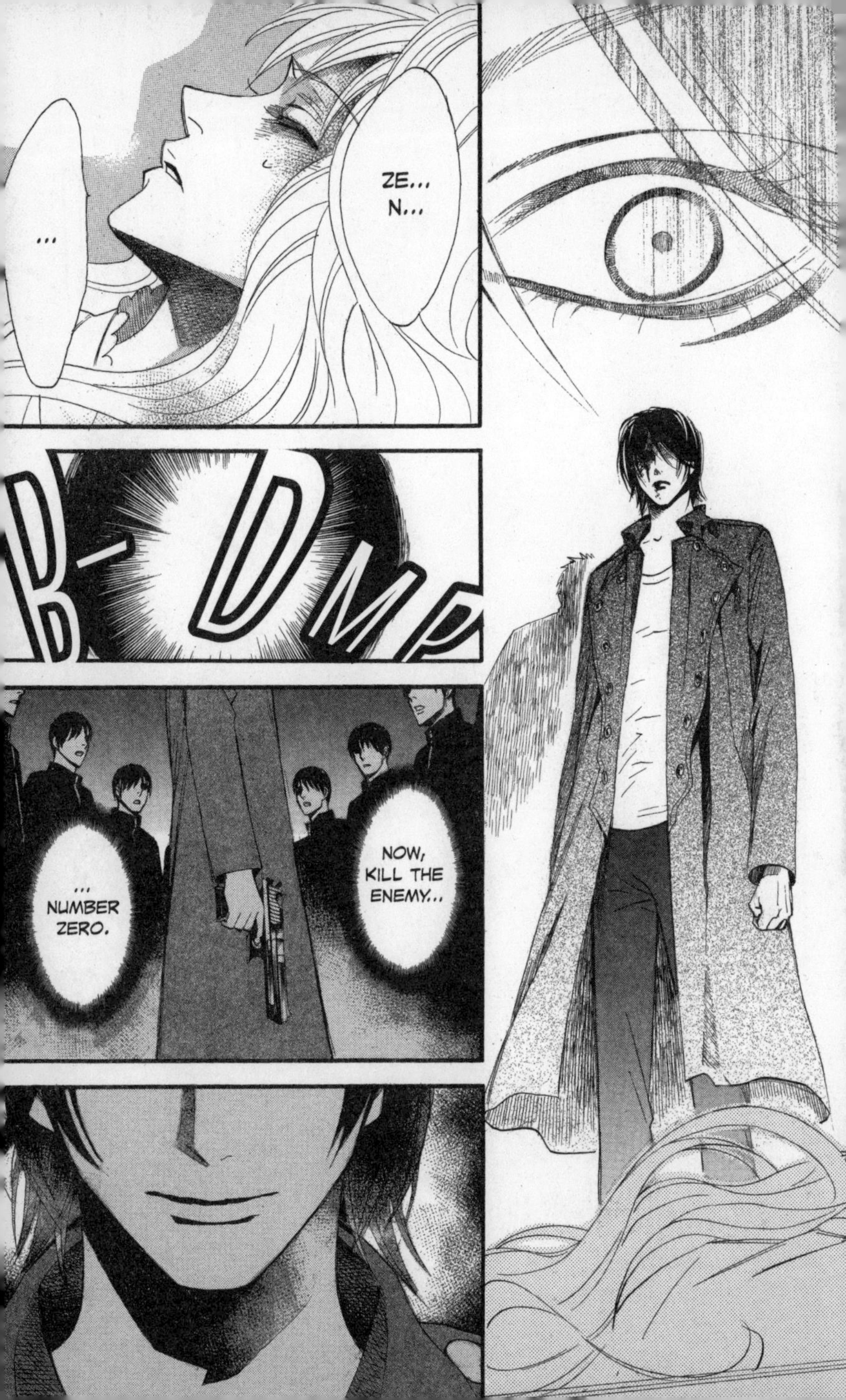
ZE... N...
...
B-DMP
NOW, KILL THE ENEMY...
... NUMBER ZERO.

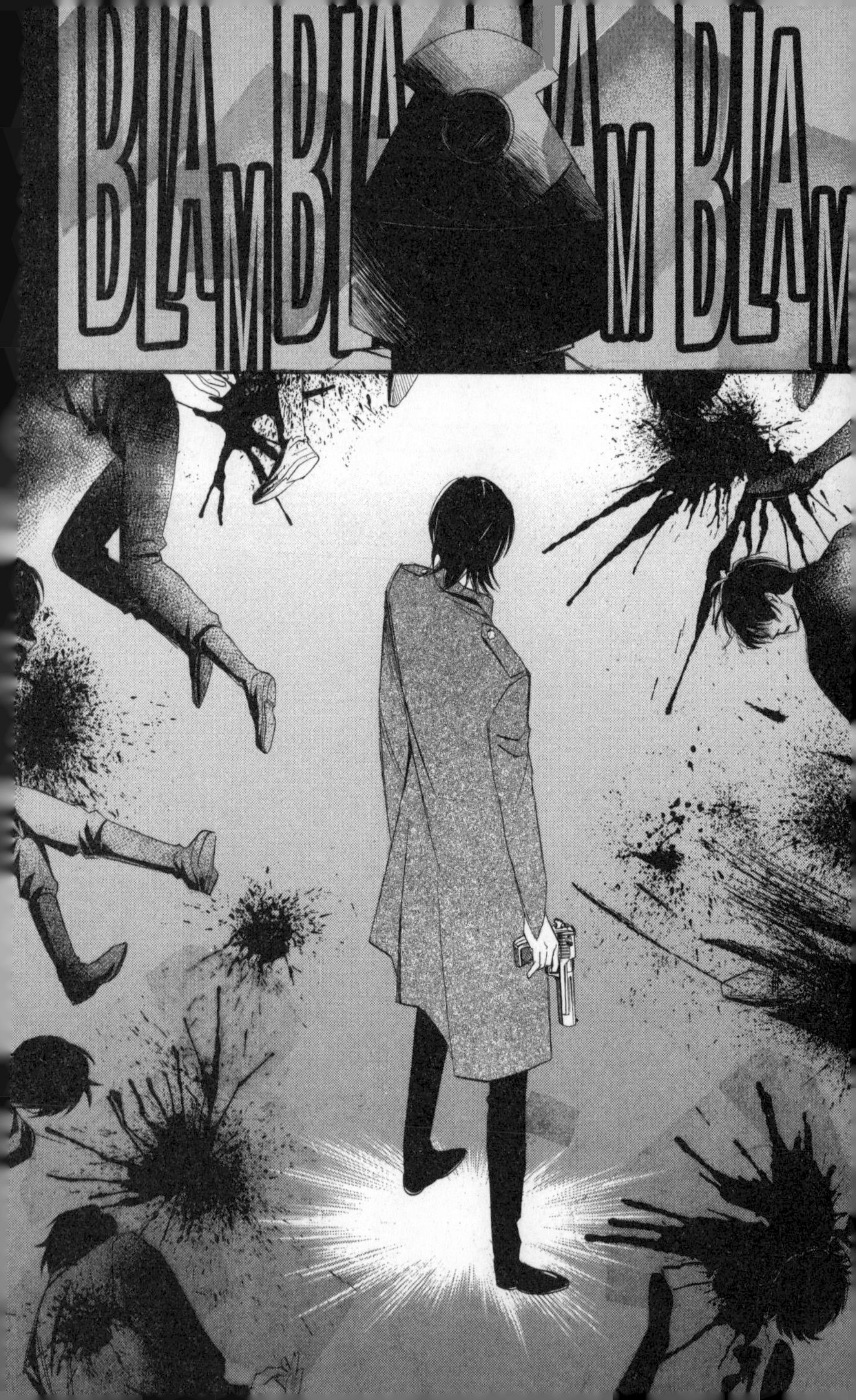
BLAM
BL
M
BLAM

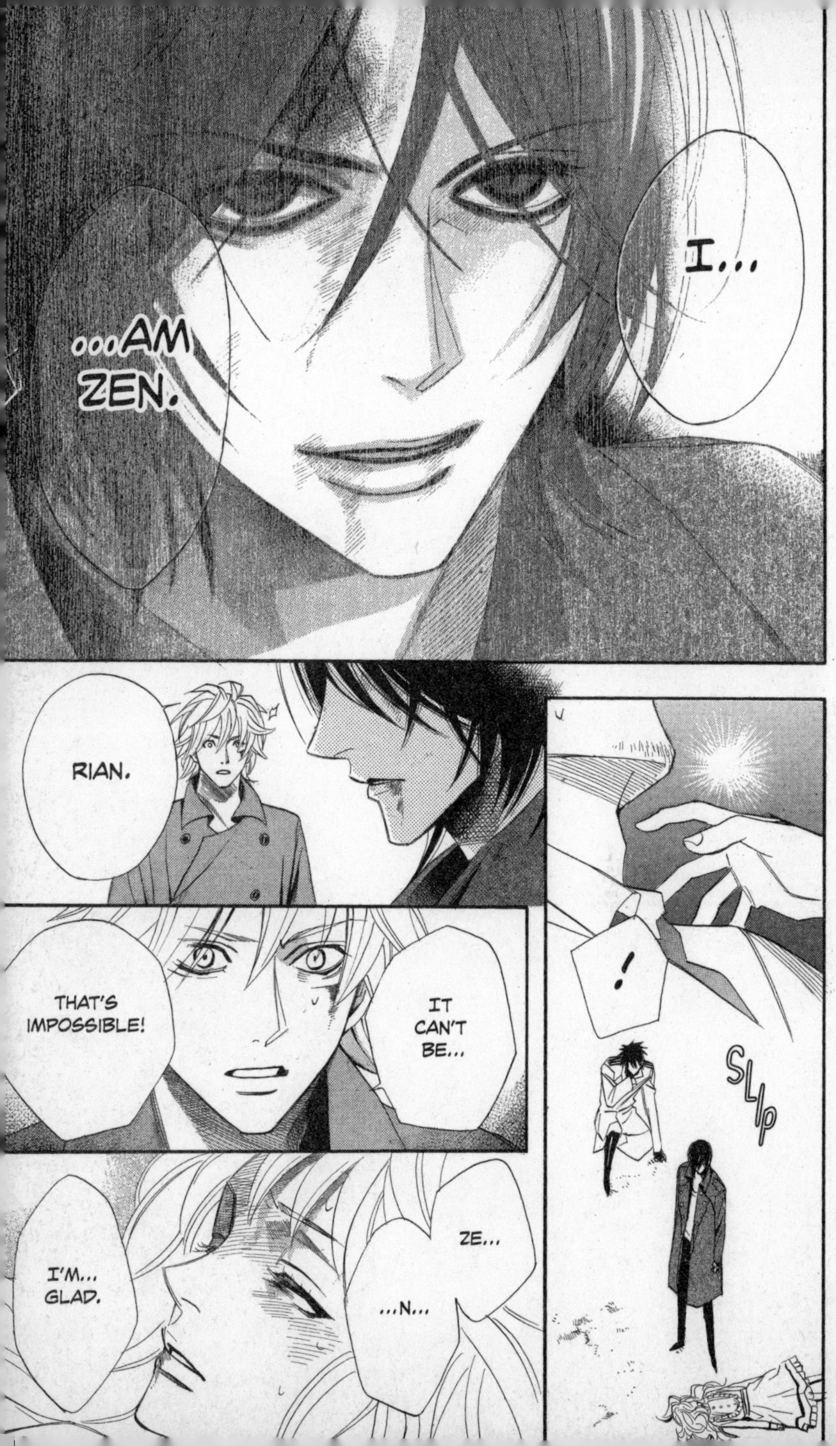

I...
...AM ZEN.
!
SLIP
RIAN.
IT CAN'T BE...
THAT'S IMPOSSIBLE!
ZE...
...N...
I'M... GLAD.

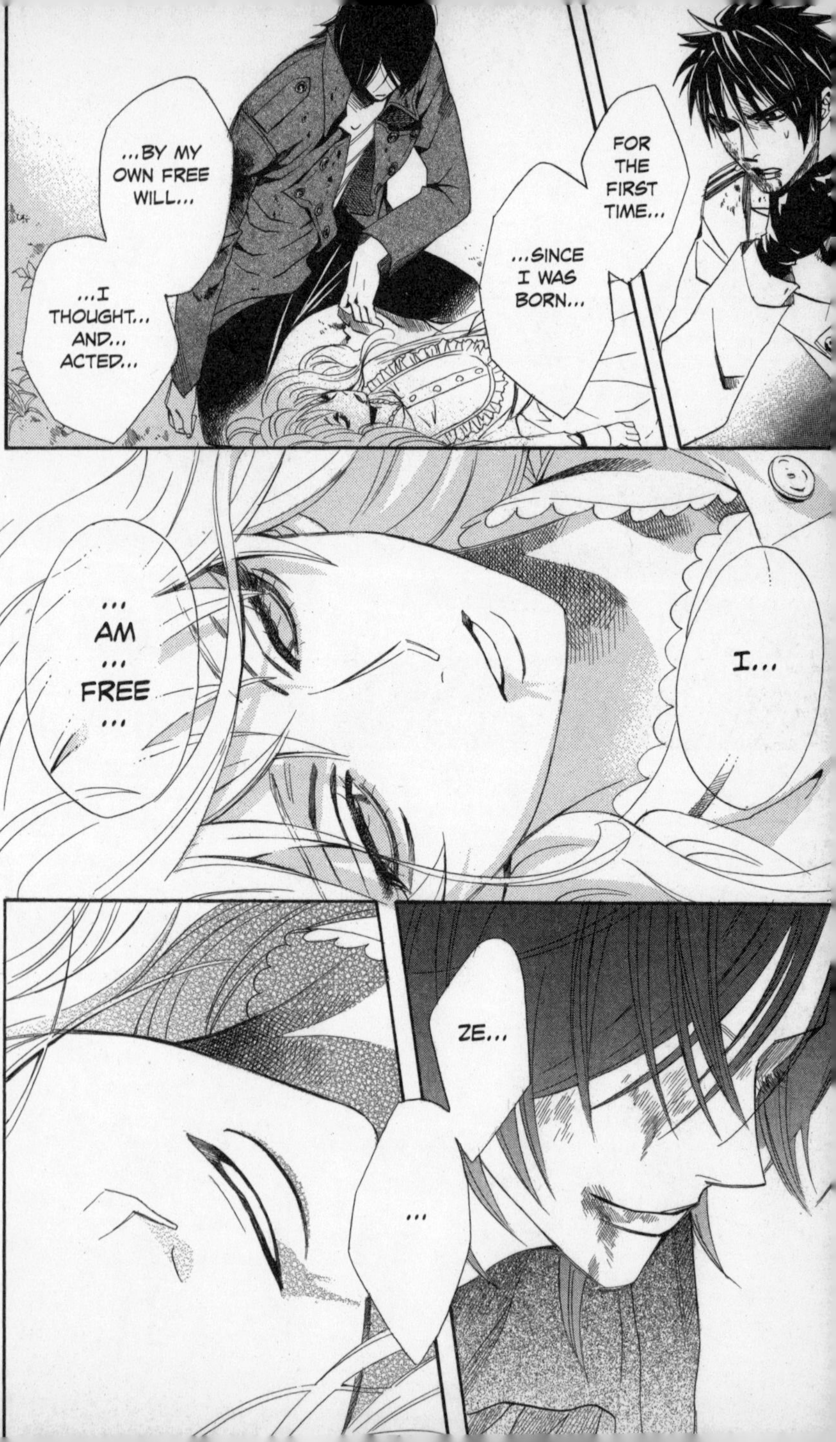
FOR THE FIRST TIME...
...SINCE I WAS BORN...
...BY MY OWN FREE WILL...
...I THOUGHT... AND... ACTED...
I...
... AM ... FREE ...
ZE...
...

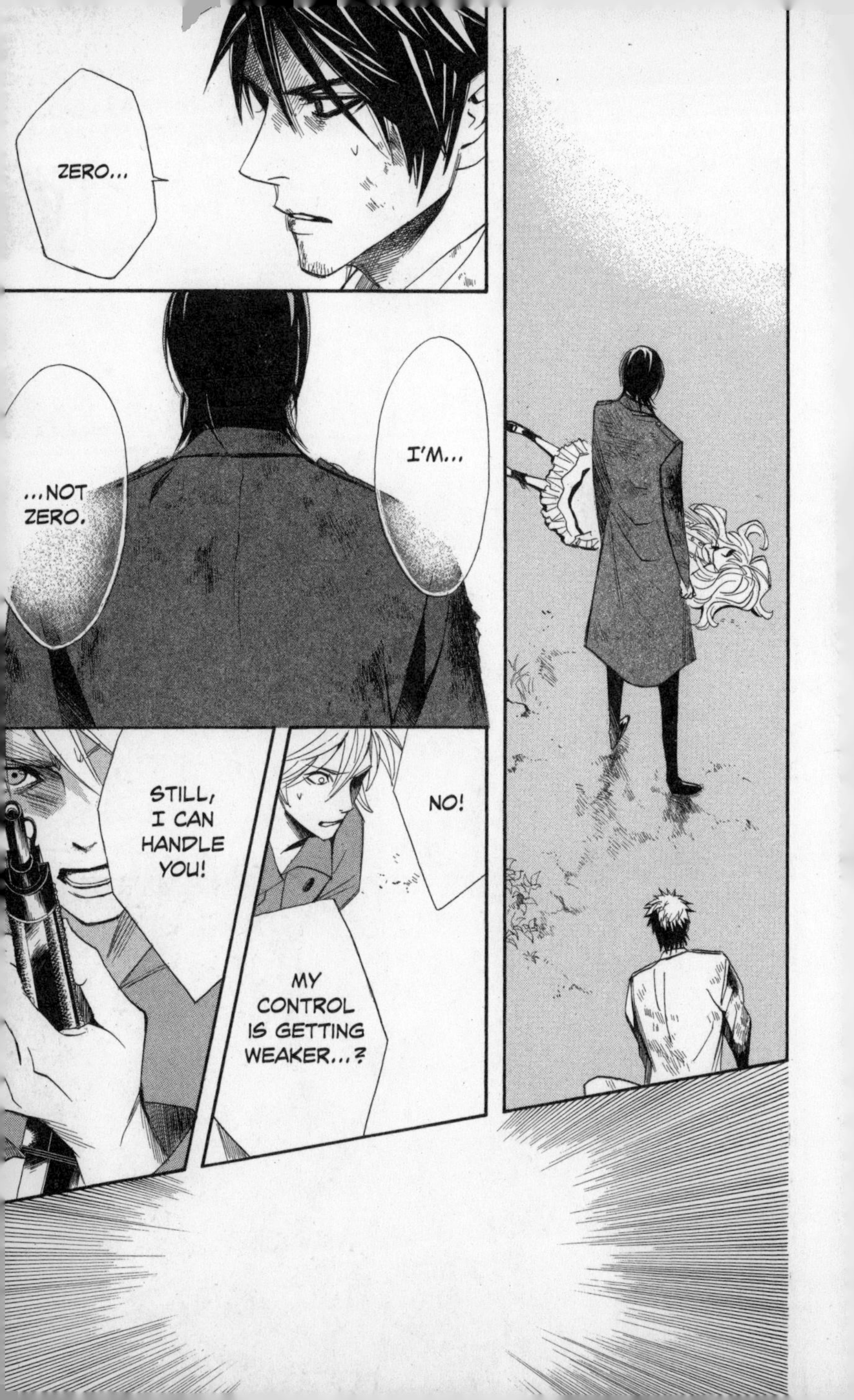
ZERO...
I'M...
...NOT ZERO.
NO!
MY CONTROL IS GETTING WEAKER...?
STILL, I CAN HANDLE YOU!

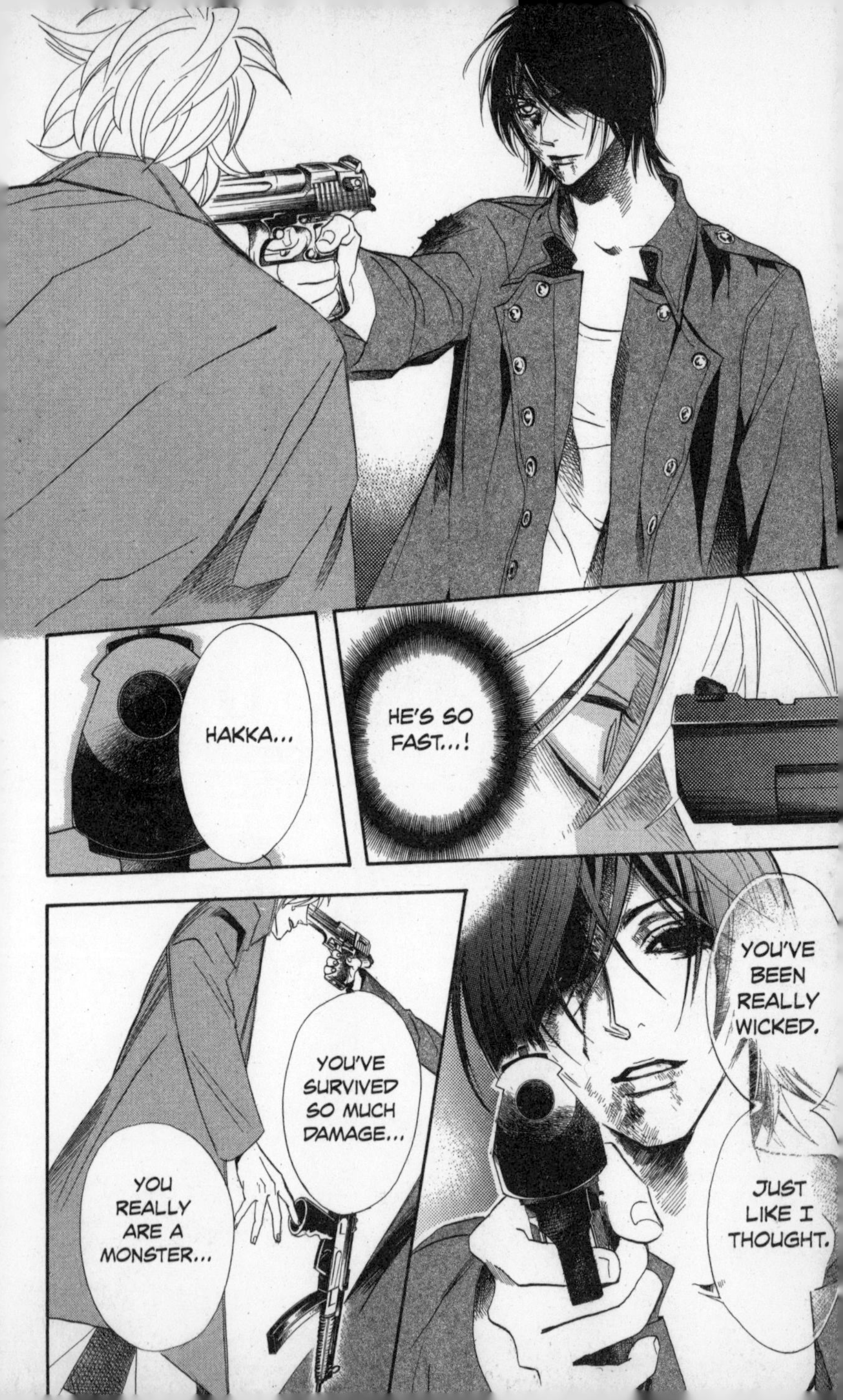
HE'S SO FAST...!
HAKKA...
YOU'VE BEEN REALLY WICKED.
JUST LIKE I THOUGHT.
YOU'VE SURVIVED SO MUCH DAMAGE...
YOU REALLY ARE A MONSTER...

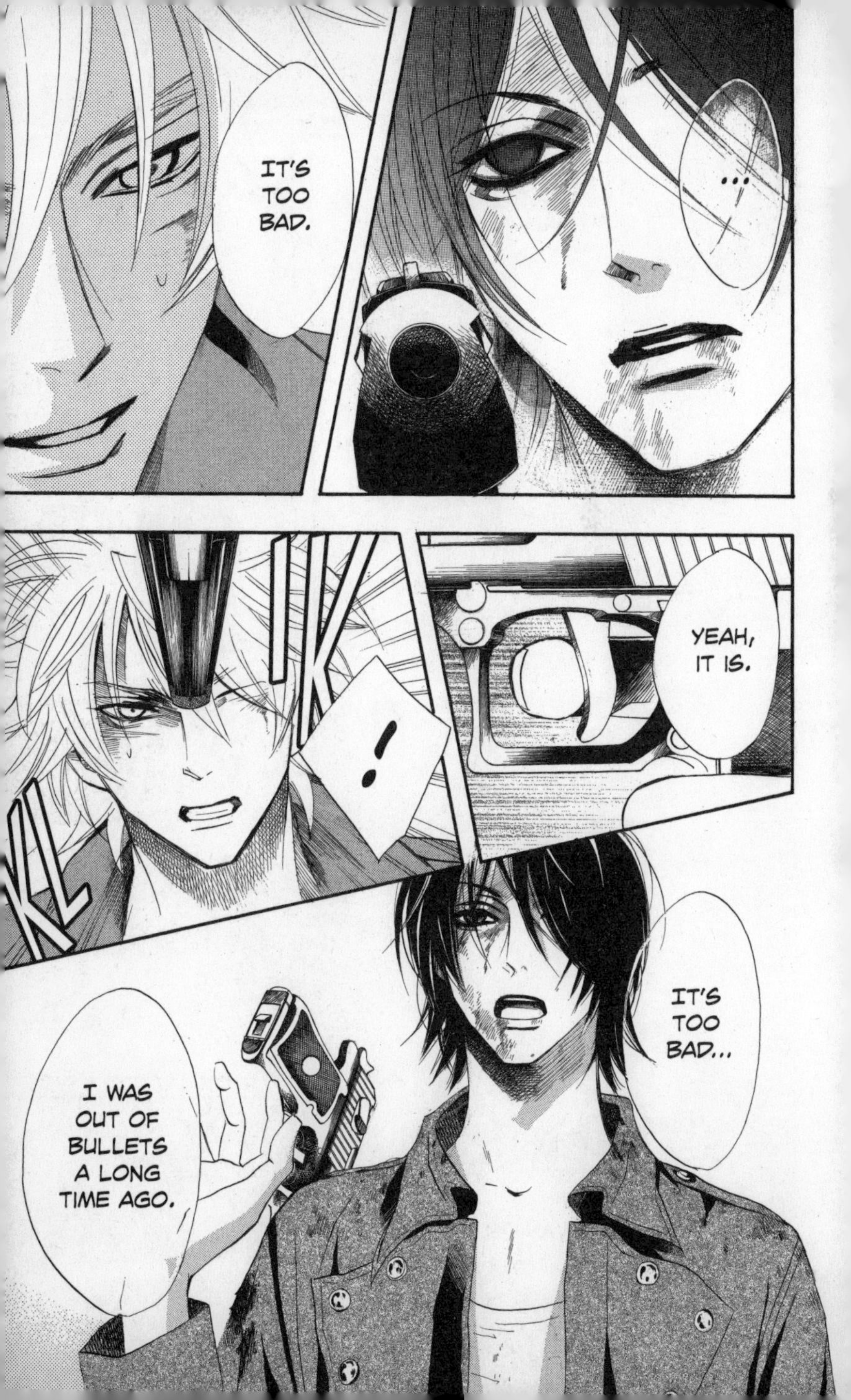
...
IT'S TOO BAD.
YEAH, IT IS.
!
KLIK
IT'S TOO BAD...
I WAS OUT OF BULLETS A LONG TIME AGO.

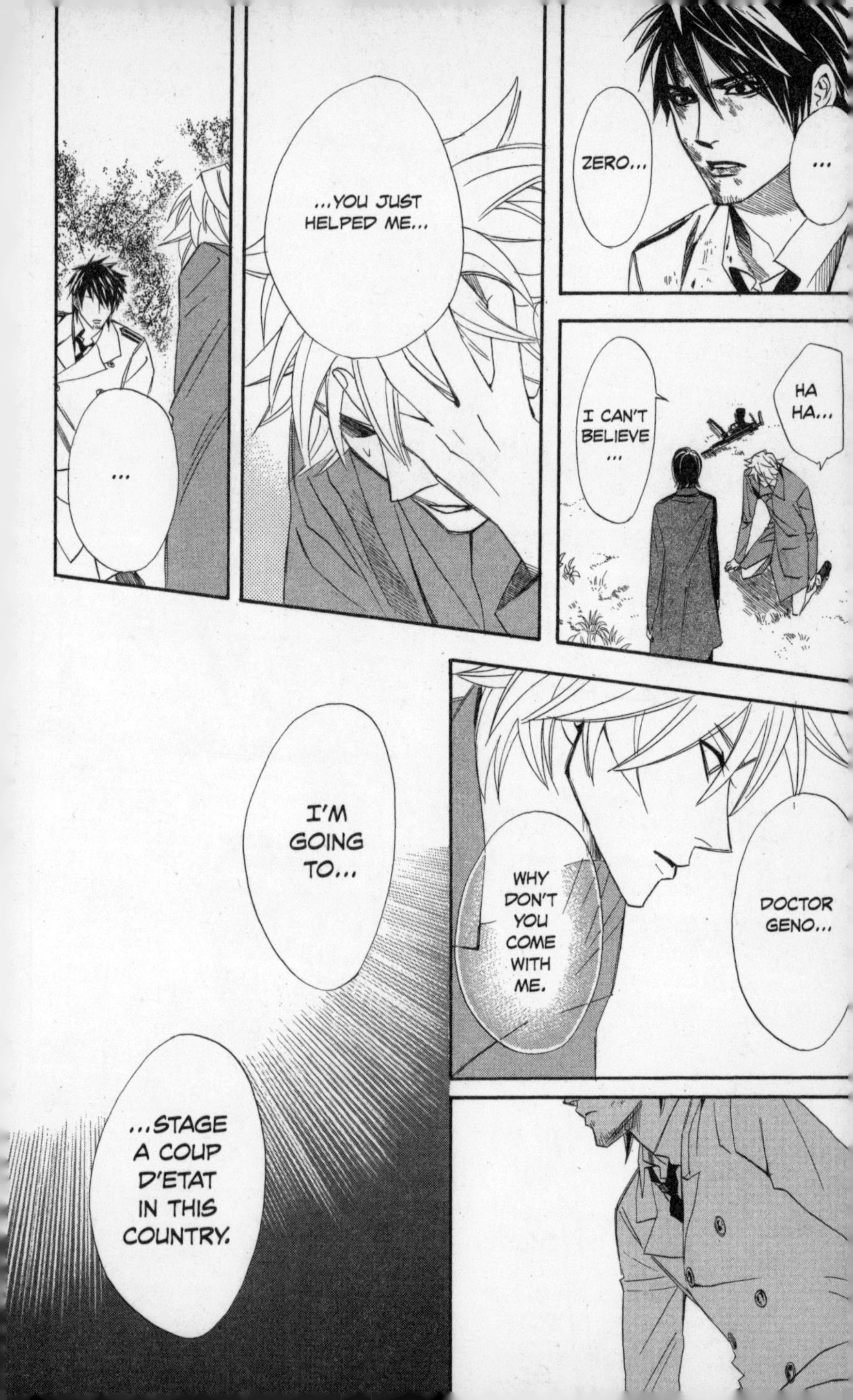
...
ZERO...
HA HA...
I CAN'T BELIEVE ...
...YOU JUST HELPED ME...
...
DOCTOR GENO...
WHY DON'T YOU COME WITH ME.
I'M GOING TO...
...STAGE A COUP D'ETAT IN THIS COUNTRY.

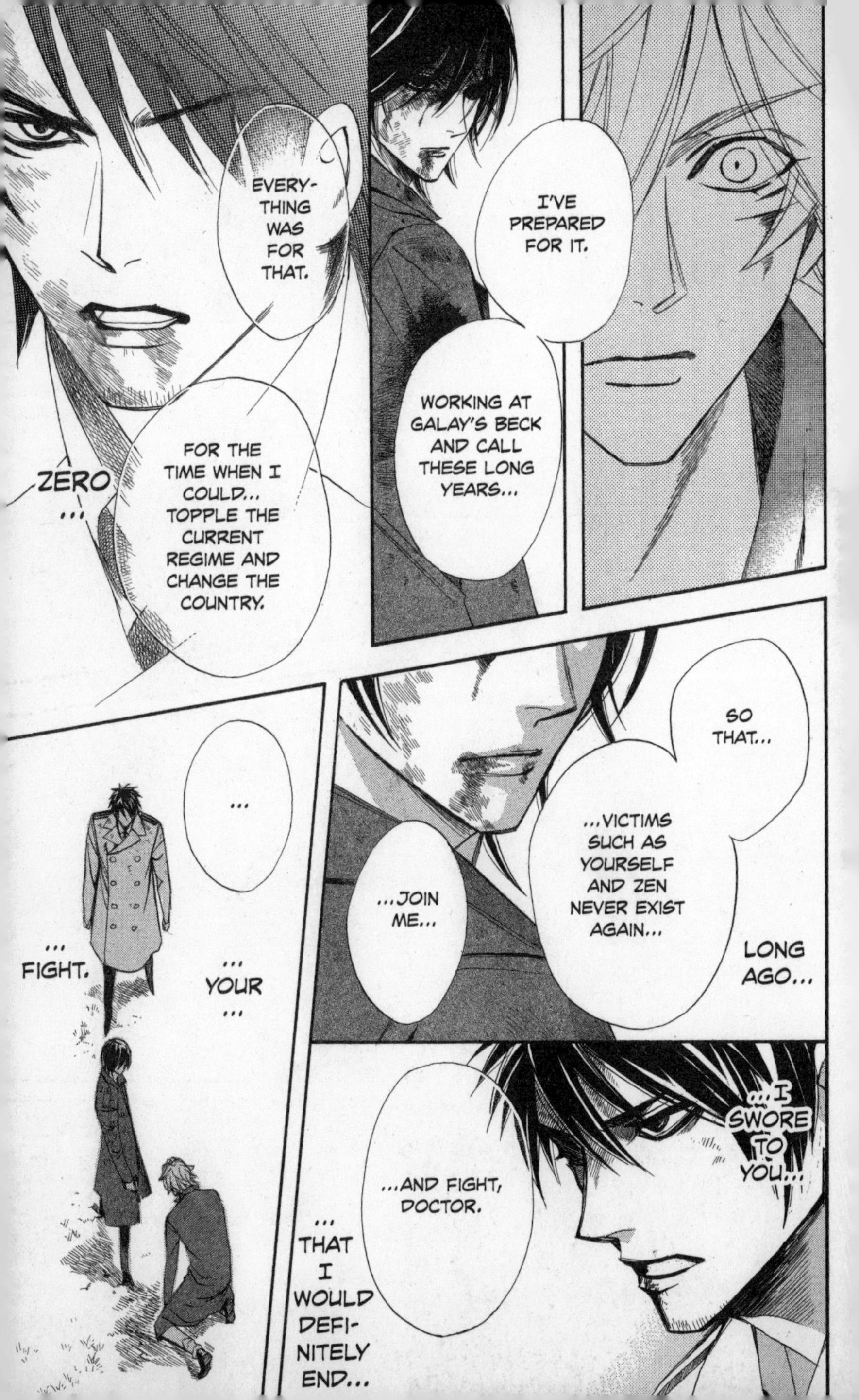
I'VE PREPARED FOR IT.
WORKING AT GALAY'S BECK AND CALL THESE LONG YEARS...
EVERYTHING WAS FOR THAT.
FOR THE TIME WHEN I COULD... TOPPLE THE CURRENT REGIME AND CHANGE THE COUNTRY.
ZERO...
SO THAT...
LONG AGO...
...VICTIMS SUCH AS YOURSELF AND ZEN NEVER EXIST AGAIN...
...JOIN ME...
...I SWORE TO YOU...
...THAT I WOULD DEFINITELY END...
...AND FIGHT, DOCTOR.
...
... YOUR ...
... FIGHT.

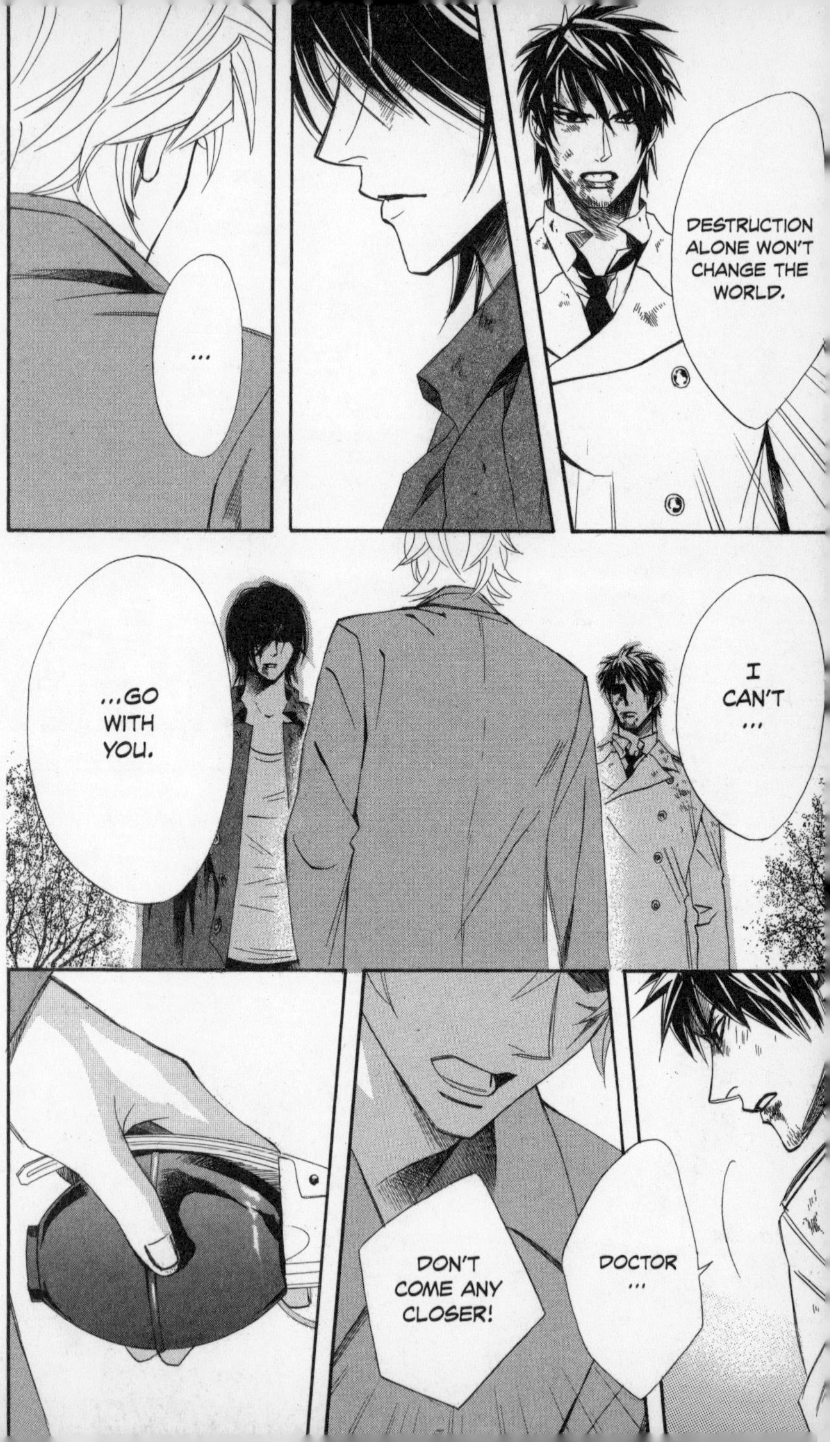
DESTRUCTION ALONE WON'T CHANGE THE WORLD.
...
I CAN'T ...
...GO WITH YOU.
DOCTOR ...
DON'T COME ANY CLOSER!

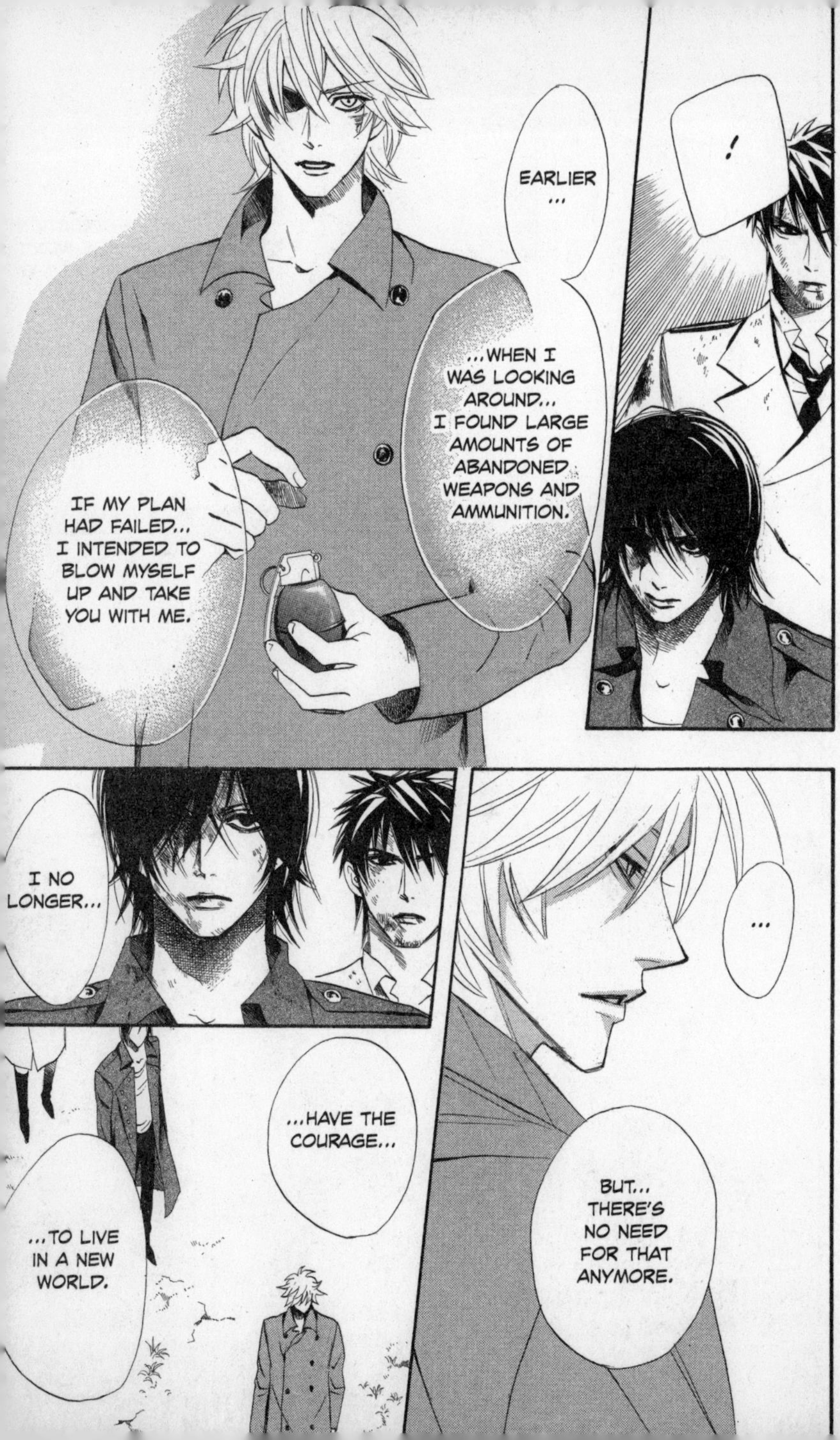
!
EARLIER...
...WHEN I WAS LOOKING AROUND... I FOUND LARGE AMOUNTS OF ABANDONED WEAPONS AND AMMUNITION.
IF MY PLAN HAD FAILED... I INTENDED TO BLOW MYSELF UP AND TAKE YOU WITH ME.
...
BUT... THERE'S NO NEED FOR THAT ANYMORE.
I NO LONGER...
...HAVE THE COURAGE...
...TO LIVE IN A NEW WORLD.

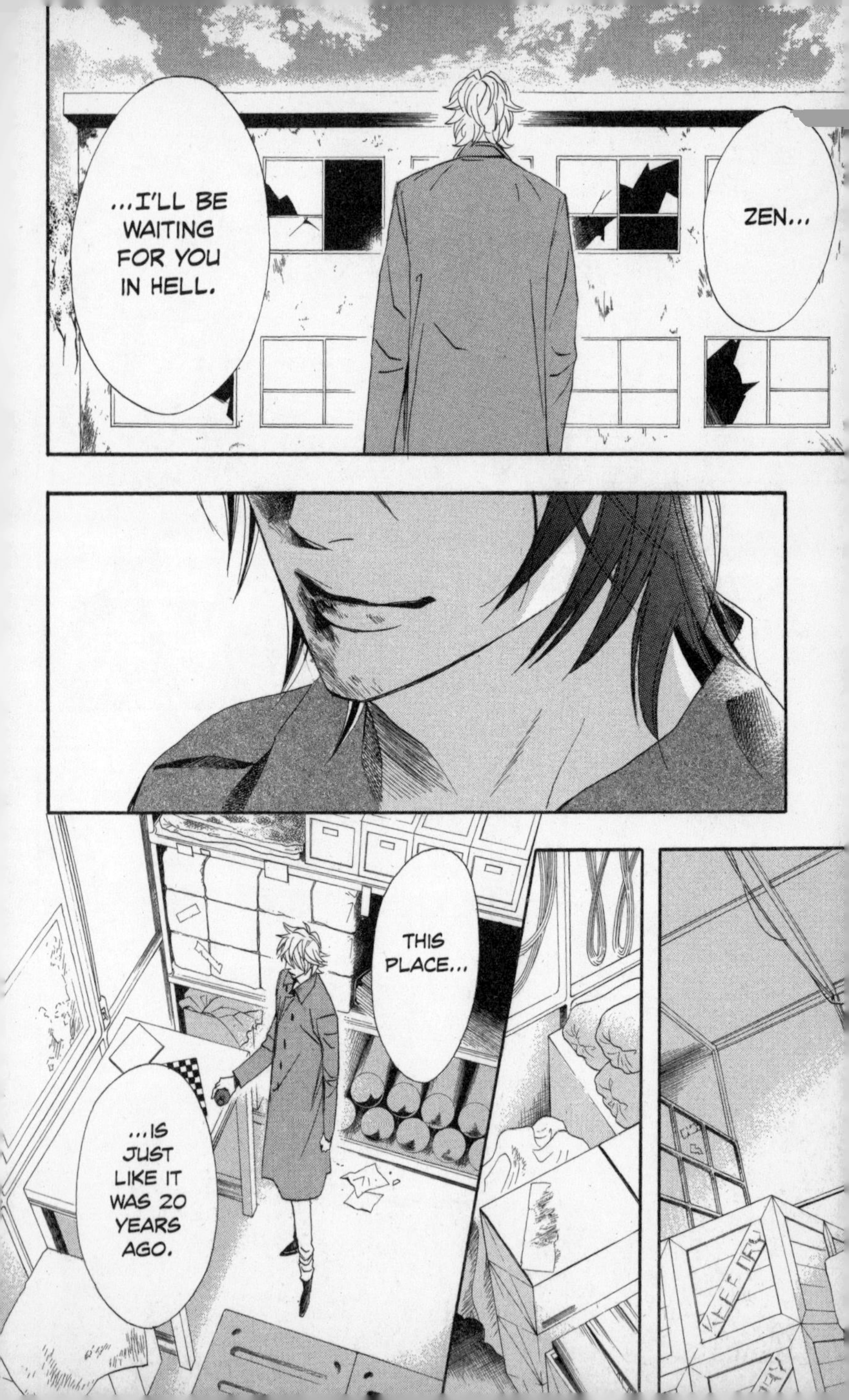
ZEN...
...I'LL BE WAITING FOR YOU IN HELL.
THIS PLACE...
...IS JUST LIKE IT WAS 20 YEARS AGO.

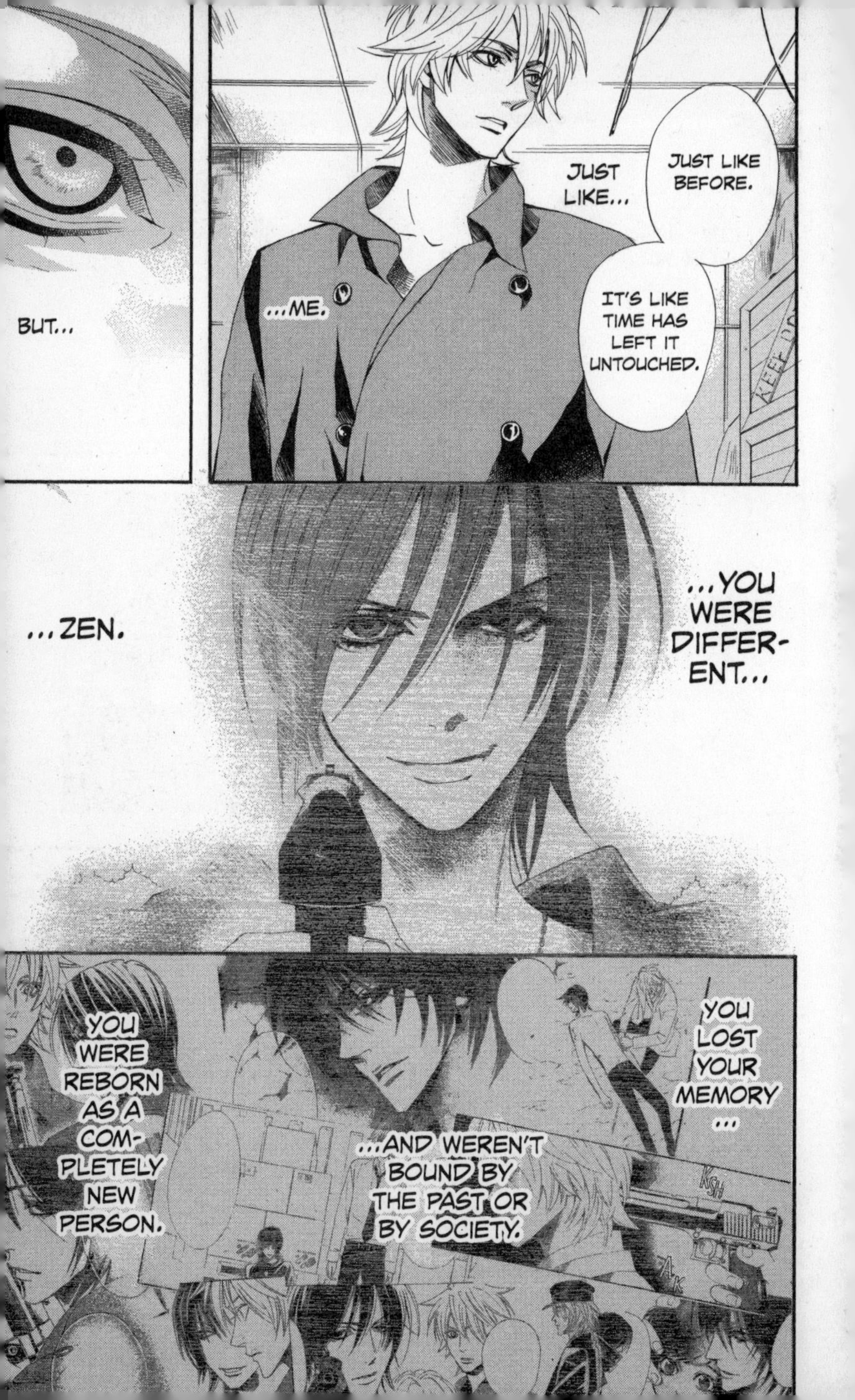
JUST LIKE BEFORE.
JUST LIKE...
IT'S LIKE TIME HAS LEFT IT UNTOUCHED.
...ME.
BUT...
...YOU WERE DIFFER-ENT...
...ZEN.
YOU LOST YOUR MEMORY...
KSH
...AND WEREN'T BOUND BY THE PAST OR BY SOCIETY.
YOU WERE REBORN AS A COM-PLETELY NEW PERSON.

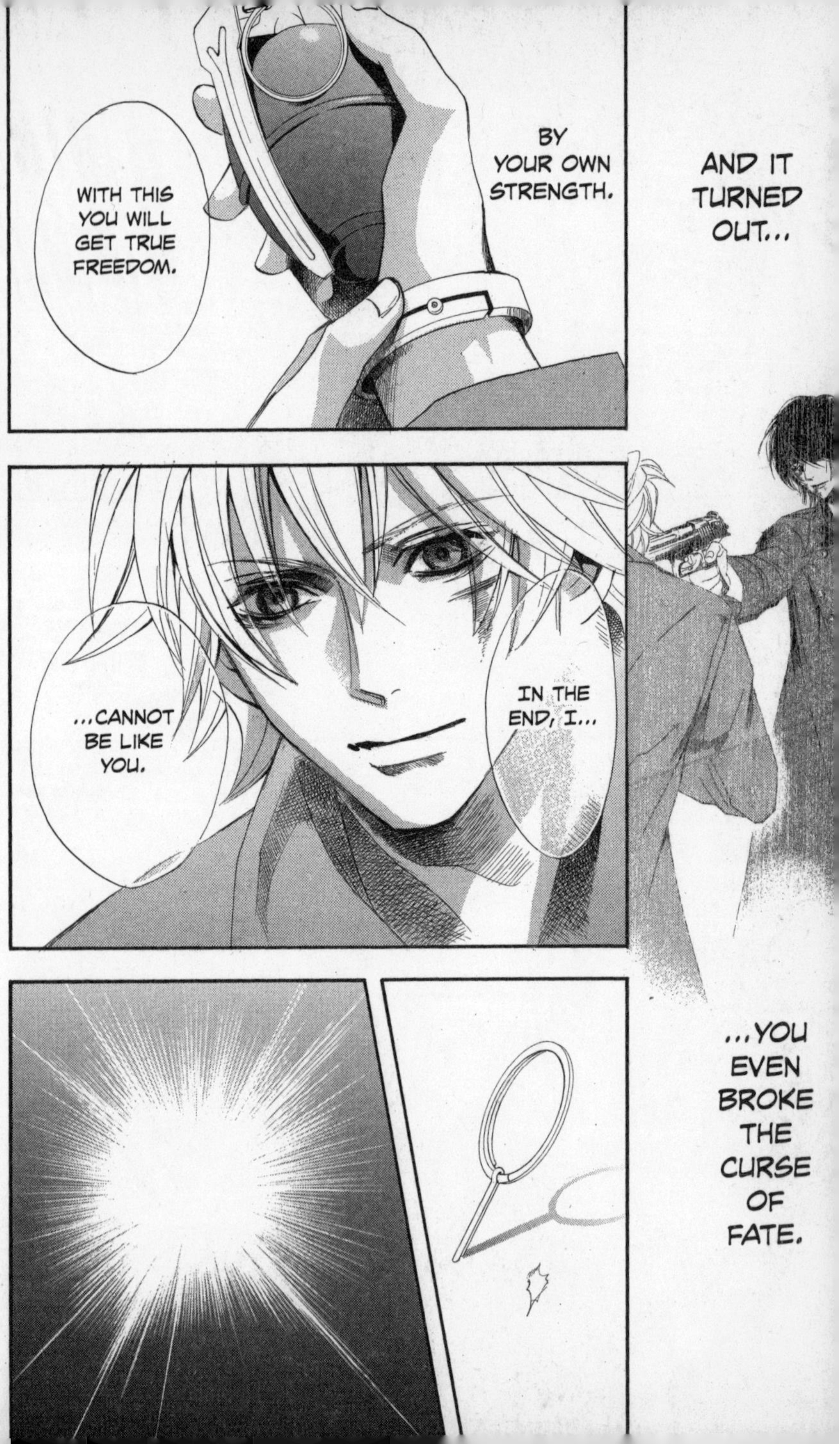
AND IT TURNED OUT...
...YOU EVEN BROKE THE CURSE OF FATE.
BY YOUR OWN STRENGTH.
WITH THIS YOU WILL GET TRUE FREEDOM.
IN THE END, I...
...CANNOT BE LIKE YOU.

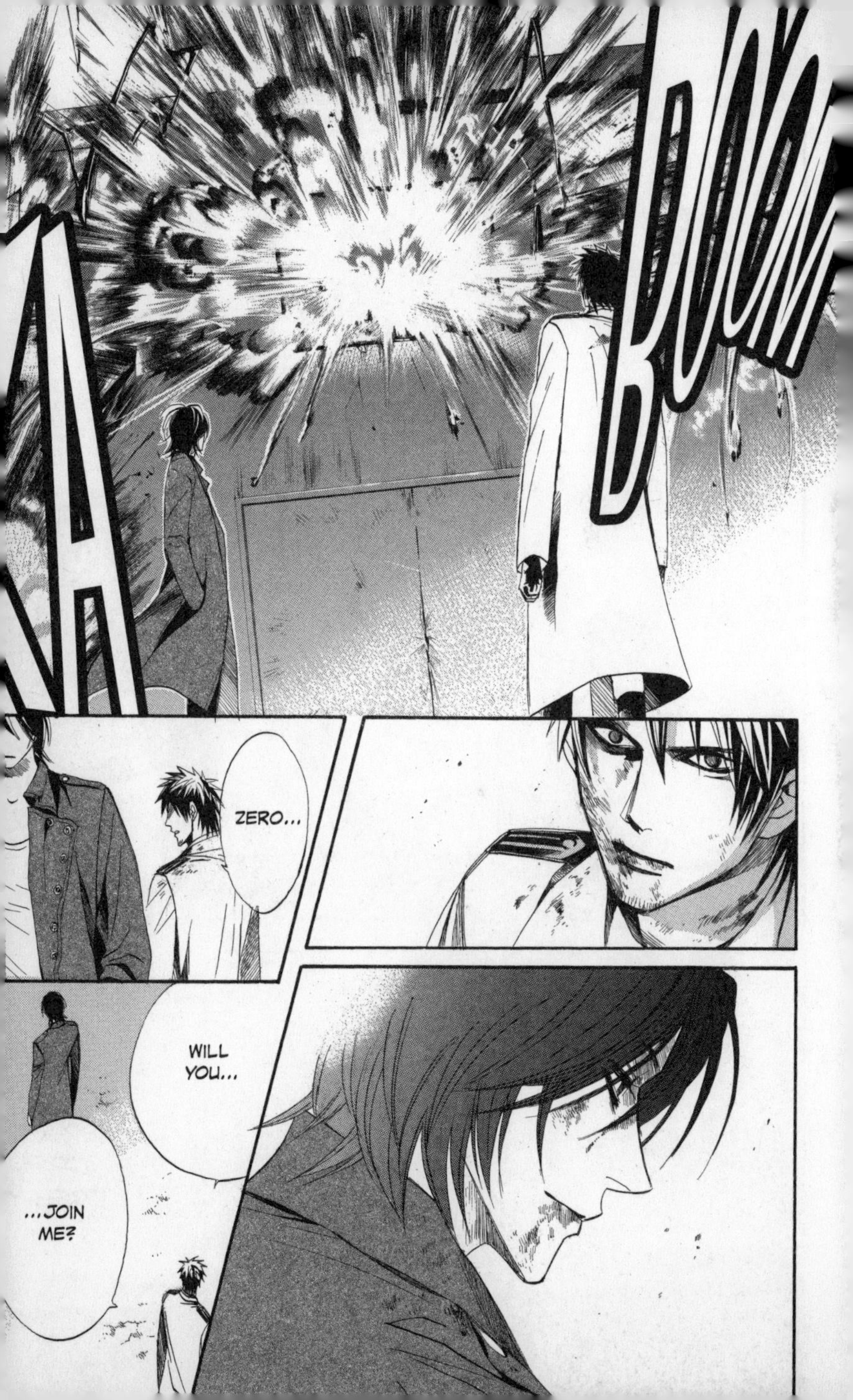
BOOM
ZERO...
WILL YOU...
...JOIN ME?

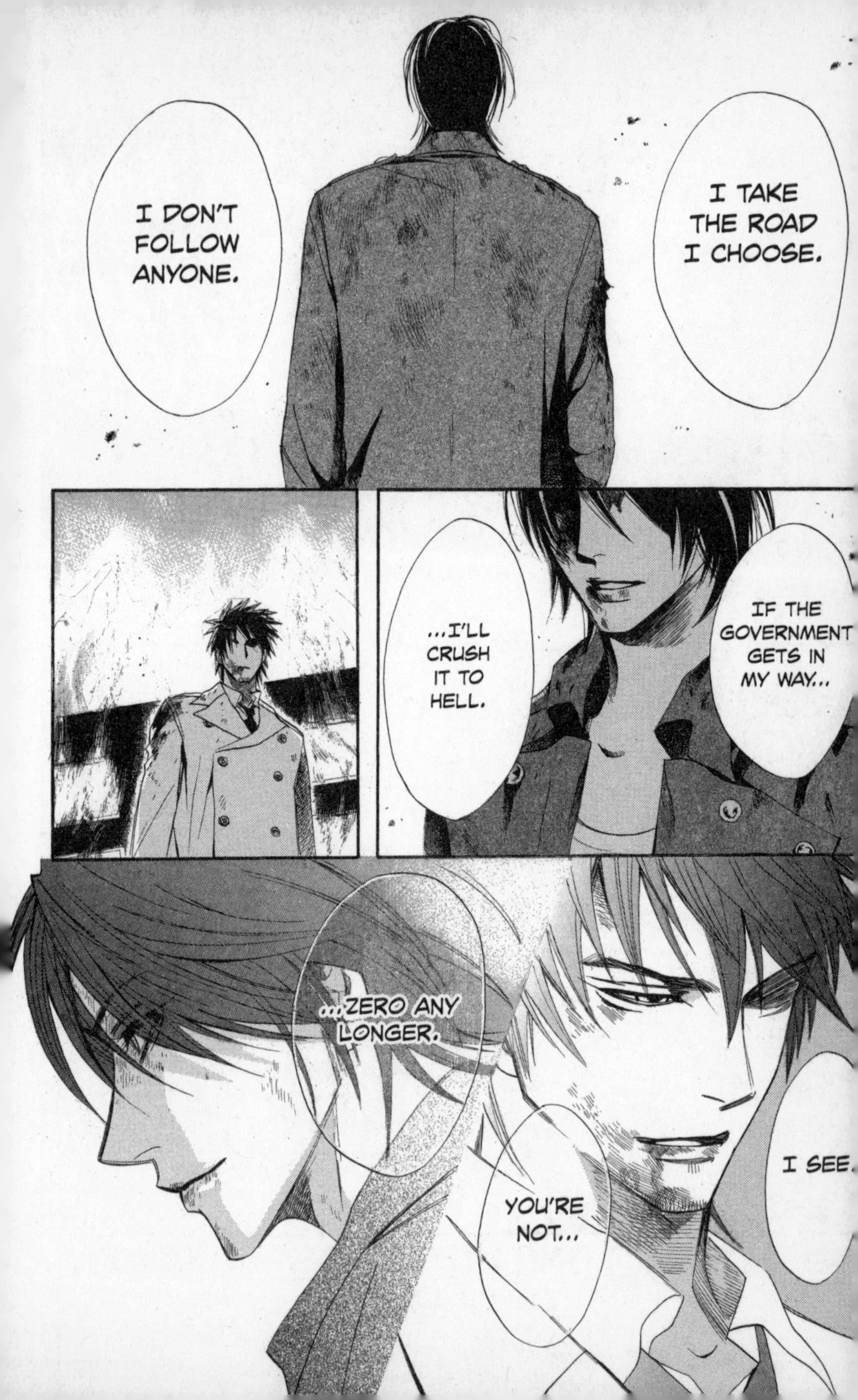
I TAKE THE ROAD I CHOOSE.
I DON'T FOLLOW ANYONE.
IF THE GOVERNMENT GETS IN MY WAY...
...I'LL CRUSH IT TO HELL.
I SEE.
YOU'RE NOT...
...ZERO ANY LONGER.

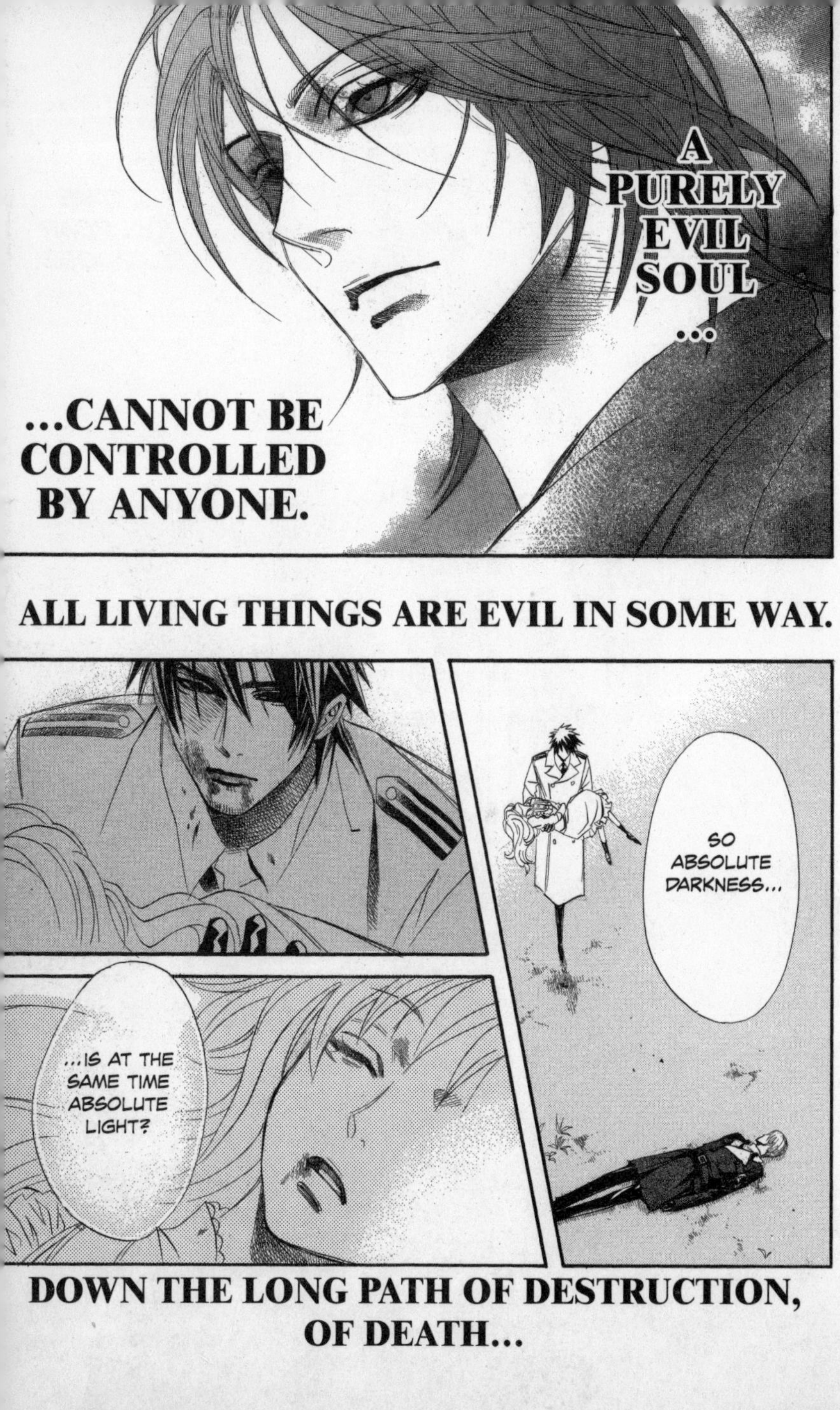
A PURELY EVIL SOUL...
...CANNOT BE CONTROLLED BY ANYONE.
ALL LIVING THINGS ARE EVIL IN SOME WAY.
SO ABSOLUTE DARKNESS...
...IS AT THE SAME TIME ABSOLUTE LIGHT?
DOWN THE LONG PATH OF DESTRUCTION, OF DEATH...

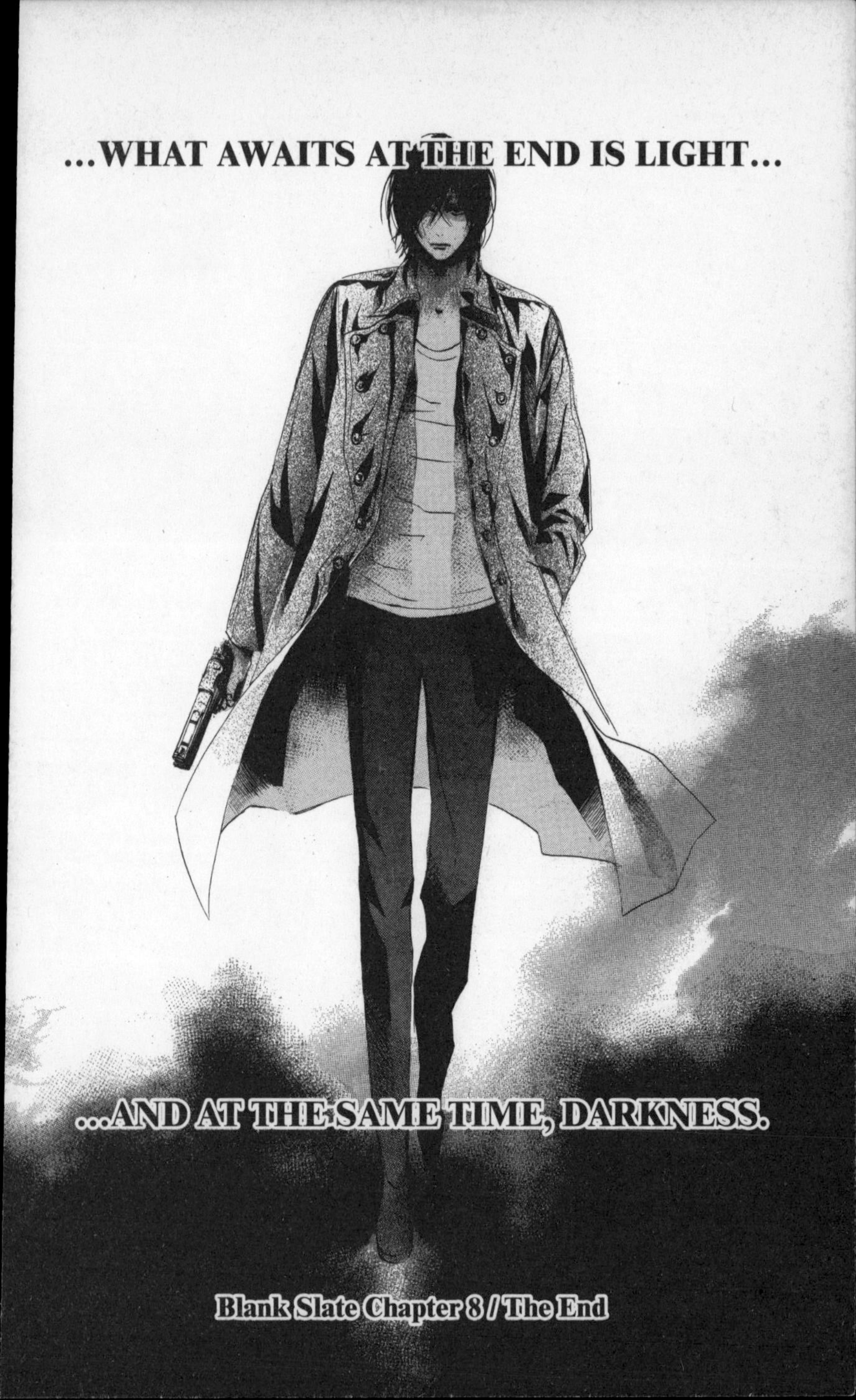
...WHAT AWAITS AT THE END IS LIGHT...
...AND AT THE SAME TIME, DARKNESS.
Blank Slate Chapter 8 / The End

ya Kanno was born in Tokyo, Japan. She is the creator of *Soul Rescue*, which has been published in the United States, and her latest work, *Otomen*, is currently being serialized in Japan's *BetsuHana* magazine. *Blank Slate* was originally published as *Akusaga* in Japan, also in *BetsuHana*.

Shojo Beat

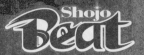

BLANK SLATE, VOL. 2
The Shojo Beat Manga Edition

Story and Art by **AYA KANNO**

Translation/John Werry, HC Language Solutions, Inc.
English Adaptation/Carla Sinclair
Touch-up Art & Lettering/James Gaubatz
Design/Sam Elzway
Editor/Joel Enos

Editor in Chief, Books/Alvin Lu
Editor in Chief, Magazines/Marc Weidenbaum
VP, Publishing Licensing/Rika Inouye
VP, Sales and Product Marketing/Gonzalo Ferreyra
VP, Creative/Linda Espinosa
Publisher/Hyoe Narita

Printed in Canada

Published by VIZ Media, LLC
P.O. Box 77010
San Francisco, CA 94107

Shojo Beat Manga Edition
10 9 8 7 6 5 4 3 2 1
[redacted]rinting, December 2008

store.viz.com

VIZ media
www.viz.com

T+ FOR OLDER TEEN

PARENTAL ADVISORY
BLANK SLATE is rated T+ for Older Teen and is recommended for ages 16 and up. This volume contains graphic violence and adult themes.
ratings.viz.com

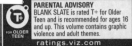